Foxtail Books

Miracles All Around Me

*The Unexpected Gifts
of My Mother's Alzheimer's*

Marsha L Burris

Foxtail Books
Charlotte, North Carolina

Copyright © 2014 by Marsha L Burris
All rights reserved, including the right of
reproduction in whole or in part in any form.

Printed in the United States of America

Library of Congress Cataloging-in-Publication Data is available upon request

ISBN 978-0-9914443-2-8

1. Marsha Burris. 2. Alzheimer's Disease. 3. Mother-Daughter. 4. Caregivers 5. Elder care. 6. Hospice. 7. Nursing homes. 8. Care for parents. 9. End of life care. 10. Growing up Southern 11. Southern Culture 12. Spiritual Growth 13. Reiki 14. Alternative Medicine

For

Rusty and Jim

Also by Marsha L Burris

Paradox of Professionalism: American Nurses in World War II

Disclaimer

Memory is a funny thing, and can be flawed. The author assumes all responsibility for any mis-remembered portions of this story. The dialog is an approximate recollection and names of the nursing home, some nursing home residents and staff have been changed.

All photographs on pages 186 through 192 are from
Burris family personal albums.

Foreword

Most everyone knows *something* about Alzheimer's, or knows *someone* who has a loved one living with the disease. Most know there is no cure, yet. The thing that is becoming more widely known than the disease itself is its impact on the caregivers of those with the disease. Caring for someone with Alzheimer's disease negatively affects the caregiver's health (physical, mental, and emotional), employment, income and financial security. But that is nothing compared to the human cost-the toll it takes watching a loved one slowly disappear.

In her book, Marsha Burris is masterful in leading the reader through the roller coaster ride that is the journey of a loving daughter caring for her mother who travels down the rabbit hole of Alzheimer's dementia. From denial to acceptance, she found that miracles are abundant every step of the way, if we seek and expect them.

With every page, I was plunged back into my own personal journey with both of my parents, who lived with dementia. Most recently, my father has moved into a nursing facility where his daily routine provides the cocoon of an ever-increasing smaller world that keeps him feeling secure and safe. This book would have helped me accept my experiences, earlier, with this new life that my Dad's dementia has caused for him and for me.

Ms. Burris helps the reader understand how the caregiving journey is isolating and lonely, making it so important for those who find themselves in these roles to seek community. The miracles of community were found at her mother's nursing home with other families and individuals living with the disease. There she learned to be present, breathe, and be in the moment in order to connect with her mother and others who knew nothing but the moment at hand.

Her journey began with the typical denial that there is really anything permanently wrong, moving through glimmers of hope that emerged each time her mother had a lucid moment. After many years, she accepted the fact that the condition does not improve. The disease makes orphans of us all. This book is a must-read for all who love someone living with dementia. In particular, for mothers and daughters, this book demonstrates through extraordinary story-telling, that the love, care, and concern of a mother truly never dies. The mother-daughter bond is eternal. Expect miracles.

Lynn Ivey CEO and Founder
The Ivey, A Memory Care Day Center
Charlotte, NC   www.theivey.com

CONTENTS

Introduction	1
Chapter One - *Shall I write a book about us?*	4
Chapter Two - *Sissies Need Not Apply*	11
Chapter Three - *Minnesota or bust*	39
Chapter Four - *Life with a twist of lemon*	50
Chapter Five - *If I have to know it…*	66
Chapter Six - *Not on my watch*	86
Chapter Seven - *Just ride it out*	104
Chapter Eight - *I looked over Jordan*	117
Chapter Nine - *Miracles all around me*	130
Chapter Ten - *It's a very small club*	147
Chapter Eleven - *Find a way to let your father go*	166
Chapter Twelve - *Thank God, even for the lice*	193
Chapter Thirteen - *They come to see me in my dreams*	211
Chapter Fourteen - *It's a poor sort of memory*	226
Chapter Fifteen - *Faith is abstract*	245
Chapter Sixteen - *Ava is born!*	264
Chapter Seventeen - *The blade that once was shiny*	277
Chapter Eighteen - *The road less traveled*	298
Chapter Nineteen - *Arden is born!*	310
Chapter Twenty - *I have been braver*	321
Epilogue - *A pesky grain of sand*	339
Letter to Caregivers	343
Acknowledements	345
Resources	347

Miracles All Around Me

INTRODUCTION

Can you tell me how to get to the dentist's office?

Rusty was a remarkable woman. I should know. She was my mother. When she asked me how to get to the dentist's office during a telephone conversation one day, I was astonished. This dentist's office was a place she'd driven to twice a year for the past twenty-four years. Now at the age of sixty-two she hadn't the vaguest idea how to get to this familiar destination and I knew then we had a problem. This was a loss of information, an inability to reason out a solution. It was not simply an item forgotten at the grocery store. Alzheimer's had fired its first warning shot.

As the outer lobes of the brain begin to die off and become nonfunctional, those with Alzheimer's disease revert, over time, to developmental skill levels comparable to that of a toddler. Knowledge is stolen from the individual in a last-in first-out fashion. Typically, the most recent memory goes first, then the less recent memory, and on and on until even recall of early life experiences may be lost. Although the symptoms were there, it may seem far-fetched that an official Alzheimer's diagnosis did not appear on our family radar for several more years. When it did, I was compelled to plumb the depths of that abyss with my mother and travel into a strange, daunting new frontier with her.

Rusty and Jim, as my mother and father were known to most people in their daily lives, were intelligent, accomplished, independent, dependable and happy individuals. They were competent parents to their four children, and good friends and neighbors. But those admirable character traits were ineffective in helping them walk the final few miles of their golden years. I stepped in and assumed a host of domestic duties on their behalf, entwining my life with theirs for the duration.

The decade of my forties is a blur. For ten years, while Mom's memory deficiencies increased and Dad's physical health slowly deteriorated, we instituted adaptive solutions so they could remain comfortable in their home as long as possible. All future professional career aspirations I held careened off course so I could focus on their care. Merely surviving the ordeal was not enough. Finding meaning in a commitment of this magnitude and in the challenges we confronted were essential, or else what was the point of all the suffering? Traumatic events can be catalysts for personal and spiritual growth, and are sometimes stepping stones to understanding our purpose. Nevertheless, my search for acceptable solutions to the various issues of Mom and Dad's aging was initially unfruitful until a series of relevant resources began to present themselves to me and my parents. I call them *miracles*. For me, miracles are not defined as magic tricks or some sleight of hand, but rather a set of unforeseen mitigating circumstances that occur by happenstance and at the precise moment to be of greatest assistance. Good luck, maybe? Divine synchronicity? Certainly they are welcomed coincidences. The miracles that assisted me in caring for Rusty and Jim were little ones, really, since no one was raised from the dead, but they were invaluable nonetheless and appropriately timed. I sought silver linings in the clouds hanging over our lives which helped me grow and permitted me to learn valuable lessons from the trials. I paid attention and journaled my thoughts on what I witnessed. Sharing them here does not remove the pain accumulated along the way but it's important to know that we need not bear our pain in vain, or alone.

Mom's Alzheimer's, Dad's stroke, and my brother's suicide are dark events in our family history. As Og Mandino states, *I will love the light because it shows me the way, yet I will endure the darkness because it shows me the stars*. In the darkness that engulfed my family, I was allowed a glimpse of illumination in the void of the blackest of nights.

My journey with Rusty and her battle with Alzheimer's must include a sketch of the woman before plaques and tangles, like the kudzu vines that grow wild in our southern region, choked out her neurons and their ability to function. But our tale is unavoidably refracted through the lens of Alzheimer's which claimed Mom's memories and ultimately her life. In telling it, I reclaim her from its clutches. At least a bit. With pure affection I resolved to protect my mother as she became less able to take care of herself and to be a witness to the odyssey we shared. Rusty made an indelible mark on my life and taught me valuable lessons until the day she died. Her instructions influence me still, and always will, unless the disease that took her bids me to follow in her genetic footsteps. If I too lose access to every experience I have had in my own life, it will not detract one bit from this love story.

Alzheimer's is called 'The Long Goodbye'.
It's a cliché only because it's so damned true.

CHAPTER ONE

Shall I write a book about us?

Rusty has slipped into the final stage of Alzheimer's. This disease effectively and irreversibly interrupts synaptic functioning in the brain; that malfunction has stolen her intellect and all of her talents, skills and abilities. My mother can no longer recall the day she fell in love or the day she gave birth to each of her four children. She has no faculty to recognize accomplishments in her life or anyone else's. The sum of our experiences molds us into who we are - the memories of those experiences enrich our lives. Losing a recollection of our milestones is a tragedy. It's a tragedy to the person with Alzheimer's and it's a tragedy for everyone who shares a connection with that individual. However, this woman, my mother, is much more than a capacious hold-all of past recollections. She lets me know this through her final gifts to me. With great effort, Mom is able to express her love when she touches my arm, gently demonstrating an understanding that we're nearing the end of this long and arduous expedition. That faint acknowledgement is enough to sustain me, for now.

Alzheimer's disease will claim Rusty's life at 73 years old. But not tonight. Tonight, I walk through the front door of the nursing facility and make my way down the critical care hall to her room. The smell of urine, mixed with chlorine bleach and freshly brewed coffee, lingers in my nostrils. It's more offensive because the attempt to eliminate its odor fails. We visitors are complicit in the pretense that all is well. Family members and friends who call on residents in nursing homes pretend that this is the best and safest environment for the care of our loved ones. God, how we hang on to that notion, and in most cases it is true. We act as if seeing the wheel-chaired amputees doesn't sadden us. We preserve the dignity of the poor soul who slumps like a rag doll in the doorway to his room by ignoring the drool that yields to gravity and rolls down his chin. I pat the hand of a resident who looks at me longingly as she plucks feverishly at the fabric of her robe. Another hand, boney and purple-veined, reaches out urgently for consolation from passers-by. I'm glad to oblige. My brief physical connection is reassuring, if only for an instant. I hear Jeopardy blaring out of someone's room. My mind grasps that it's Alex Trebek's voice and I hold on to it. It's normal. It's a normal sound in an abnormal environment and I want it to drown out the rhythmic pulse of the oxygen-assisting machines and the moans emanating from rooms I have to pass to get to my mother's bedside. Words of instructions fill the hallway as a disembodied voice escapes from a loud speaker: *Telephone call at the main desk for the 200 Hall nurse…* A wheel on the med cart desperately needs oil, and I think that if I had to live here I would never get any sleep with so much racket.

I arrive at Mom's room and sit down beside her bed. I don't know what little time I have left with her or I would be in a great panic to get everything said and done before the clock runs out on us. One moment I'm afraid, unreasonably, that these duties and responsibilities I've assumed on Mom's behalf will never end. Then the next moment, I'm more afraid that they will.

I was not cut out for the caregiver role. In fact I was an unlikely candidate for taking on Mom and Dad's welfare since the sight of blood makes my knees weak, and just hearing that a loved one has the flu brings on sympathy symptoms. Of course, there was that one time when I was five years old and Mom helped me set the broken leg of a chicken. We raised fryer hens and one of them had an unfortunate incident in its coop. I was sensitive to its plight and I asked Mom to help me fix the broken leg. We set the hen on the dining room table for the procedure. Mom guided my hands to frame the fractured little bird leg with two Popsicle sticks. So, other than Operation Chicken Rescue, I harbor no natural nursing tendencies and I successfully dodged all health care related roles for the next forty-five years. At Mom's side I consider that perhaps the caregiver role is finally growing on me. As I sit with her each evening after work, I'm now more at ease, confident even, as I feed her in comfortable silence. We've carved out a little haven of peace here in her room. Our gaze becomes fixed on each others' eyes. I feel as if she can see into my soul. With all of her senses stripped, she is no longer engaged in any tangential activities taking place in the hallway. "I'm not nosey," she would counter any time I called her out on what I thought might be snooping behavior in her previous life. "I'm just interested!"

Mom is no longer nosey and she's no longer interested in what's going on outside the scope of her immediate surroundings and I feel that she is focused only on me, at last, and I revel in the attention. At the moment, nothing else exists, nothing else matters in this world except the two of us. My logical mind knows this is not true, but my sentimental-daughter-mind hangs on to the belief like it's a life raft. The reality is that Mom is not capable of doing anything for herself at this point. She has no awareness that life-sustaining activities must be performed for her. She's unable to feel exasperation or anger if she's not fed or bathed. What a huge departure from the old Rusty, the big strong, beefy Rusty. How I wish she would instruct me to get in the kitchen and lend a hand so all these people will be fed tonight.

Mom can't tell me how she feels, but I deduce from her facial expression that she is physically uncomfortable from having to sit in one position for lengthy stretches of time. I fret that if the nursing assistants don't get her up and dressed and into the recliner-like Geri-chair, she will lie in bed in one position staring into space all day. But they do get her up. Each day. And they tend to her basic needs with love and care. I am grateful to them. I love them because they love Rusty.

Mom's eyes meet mine again and mine fill instantly with tears. I have little control over my emotions these days. I haven't seen tears well up in Mom's eyes for almost three years now. Perhaps Alzheimer's takes away the ability to cry. Or maybe the need. I wonder if that's a compensation or a curse. To be able to endure these heartbreaking circumstances we're in, I must look for any redeeming qualities lurking behind the difficulties.

The concept of seeking a silver lining in the dark cloud that is Alzheimer's is not my own. I adopted it only after reading *Elegy for Iris* by John Bayley. Bayley wrote this tribute to his wife, Iris Murdoch, the well-known Oxford professor and novelist who fought valiantly against the encroachment of Alzheimer's into her brilliant mind. A friend gave the book to me hoping that reading someone else's experience as a caregiver to a loved one with

Alzheimer's would help me deal with my own. I couldn't read it. It sat idly in a corner of my bedroom for a year. Why would I read about this horror when I was living it? Fun books, I could read. But nothing complex, certainly nothing realistic. Following complicated plot twists were beyond my paltry powers of concentration. Feelings of guilt eventually prodded me to read the book so I could return it to its owner. I'm glad I did. Bayley's message was clear. Advantages are connected to the adversities we face in our lives. But I challenged his premise at first - my own inner voice screamed, *No way! Absolutely NO good can come from Alzheimer's.* I saw no potential reward for what my family was going through. In time Bayley's message resonated with me and I determined to uncover the compensations within our own experience. Bayley's story proved to have great value for me. If there was the faintest possibility that I could look at the effects of the Alzheimer's experience in a more productive way as it stole my mother's life, I would attempt to do just that. I relied on Bayley's example to reframe Mom's Alzheimer's experience from a hopeless tragedy into a life-altering challenge to be managed. I began looking for gifts and benefits concealed within our own trying circumstances and I became a believer. Instead of hating every minute that Mom's brain was being stolen from her, I made a conscious decision to seek evidence of anything positive in the developing Burris family state of affairs.

The pain of losing Mom and witnessing Dad's physical decline did not disappear because of the shift in perspective but it meant that I salvaged some good times and was able to maintain a meaningful and significant relationship with Mom, and with Dad, as long as they lived. I would not have done that if I had not consciously been on the lookout for redeeming qualities embedded in the circumstances of the disease. Indeed, I would have only dreaded each waking moment for the duration of my caregiver days.

Bayley's message was the first of many miracles introduced into my life. These unexpected random forces, which appeared without conscious input or precipitating action on my part, helped me tremendously during the roughest patches of caring for Mom and Dad. I considered Albert Einstein's observation that there are two ways to live your life: *One, as though nothing is a miracle; the other as though everything is a miracle* and I chose the second outlook for my own. I found it preferable to becoming bitter from an unending spiral of grief, which is my natural approach, and I became determined to find a way to place this wretched experience in a positive light.

Sitting here beside Mom, I try once more to turn tonight's burden into a blessing. We've been at the end stage for only two years – an eternity in Alzheimer's time. The end stage is not necessarily the end of life but it is the point at which many of the bodily functions we take for granted begin to fail. The brain ceases to send or receive messages for activities that we engage in without conscious thought. For instance, Mom can no longer walk, and she can't feed herself. She doesn't comprehend that food is needed to sustain life. However, she still reaches playfully for the little plastic cup I use for her 'health shake'. I occasionally give her a cup to hold, but I give it to her empty because I don't want to have to clean up a puddle in her lap. She takes it and swirls it as if she's swirling ice in a freshly poured glass of iced tea. Occasionally, she reaches for the straw too. I'm wary that she might poke it in her eye and I think that I wouldn't give such an instrument of potential danger to a two-year-old child. But she's not two - she's my mom - so I give it to her. She stabs it into the air. Now she's a lecturer, trying to make a point. In her former life as a healthy vital intelligent woman, Mom would hold a pencil in this manner as well. I know I won't give her a pencil. That's going too far.

Other than the occasional involuntary word, Mom is no longer able to speak. At times she's able to mumble something to 'them'. A distant look in her eyes tips me off when she begins to interact, using sounds and gestures with someone, possibly many *someones* that I cannot see. I'm inclined to dismiss their existence, but they are present and real to Mom. I see the evidence of them through her, so I assume she is surrounded by the spirits of her loved ones. I do not know who they are but even though Mom can't engage in a give-and-take conversation with *me*, she certainly knows *them* and enjoys *their* company. I'm envious of them and the fascination they hold for Mom.

And yet, she finds ways to communicate with me as well. Mom connects with me at an instinctual level, which is emotionally moving and never fails to touch my heart because of the effort I know it requires of her. If she senses that I'm upset or particularly emotional during my visit with her, she will reach for my face and stroke it lovingly. Friends have asked me if Mom reached a point when she no longer knew who I was. I'm convinced that although she could not utter our names, she still knew and recognized her children. I believe she always knew that we are *hers,* we exist because of her and that she continued to know and love and trust us. Surely she wouldn't be capable of loving us so much if she didn't know us from the mailman.

Tonight, as usual, I continue to tempt Mom with food. She has no way of knowing whether this meal is breakfast, lunch or dinner. If I get a spoonful of mashed potatoes loaded toward the center of the spoon and position a little bit of vanilla pudding on the tip end of the spoon so that it's the first hint of flavor that reaches her mouth, I can daub it ever so gently onto her lips. When she tastes the sweetness, it persuades her to take a bite. Alzheimer's causes its victims to have a sweet tooth. They may have little interest in nutritious vegetables or meat, but they will kill for a cookie.

Nothing is new with this visit. Nothing is different tonight. This is a ritual I've repeated for three years and I never mind the process of feeding Mom. It's therapeutic. It's a connection. And it gives me the illusion of being helpful. Sometimes I do wish I could hurry her along to finish her meal more quickly because I rarely get out of her room before seven or eight o'clock in the evening. After I leave her I must make my way home, eat my own dinner, and do all of the other little chores that require my attention to prepare for my job at the university. But, tonight, I sit back and take a deep breath. I accept that the amount of time it takes to feed Rusty her meal is but a drop in the ocean compared to a lifetime of care she showered on her family, her friends, her community. And me.

I look up at Mom and get her attention. "Shall I write a book about us?" I ask her.

She nods her head, yes. It's little more than an involuntary jerk, but it's the go ahead I need. *I don't need her permission...,* flashes briefly through my mind. Only a moment later I think that maybe I do need her permission after all. This story wants to be told – I will tell it. It's a pact we make and she finds ways to keep me on track in the future.

As I contemplate writing a book of our experiences, I think that it's too fresh to be able to describe the accumulation of pain from all the events that led up to this moment. I'm one of the walking wounded, and I question why I would want to pick at the pain until I make it sore. If I wait for the right time, though, I may forget the real, raw and profound feelings - and *those* are the feelings that are important enough to share.

I lay my head in Mom's lap and give in to her comforting and loving pats on my back. She plays with my hair and I feel like a child again. Her child. It's as if no fundamental reversal of roles has taken place; only the natural order of mother comforting daughter. My tears flow freely. I ponder where the time went? How did we get here? How did we get here so fast?

CHAPTER TWO

Sissies Need Not Apply

Growing up with Rusty was like riding the *Scrambler* in an amusement park. Every day. Like the Scrambler, Rusty has a fast pace and is unpredictable. Having Rusty for a mother is not for sissies.

Besides me, Rusty and Jim's children include my sister and our two brothers. I was born three years after Barbara and two years before Robert. Andy came along a decade after me. The house we moved into when I was four became the family home for the next thirty years. It sat on a corner parcel of land carved out of Mary and Osborne Yeomans' dairy farm in Newell, North Carolina. Newell was a dot on the map at the outskirts of Charlotte. This community developed when Cotton was King and it flourished along the railroad tracks like the Queen Anne's lace we gathered into bouquets as children. Those of us who grew up there enjoyed the best of two worlds; the advantages of an idyllic rural life mixed with the amenities provided by our proximity to a developing and growing banking city.

Dad was raised in a small textile mill town east of Charlotte, with a younger sister as his only sibling. His parents provided a stable, tame environment for them to grow up in. Our grandparents lived long enough to see us, their grandchildren, become adults. We adored them. The feeling was mutual. Dad saw active duty on a PT boat in the Philippines during World War II and met Mom in Memphis after the war while taking a diesel mechanic course courtesy of the GI Bill. He brought her back to North Carolina to be his bride and although Mom loved Memphis, she was never nostalgic enough to return. During our growing up years, Dad worked at a large automobile dealership in Charlotte as Vice-President of the service and parts departments. His Ford Motor Company connections led Dad to pit-crew for

Ned Jarrett and Darrell Derringer during their NASCAR heyday. He coached Little League, Pony League and Legion Baseball teams. The man loved baseball and played catcher in high school, college, and on a semi-pro team after that. He shared his talents and skills with the boys in the community and enthusiastically helped them reach their potential. Dad enjoyed hunting, golfing, watching John Wayne movies and playing practical jokes at church. Jim was a quiet fellow, and although he was a true introvert, he could be called upon to emcee company functions when needed, and he readily assumed other leadership roles when invited. A man of few words, Dad commanded respect and we took notice when, on rare occasions, those words were quietly uttered.

Mom's childhood and family structure was the polar opposite of Dad's. His world was sound and secure. He had no reason to doubt that meals would reliably appear on the dinner table every day. By contrast, Mom's family could never be as certain. Her family's access to the meager resources of the depression-era South meant that although Mom called Memphis home, her family moved frequently, living a gypsy life, while her father chased promises of a locksmith job wherever they took him. At six, the innocence of Mom's childhood was abruptly cut short when her father was killed by a drunk driver whose impulsive and reckless choice to get behind the wheel of a car forever changed this family's life. Tragically, Mom's mother would suffer the same fate eleven years later. These experiences formed Mom's outlook on life as one that is harsh and unkind. She believed that the solution that ensured survival was to get tough, and the magic pill to remedy an unpredictable human existence was *work*.

To stack the odds in favor of protecting her children from the same harsh realities of life that she had known from her own childhood, Rusty resolved to control all aspects of our lives. If only we would listen to her and heed her instructions, she believed, she could manifest order, and thus safety, while raising four kids and directing us as her work force. She had good stuff to work with, if I do say so myself.

For starters, there was my sister, Barbara, who is smart, witty, and stylish. It is her way to surround herself with beauty. She was a Rainbow Girl and was chosen to attend the Governor's School in Raleigh for academically gifted high school students. As the first-born of the first-born, there are many photographs of Barbara in various poses wearing attractive tams atop thick brown naturally curly hair and fluffy white fur muffs protecting her tiny little hands from the elements. In first grade, she starred as Suzy Snowflake in the Christmas Pageant. She was comfortable with the only-child status.

Like Dad, Barbara is most content in solitary activities. They both care deeply for their friends and family and yet find little reward in spending time in crowds of people. When they are in large groups, usually by no choice of their own, they delight in observing, rather than participating. On occasion, Barbara allowed me into her inner world. We shared a bedroom when we were very young, and instead of sleeping as Mom intended, we made up games to play. One of our favorite games was a particularly amusing and satisfying *What-If* game. It went like this: 'If you had all the money in the world - *and everybody else did too* – what would you buy?" My sister insisted that we include the caveat 'and everybody else did too' because she couldn't conceive of having wealth, affluence and prosperity if it excluded anyone from experiencing the great and wonderful things that we ourselves enjoyed. I agreed with her unconditionally. If even one poor soul had less than we did, we wouldn't have enjoyed the game at all. My sister and I desired utter fairness for the entire world. Weren't we adorable?

Robert, my brother with chocolate brown eyes full of basset hound sadness, was born two years after me. He was the brooding misunderstood, 'James Dean' of the family. Mom didn't allow any of us to brood or to be misunderstood, though, so it was extremely frustrating for him growing up. Since we were close in age, we were great playmates and companions when we were young. Robert and I played countless made-up and make-believe games, too. Obviously, I was eager to employ my imaginative skills with anyone who was agreeable. One of our favorite games was *Bravest Man in the World*. Even though we were not yet politically correct enough to employ gender-inclusive terminology, girls were allowed to participate. The game had to be played outdoors and in the pitch-black darkness that only living in the countryside provides. Together we stood on the edge of the concrete patio attached to the back door of our house and looked outwards into the void that stretched beyond us. The goal was to see how far into that mysterious and terrifying blackness we could run before turning back and high-tailing it to the house. The one who could go the farthest won the title, *Bravest Man in the World*. Oh, how I coveted Robert's claim to that mantle of heroism.

Robert was also athletic, and like Dad, the catcher on our school baseball teams. He was also on the high school wrestling team. He was a hunter and a fisherman, and was attractive to the girls who claimed that he understood them - a trait he somehow dropped at the door when he got home. Robert joined the Navy immediately after high school graduation and attended Corpsman school where he excelled in the medical field. A Naval Corpsman is similar to being a medic. Robert's sensitive and caring side, concealed from public view, found an outlet in the Corpsman job where he received a wealth of positive recognition for his efforts. We thought he would make a career in the medical profession, but after his tour of duty ended, he joined the automobile world, also like Dad. Robert married early in his Navy career and his son, Tony, was born while Robert was stationed in Charleston, South Carolina. Robert always seemed to be searching for some elusive thing. He believed that none of us would, or could, understand what that thing was, and he never shared details about his search. I suspect he didn't know precisely what he was looking for. At any rate, he never found it.

Andy's the baby. At times, we still call him Little Andy even though he's the tallest member of the family at six feet, four inches. He gracefully sports Tom Selleck good looks on that frame. He was born ten years after me and was most welcomed by a family who excitedly anticipated his arrival. As an infant and a toddler, Andy was my own special baby doll. Barbara, already in her teens, had important social commitments occupying her leisure time. At ten years old, I didn't have a life and since I was available, I became the designated babysitter by default. At that age, I wasn't quite strong enough to hold him any other way than perched up on my hip. I looked as cool as a band-aid repair job on eyeglasses. He called me Na-Na – not 'Nana' like the grandmother name but *Nanh-nanh*. Which apparently is short for *Marsha*. I don't know. Of course my sister modified it to sound like 'Nanner' which pretty much stuck.

I'm not exaggerating when I say that Andy grew up the most

personable and charming of us all. He's yet to meet a stranger and if he ever sees you stuck in a snowdrift, rest assured that he will get you out. At thirty-five, he married an extraordinary woman and is an attentive and devoted dad to two precious daughters. He has overseen land-grading operations for most of his adult life and as the child who digs in dirt for a living, it's possible that his career choice is the one in which Mom took the most pride. Good solid work. And according to Rusty, there's no finer occupation than to be digging in God's earth.

And, me? In one of my first clear memories, I am standing in the carport of our new house, not yet five years old, when I noticed a small yet majestic woman walking down our driveway. It was Mary Yeomans, our new neighbor who we would shortly adopt as our beloved *Mam-ma*. My cowboy outfit, complete with a pair of silver-painted die-cast western pistols holstered and strapped to my waist along with a pair of authentic cowboy boots, gave me an air of confidence. When she got within earshot, she called out, "Hi, hi! And what is your name?"

I propped my booted foot on the step, rested my elbow casually on the elevated knee, and answered with all the pride my slight stature could muster. "I'm Marsha Lorraine Burris." We bonded that day, Mam-ma and me. She was my first friend in Newell.

I loved school as much as I enjoyed welcoming new friends into our family, even though I suffered some disappointments there. I had eagerly anticipated the school year when I would take Latin as Barbara had done, but without warning some educator deemed the merits of this course nonessential and struck it from the offerings when it was my turn. My disappointment over that slight has never diminished and it was not the only curricular snub I encountered during my public school career. I was prohibited from using a slide rule in math class, too, because of the introduction of the electronic pocket calculator. Life is not fair, even when you have generously wished that same virtue for the entire rest of the world.

My attraction to dead languages and out-dated methods of mathematical calculations suggest my love for the life of the mind and the knowledge that books provide us. I've always been an intellectual. I'm not all that smart, but I *am* naturally drawn to the scholarly pursuits found within academia. Yes, I'm the one who loved homework. I loved college. I loved graduate school. And I worked at a university for twenty years. It's possible that I was left on my family's doorstep by a band of gypsies. Or nomadic academics.

Once, Mom called me on the telephone and said, "Hey there, how are you doing, and how's your nose?"

"My nose?" I responded with surprise.

"Yeah, I thought you probably have it stuck in a book and it might need a rest..." *Ha, ha.* Dear ole' Mom.

Mom was an avid reader herself, but only if she could rig a stand to prop the book open while she ironed or cooked dinner. Mom maintained the home front with vigor. It was an occupation for which she was especially well-suited and she organized her life, and ours, around it. I use the term *home front* purposely - we were like the National Guard, Mom's personal reserve unit, mobilized for active duty whenever she raised the call for action. Rusty was as strong willed as any drill sergeant and ran her household and those who resided therein firmly and effectively. Mom believed that if you worked hard enough and fast enough, you could keep a step ahead of hardship and outrun pain. In this mission, Mom was not shy in sharing the work. She thought up and distributed endless tasks among her progeny. And therein lay a major conflict between this mother and her children because we didn't experience hardship. We had food, shelter and security. The only hardship, as we recognized it, was nonstop toil imposed on us by Mom. Whereas she thought work equaled freedom, we viewed work as anything but that.

Because of poverty and the experience of losing parents at a tender age, Mom recognized how vulnerable we humans are and how precious life is. Being exposed to these hardships as a young child produced one tough nut in the form of our mother. Describing Rusty completely would fill volumes, so I'll summarize. She was decisive and confident which made her a little bit bossy. She rarely questioned herself but once confessed that she wished she had more patience. She relied on God to grant that virtue to her in His own good time and found just enough patience to wait for it to happen. Which it did, years later. To Rusty, things were either right-or-wrong, black-or-white. She was no fence-sitter.

No doubt that these are the qualities that Dad found

attractive when they met in Memphis. He admired Mom's predisposition to lead and dominate the domestic realm of his life and in that domain he relinquished authority. Or perhaps Dad surrendered authority to Mom at home as a separation of powers, common in the 1950s, when he realized Mom's confidence in her home-making and child-rearing abilities knew no limits. It was chiefly recognized that Mom was a woman who had the answers and she couldn't understand why everyone else didn't see things her way. Life was a lot easier for us all if we followed Rusty's lead.

The complex characteristics that formed Mom's personality seemed to contradict each other but she reconciled them masterfully. She was loving and supportive but also strict and scary. She loved to have fun, but work always came first. She was serious about, and devoted to, her faith but often misbehaved and giggled in church. She was extremely knowledgeable and well-read in a large range of subjects but was defensive if anyone questioned the extent of that knowledge. As a child who frightened easily, it would have been helpful if Mom had been a calm, consistent and nurturing soul, but Mom didn't do anything the easy way. She was a Scrambler and she never questioned her own authority.

Barbara and Robert did, though. They stood up to Mom and even sassed her at times. If they perceived unfair treatment, they rebelled, usually without success. Andy used diplomacy in his approach to seeking redress and got good results with that but it was much later, after Mom had mellowed some. I saw Rusty-Almighty as the Borg. Resistance was futile against her powerful omniscience. My strategy was to assimilate, get along, acquiesce, and wait for the perfect time to escape. To some, that strategy was viewed as cowardice, but I just wanted to survive. At least that was my perception. From Mom's point of view, she was being protective. She called us her *Chickies*. After we grew up and had homes of our own she telephoned us weekly to make sure her *Chickies* were safe. Mom's hands-on parenting technique was proprietary and she was forever willing to clean our faces with spit on her thumb. We improved our duck-and-weave tactical moves to escape her reach, but she never stopped trying. Thus are the possessive qualities of a mother for her children.

During our younger years at home, Mom conscripted our aid in confronting the enemy, namely, dirt in the house. Laundry was to be washed and ironed, weeds needed to be evicted from the garden, three acres of lawn were to be mown, just to name a few. These aggravations challenged Rusty's attempts to establish order. Much of the time, we only added to the disorder. *Be useful!* This was Mom's mantra, her call to arms. Mom seized every opportunity to teach us to take responsibility for ourselves, contribute to our own upkeep and to be self-sufficient. To drop the ball on any one of these qualities made you... a *lazy heifer*. No lie. That was the worst name you could be called in our family. If you lingered in bed until eight o'clock on a Saturday morning, you were a lazy heifer. Recently, I was on a road trip and I saw a cow lying on her side in a beautiful green pasture.

"There it is!" I shouted to my traveling companion. "The lazy heifer! There's that blasted lazy heifer right there." I thought she looked quite comfortable and content, however, and I frankly didn't see what the big deal was at all. To this day, I sometimes lie in bed until 8:05 on Saturday mornings – just because I can.

With Rusty, a state of laziness was not acceptable, and lazy we were *not*. And neither was she. Mom was no hypocrite and she definitely practiced what she preached. That woman could do *any*thing. Rusty was a doer, a fixer, and most of all, a creator. She was a dressmaker who sewed gorgeous and stylish clothes for some of the society ladies in Charlotte. With vigor, she planted, harvested and preserved incredible vegetables, second in grandeur only to the flowers she grew and nurtured. Often, her artfully arranged flowers found their place in the sanctuary of our church on Sunday mornings. Through the years, before this appalling disease seized Mom's brain, Mom was active in community and church affairs. The robust Rusty was constantly in motion and always with people. Her friends were like the stars in the sky – scattered far and wide, and too numerous to count. Friends were family to her. There was no distinction. Barbara, Robert, Andy and I shared Mom with a host of siblings. And as I mentioned, Mary and Osborne Yeomans, who owned the dairy farm where our house was located became an essential part of our family. They were surrogate parents to Mom and adopted grandparents for us. They were our closest allies. As our two families merged we went through good times and bad; sickness and health, injuries, births and deaths.

After living a nomadic childhood Mom chose this piece of real estate in Newell for putting down roots. We children believed that in this fairytale-land anything was possible, including the best tasting milk and cream and butter ever manufactured by man and bovine. No lazy heifers grazed in Mam-ma and Pam-pa's fields. A spring-fed pond in one of the fields provided water for the cows. Oh, how wondrous a universe is a pond! To our kid-sized perspective, it was huge. And mysterious. Cattails grew at the edge with their velvety corndog shaped spikes that could be used in swashbuckling pretend sword fights. The brown murky water hid sea serpents and monsters from our keen eyes. It smelled of mud and muck and mire, if mire indeed does have a smell. It was located two football field-lengths from our house and was surrounded by blackberry bushes. In the summer we hiked across the pasture and down to the pond to pick blackberries for hours. Our haul, when placed in Mom's capable hands, yielded the most scrumptious blackberry cobbler in Newell. Picking the berries was treacherous, though, and fraught with danger. There were snakes in the bushes so we carried sticks to beat the ground as we walked which we hoped would frighten them away. Worse than snakes (*worse?*) were the chiggers which find their way to the most delicate areas of your skin and itch like the devil. In order to pick blackberries, a few precautions had to be taken. Long pants and long sleeves must be worn – a torture in the hot southern summer, but essential. Pants legs and cuffs of the shirt were to be duct taped and sealed to the skin. And then any skin left exposed was to be slathered with Vicks Vapor Rub. I'm not aware of the originator of the chigger-defense procedures but I suppose it worked, since I don't remember too many horrible bouts of infestations afterwards. I wonder how we were ever brave enough or had the energy to pick any blackberries after all that preparation.

    Pam-pa stocked the pond with bream and some sort of bass. Robert and I loved to fish there when we could sneak a little time away from our chores. Buzzards glided high overhead in lazy circles. Crows cawed boldly from their perch in nearby trees. We imagined that one wrong move would make us their dinner. It kept us on our toes and motivated us to employ survival techniques. For fishing tackle we had an old cane pole, a fish-hook made from an opened safety pin, and a slice of Sunbeam sandwich bread. Mom showed us how to gouge the soft middle out of the bread and knead it into little spheres. Voila! We had bread balls for our bait. Bream reportedly like it, but not the ones in our pond. We'd sit and tempt the bream with the bread balls for hours on end but they seldom, if ever, were coaxed into taking a nibble. We found out later that Mom hated cleaning fish and secretly applauded our failure to bring home a catch.

Robert and I would get bored with our fishing adventure eventually and give it up to play fanciful games we invented, although I swear we had real toys. Once, Robert decided to wade into the pond for an extra bit of fun, but the mud at the water's edge was soft and yielding. He got stuck up to his knees. I swung my pole over in his direction so he could grab hold of it and I got him out. I wasn't as lucky when, one day we were playing 'Jump the Creek'.

A creek ran through the woods located beyond the pond and across the far side of the pasture. It was another magical place that we were, by some miracle, allowed to play in occasionally without adult supervision. When Dad did accompany us and if it was spring time, he would let us play on young trees running with sap. He would bend them down for us to grab, then he let it go. Returning to its upright position, the spindly little trunk would fling us into the air like a catapult. If we were lucky we landed in his arms or on the leaf-strewn forest floor. Where was Rusty on these outings?

Because Robert and I felt expertly knowledgeable of all things woodsy, we seized every opportunity to march down to explore our favorite destination. At no place was the creek wide enough that we couldn't jump across it in one leap. And at no place was it more than ankle deep. But that wasn't challenging enough, so we took steps to increase the danger. There was one particular place where the creek made a diversion around a tiny rise of land the size of our dining room table. That was our 'island'. Merely leaping over the creek to the island was lame. And unimaginative. The preferred method of transport was to use a rope stretched tautly from mainland to island. By using the hand-over-hand maneuver, we could safely cross the treacherous ankle-deep rushing waters below us. One day, a friend of Robert's was with us and when we instructed him on this mode of conveyance across the creek, the friend suggested that it would be much more fun if two of us held each end of the rope while the other one crossed rather than relying on knots and trees to steady the line. We had to agree.

I took the initiative and crossed to the island first. I untied the rope on my end while the friend untied it on his. We held it taut between us as Robert grabbed hold. He worked his way backwards over the water, hanging on by his hands upside down and looking a little bit like a 'possum hanging from a tree limb. Just before he made land-fall, I got a bad case of the giggles and let my end drop. Butt-first, Robert plunged into the creek. We were young and our bones were spongy and we were never injured even after being flung from saplings or dashed upon river rocks. Thank goodness Robert was okay other than feeling let down, literally and figuratively.

Our initial reaction was, *Oh no! Momma is going to kill us for getting wet and muddy.* But I had a plan. I recommended he take off his jeans while I ran wildly through the woods, trailing them behind me hoping that the air circulating through the fabric, because of my swift movements, would dry them before suppertime. As Robert stood on the island in his jockey shorts, I could see in his expression that it was possible he would never forgive me for this one.

When we were not off having adventures on our own, we were found at Mom's side, in one of her gardens. Nearly every sunny week-day in spring and summer, Mom worked the fields with Pam-pa or used her mattock to break up the hard red clods of clay at home to create a new flower bed. In Mom's childhood, her series of family homes had only dirt yards, the size of postage stamps. Grass costs money and takes time to cultivate, scarce commodities for her family. This fact did not stop me from daydreaming about how wonderful it would be to go out, sweep the yard, and be done with lawn-related chores for that day. I had not considered that Mom never experienced a stable place she and her family could call their own and where she could feel secure. But now Mom had the luxury to plant pretty things and surround herself with the beauty she didn't have growing up. She called this patch of earth her own and became a good steward of it. I believed then, as only a child can, that she sure was lucky to have the sibs and me, the *work force*, to make this world of beauty happen for her.

Mom was on intimate terms with her dirt and clay and worked

without gloves as she dug in it. After hours of toiling in the garden soil with her fingernails chipped, dirt embedded underneath them, it took ages for her to scrub her hands clean and repair the damage. "Wear gloves!" I suggested helpfully. But gardening was a spiritual experience for Mom and my rebukes fell on deaf ears. She couldn't bear to feel any barrier between her and her beloved earth. She would no more consider placing gloves on her hands to separate them from her flowers than she would wear gloves to change diapers on her babies. Once when I was concerned about the possibility of colors clashing in one of her flower beds, she responded with, "Look at all of these flowers that God put on this earth. He never worries over 'clashing colors' and neither will I. Beauty is beauty."

My sister and I used God's earth to bring us beauty too. Mom planted a row of bearded iris that defined the border between our lawn and the field of alfalfa that lay between our property and the Yeomans' farm. The iris bed was three miles long, or so it seemed to Barbara and me when we were ordered to weed it. *Stupid iris.* Sweat poured from every pore of our bodies as we baked in the hot North Carolina summer sun that, incidentally, corresponds to North Africa's latitude. My sister's intellect was not diminished, even under these severe climate conditions. She discovered that by rubbing the red clay up and down our legs, it gave us an instant tan. And not *just* a tan, but a reddish, coppery glow that we believed approximated the hue we imagined pigmented the skin on the indigenous Cherokee peoples from whom we were descended on Mom's side of the family. We were pleased with ourselves and with the result of our efforts. We were not as concerned that our beauty applications slowed down progress in liberating the infinite iris tubers from the encroachment of crabgrass. And incidentally, didn't God create crabgrass too? Who were we to second guess where crabgrass should and should not grow? Mom was not pleased with our reckoning on the merits of crabgrass growth within her iris border and she was livid when our mud-tans stained the tub in the wake of our evening baths. To this day, my sister and I harbor a love-hate relationship with bearded iris, but we look affectionately upon North Carolina red clay.

Mom preferred her own tan to be natural and to be naturally derived from the sun. And using nature to divine God's will came, well, *naturally* to Mom. Once, when one of our dogs died, I was concerned that he would not go to heaven and it upset me. I had heard at Sunday school that only human souls were allowed into heaven and it didn't seem right to me. I went to the expert, Rusty-Almighty.

"Can you imagine a heaven without dogs and cats and animals of every type?" she asked me. It was an earnest question.

"No," I admitted.

"I don't think God would devise such a bland environment for us to dwell in for eternity." As always, her proclamation was final.

Clearly, Mom was never happier than when she was *worn out* from working in the garden. Flushed from the heat. Sweaty and dirty. She loved it! She complained loudly that much work needed to be done but behind the complaints was a woman totally in her element engaging in work and accomplishing tasks that she found quite satisfying. Mom designed her flower gardens in her imagination, sketched them out on notebook paper, and then directed the action needed to make her images became reality. She did this with the help of her young army, namely us, her children. And as children, although our mother grew lovely flowers that bloomed almost all year long, we often picked wild bachelor buttons and daisies and Queen Anne's lace for her from the fields along the railroad tracks near our house. We took delight in bringing bouquets to her and declaring, "We know you have your own flowers, but here are some more for you." Mom assured us that flower-lovers never have too many flowers and more are always welcomed.

To grow award-winning vegetables and flowers, red clay (also good for fake tans) required amendments in the form of cow manure. Conveniently, Pam-pa had cows, and his cows were obliging. One of our family activities included shoveling the stuff into the farm wagon and hauling it to its destination. "Gotta have a little manure to make things grow," Mom sang proudly as we groaned over having to shovel cow pooh. "We *need* the manure. Fertilizer is God's gift and it makes things grow," she assured us. "Wonderful things come from manure! And it's free!"

I did not understand the broader significance of this concept then. I would come to learn that because of the dung that life flings at us at times, we are able to grow and then harvest the best that our experiences can produce. It would become a metaphor for my life.

Mom had a talent for making deals and driving hard bargains. She not only made deals to acquire free cow manure, she scrounged and bartered for shrubs, flowers, fruit trees and other plant life. She dug up a Black Cherry tree seedling from Pam-pa's orchard and re-planted it in our back yard. When it didn't bear fruit, Pam-pa suggested that she should cross-pollinate it with another cherry tree. Mom had believed that the trees at the farm were near enough to be equal to the task of providing the necessary pollen to her little transplant, but alas, they were too far away to accommodate. She only wanted the one tree in the yard, a second one would destroy the symmetry she desired to produce, symmetry being one thing she believed she could improve upon after God had created the heavens and the earth. She would not be thwarted in this plan. Mom marched up to the farm, got permission to cut a good sized blooming branch from the parent black cherry tree there and brought it back home with her. She proceeded to wave the pollen-laden branch wildly as she marched about the young cherry tree like it was a Maypole. The artificially forced pollination of the cherry tree was successful and we enjoyed a grand crop of cherries that season. The Burris family continues to live with the indignity that our mother was a cherry tree pimp.

As for us kids, our summers were spent pulling weeds in that endless row of iris and in the rows of beans and corn in the vegetable garden. Mowing the massive lawn with a push mower took us several days to complete from beginning to end, and then it was time to start over again. We mowed grass in the morning and we mowed grass in the evening the entire summer. Ironing, as a domestic chore, was at its zenith during my childhood. Cotton shirts without rayon or dacron or whatever it is that makes them wrinkle-free had not yet hit the market. Dad's work shirts were sprinkled, rolled into balls, and placed on the bottom shelf of the refrigerator. *Why is this?* I didn't think to ask then, but I *do* know that I was a skilled ironer and while ironing I could sit on a stool and listen to the radio – a chore made in heaven for this naturally lazy heifer.

With seemingly unending chores, we kids still found time to lie in the side yard and gaze at the wisps of clouds as they drifted across an endless sky in an ever-changing kaleidoscope of shapes. Bunnies, witches, bicycles, four-leafed clovers... Four-leafed clovers!

As we rolled in the cool grass of that little side yard, we searched for four-leafed clovers. And, we found them, too. The clover, ever yielding in lucky charms for us, was also hospitable to bumblebees. Since we romped everywhere during the summer with bare feet, this meant we had scores of bee stings. The traditional country remedy for bee stings was a poultice made from a mixture of tobacco juice (yes, spit) and baking soda. Mom never shied away from either the chewing or the spitting. Oh, she of many talents... Other skills included repairing tractor malfunctions, mitering joints for interior trim-work, and then adorning herself glamorously for dinner and dancing in a taffeta, chiffon, or sequined cocktail gown designed and made by her own hand. Mom slipped effortlessly from the down-to-earth cotton shorts and sleeveless blouse uniform she wore working in the yard, to evening attire of stunning beauty.

As children, we knew Mom was off for a night on the town with Dad when we heard the rustle of her brocade dress against silk hose. If we caught a whiff of White Shoulders faintly dabbed onto selective pulse points we knew Mom felt sophisticated. It was a sassy splash of Jean Naté for everyday wear. Besides looking and smelling dressed up, Mom *sounded* dressed up as well. A mink stole, satin high heels, and elbow length gloves rounded out her ensemble. With hair coiffed, and lipstick and mascara deftly applied, she was a beauty - a raving beauty. Mom was beautiful because she created a style that was distinctively her own and reflected her personality.

Rusty possessed poise and displayed certainty and confidence in herself and her abilities. She displayed anxiety only when confronted with heights, snakes or speaking in public. Other than these three things, nothing else frightened the woman. The force of her personality, alone, gave her great sex appeal. She and Dad were a good match. Jim's tall slender figure was quite dashing in a bright red cummerbund surrounding his trim waist - a cigar and drink in hand. With salt and pepper hair, Dad was an attractive man, an elegant man. Think Cary Grant or George Clooney. My sibs and I remember those days fondly as the 'Dean Martin Era' because our parents commanded their niche in the late 1950's and 1960's as Dean Martin and Ann-Margaret commanded theirs.

Mom and Dad met friends or colleagues at supper clubs or fine restaurants that provided live music and a dance floor for the foxtrot crowd. They attended company parties and parties hosted by some of the movers and shakers in Charlotte. What fun Mom had at these cocktail parties. She drank little alcohol, having more fun without it. In fact, choosing water over whisky is how the nickname *Rusty* was bestowed upon Mom. Back in Memphis, when going out with a group of friends, they would tease her that drinking so much water would rust her pipes. Then they pointed out that the rust had already set in by indicating Mom's reddish auburn hair as evidence of it. Mom loved it.

At a party, Mom used her sobriety to interact playfully with those who did enjoy a cocktail or two. One of her favorite tricks needed a prop. She owned an enchanting gold-tone cigarette holder. *Enchanting* because it telescoped from five inches to well over a foot. Rusty cast a spell with that thing. She started out with the holder fully collapsed, then as the evening wore on, and as the partiers imbibed more and more of their host's cocktails, they were mesmerized by watching the thing grow magically, subtly, little by little, until it was at its full length. If Mom didn't have the cigarette holder, she would use a trick that her mother had taught her. She took a bobby pin from her French Twist, straightened it and inserted it into the end of a cigarette. As she smoked the cigarette (employed strictly as a prop at this point) she didn't tap the ash out into an ashtray; she allowed it to accumulate. As the ash got longer and longer, her friends would be riveted to her cigarette to see how long it would grow before it fell. All the while Mom chatted and waved the cigarette for emphasis, enjoying herself immensely.

Mom was an intelligent woman by any measure but believed that higher education was cheating. A short-cut. Formal education, especially at the university level, was a waste of time as it infringed on time that could otherwise be used for manual labor. While we were in primary and secondary school, though, we got out of doing a lot of chores by claiming we had homework. Trust me when I say that *good grades* were expected, and trust me when I say that I played the homework card a lot.

But, to Mom, no government-provided education compared to self-acquired knowledge obtained outside the classroom. It didn't cross her mind that others may not believe as she did. In any case, I took every opportunity to glibly pronounce that a self-taught person has an ignorant teacher. Mom didn't complete her last year of high school, which was not unusual for her generation. She stopped out early to work as a waitress and contribute to her family's household finances. I think she was a little sensitive about her lack of formal education, even though she was intelligent - more intelligent than I wanted to give her credit for when I was younger.

Apparently Mom absorbed her vast knowledge through osmosis because nothing learned from a classroom could measure up to the lessons learned in the school of hard knocks, her own personal Alma Mater. Of course, that attitude doesn't explain how she could be on intimate terms with Latin names for every flower in her garden, or how she understood and recited to me, on one occasion, the Archimedes' Principle of Fluid Displacement. When I was in the eighth grade, I came home from school one afternoon fresh with this new tidbit of information to test Mom with. It was my purpose in life at that point to demonstrate my superior intellect. I placed a small potato in a glass of water and set it on the kitchen counter. As the water level rose, I asked her what this phenomenon was called. Her hands were working a flour-and-shortening concoction that was to become biscuits unsurpassed on this planet and without skipping a beat she said, "Oh, that's called displacement. It's one of those principles that Archimedes discovered." She blew a wisp of hair off her forehead and continued with supper preparations.

Regardless of her own beliefs, Mom understood that I had a drive to pursue academics and she was proud of me in her way for any awards I won as a result of my efforts. As a five-year-old child, I would sit on the floor by Mom's side while she did finger work on the dresses she made for her customers. I read out loud to her from Little Golden Books and she would help me only when I was stumped by difficult words. Mom quizzed me in preparation for Spelling Bees in vain since I'm a notorious bad speller. I lost my chance at glory by misspelling k-i-t-c-h-e-n. I maintain even now that the 't' is not essential.

After I learned how to write, I was often found with a volume of Funk & Wagnall Encyclopedias spread across the dining room table while Mom prepared supper. I turned our dining room into a medieval scriptorium as I methodically perused the pages until I spotted a familiar word or a particularly interesting topic and proceeded to copy each sentence directly from the article, by hand, into my wide-ruled writing tablet using a fine-nibbed fountain pen. Funk & Wagnall's are a little sophisticated for a primary schooler, true, but they were more intellectual and serious than World Book, if serious intellectualism is measured by word-length, difficulty, and the intensity of ink smudges on fingers. Mom would call out from the kitchen, "Whatcha doing there?"

"Research," I answered. Deadly serious.

Thus were planted the seeds of my 'professor' phase of childhood. When I reached my tenth birthday, Mom provided me with my very own leather briefcase. Not a book satchel. Not a box-style attaché case. Not a book *bag*. But a genuine, full-sized, top-loading, *classic*, lawyer's briefcase. Actors carry them in movies to look *professorial*. I loved that briefcase. It was one of my prized possessions. It ranked up there with my cowboy boots in importance. I carried it with me to school every day. On Fridays, at three o'clock in the afternoon, you could find me re-organizing the briefcase. After a hard week of preparing for spelling bees and memorizing multiplication tables, it was necessary to prepare for the new week ahead.

School was not only fun and games. Pressures of life encroached on our idyllic days. It was the Age of Sputnik and during the autumn of 1962, there was much to be afraid of for us school-aged children. The Cuban Missile Crisis caused political tensions and heated things to a point that our teachers were obliged to instruct us on how to survive a nuclear war. Our safety would be guaranteed in two phases. Phase One was tricky. If there was enough warning time before bombs hit Newell, we were to be evacuated to New London, North Carolina, which was located thirty minutes east of us. Why this was much safer than Newell I would never learn, but I totally bought into the efficacy of such a plan. Phase Two was simple. If there was not enough warning time for us to evacuate to New London, then we would be forced to employ the classic protective-desk strategy for our defense against atomic attack per instructions from the Civil Defense program called: *Operation Duck and Cover*. The procedure went like this: At the first sign of a bright flash, duck under your diminutive school desk and cover your head. That was it. That was all that was required for us to be safe. That was all that stood between our little bodies and the horrors of searing temperatures and the tremendous devastation created by the force of the blast.

One wealthy family in Newell had built an authentic Fallout Shelter in the back yard next to their swimming pool. But rumor had it that the thing was too small to hold more than its own family members. The rest of us were out of luck if we wanted to be safe in Newell and we didn't have a desk handy. But something puzzled me. One afternoon, after getting home from school, I sat outside under a young oak tree in the side yard and pondered the fate of my mother and myself. My fear wasn't the after-effects of an atomic bomb. I knew I'd be safe. I had access to a desk. My mom did not. In the event that my desk would not be necessary for immediate bomb-shielding, I would be sent to New London for shelter. My mom would not. It was inconceivable to me that the invasion would come any time other than during convenient school hours where we would be at the very place which afforded us the most protection. My mother would not have the safety and security of a desk or a bus ride out to the small town two counties over. What would she do? And if I *was* evacuated, how in the world would she ever find me again? I could construct no satisfactory solution. So I cried.

Mom saw me and came outside to ask what the problem was. She didn't like for us to have problems. Or to cry. She encouraged us to be trouble-free when possible. I told her what worried me and she immediately sought to allay my fears. In her booming baritone, usually saved for Sunday morning hymn-singing, or calling us to supper from four miles away, or to demonstrate her mastery over atomic bombs, she explained, "First of all, I'll be just fine. I'm too mean to ever be killed by anything as silly as communist bombs. Plus, I have plenty of things to duck under here, namely the kitchen table. Don't think for a minute that your school has the only means of defense available. And as for the evacuation, I *will* find you no matter where you are taken. You can depend on that!"

And I did. She was big and strong, permanent and everlasting. And smart, too. I believed her with all my heart. I no longer feared our separation because of a ridiculous atomic bomb.

Mom consoled me at other times, too, especially when I was

forced to confront serious real world facts of life. When I hit the age where one's friends attempt to disabuse their peers of the notion that Santa is real, I asked Mom to address the subject. She simply stated that when I no longer believed in Santa, Santa would no longer bring me gifts at Christmas. That was that. As I sit here writing this, I declare that I believe, unequivocally, in Santa Claus.

And once, after a family member died, I confided to Mom that I was afraid of death for myself and that I was afraid of her death as well. Camel cigarettes, unfiltered, burned perpetually while perched on the lip of a Bakelite ashtray within Mom's easy reach. Often, they burned themselves out without notice. Other times, she reduced them to short stubs after several lung-filled intakes. In the 1960s, we already suspected that smoking cigarettes was harmful to humans. Each one of her children begged her to quit the habit.

"I will not quit." No hesitation. She knew her own mind. "These cigarettes are pure tobacco, untainted by filters or chemicals such as menthol. A natural product like this will not give me cancer."

"But if it does," I whined, "it'll be hard to stand by and watch you suffer…"

"If smoking does give me cancer," she swore, punctuating her words with determined jabs of the cigarette into the space between us. "I promise you will *not* have to sit by my bedside and watch me die a slow and painful death. I hereby let you off the hook."

Fate is a funny thing, and she did not get cancer. And yet I still watched on as she died a slow and heartbreakingly difficult death. At the time of this exchange, though, I was relieved. Her word was law. "Besides," she added gently. "God does something to help us get ready when death approaches. Something happens inside of us that makes us not so scared, not so frightened. Death is not horrible. It's only the other side of life. It's like going home… it's simply going home."

This advice would be helpful several decades hence. Mom closed her message with this exclamation. "Cherk up!" (This was Mom's unintentional but no less endearing, combination of perk-up and cheer-up, and always made me laugh.) "All this obsession with death has got to stop because I'm not *going*. I like it here too much and I've decided that I'm not going to go. And if it winds up that I do have to go, it's a long way off. I'm going to live to be a hundred at least." I believed her on this too. I was a gullible little kid.

As I dealt with the dilemmas introduced to us kids by the Cold War, and as I imagined myself the youngest briefcase-toting professor in the world, I also flirted with aspirations of becoming a Mad Scientist. Now, anyone can dream of being a general scientist of non-descript species, genus or phylum. I was a budding *Mad* Scientist. A chemical factory near our house churned out mysterious noxious fumes 24 hours a day. I wanted to be a part of that. I imagined bookish, determined and extremely intelligent people working there in crisp white lab coats, *briefcases*, and their own chemistry sets. I imagined these professionals creating chemical concoctions that a normal person wouldn't be able to envision a purpose for. I threw myself into this new calling with intense dedication and I must have boldly mentioned the scheme to Mom because she made me a crisp white lab coat of my own, and Santa brought me an A.C. Gilbert Chemistry Set. I credit this gift in steadfastly maintaining my belief in dear Santa. And I credit Dad with completing my Mad Scientist attire by donating an old pair of plastic safety goggles from work to my enterprise which, when tightly cinched around my head, deformed my cheeks and upper lip into a hideously mashed up mass of facial features that resembled the profile of a duck-billed platypus.

Since Mom insisted on having a pretty, clean and tidy household, I was exiled to the attic to set up my experimental laboratory. That is where I performed my top secret Mad Scientist experiments. The attic was the perfect setting for carving out a private place to work since nobody else in their right mind would sit in such hot and steamy surroundings for any length of time. In the summertime our attic heated up to triple digits. Alternatively, I could have worked in the cooler and larger crawl space under our house, but I didn't relish sharing digs with the spiders. So on any given day when I had free time, I would suit up, release the pull-down stairs, and climb into the attic for a bit of chemistry-set mayhem. The blonde boy with his dad portrayed on the cover of the metal casing of the chemistry set did not discourage me. I had not yet heard of Marie Curie, but my laboratory would have rivaled hers or the blonde kid's. My chemistry set had little built-in shelves that contained numerous bottles of brightly colored powders and crystals. The set included a metal rack which held several clear glass test tubes. I had tweezers, tongs, litmus paper, and other essential apparatus, or would that be apparati? The instruction manual listed a variety of safe projects for apprentice Mad Scientists to practice, but the Burris family is not known for its devotion to reading instructions and I followed suit. In my own innovative experiments, I created chemical potions of which the average individual could not conceive. I was never quite sure of the purpose or usefulness of my homemade brews but they were original. I sat in that humid hot-house attic for hours on end, in my lab coat, and my goggles. After I had designed and implemented the day's experiments, I wrote up the results in a composition book. And when I was coerced to come down at last, I was a sweaty puddle. I descended into the living quarters gasping for oxygen, perspiring more profusely than if I were weeding an iris bed, with my naturally curly hair frizzed out to stratospheric proportions. That my sibs would roll on the floor laughing at the sight of me mattered not at all. Mad Scientists are misunderstood in their own time.

Sweltering summers in the south during an age when central air conditioning in our homes was rare, called for creative problem-solving in our attempts to stay cool. On hot summer evenings, Mom typically made cold suppers for us to eat at the picnic table on the patio under the awning. I fondly recall home-grown tomatoes stuffed with tuna salad as a favorite. The house would be stifling from the midday heat and it was quite pleasant to sit outside when evening brought the relief of cooling breezes. Probably the only other time we did not eat at the dining room table as a family was when Mom presented her famed Friday night fish fries on the floor of the den, covered with newspaper, in front of the weekly televised Rawhide episode.

Eating inside at the dining room table was usually fun, too. Dad was a student of history, and at the supper table, he quizzed us on various events as well as other bits of trivia like naming each of the state capitals. He loved to give us clues. *"J'you know* (Juno) the capital of Alaska?" At dinner, we were more or less allowed to engage in open, unrestricted conversations. What was *not* open for debate was Mom's rule that every crumb of food on our plates would be eaten. Starving children somewhere in the world would appreciate having a fraction of our bounty. We would have shared, but that wasn't an option. If we did not consume our food quickly enough, it would elicit Mom's ire and a swift reprimand represented by three sharp strikes of her fork on your plate followed by a one-word command: EAT! The command accompanied a thrust of the fork in the general direction of the guilty party. Obviously, we learned early on that while discussing topics of world events at the supper table, we better be *eating* supper too. Mom's stern food-eating policy and implementation was occasionally derailed when her totally involuntary and distinctive pepper-induced sneeze manifested suddenly. Without warning, that thing erupted, shrill enough to puncture an ear drum and it sounded like, CHAW! Not a dainty, delicate or elegant *a'choo*. It was a great big earth-moving two-syllable high-octave CHAW! And it was invariably just one sneeze only. More than one at a time would not have been funny. Trying to top Mom's laughter provoking sneeze, we countered, not with 'Bless You', and not with the accepted German equivalent 'gesundheit' but a derivative play on words my sister manufactured, "G'zoonie, Goonie". In retrospect, I realize it tickled us more than it did Mom.

During our summertime al fresco dining, we were allowed a few liberties not granted to us at the dining table (g'zoonie-goonie blessings excepted). Many times before we finished our meal, Pam-pa would cut a freshly harvested watermelon into pieces and call us up to the farm to share it with him. He literally 'called' from across the field. He had no reason to use a telephone because he could see that we were not inside the house to answer it. And we were allowed to run to him without considering the consequences of unspecified hungry children. One particular invitation was memorable. As soon as we heard Pam-pa's shout, the family took off through the field. I had lagged behind them because I wanted to put on my new tennis shoes. I made up for lost time by running up the path between our two homes at lightning speed. This brand new pair of Keds may not have been PF Flyers of the 'Run faster, Jump higher' fame, but you couldn't have guessed it by my momentum. As I ran full-speed-ahead with my head down to prevent wind-drag that would slow my progress, I had only one theme running through my thoughts:

I am running faster than I have ever run before...
I am running faster than any other human on earth...
I hope everyone is looking at me as I run, so they can witness this amazing feat...

I *knew* all eyes were focused on me and marveling at the swiftness of my strides. I *knew* they were thinking exactly what I was thinking: *Wow, she sure is running fast!*

When I regained consciousness on the sofa in the living room back at our house, I realized that running with my head down and my eyes following every move my Keds made, meant that I did not see the cast iron lawn furniture that put a major lump on my forehead before it knocked me out. I have no recollection of receiving sympathy from any family member that day.

The cool thing about growing your own food, including watermelons, and having a mother who is artistic and never wastes anything, is that she carved charming baskets from the watermelon rinds, then re-filled them with melon balls as a treat for us. It was labor-intensive, which was an attraction for Mom. No effort was too great for her and no item too small to re-purpose. She never wasted even a nut shell. In fact, she would take an English walnut shell, line each half with a piece of delicate fabric from her sewing room (also known as the utility room) glue it into place, make a tiny little pillow, and present it to us as a little Thumbelina bed. We placed these little beds on our bedroom window sills to attract Thumbelina to visit us. We stayed awake long into the night waiting for her to materialize. She would have had easy access since we slept with windows and doors wide open. Like most homes in Newell at that time, our home was never locked (they are now, so don't get any ideas). I wasn't even aware that a door key existed as long as I lived there so there was nothing but the screens between us and the mosquitoes, which was a more imminent threat to us than two-legged intruders. With every entrance unencumbered by any sort of fortified barriers, we knew that when Thumbelina appeared, she could tuck herself into bed without impediment.

While waiting for the elusive little fairy to arrive, I passed the time listening to the night sounds of crickets, katydids, freight trains, dogs barking in the distance, and undetermined rustling in the grass under the window. *Thumbelina?*

One particular sound was a bit disturbing. Our volunteer fire department had an old Decot siren which, when set off, began on a low note and slid up the scale an octave into a crescendo where it persisted for agonizing minutes before working its way back down the scale again. It sounded like the air raid alerts I had heard in wartime movies which warned of impending bombings of allied cities. Hearing the alarm set off in the middle of the night to notify the volunteers of a fire or other danger, prompted recurring nightmares. I suppose this siren would also have been designated as our civil defense warning in case there was a need to evacuate ahead of a nuclear holocaust. I never became inured to that mournful warning of peril.

I had other recurring dreams. Some silly, some terrifyingly grim like *The Foot Grabber* dream. Yes, my dreams have titles - it makes them easier to remember and report on in any conversation. For instance, I can say, "Oh, I had the 'Foot Grabber' dream again." And, "Yes, last night, I dreamed the 'Hospital Robot' dream again." And so on. Anyway, in the Foot Grabber dream, I'm walking from the kitchen in our house, down the brick steps to the 'outside den'. The outside den was converted out of the carport and it was closed in with floor-to-ceiling louvered windows that made a nice cool, breezy, gathering room in our air-condition-less house. As practical as they were, washing them, like weeding that blasted iris bed, was a time-consuming chore. Mom made quite sure the devil never had access to idle hands at our home. But, back to the dream. In the dream, I'm going to sit on the sofa and watch television. As I get near the sofa, a man's hand reaches out from underneath it to grab my... yes, you guessed it, *foot*. See why titles are useful?

In reality, the sofa was low to the floor with not enough space for even the cutest and most benign little dust bunnies to collect, let alone a foot-grabbing adult man. Nonetheless, it's a spooky damned dream to have in the dead of night. And it spooked me that I dreamed it more than once, believing it to be a 'prophecy'. Reason told me that no adult could fit under our sofa, and that there was no cause for me to be frightened, but a glitch in that same rationale commanded me to believe that he actually could fit under *my bed*. Since I'd been warned, I felt the need to guard against a real occurrence. Dreams may be off by only a small amount, for instance the actual piece of furniture under which a foot grabber will hide as he lies in wait to grab young, innocent feet. Therefore, it was necessary for me to take extreme caution before getting in my bed each night. The precautions I felt necessary to take were these:

Step One: Search the closet. Yes, stay with me here. You see, the foot grabber could hide there until making his slithery move behind my back to slip under the bed. Checking the closet was vital to my pre-bed ritual. After checking the closet and proving to myself that it was clear, I then proceeded to Step Two.

Step Two: Check under the bed. This was the hard part. I would throw back the covers, do a two-step backwards, bend at the waist (never kneel, you can't get back up and run quickly from a kneeling position – who said I can't think out a well-reasoned plan of action?). Peer under the bed, quickly but thoroughly, because you don't want to have to duplicate this step under any circumstances. It was enough that this procedure had to be performed every night, I sure didn't want to wind up engaging in the obsessive-compulsive behavior of doing this thing *more* than once a night.

Step Three: Turn off the light. After determining that the coast was clear, I had to retrace my steps back across the room to the wall where the light switch was located, and I had to do it without taking my eyes off the space between the floor and the bed because who knew how quickly the foot grabber could scoot into position and successfully complete his plan to grab my foot as I climbed into bed.

Step Four: Leap into bed. After walking back to the light switch and turning it off, I took a flying leap into the bed that was six feet away. My ankles weren't in the same zip code as my bed when they lost contact with the floor and jumped high into the air, landing safely onto the island of protection – the surface of the bed itself. Mission accomplished. Relief. Then a quick silent reminder to myself before drifting off to sleep: Do NOT let your feet dangle off the edge of the bed at any time during the night.

Unknown to me Robert acquired information related to this nightly ceremony of mine. In short, somebody I had told the dream narrative to ratted me out. And Robert, of course, had no choice but to use it against me. He didn't taunt me, or call me names. No, that would have been unimaginative. What he did was to lie in wait for me, under my bed, until I launched into my shenanigans. In essence, he became the foot grabber himself. So, on the night in question, I went through each step as usual, and as I got to Step Two and pulled back the bed covers, never-ever-in-a-million-years did I expect to see a face. Because logically, THERE SHOULD BE NO FACE. And yet, THERE WAS A FACE. The moment I saw this face, I knew it was Robert's. My rational brain said: *Great, stoopid ol' Robert's hiding under my bed*. My reptilian brain, however, took total control of my emotional and physical response. I screamed. No, I didn't just scream, I bellowed out a blood-curdling scream without restraint. And I didn't merely bellow out a blood-curdling scream without restraint. I jumped outside of my body and watched myself as I bellowed out a blood-curdling scream. My psyche detached from my body as I observed myself jump about three feet straight up into the air, as I screamed, blood curdlingly. From that position, I saw Robert cringe in terror as he witnessed the demon possession of his sister because of this prank, but I couldn't do anything but look down at the scene and observe. After some time passed, I don't know, say five minutes? Five seconds? Five hours? Total time-warp here. Anyway, Mom eventually came into the room and grabbed my shoulders. It was enough to bring me back into my body. Robert was up and out from under the bed by this time and trying to convince me that he was sorry and that he had no idea what the outcome would be. *I guess NOT!*

Mom wanted to know what the hell was going on. Robert explained. He told the truth. I had no words. In fact, I had screamed so hard that I ejected my voice box out of my body and it had taken up residence somewhere under the bed where the real foot grabber would find it one fateful night. And it would serve him right, too! Aunt Ruth, Dad's sister, who was visiting from out of town, had been in Mom and Dad's bedroom with Mom moments before the incident occurred. They were looking at something –I don't know what– but as Ruth stood there listening to Robert explain the cause of the ruckus, she breathed a huge sigh of relief. She interjected, without invitation, I might add, "Whew. Thank God! Thank God it was only a prank, because when I heard the screaming, all I could think of was that communists had gotten into the house."

Robert consoled me. He sat on my bed with his arm across

my shoulders for the longest time. He's never hidden under my bed since but we had many more opportunities for fun and high jinks.

CHAPTER THREE

Minnesota or Bust

Nothing bonds a family better than fun and high jinks, unless it's an expedition to a foreign culture. Mom drove us 1,300 miles to northern Minnesota to visit her only sister during summer vacations when we were youngsters. Our Aunt Virginia moved there in the late 1940s after marrying one of its native sons. There, she and our Uncle John grew a nice large family together. After my siblings and I were grown, other priorities bumped ahead of further escapades into the North Country until Aunt Virginia began her battle against breast cancer. Even though Mom was only sixty-two, my sister and I had noticed an uncharacteristic slowing down of the Rusty-machine so we hatched a plan to take Mom on a road trip to Minnesota for a Parker sister reunion. We had an inkling of what the future held for our aunt, but no comparable feelings of dread for Mom - the concept of Alzheimer's had not yet made itself a resident in our consciousness. Nor had the diagnosis of clinical depression which would be the initial explanation of the changes she experienced. Mom had lost considerable weight and was smaller than I had ever known her to be in my life. She was frail enough to occasionally rely on a walking cane for support and she was somewhat forgetful but nothing more noticeable than what could be explained away by fatigue or stress. However, this was a turning point in Rusty's trajectory through an otherwise active life and a significant departure from the usual *confident* Rusty. With these changes, Mom was reluctant to take the lead in our travel plans and deferred to Barbara and me over issues such as the route we would drive to Minnesota and when and where we would stop for meals. This was fresh territory for all of us.

Mom had planned and executed the Minnesota road trip countless times before on her own since Dad typically did not take extended periods of time off from work. As the only adult with three, and then four children, she was in control. *She* knew the way. *She* knew the schedule. Rusty was up and on the road at daybreak. Air conditioning was not standard in most automobiles then and getting a certain number of miles under her belt before the afternoon heat made us ill as hornets was appealing. We stopped for picnic lunches on the side of the road, and by mid-afternoon, we checked into a room at a motor court, lured into its parking lot by a colorful neon sign advertising an outdoor pool. If we didn't have air conditioning in our automobile, then you know we didn't have DVD players or video games. Boredom and restlessness produced many *he hit me-she looked at me* skirmishes that Mom had no patience for. Basically, if she could swat all of us at once, she felt she had demonstrated a keen advocacy for justice and fairness and we were to be grateful it wasn't more.

But the swimming pool! The prospect of a swimming pool waiting for us at the end of our day's journey lulled us into a state of unnatural compliance that went against our puerile temperament. The promise of splashing about in ten feet of chlorine water as a reward for being cooped up in the car for hours was the inducement for us to behave. And Mom joined us. It was fun to see her un-self-consciously enjoying herself. Athletic and energetic, Mom was the picture of health and vitality. Yet, driving for hours with rowdy children tensed up her muscles for some reason. Those same muscles relaxed in response to the physical exercise that swimming provided. Mom was nature-woman. No aspirins or other chemicals for her. She determined to be healthy through the natural healing powers of her own mind-over-matter. Rusty was organic before organic was cool.

Still, we had little sympathy for Mom. In our world it was parent *versus* child, and neither faction held much compassion for the predicaments of the other. From our point of view, adults could do exactly as they wanted; Mom's position was that kids only ever wanted to have fun, thereby rendering us incapable of appreciating the sacrifices made on our behalf. Mom probably had not known carefree larkdom since her father's death. As the traditional bread-winner of the family, his being snatched away prematurely imposed dire economic straits on her family. We, of course, had not tasted any responsibilities of adulthood and believed the world should indeed revolve around us. During swimming time, at least, we enjoyed a détente. Mom swam and enjoyed her healthy, agile body. We played and enjoyed our freedom from the chores we would have been doing if we were home.

During each day's tediously long ride that propelled us ever closer to Minnesota, we were not left totally to our own devices for fun. Weeks before our trip, Mom bought games and books for us. We typically didn't receive toys and gifts other than birthdays and Christmas, which were quite generous, but this was an exception. Little Golden Books and Car Bingo were favorite amusements of ours, as was Wooly Willy, a cardboard game with magnetized metal shavings that could be positioned over a picture of a man's bald head to produce hair, sideburns and mustaches. A Magic Slate board was also part of our inventory of fun. This toy was a writing tablet that used a sheet of film over a black wax backing that could be written or drawn upon with a stylus and then erased by lifting the film away from the backing. This action could be repeated indefinitely, making it a most practical plaything. I think cave dwellers had similar gadgets. Coloring books and fresh packs of Crayolas rounded out our onboard entertainment except for the one trip where we had an Etch-a-Sketch. Very high tech.

We were eager to see this cache of fun as soon as Mom brought the items into the house, but she was adamant, "No touching or looking at the books and games before the trip!" She knew that if we had access to our road-trip diversions, the mystique would be diminished and we would, no doubt, resort to being unruly little monsters. Mom's plan worked, and grueling hours and days on the road were improved dramatically by her foresight. To this day, I cannot pass up the lure of a Little Golden Book or the siren's call of crayons and coloring books.

After what seemed like a lifetime on the road, we arrived at our cousins' house in Keewatin. We marveled at the close family resemblance Mom and Aunt Virginia shared. Both had thick, naturally curly hair. They both actively nudged their reddish-auburn color toward the *reddish* end of the spectrum – Mom's only concession to better living through chemistry.

Upon our arrival, my sibs and I were treated like royalty. Or novelties. Our cousins were exotic to us, too. We were worlds apart and there are scores of differences between our cultures. The village of Keewatin is strategically located in the Mesabi Iron Range, famous for its taconite mines. Traditions and customs there are vastly different from the ones we grew up with in Newell. At home, our rural location meant that we could only go as far as our little legs could pedal our bikes. And even then, we were only at someone else's farm. Here in Keewatin, we could walk a block and a half across the railroad tracks and be in the middle of town – a town where kids could walk into a Malt Shop and order a Chocolate Malted Milkshake, *Malted* for short. The fact that kids could get one of those without a parent accompanying them was the ultimate freedom and it caused me to imagine that I was living inside an Archie comic book.

My cousins' hometown occupies three square miles and probably had a population of around 1,200 people in the 1960s. My high school had more people, so it's safe to say that everybody knows everybody there. Certainly, residents know when visitors turn up. My uncle was Chief of Police there and the Carroll family was active in church and local affairs. On any given day, when walking down the street with our cousins, going to get, say, a *Malted*, someone would shout at us from across the way, "Hello, are those your cousins from Carolina?"

"Yes! They're here, finally." Our cousins seemed to be quite proud of us in spite of our *To Kill a Mockingbird* mystique.

"Say something 'southern'!" Their friends would demand.

"Hey." We obliged by stretching this small word to two or three syllables. We southerners treat vowels with much more respect that northerners do, giving them the full value they deserve. For good measure, we'd whip out the classic Dixie greeting. "How *ya'll* doin'?"

"Oh gosh. It's just like in the movies."

Speaking of the movies, going to the movie theatre in town was another treat for my sibs and me when visiting our cousins. We roamed free at night to attend black and white, science fiction, and horror flicks. The great films of the 1950's and 60's included such blockbusters as *Creature from the Black Lagoon*, *Godzilla*, *Night of the Living Dead*, *Invasion of the Body Snatchers*, *The Day the Earth Stood Still*, *The Giant Claw*, *The Blob*, and *Attack of the Giant Leeches*. For crying out loud, where was *Mary Poppins* or *Peter Pan*? I can remember only alien invasions and mutations. This was the Cold War era after all and the entire world feared a nuclear meltdown, communists hiding under the bed, or world domination by malformed invaders. I knew we'd be protected from the effects of a communist-initiated nuclear blast if we hunkered under our desks at school, despite our mothers being vulnerable and unprotected at home. But the cloak of faux-safety will not save earthlings from intergalactic marauders.

On these movie nights, I never stopped to wonder what the adults were doing while we were at the movies. I thought their lives began only when we were present and stopped when we were gone. They were boring and un-fun most of the time anyway - we couldn't imagine that they were having a secret good time on their own. I figured they were probably taking naps since we made them so tired.

Minnesota is the Land of 10,000 Lakes and there is no shortage of swimming and shoreline picnic opportunities. We never made it to all 10,000 of them but I remember a few of them like, Swan Lake, Twin Lakes, and Nameless Lake. At Wolf Lake we shared swimming space with gigantic home-grown leeches. Since this lake was handy, there was no need to drive all the way to Leech Lake (official name). Regardless of our destination, we all shared duties in the massive mobilization of food, supplies and materiel necessary to provide for Mom, Aunt Virginia, Uncle John, and upwards of ten to twelve kids as we took advantage of lakeside recreational features.

My sister and I reminisced about these good times during the current trip to Minnesota. We knew this visit would be quite different - we were going to say goodbye to our aunt, the person in our lives who thought we were perfect in every way. In spite of the reason for our visit, we found ways to enjoy the trek with Mom. She, however, was not completely content that my sister and I were in charge of planning and navigating the route, and that we made up the ground rules. The two basic rules were simple, and (we thought) easy enough to follow.

Rule #1: No smoking in the car.

Rule #2: No negative talk about Dad.

"What on earth will we talk about then?" Mom complained.

"*Any*thing else" we countered.

"But he's my husband. I can say whatever I want about him."

Mom loved Dad and she never said horrible things but she could be a little critical and this was a typical exchange:

"Your father doesn't even know how to wash dishes right."

"But he washes them, right?"

"Yes, but he doesn't do it *right*."

"He's our father and it hurts us to hear these things – besides if he's as incompetent as you claim, why didn't you divorce him?"

"Because I love him. I wanted to spend my life with him. There's room for improvement in the dish-washing category, though."

"Okay, you're welcome to your opinion, but we don't want to hear you voice it."

"It's not an opinion. It's a fact."

"Okay, we don't want to hear negative facts."

"Fine. I'll sit back here and you won't hear a peep out of me." She turned her head in an *I'm-above-it-all* attitude. She gazed out the car window and into the distance, appearing to watch the scenery roll by. Since we were unsympathetic to her plight as someone who must endure Dad's dish-washing ineptitude alone, she tried to ignore us as long as she could. Only two minutes later, seeing a pretty bloom along the side of the road, Mom forgot all about being peeved with her traveling companions.

"Look at that magnificent flowering Quince!" she exclaimed. "It's the most gorgeous one I've ever seen!" Rusty had lost none of her enthusiasm for roadside diversions.

We logged twenty-four hours on the road from North Carolina to Minnesota, chewing up the miles and spitting them out as we talked and laughed and cried. Mom accepted that she couldn't smoke in Barbara's car, but she realized early on that we couldn't refuse her a bathroom break which brought with it a cigarette break as well. Crafty. Once, when we were telling jokes, we got Mom laughing so out of control that she wet her pants. She blamed the incident on us, which we agreed was entirely our fault, but she used it to her advantage to get another break. And more cigarettes. She merely threatened to lose control of her bladder again and we stopped at the first opportunity. Smart ol' bird. During the break and after returning to the car in a speedy fashion, Mom would light up then sit on the back seat with the door open and smoke her cigarette. She would keep the cigarette *technically* outside of the vehicle. We took one bathroom break at a rest stop on a highway in Ohio. It was an outhouse. An outhouse for a rest area? No lie. I have photos.

We finally crossed the state line into Minnesota. The Mississippi River has its origins there. Mom, Aunt Virginia and their brother, Jack, lived on or near the *Mighty Miss* during their growing up years in Memphis. We had been told river stories since we were tots. In anticipation of this occasion and to commemorate it, I had dubbed a cassette tape with Patsy Cline's greatest hits as a surprise. Mom loved Patsy Cline. She loved her music, she loved her story. We grew up listening to Patsy's music on our phonograph along with Doris Day, Gentleman Jim Reeves, Frankie Laine, and others. But Patsy held a special place in Mom's heart – I popped the cassette into the player and we sang our hearts out in celebration as we drove along the bridge that crossed the river. We sang without missing a word or skipping a beat. It's a memory of Mom that I hold dear. We had no sense yet that the condition of Mom's body and mind would deteriorate shortly and in retrospect, I'm glad I maintained my blissful ignorance a little longer. We three Burris women were completely in the moment with little care for what the future would bring our own family. In fact, I thought at the time, *it doesn't get any better than this.*

We would spend the night with our cousin, Virginia Catherine and her husband, Bruce, in Edina and from there we would drive together up to the Iron Range the following morning. Once again, we were treated like royalty. The next morning, we organized ourselves into a tiny convoy to Itasca County. I rode with Virginia Catherine; Barbara and Mom followed. Aunt Virginia was being discharged from the hospital on the day of our arrival so Barbara and Mom drove directly to the hospital to greet her there and accompany her home. Virginia Catherine and I drove directly to the house.

After we greeted each other, Aunt Virginia put away the groceries she stopped to buy for us. Her head was bald as a honeydew melon from chemo-treatments. She covered her head with a wig worn at a rather jaunty angle, but it made her scalp itchy. She took a hank of the artificial hair and worked the wig back and forth to scratch the itch. It was a funny sight to see her move that thing across her head like tectonic plates moving across the globe during a seismic shift. She said it was an irritating thing to put up with. We told her to take the blame thing off. We didn't care about her old bald head, we were just glad to see *her!* Besides, Mom had made Aunt Virginia several turbans for such an occasion. Mom whipped them out on cue. She had sewn a terry-cloth one for that just-out-of-the-shower look. She had made a couple of soft cotton ones for casual-dashes-about-town. And the *pièce de résistance*? A turban made from lamé. Aunt Virginia's eyes lit up when she saw it. Aunt Virginia *loved* any fabric that was shiny and flashy. If it wasn't shiny or flashy, red would do. This turban jumped to the front of the line. She snatched off the offending wig and wrapped the turban-of-honor around her head with flair. She wore the other ones in turn throughout our visit, but none of them lifted her spirits more than this one did. I can't imagine what must have gone through Mom's thoughts as she lovingly made these turbans for her big sister, for her *Ginny*.

Cousins came by to greet us over the next days and we visited Gramma Carroll next door whenever the whim hit us. Aunt Virginia pulled out boxes of photographs and placed them on the dining room table. She used the same system of photo organization as Mom did. It's the same one I use, too. Each snapshot she pulled out of the cardboard box of loose photographs had a story. Aunt Virginia remembered conversations, fashion details, hair styles. Everything. Her memory became more acute as she neared the end of her life, while Rusty's became vague and eventually non-existent as she neared her own. But for now, Mom continued to have a healthy enough recollection and any fuzziness she experienced she chalked up to her 'little memory problem'.

On previous visits, decades earlier, Rusty would have been looking for work to do – something useful, something more productive than sitting, and talking. During this turning-point visit, Rusty was content to enjoy the company of her family. A miracle? This was perhaps one of the first to come to my attention. She sat at the dining room table with the serenity of a Zen monk as we looked at photos and listened to Parker family history. Mom had mellowed and she demonstrated a quiet inner peace that permitted her to sit and be with us, patiently.

My cousins couldn't believe how tiny and frail their Aunt LaVern had become. I was glad that they remembered her as a larger-than-life, glamorous, and statuesque woman. I had always seen her this way too, but I had begun to question my own memory. It's nice to have corroboration. And although Mom's physical stature was shrinking, her spirit and countenance continued to be titanic.

We burrowed through the piles of old black and white photographs. I held one up. It was of a matronly-looking sour-faced woman. She had a bun pulled back so tight that, it almost made her smile. Almost, but not quite.

"Who is this?" I asked my aunt.

"Oh, that's your grandmother. *My* grandmother, actually. Your *great* grandmother, Belle Payne. Her name was Pearl Isabelle Payne. I was named for her: Virginia Isabelle, as your mom was named for our mother: Lottie LaVern."

But back to the photographs. "This is our Cherokee connection, then? This is the Cherokee Grandmother who married the man from Paris, France?" I asked.

"That's the one. His name was Edmond DeMaris." Aunt Virginia pointed at a serious-looking tall slender man with a long, dark handle-bar mustache. He stood beside Belle Payne on the field of a farmstead.

"She doesn't look very Indian-ish to me," I observed. "Or Native-American," I corrected myself.

"Did you expect feathers and a papoose?" My aunt replied matter-of-factly.

"Well, yes. Actually, I did." And I expected long silky-black hair, a glorious golden-red tan, buckskins, and a *princess* title as well. I didn't voice this, but I *did* expect it. My sibs and I had not ever seen photographs of this set of grandparents, and the made-up image in my mind was a little different.

"That's the stuff of stories. This is how real people looked."

Stories that Mom and Aunt Virginia shared with us at the dining room table helped make connections to grandparents and great grandparents we never knew. Aunt Virginia corroborated stories we grew up hearing from Rusty about their mother, Lottie. After their dad had died Lottie took the small insurance benefit and bought a used car with it. Since she didn't know how to drive, Lottie made a deal with the salesman; she would buy the car from him if he taught her how to drive. Few job opportunities existed for a widowed woman in 1936 who needed to support a family. Threatened with the prospect of having to place her children in an orphanage, Lottie became entrepreneurial. She used the car and the newly-obtained driving skills to run a jitney service.

A jitney service, as Mom explained to us when we were old enough to ask, was an auxiliary form of transportation. In Memphis, the bus service ran to the city limits and stopped. If you needed to travel further on into the county, a jitney – or privately owned car – would collect you and take you to your destination. It was a dangerous business, especially for a woman, so Lottie Parker carried brass-knuckles as protection. I know this part is true because Mom inherited them. I was a little bit scared of this grandmother even though I never met her, but her memory lived in our household throughout the subsequent decades. Aunt Virginia backed up Mom's stories that we half-suspected were fabrications. And if not fabrications then at least amplified for our benefit. The tales were colossal, there's no doubt about that. But they were true. Aunt Virginia added to the stories, and we comprehended that Mom had been quite restrained in telling the tales to us over the years of our childhood.

We stayed with Aunt Virginia for two weeks. In that time, we had family cook-outs and we visited the homes of cousins who lived nearby. We spent hours sitting with Aunt Virginia in her living room, telling stories and reminiscing. She and Mom spent time together, just the two of them. We behaved as if our day of departure would never come. As each new day of our visit dawned, I subconsciously maintained the perception that we had plenty of time - our minds always delude us into thinking we have more time. But the moment to say goodbye did come. It was hard on Mom, naturally, to believe she was seeing her sister for the last time. It was difficult for Barbara and me, too. Aunt Virginia loved us so much. Our aunt, always, *always* treated my brothers and sister and me as if we were the sweetest and most adorable and delightful children to ever walk the earth. In her eyes we could do no wrong. No price can be placed on that. It's good to have somebody in your life who believes in you to the extent that they cannot imagine you being less than a pure Angel. I did not want to say farewell to my aunt. I did not want to think of a world without her in it.

Even so, I treated the last hug and wave goodbye as lightly as if we were merely running up to the corner market for bread and milk. I guess we do this so that we don't make a scene or collapse into hysteria. Mom and Barbara were being brave too. But I hope when it's time for me to die, somebody will cry in my presence to let me know that my leaving causes some pain. I hope friends and family won't wave nonchalantly as they get into their automobile to go home and shout at me: 'Take care!'

I never saw my aunt again. But Mom saw her two more times. She met Aunt Virginia and Uncle John in Memphis for a family reunion and then once more in Keewatin the following February. Aunt Virginia was nearing the end of her struggle against cancer but Mom's visit meant the patient rallied and improved. Mom came back home after a 'good little visit' but flew back once more, for the funeral. Mom accepted this loss as she had other losses in her life. It was part of life for her and she took it in stride. I remembered her telling me when I was a child, that when it's time to face death, God finds a way to help take away the fear of this unknown destination. If Rusty says it's true, then it's true. There is no doubt that her faith comforted her but I was no comfort to her at all. I had no idea how it felt to lose a sibling, but I would find out.

It is a testament to Mom's pluck, and evidence of my ignorance of the real state of her mental health, that I encouraged her to traipse off to Tennessee and Minnesota on her own. Our family still worked under the mistaken impression that Mom's changes in personality and the decline in her characteristic boldness was only a phase, a consequence of age and nothing more sinister. But she was only sixty-two. Not even retirement age. Nevertheless, the weight loss, the forgetfulness, and the subdued temperament were uncharacteristic. We were concerned, but only as much as anyone would be for a loved one. A blissful cloud of ignorance protected us from believing that anything more daunting than Mom growing a little older was taking place.

CHAPTER FOUR

Life with a twist of lemon

Aunt Virginia died on her brother's birthday. Mom came home from that last Minnesota trip filled with grief but no less determined to live her life to the fullest. A lifetime of memories helps sustain us when we lose our loved ones but Mom's personal cache was being depleted daily. It's not true that women can't keep a secret. A generation of stories and events judged private by these sisters, was guarded and protected by LaVern and Virginia from all mortals on earth for eternity. By a bizarre quirk of fate the last seeds of the Parker family memories were to be left behind in a field that would soon lie fallow. It's ironic that Mom's family history, including secrets great and small would reside with her alone, entrusted to the one who would eventually have no capacity to retain the stories. I kick myself that I did not think to ask more questions about the Parkers while there was still time.

Rusty relied on the walking cane as she became more unsteady on her feet. Once she told me, "One doesn't *use* a cane, one *wears* a cane; although a man may 'sport' a cane". She was referring to a time when a walking cane was a fashion accessory not an orthopedic device. All the foremost English walking cane dealers will tell you the same thing. I think Mom had a British past-life persona that seeped into her current life on occasion as she also used other British phrases such as, *that's like carrying coal to Newcastle*. So, she *wore* a cane. She actually looked quite distinguished with the cane and I think she knew it. She used it proudly for support as she walked and it gave her confidence that she otherwise no longer had. And if the cane attracted attention, the more the better as blending into the environment, chameleon-like, is not a Rusty-trait. Her Sunday hats were the talk of the congregation back when hats were in vogue at church.

Outrageously plumed affairs, they were. And she wore the cane with as much flair as she wore those hats. She could also use the cane to punctuate any point she wished to make, like when she wielded a straw or pencil in a more scaled down display of dramatic emphasis.

I was busy making my own points in the Western Civ history course I taught at the university. The need to prepare lectures prior to standing in front of thirty-five pairs of eyes kept my mind occupied, focused and engaged and it was a much needed distraction from my parents' flagging health. Neither Dad's physical struggles nor Mom's diminishing problem-solving skills boded well for a long-term plan to keep them living independently in their own home.

Dad could have taught my history course as well as I did. He loved history and his intellect never dulled with age even though his body declined slowly and progressively in his seventies. Arthritis in his hands, knees and back affected his mobility but the macular degeneration diagnosed in both eyes was debilitating. The loss of central vision explained why Dad was not able to bring much of what was in his line of sight into focus, seeing only shadows at times but generally missing entire portions within his line of sight. The resulting impairment meant no more driving for him. It was a sad day when Dad had to give up driving Li'l Whitey, his beloved white Ford Ranger truck. Charlotte is a city spread out past its capability to provide basic and convenient mass transit services (or sidewalks) to all its suburbs, even if its citizens *were* likely to adopt that mode of transportation – which Jim and Rusty were not. In Newell, a car is the primary means of transportation, but more importantly, it is *the* symbol of independence. Not having that ability means you're at the mercy of friends and family for help to run errands. Not to worry, though. Mom could drive them to various places like the grocery store, the local convenience store, church, and Hardee's. All the important places.

Relying on a walking cane did not diminish Mom's enthusiasm when I mentioned that I needed to paint the exterior of my house the autumn after Aunt Virginia passed away. I took some time off from work to do the project and to enroll in a Latin language course on campus. I used a host of Latin words in the course I taught and I wanted a firmer foundation in the language. Also, I yearned to gain parity with Mom's botanical taxonomic proficiencies. At last I would put the regret for not acquiring this skill in high school to rest.

I looked forward to completing both the Latin course and the house painting during my vacation. My one-story house had rough cedar-board siding on it that gave it the appearance of a rustic cottage, but it had been a decade since its last coat of stain and I wanted to protect the wood against the coming winter. When Mom volunteered to help me, childhood memories of her as a tough task-master could not be quelled, even though my adult self thought it would be fun for us to be together. On my own, I had developed a different, that is to say, slower work pace than the one I was taught as a child. I didn't relish any 'lazy heifer' accusations in my own home. But, I couldn't have been more off the mark.

"What time do you want me to come over in the morning?" Mom asked as we made plans. Mom was an early riser and could get the bulk of her chores done before lunchtime, or even dawn. A brief nap after lunch energized her to finish whatever work couldn't be done the next day, which was all of it, actually. I pondered my answer.

"Um...," I hesitated. "We could get going about seven o'clock, I guess. Or seven thirty." I found my courage and boldly pushed my luck, by thirty minutes.

"Seven?" Incredulity in her voice. I re-set my inner clock. Backwards. My courage waned. Mom continued. "That's much too early. I have to get your father's breakfast before I come over and you need to have a little leisure time before we start – it's your vacation, after all."

W*here-is-my-mother?* I thought. I was unaware that the word 'leisure' was in her vocabulary. The voice on the phone was Mom's but her outlook was unfamiliar to me. Had aliens come down and inhabited her body? Images from the Keewatin movies flashed in my mind.

"Why don't I plan to be there around eight or nine? You have the coffee going and I'll bring ham biscuits." I liked the plan immediately.

Mom arrived at eight-thirty each morning. We enjoyed our breakfast and then we painted. I used a roller and stood on portable scaffolding to reach as high as I could. Mom used a brush and cut in the edges but only as far as she could reach from *terra firma*. Mom complimented me on the home-owner skills I had acquired since I had struck out on my own. We painted in silence while birds sang to us and we chatted casually when it suited us. We stopped for refreshments when we needed them. For lunch, Dad was to fend for himself. We made our own sandwiches and sat in lawn chairs at the top of the driveway in front of the garage and in the shade. We ate and chatted. I cannot remember a conversation we had. But I remember thinking as I did the day we drove into Minneapolis singing Patsy Cline songs, *it doesn't get any better than this*.

Mornings were invigoratingly cool, then pleasantly warm by afternoon. Other than that distinction, the days ran into each other. Mom left early enough in the afternoon so she could rest and recover for the next day. Sensible woman. I spent the remainder of my time completing conjugation, declination, and translation homework. I appreciated having time to prepare. Latin is hard. As we began to complete the trim work on the house, I was sad to be near the end of our project.

With the exterior of the house protected and my Latin skills up to snuff, I looked forward to the Christmas holidays. My brother Robert invited the family to his house for our celebration but it was there that we had a first-hand peek at some real problems plaguing Mom. Considerable personality changes began making major departures from the *old* Rusty way of doing things. Mom acted so out of character, we had to stop and take notice.

Robert had prepared a wonderful feast for us all. Mom and Dad rode with Barbara and Andy to his house. My best friend Donna and her son Josh came with me. Josh is my godson and together the three of us have shared a home since he was a toddler. Dad's sister, Ruth and her husband, Ben were there as well. Ruth showed no fear of communists hiding under Robert's bed so it was a fun day. Then, for some unknown reason, Mom became upset and demanded to go home. She couldn't describe why, only that she felt trapped and needed to go home. It was extraordinary that she insisted on this because she was never given to dramatic displays of emotion before. In fact, she discouraged dramatic responses to uncomfortable situations as signs of weakness, characteristics which should not be displayed in public. On this occasion, unable to hide her anxiety or mask her distress, Mom threw that rule out the window. The irrational behavior was new and it was a red flag. We just didn't know what was being flagged. Barbara and Andy took Mom and Dad home. Barbara called me after she and Andy had a chance to calm Mom down.

"Andy was so sweet and gentle with her," Barbara told me. "He sat down by her side, held her hand and encouraged her to tell us what was bothering her, but she couldn't describe how she felt or what actually upset her."

We took more notice of the daily challenges Mom faced from then on. Rusty had always stood up to, and overcome any challenge that stepped in her path so this was a major departure from her usual personality. We were oblivious to the plaques and tangles forming in her brain. Shortly after Christmas, Mom called me at work. "Would you mind taking me to my doctor's appointment? Your father said it would be fun if the two of us went together."

Thanks a lot Dad. I detected a conspiracy. But could it be that Dad believed Mom needed protection, a taxi, and someone to listen and remember the doctor's orders? I agreed to take her. We needed to find out why Rusty was experiencing anxiety attacks. The doctor gave Mom a physical exam and did some blood work. Afterwards we sat in a café and Mom bought me a chocolate milkshake, although she neither ate nor drank anything herself. I was happy to be with Mom on this outing. Taking her to the doctor's office was a small price to pay for such a lovely afternoon. Jim, in his quiet little way was right after all. And still, I remained blissfully ignorant to what was ahead of us.

The results of Mom's blood test showed no signs of any physical illness so the physician defaulted with a diagnosis of clinical depression as the culprit causing the behavioral changes. Mom was thrilled. *What?* She beamed with pride as she accepted this thing that now had a name, this thing that was the source of her suffering. When Mom's physician prescribed an antidepressant, we all felt better. Especially Mom who now had an explanation for her problems and it was no fault of her own. From then on, Rusty spoke of her depression as if it were a dear friend.

"You're losing weight," I'd say to her.

"I'm not eating as much as I should. I don't have much of an appetite. It's my *depression*, you know - a chemical imbalance."

With her mind-over-matter attitude, Mom had never owned up to illnesses before this. Often, I thanked my lucky stars that we, her children, were not born with major infirmities or she would have accused us of faking the illness to get out of work. That was the younger Rusty, at any rate. Not the mellow one who emerged after we grew up and left home. That she was now able to acknowledge even a smidge of imperfection was psychologically healthy for her and for me. It made her more human. From then on, I went to every appointment with Mom and I drove Rusty and Jim to all events that were not the routine grocery store. If their destination was unfamiliar, I was their taxi. It was not always convenient, but it put my mind at ease.

Being chauffeured around town didn't mean the old Rusty, my real mother, was lost. She still had plenty of grit in her. Her brother, Jack, lived only ten miles away. Since he had been just fourteen when their mother died, Mom and Aunt Virginia had shared responsibility for his care; the pattern established then continued throughout his adulthood. Now he was diagnosed with liver cancer and although Mom herself was experiencing the dulling of her sharp intellect, she accepted responsibilities for his care.

After surgery, Jack required the comprehensive care of a nursing home. With little chance that he would recover sufficiently to be on his own again he would have to vacate his apartment. It was up to Mom to physically move his belongings out. Mom told me when the day of the move would be but she did not ask for help. She intended to take care of her brother's affairs on her own. Four and a half years later, when we cleared out Mom and Dad's house for the same reason, I came across a collection of paperwork for Jack and only then did I realize how much of Jack's legal formalities Mom had been dealing with. I had become involved in something similar with Mom and Dad's affairs and discovered that dealing with Social Security and Medicaid departments are complicated and tricky. It's amazing that she found the mental and physical resources to fulfill countless tasks on behalf of Jack. But that was Rusty's way – to be amazing. At the time of Jack's situation, I *did* appreciate how large the task of clearing out his apartment would be so I volunteered to help. Jack lived only six more months.

Andy and I accompanied Mom to the funeral home to make arrangements for her brother. We sat in the director's office who was, not surprisingly, an old friend of Mom's. Mom described exactly what she did and did not want done for her brother then wrote the man a check from a personal bank account that she and Dad kept for emergencies; Jack had no life insurance policy.

Before going home, Mom and Andy and I sat on the brick wall outside the funeral home. We discussed bits and pieces of Jack's history while Mom smoked a cigarette. The minister from Mom and Dad's church was already at the house when we got there. He said a prayer and then proceeded to tell us how he wouldn't be available to preside over the service when Mom wanted it. Mom explained politely that she wanted a simple graveside service the next day in our church cemetery where Jack would be buried in the Burris plot. She stated that the prayers and scriptures required for this service could be said by any member of the clergy. But ministers can be territorial. He told Mom when he *would* be free. Mom quietly stated that those times would not be acceptable to her as she showed him the door. *Go, Mom!* A nugget of her feistiness remained. Mom and Andy were friends with another minister in Newell, and they had both always taken great comfort in his gentle loving manner. He was suffering from the early effects of Alzheimer's himself, but he remembered Mom and Andy, and was delighted to quote the suitable scriptures as we lay Jack to rest. We buried Jack on a sunny autumn day. Mom was sad, of course, but also accepting of the circumstances. I think she may have felt relief that her brother's worldly suffering had ended.

"How are you doing, Mom?" I asked a couple of days later.

"Fine," she replied but not in a dismissive way. "I'm sad, but I'm okay."

"I know you're the last of your family now. You're the only one left and that's got to be difficult."

"Well, it had to be somebody, didn't it? I'm glad it's me." I love my momma.

Even with extra responsibilities, I found opportunities for recreation. I hiked and biked but more importantly, I made time to canoe. The moment my paddle dips below the surface of the water, I know I'm home. Being on the water rejuvenates me. The nuance of each wave that passes below this self-propelled craft is like being part of something divine. I feel independent and free. Same with cycling. Gentle breezes and summer fragrances wafting across the water is what I imagine heaven to be. Yet all good things have a flip side.

During one outing a microscopic water-borne parasite that I somehow ingested while canoeing attached itself to my intestines making me terribly ill. It was months before my doctor figured out what was causing the problems. She believed initially that I was experiencing some sort of irritable bowel syndrome because the symptoms were similar and I was under a lot of stress. After a couple of months of *not* responding to treatments, the doctor decided the signs pointed toward Giardiasis. Medicine has never claimed to be an exact science.

Before I could gain back the capacity to eat more than two Saltines for a meal, my nephew, Tony, came to live with us. Tony's personality was suited for an urban environment so when my brother Robert moved his family to a small rural community outside of Charlotte, Tony found it difficult to adapt to his new surroundings. Add to that a variety of issues he was dealing with at home that we were not aware of. Unknown to me and the rest of the family, Robert suffered from alcoholism. It's a destructive disease, and as a result, Tony became collateral damage. He quit attending any of his high school classes and spent most of his time on his own. Donna, Josh and I offered to make a place for Tony in our home. By living with us, he could return to the high school he had gone to in Charlotte. Robert was dead-set against this arrangement so we waited for Tony to turn eighteen when he could make the decision for himself. He moved in with us the week-end after that birthday.

Tony dreamed of joining the Navy as his dad and granddad did before him, but the Navy accepted only a high school diploma, not a GED. Donna made several telephone calls and discovered that a high school diploma program for adults was offered by our community college and signed Tony up. Our new family arrangement was fun. Josh and Tony are one year apart and they had always been involved in each others' lives – they were, and are, as close as cousins or brothers. Many times, the two of them would regale Donna and me with stories of their exploits that had us rolling in the floor. They endured, with grace, living in woman-land (as they called it). But some of our time together was stressful. Much of my time and emotions were being spent on taking care of Mom and Dad. And though I was determined to accommodate the needs of my parents so they could stay in their home and maintain their independence as long as possible, it put more strain on me than I was able to comfortably handle. I had no time to myself which meant that I was unable to repair frazzled and jangled nerves before the next round of events needed my attention.

Tony's predicament was important, though, and in our occasional heart-to-heart chats I learned that his childhood circumstances were vastly different than I ever knew. Living with an alcoholic father created more than the usual arguments. It meant unreasonable expectations and the reversal of roles.

Including Tony as a member of our household was the right thing to do, but I was unqualified to offer my nephew the salve he needed after such a traumatic childhood. My inner resources were dwindling and I withdrew from everyday reality as much as possible each evening. After seeing to the most imminent chores for Mom and Dad, I closed myself off in my darkened bedroom, slipped under the protective covers of the bed and watched something mindless on television. Donna handled the daily chores in our own home. She cooked most of the evening meals while Josh and Tony took turns preparing some of our dinners as well. At times I lashed out hatefully at an innocent remark one of them made causing irrational and senseless arguments. I knew inside that I was spiraling out of control and that my reactions were inappropriate and out of proportion to what they were saying to me, but I couldn't stop the words tumbling out of my mouth. I wanted to leave. I wanted to escape. Life was unbearable and I wanted to be done with it.

When I gave voice to these sentiments, Donna was furious. And rightly so. She threatened to leave me to my own misery if I didn't seek professional help. And I did. At least I tried. I talked to my GP and I consulted a therapist. I explained my situation and how the sadness made me feel like I had no energy for things I had previously thought were fun. And I was convinced that things would never improve. Ever. Eventually, I was prescribed medication that would calm my irrational thoughts and give me the resources to plod through the unfortunate circumstances that consumed my life. It was too late to help control the tension growing between Tony and me, and I will always regret that I couldn't have been more patient, loving and kind.

Shortly after Tony moved in with us, Tony's dad received a third DWI, a driving while intoxicated citation. I was unaware that Robert had already received two previous ones. We were angry that we didn't know the extent that alcoholism had taken over Robert's life. It's sad and disturbing when a loved one suffers, and it's devastating if someone you care for winds up incarcerated because of poor decisions. But we were hopeful that this would be the wake-up call that Robert needed to get his life back in order. We were also relieved that he was now off the streets before he could harm himself or anyone else, and we were optimistic that he could get help dealing with the alcohol abuse.

As Rusty and Robert hit roadblocks in being able to manage their lives, mine improved because of the antidepressants. I returned to searching for proactive ways to deal with Mom's deteriorating state of mind. Mom's physician felt Mom's response to her antidepressants was not what she had hoped for so she recommended the services of a mental health professional as the next step. She thought psychological testing would give us a better picture of Mom's problems and I agreed especially since Mom was processing the death of a brother and sister to cancer, *and* having her son in the pokey. She was also having to come to terms with Dad's health issues as well as her own. I set out to see if Mom could get diagnosed with something for which there was a more concrete fix. Perhaps a psychiatrist could pinpoint Mom's psychological or neurological problems. At times, life's circumstances throw too many rocks into our path; a little help to get over them makes a difference. The psychiatrist fell in love with Mom instantly. She thought Mom was absolutely wonderful. This is the Rusty-phenomenon.

"I don't think she's got Alzheimer's...," the psychiatrist stated boldly.

Alzheimer's? Who said anything about Alzheimer's?

My mind skittered away from that topic immediately after I allowed myself to feel relief that Mom's problem was not *Alzheimer's.*

"...but your mother has had some dramatic events to deal with lately," she continued. She was oblivious to my recoil at her use of the term 'Alzheimer's' for what my mother did not have. I thought these people were supposed to pick up on body language. "I think she would benefit by talking to a therapist and working through the issues that are on her mind."

She recommended a colleague, Mary Bobis, who had an office in the same building. I recognized the name immediately. I had seen her sixteen years before because of another personal crisis. I held this person in high esteem and I enthusiastically jumped at the opportunity for Mom to work with her. I took Mom to her first visit. I accompanied her to the office door and told her that I would wait for her in the courtyard. After her hour, Mom came out of the office and we walked out to my truck together. We stood for a moment before getting in. I asked her how helpful she thought the appointment was.

"I feel much better," she declared. "That woman is so smart! At last I can open up my heart and confide in somebody who understands - who *totally* understands me."

Years earlier when I confided to Mom that I had sought help from a therapist for coping with stressful hiccups in my own life, she didn't talk to me for two weeks. It was as if I had told her that I was a mass murderer, and she needed time to decide whether or not she wanted to admit knowing me. After *her* appointment, she fairly gushed over her own therapy experience. I didn't remind her that she shunned me for doing the same thing. But I did seize the chance to mumble under my breath, "Congratulations, you've just been shrunk!"

Rusty began a series of appointments where she was able to safely confront the difficult concerns in her life. I would normally drop her off at the appointments then go have a cup of coffee and read for an hour until time to pick her up. After one of these appointments, I could tell that she'd been crying. I hugged her and said, "Wow, you must have had a successful session if tears were shed." Success of a therapy session is based on how many tissues have been used.

"Oh yes," she admitted enthusiastically. "Mary says that I never gave myself time to grieve after the death of my father and mother. And I need to grieve for my sister and her battle with cancer, and I need to grieve for Jack and for Robert's battle with alcohol."

"That's wonderful, Mom. Now that you've gotten started, you

can begin to heal. And, you can begin to deal with the depression."

"Oh, no! I'm done!"

"What?"

"I'm done."

"You're done?" *Incredible.*

"Yes, I sat there and cried for a solid fifty minutes. Now, I'm done and I feel so much better." *Why can't I be on the Rusty fast-track mode of psychotherapy?*

Therapy did not transform Mom back to normal. And handling basic housekeeping and cooking duties did not improve. One evening, Andy called to share his concerns.

"She-is-driving-me-crazy!" He shouted into the phone.

I could understand how living with Mom and Dad could send Andy into a tizzy.

"Uh oh. What's going on now?"

"She is going to burn the house down. I know she's going to burn the house down, and Dad just sits there watching TV."

I was silent. He continued with a description of food being left on a burner until it was charcoal and how he found food in the refrigerator fit only for a Petri dish.

"Marsha, I've been talking to some of my friends. I hate to say it, but we wonder if she might have Alzheimer's. Can we get her tested or anything?"

There it was. That word again. The hands of time stopped. I felt a little sick as a few niggling things dropped into place. My aversion to the word in the psychiatrist's office was an indicator that, in the back of my mind, I must have believed there was some validity in her use of it. Deep in the recesses of my mind, I had thought the same thing, but was not brave enough to confront it head on like Andy. A huge *huh oh* flashed into that place where we comprehend reality and then the earth stopped turning on its axis for a moment. A seismic shift took place in the Burris world, and then everything, *everything,* was different.

We now had to face reality. One major course of action had to take place before any other. I no longer had faith in Mom's current physician so we fired her. Time was wasted when we could have been proactive on Mom's behalf. We could have already instituted practical ways to mitigate the true cause of what was destroying Mom's personality and cognitive skills. I had her records transferred to Dad's GP and we began to get more aggressive with Mom's care. The doctor made no attempt to officially apply the label of Alzheimer's to Mom's problems but he treated her symptoms as if that was the diagnosis. He said that there was no way to know for sure if a person has Alzheimer's, but he could order diagnostic tests to rule out other explanations for the altering of a person's psychological makeup.

The first test was an arteriogram to determine if there was a blockage in the carotid artery that might restrict a sufficient flow of blood to her brain. *No problem there*. An MRI of the brain ruled out the presence of a tumor that would affect her personality. *Nothing out of the ordinary there*. Physical exams and diagnostics failed to show any physical problems so Mom's doctor prescribed the medication, Aricept. He declared that it might help, and it certainly couldn't hurt. Aricept is the brand name for donepezil HCL. One of the chemicals in the brain, Acetylcholine, helps maintain the memory process. It plays an essential role in many brain functions such as memory. If that chemical breaks down, or if the levels decrease, memory loss occurs and learning can't take place – key symptoms of Alzheimer's disease. Aricept helps prevent that breakdown by increasing Acetylcholine levels and thereby assisting the nerve cells of the brain to communicate with each other more effectively. Aricept appeared to slow down Mom's memory degeneration. Like her physician, Mom would never use the term Alzheimer's. She called it 'her little memory problem'. But now we had a better course of action to mitigate the problem.

I took on additional responsibilities for Mom and Dad but I received pleasant payoffs in return. For example, I was included in the gathering of Dad's fellow World War II PT boat veterans when they held their reunion in Charlotte. PT Boat reunions are held in various cities across the United States, how exciting that this one would be held in our own backyard. We grew up hearing many stories of Dad's war experiences. Now, his fellow PT Boaters would no longer be mere imaginary characters in my mind, especially 'The Admiral'. That's what Dad called him, 'The Admiral'. I didn't know his full name until I was an adult. As a child, I thought there was only one admiral in the whole world, a legend, and Jim knew him.

"Call Marsha and see if she'll drive us to the Adams Mark Hotel for the reunion," Dad instructed Mom. Mom, who never took instructions from Dad before, was now pleased to do whatever somebody else thought up, as if she was glad that someone somewhere was able to think things up at all. She called me at work.

"Your father thought it might be a good idea if you could drive us uptown to the reunion next week. Do you think you could do that?"

"Will *the Admiral* be there?"

"Buzz!" This is not the sound a bee makes. This is the nickname Mom called Dad, a nickname he earned when he was in the Navy, a nickname he used in Memphis after the war where these two met before they got married.

"Buzz," she yelled again loudly at my hard-of-hearing father. I jumped out of my skin. "Marsha wants to know if the Admiral will be at the reunion."

"Yes, of course. No other reason to go, if he's not there," Dad gruffly replied as if everybody shared his reality. *Pay dirt*, I thought! Now I had my chance to meet these men in the flesh - no way would I miss out on this opportunity.

"Count me in," I told her. I immediately dashed off a note to the Admiral to request a meeting time. I realized that everyone there would probably want to get together with the Admiral and his wife, and I wasn't going to miss out. We had his personal address because he sent a Christmas card every year since Dad had been discharged from the Navy in 1946, a treasure that Dad looked forward to every year as if it were…, well…, Christmas.

The day came. We arrived early and quickly met up with Rear Admiral John Harllee and his lovely wife, Helen. This man, who was a living hero to my Dad and stood ten-foot tall in my mind's eye, was shorter than me and I'm 5-foot-3. He looked up at me with rapt attention, grasped my hand in his, and proceeded to tell me how wonderful my father was. I fell in love with him immediately and understood in an instant why men followed Admiral Harllee into battle and revered every Christmas card they received from him.

The Admiral led us to the dining room where he'd reserved a table for us. I followed behind him respectfully as he shuffled gingerly along the corridor. We sat down and ordered drinks, then chatted formally for a little while. It was lovely to have this man's attention. I was honored. Then several other devotees of the Admiral came in and joined us. The conversation became more comfortable after we went around the table and introduced ourselves. Briefly each man described which PT Boat he'd served on, and what he'd done in the intervening five decades since the end of the war. My own biography, though graciously inquired about, was short. The other biographies were, of course, much more exciting by comparison. They had my attention. After two or three of the men explained how they had earned law degrees from Harvard after returning home from war, I looked at Dad questioningly. Dad had gone to diesel mechanics school in Memphis, Tennessee after the war, thus the subsequent meeting of my parents in Mom's hometown, and Dad's resultant automobile career. In a flash of imagination, sitting at the table in the Adams Mark that afternoon, I daydreamed about the life I would have enjoyed as the daughter of a Harvard lawyer. I dreamed of the country clubs, the tennis frocks, and how I would surely have been taller, thinner and blonder too. I returned my attention to the individuals at the table, especially the individual who was my dad. He looked directly at me and said, "I could have gone there too. The Admiral got us into any college we wanted."

"And you chose diesel mechanics school. In Memphis." I had never had cause to question this decision of Jim's before.

"It's what I wanted. I was good at it. And, I met your mother there, so everything turned out alright." He winked at Mom.

I had to agree.

The men continued with more stories. One of the Harvard attorneys had a law practice in Washington, D.C. He was a loyal Republican and fairly conservative in politics and outlook. He had participated in some capacity in several White House administrations, the details of which now escape me because the story he told us shoved them right out of my brain. He related how during the Clinton administration he had been invited to one of the breakfast meetings. Whatever opinions are held for President Clinton, by most accounts he is considered personable and engaging even though the Monica Lewinski incident rushes to the forefront of most conversations related to him. Dad's PT boat pal had one such story. He described the breakfast table and all the attendees present.

"When Clinton talks to you, he talks to you directly, he makes eye contact," he said. "And when he talks to you, you feel like you're the *only* person in the room. In fact, you feel like the *most* important person in the world. As Clinton was addressing me that morning at the breakfast, I thought to myself 'Hell, *I'd* sleep with him'. If I found him hard to resist, I know that poor Lewinski gal didn't stand a chance!"

What a miracle that I was able to be a part of this experience. I'm grateful that I could spend the afternoon in the company of these fine gentlemen, Mrs. Harllee and Rusty. Theirs was a noble generation. To hear the stories of their war years and reminiscences of their lives since then, gave me a new understanding of my dad and his war experience.

The Admiral stayed in touch with me until his death. He outlived Dad and sent me a sweet note when I told him Dad had passed away. "Your dad was a hero," he wrote in the sympathy card. The Admiral would know.

CHAPTER FIVE

If I have to know it...

Jim was a hero - in wartime and in our family too. He was a loving husband, father and grandfather although saying the words 'I love you' seldom, if ever, sprang from his lips. Nevertheless, he showed his love in a variety of ways. For instance, when I was ten years old and preparing for my first Girl Scout camping trip, Dad took me to the local Army-Navy surplus store to buy me a pair of hunting boots. Comfortable footwear for active girls, were practically unheard of in the early 1960s. Culture in the 1950s and 1960s maintained a pretty sharp defining line between genders, but Jim Burris was a sensible fellow who occasionally thumbed his nose at conventional ideas. So, inside that male bastion of fashion that was the Army-Navy store, I was fitted for, and walked out with, a pair of leather lace-up hunting boots like he and Robert wore. I kept those boots long into adulthood. I discarded them only after they fell apart and threatened to infect my other footwear with dry rot.

I spent a lot of time wishing those good old days were back. I wished Mom and Dad were still independent. I wished that it wasn't essential for me to be involved in the details of their lives. And I bet they out-wished me by a mile. However, our family had much to be grateful for. One significant milestone which called for celebration was Josh's graduation from high school. Friends and family joined in the festivities. Mom was there, of course. She wouldn't have missed it for the world. Josh and Tony had equal grandson rights with Jim and Rusty. Barbara and her best friend, Peggy, drove down from Virginia for the festivities too. We ate celebratory pizza which prompted a gallstone attack for me. Surgery was quick and relatively painless due to the laparoscopic (and therefore minimally invasive) nature of it. Josh and Tony greeted me at home after I was discharged from the hospital.

Standing on the front porch as Donna and I pulled into the driveway, their faces reflected uncertainty in knowing what to say as I slowly hobbled to the front door. For them to be there was enough. Mom came over with homemade chicken soup. I was pretty groggy from the anesthetic but I remember being amazed that she was still able to find her way to our house from hers. There were many and varied twists and turns in the short distance between our two driveways and I wondered how long it would be before she could no longer find her way to my house. It wouldn't be much longer, as it turned out.

Late summer, after my remarkable recovery from surgery, Donna and I took Josh to Appalachian State University in Boone, NC where he would matriculate as a freshman. Moving him to his dormitory, Donna and I watched him enter the world at large, the first of his many capable steps into adulthood. We helped haul his belongings up several flights of stairs to his room, then bid him farewell. We cried. But we knew he'd be safe. He is a resourceful problem-solver but he had been the center of our lives for eighteen years and we would miss his sublime presence at home.

On the bright side, Tony was still with us. I loved having him there despite our different points of view on his education. For me, school was simply a matter of attending classes, sitting for exams and receiving a diploma. For Tony, staying in a class when he experienced personality clashes with the professor or other students was untenable. I saw the conflicts and disagreements Tony faced everyday at school as roadblocks to his success that needed to be overcome so he could proceed through the diploma program. He saw school as part of his social and cultural environment to be experienced fully and as important as anything learned from a book. I thought Tony was lucky to have the opportunity to further his own education and I had little sympathy for what he was going through. My own academic aspirations had been squelched because I could not justify leaving Mom and Dad. Clearly their health would not improve and the two doctorate programs where I intended to apply were both out of state. Alzheimer's does not get better with time. Neither does arthritis and macular degeneration. There's no known cure for the enfeebling effects of aging. I grieved, without realizing it, the loss of my mother and father as adults and as parents as well as my own professional ambitions. Rational thoughts and inner resources failed me, and I felt as if I had lost the freedom to determine my own future. Seeking fun and recreation was out of the question because it required energy and I was out of steam. As my sorry outlook escalated, counseling sessions educated me in how to access some much needed coping skills. Possible positive ways to deal with the areas I found difficult were suggested to me but before I could put these ideas into practice and before I was able to make progress in the right direction, the friction between Tony and me ruptured our relationship to the point where he moved out of the house. We learned later that he completed his high school diploma and joined the Navy on his own, fulfilling his long-held dream. We were proud of him but it would be several years before we saw him to tell him so.

Antidepressants smoothed out my mood swings enough to get me through the events being thrust at me from every direction, but of course it didn't fix the general state of affairs that I saw as the train wreck of my life. On one of my sister's visits, we were walking in my backyard having a chat when I must have made a sour reply to something she said. She asked me, not unkindly, "Are you *ever* happy? Is there anything at all in your life that you enjoy?" My simple and honest reply was, *No*.

Even with a glass half-empty perspective, my life was sprinkled with many good occasions for celebration. Mom and Dad's fiftieth wedding anniversary was upon us. Under normal circumstances this should have been a wonderful opportunity to honor Jim and Rusty's rather successful partnership but the specter of Alzheimer's dampened my enthusiasm for any festivities. Mom was losing weight, losing strength and stamina, and she looked more delicate than ever. Mundane household tasks confused her, if she remembered to do them at all. And yet, Dad insisted on having a party. My sibs and I hosted a reception for their Silver Anniversary and Dad wanted a reprise of those good times for the Golden one. Jim was a quiet, introverted man, but he loved a party. His favorite pastime was sitting back and watching Mom and the rest of us have fun. We obliged. Jim and Rusty may have been shuffling toward their declining years, but Dad insisted they go in style.

I was totally against the party from the beginning, party-pooper that I am. I was drained from the extra attention Mom and Dad needed and I didn't know how I was going to pull this off. Barbara came to the rescue. She and her friend, Diane, planned the entire affair. My job? Just show up. This was no minor miracle to me! The commemoration of my parents' half-century of marriage was an amazing moment in their lives as friends and family visited and wished them well.

Tiny triumphs and small pleasures buoyed my spirits. On Friday afternoons Dad would call me at work and ask me the following question as if he hadn't called and asked it a dozen times before. It pleased me to play along.

"What are you and Donna doing tonight?" he asked.

"Nothing. We don't have any plans. Why?"

"I wondered if you might want to go to *Captain D*'s tonight. Your mother likes the fish platter from there..." *Subtle hint.*

"Sure, we can do that. What do you want me to get for you?"

"Come by, pick me up, and I'll ride with you."

Dad rode shotgun with me the four miles to the restaurant. He always insisted on paying for our meals, an offer I couldn't resist. It didn't cost a lot of money, but Dad's thoughtfulness touched me deeply as did the pleased expression on his face. He sat in the truck while I went inside to place the order. We arrived home with our fish dinners as proud as if we'd caught the fish ourselves and fried it up. Mom's interest in food had vanished – I think she no long felt the sensation of hunger. She had a sweet tooth, though, as Alzheimer's sufferers often do, but she had no interest in eating healthy, nutritious food until someone sat down with her and engaged her in conversation. Then she ate ravenously. Donna and I joined Mom and Dad for as many meals as possible.

On Friday nights, Mom and Dad would eat half of their fish platters, then reseal the Styrofoam containers and save the rest for Saturday's lunch. It was frugal of them to make two meals out of the one, which made them gleeful, and I was happy knowing that they would have a fairly nutritious meal the following day without my participation.

Rusty never admitted to being upset or frightened because of the synaptic misfirings in her brain. She may have been in complete denial that Alzheimer's was encroaching into her heretofore independent life, but it's more likely that she was adapting to the new course her life had taken with grace and acceptance. Mom must have been aware that her faculties were being diminished, although she never demonstrated self-pity. Her dependence on me expanded though, and she made no decisions without consulting me first. I was grateful for that development since it was becoming more difficult to get her and Dad out of the fixes they got themselves in. For example, after seeing advertisements for life insurance policies, Mom bought extra coverage with a simple telephone call to the 800-number when their existing coverage was ample. I could make arrangements to cancel the policies only after I detected the purchases from reconciling their bank statements. Their fixed income covered their needs adequately but there was no surplus of income to spend on non-essentials.

Other emergencies included frantic phone calls from Mom when she was unable to find her handbag. We usually found it stashed in the corner of the living room behind a chair, protected from *thieves* who may come into their house for that very purpose. Once, I needed a frying pan to make supper for Mom and Dad. I looked in the usual places, to no avail. When I asked Mom where I could find it she replied, quite frankly, "I don't have any frying pans." Balderdash! All southern women have frying pans. We inherit them from each preceding generation; from great grandmothers to grandmothers to mothers to daughters. I was on the verge of getting upset over Rusty's denial of owning a frying pan but when I opened my mouth to call her out Donna pulled me aside and said, "If she remembered where the frying pans are kept, she would tell you. You want her back the way she was, but that's not going to happen. Since you know it's not going to happen why don't you leave *your world* and go into *her world?* Find a way to go where she is now. It could be a pretty good place, and you might find that you like it there."

I wasn't interested in finding a *good place*. I was more interested in being in a snit. But I considered what she said and since I had absolutely nothing to lose by giving this unique concept a chance, I vowed to examine future situations from Mom's point of view.

Mom's legs began hurting her which hindered even a walk up and down the grocery store aisles. We consulted her GP and he concluded that Mom's smoking habit restricted oxygen to her legs causing the pain. The irony of this, he explained, is that the nicotine in her cigarettes was a benefit to Alzheimer's patients. (I've since read several sources that assert the opposite.) After over fifty years of smoking, Mom agreed to stop. Incredible. But she did *not* want to lose the use of her legs. Nicorette gum helped with the cravings, and I drove over to her house on weekdays during my lunch hour so we could walk through the neighborhood together and built up her strength. Those were the best lunches of my life because they allowed me the opportunity to witness Mom's new world and participate in the awe and wonder that she experienced as she interacted with her surroundings. A Zen experience for us both.

We walked arm in arm around the circle that Mom and Dad lived on. It took us about twenty minutes and we alternated our route one way then the other depending on the day and our whimsy. Leisurely chats without any agenda only heightened the fragrance of the blooms we passed. Those were perfect days – days I would not have shared with Mom if there had been no need for my help. On one walk, Mom looked up at the sky and pointed. High in the stratosphere a jet plane trailed white vapor in its wake. The jet making its way to some distant place was so small it was invisible to our eyes. I don't think she understood what it was, or what caused it. So what? She looked at it as through a child's eyes, without scientific interpretation. She looked at it in amazement. She saw only a pretty design in the heavens, already made gorgeous by white clouds against the backdrop of a Carolina blue sky. She stopped suddenly and said, "Oh, my. Look at that. Isn't that the most beautiful thing you've *ever* seen?"

No. It wasn't. The most beautiful thing I'd ever seen was the look of wonder on my mother's face as she experienced this simple vision. I was in her world. And, it was marvelous. This singular moment in an otherwise daily routine was a benefit of our special circumstances. Many times after that day I saw Mom look up and notice the vapor trails of other airplanes and every time she was thrilled by it. I never told her what caused the phenomenon. It would have taken the magical enchantment of its existence away. Who tells a child there's no Santa Claus or Easter Bunny or Tooth Fairy? When I look up and see similar white streaks across the sky today, instead of seeing a natural phenomenon that can be scientifically explained, I see the magical brush strokes of an artist and I feel Rusty near me. I know she's now a part of the condensed water vapor made by the exhaust of aircraft engines as she is a part of me and everything in the universe, and it's good.

Beautiful experiences like these helped a little as we faced a bleak future. We watched helplessly as Mom's reasoning skills deteriorated to irrevocable levels. Once upon a time, there was nothing that Rusty, healthy Rusty, beefy Rusty, could not do. She had no doubts that if it *could* be done at all, she could do it. If she didn't possess the knowledge of how to swap out the solenoid on the riding lawnmower, she found out who did and wrested the information she needed from that expert. This was decades before the Internet where we now type in a few key words and facts are spat at us within seconds. I could still recall at this point of our journey, the Rusty who completed any project capably. And I missed her. It broke my heart to watch as the bits and pieces that made up Mom's personality vanished gradually, progressively. One day as I dropped off groceries, I stood in her kitchen and watched as she painstakingly stored each item behind cabinet doors. I secretly wondered if she would find them again. Fingers of sadness gripped my heart making unwanted tears surface. Mom saw them and came to me.

"What is it, honey?" She put her arms around me and pulled me to her as I cried. I let the fears and anguish I felt towards this damned disease, and how it was affecting my mom, spill onto her still-capable shoulders. "What's the matter?" she encouraged me.

My first inclination was to cover up my pain, make an excuse, claim to have something in my eye, feign braveness. But I found my voice and I recognized that the moment was a genuine opportunity to face this monster head on. I opted for the truth like the time I admitted to her that I was afraid I would be safe from nuclear holocaust and she wouldn't.

"I'm afraid, Momma."

"What are you afraid of, honey?"

"I'm afraid of where all of this is heading…," I had taken a step back and I flung both of my hands wide as if to embrace 'all of this'. Then I shrugged my shoulders in resignation, searching unsuccessfully for the right descriptive word for 'this'. She knew what I meant. She said, "I know. It's hard. But it's okay. It's all going to be okay. There's no need to be afraid."

Of course I believed her. The Great and Powerful Rusty had spoken. She was inside this frail, forgetful, mother of mine. Somewhere. And I trusted that the essence of Rusty knew what was best as she had always done throughout our family's life. In spite of this shared moment I began leaving the old Rusty behind more and more. I followed the newly emerging one into new, unfamiliar territory.

As Mom's memory blips, as she called them, became more frequent, the enduring qualities that formed her personality remained recognizable. But what was going on in her head at the physical level? Plaques and tangles forming inside her brain wreaked havoc and erased seemingly random memories with no rhyme or reason that we could detect. Without the glue of memory to connect the dots of our daily activities, confusion is likely. One such example of this process emerged when we made the decision to have Mom fitted for a denture.

Rusty continued to be diligent in her dental hygiene. She followed her daily ritual of brushing and flossing, but periodontal disease ended her success against the Parker family genetic odds to keep her pearly whites. It was a sad day when her dentist recommended the new treatment plan. I tried to talk him out of it and stated a case for why we shouldn't take this course of action. I thought Mom's state of mind wouldn't be able to grasp why she must have her teeth pulled out and a big plastic masticating apparatus placed in the void. Mom and her dentist had enjoyed a long and trusting relationship over the years and he understood my point, but he convinced me that there was no time like the present since the situation would only get worse for Mom. Without the ability to continue the rigorous routine, he explained, her teeth would become too unstable to eat even soft foods. I was persuaded to go ahead with the procedure while we could reason with Mom and she could understand what the modifications to her current dental status would mean.

With Dad's agreement, I sat Mom down and explained what we needed to do. Mom reacted stoically and resigned herself to accept what had to be done. She displayed incredible courage and once again adapted to life's zings as the effects of Alzheimer's crept in. Mom must have understood what was being stolen from her, but if she realized it, she didn't confess it to me.

The Friday morning of Mom's appointment arrived. I drove over to her house early and she met me outside. She knew where we were going and what was going to happen. So did I. I had worked in a dental laboratory before my career at the university and knew the steps necessary to replace natural teeth with a denture. The dentist makes a plaster cast of your mouth before the extractions are made, usually a couple of weeks before the extractions are done. The plaster cast is sent to a dental technician who cuts the teeth off of it leaving an approximation of how the toothless gums will emerge. Then a denture is constructed over this reproduction and sent back to the dentist's office for a fitting on the day the teeth are pulled. After the denture is in place, the raw gums form to the interior structure of the denture and hopefully fit snuggly like a hand in a glove. After a week or two, the gums heal and recede. In a follow-up appointment the dentist refills the interior of the denture with more acrylic for a custom fit.

All went well during the extractions procedure. The dentist was pleased with his work and Mom didn't seem to experience much pain. Her teeth had loosened to the point where little pressure was necessary to lift them out of their sockets. The instructions were to take the denture out before bedtime and swish with luke-warm salt water but to put the denture back in and sleep with it in place. The process was to be repeated for a couple of days, especially after meals. If she felt discomfort she could take Tylenol. The dentist called her at home that evening to see how she was doing. It meant a lot to her, and to me, and I went to bed that night believing that although this was a miserable milestone in the life of my mother, it went pretty well.

First thing the next morning, a Saturday, I got a telephone call from Jim. Dad didn't use the telephone often because he had difficulty hearing the conversations, the exception being Friday night *Captain D*'s invitations, so a huge *uh oh* ran through my thoughts.

"Honey, do you think you can come over here and talk to your mother for a little while?" he asked me without preamble. There was urgency in his voice.

"Sure Dad. What about?"

"It's this denture. It's upsetting her. Maybe you can calm her down."

Donna and I jumped in the car and made the six-minute trip in five. When we went into the house, Dad was sitting at the kitchen table inside the back door, deflated.

"She's in the bathroom. I don't think she understands that she now has a denture. I tried to explain…" He looked like he might cry with little provocation. The pain in his face told me he was at his wit's end for knowing how to deal with this development. Even a hero like Jim had a big old soft spot when it came to Rusty.

I walked through the house to locate Mom. I tapped on the closed bathroom door.

"Mom," I called to her. "It's me, Marsha. Let me come in, okay?"

With some coaxing, she opened the door. Standing at the bathroom sink with the water running, Mom held the denture in one hand and tried to staunch the flow of blood from her mouth with the other. She had the look of a wild animal caught in a trap, fighting desperately to escape.

"What's happened to me?" she cried. She was looking at the black hole of her toothless mouth in the mirror over the sink. "What happened? Where are my teeth? What happened to my teeth? Why am I bleeding? Just look at me!"

The void in her mouth created by removing the denture gave her face a sunken-in appearance, drastically changing her looks and aging her at least a decade. She was in a state of panic and could not construct a suitable explanation for her predicament. I can't say for certain whether or not I drew back in horror when I saw her. The massive amount of blood unnerved me and made me feel sick. The drastic change in her looks shocked me because I had only seen her after the denture was fitted in the dentist's office and had consoled myself that not much had changed after all. I was wrong.

After my initial shock I slipped into fix-it mode. Calm washed over me and I knew I had within me the power and ability to help Mom come to terms with this problem. This was a tiny miracle I didn't appreciate at the time.

"It's alright, Mom. I know there's lots of blood - but you're not injured. It's your new denture. See?"

I adopted the tone mothers use when trying to convince a

toddler that their skinned knee is actually fun and exciting. I took the denture out of her hand and rinsed it off under the running water. I held it up for her to see the white plastic teeth imbedded in the pink acrylic.

"The dentist had to pull your teeth so that this would fit and you can eat better."

"No he didn't. What are you talking about? I haven't been to the dentist."

After a night's sleep, Mom had become disoriented and memories of the previous day had ceased to exist. When she woke up on the following morning, she found an alien object in her mouth, having no recollection of how it got there, she did the only thing she knew – she pulled the damned thing out. Mom disturbed the delicate and tender sockets where the teeth had been extracted and dislodged the clots that form in those areas after the procedure. Much to her horror, and without a logical explanation available to her brain, she realized that her teeth were gone and the blood that had puddled inside the denture poured out of her mouth.

"Mom, listen to me," I started to explain quietly. "You've been having problems with your teeth. Yesterday, you and I went to the dentist together. When we got there, the dentist pulled your teeth and made you this denture." I held it up again for her to see. Evidence.

"You have to trust me on this. It happened."

She took my explanation on pure faith because she had no way to access the experience for herself. I encouraged her to swish out her mouth with warm water then I sat her on the toilet while I talked to her. She cried so hard, I couldn't get her to listen. She put her head in her hands and sobbed. Dad came back to the bathroom and peeked inside the door. I was making little progress in getting Mom calmed down and I hated letting ol' Jim down. I knelt on my knees in front of Mom and put my arms around her. I let her cry on my shoulder for a while. Then I asked her, "What's the matter, Mom? Tell me what's upsetting you."

"I look horrible. I look ugly. Your father's not going to want to look at me." Her words were sloppily formed without teeth for them to glide over.

Dad leaned in. "I told her that she is beautiful to me and she will *always* be beautiful to me." He spoke these words tenderly.

"See, Mom? Daddy thinks you're beautiful. He loves you."

"He does?"

"Of course he does."

"Tell her there's nobody else on earth who is more beautiful to me than she is."

On one hand, this was the sweetest thing I'd ever witnessed. On the other hand, this was getting to be weird. Dad was standing only three feet away but there I was, doing the he-said she-said thing. I hadn't done that since eighth grade and I didn't like it then either. And like a 14-year-old hearing her parents say gushy things to each other I thought I was going to die of embarrassment.

Mom composed herself. I slipped the denture back into her mouth. Dad went to the kitchen to make a pot of coffee. Mom checked herself in the mirror and said, "I don't recognize myself. I look in the mirror and it doesn't look like me. It's not me..."

Did she expect to see a younger, vital woman reflected back at her? Had she forgotten the intervening years that produced this mature woman? I could only speculate.

Increasingly I put out fires for Mom and Dad. Another phone call at work from Dad went like this: "What're you doing on Thursday?"

A trick question? Dad liked to ask trick questions. I knew that if I said "nothing particular" or "going to work, as usual" he would counter gleefully with "Wrong. You're going to... *fill-in-the-blank.*" So I cleverly answered, "I don't know- what *am* I going to be doing Thursday?"

"Take me to get a colonoscopy." *Oh joy.*

"Just up to University Hospital, not far, probably won't take the whole day."

"What time do you have to be there?"

"Seven in the morning. They'll do the procedure at eight, but your mother will have to go with us since she can't stay at home by herself. She'll forget where we are and I'm afraid she'll get scared."

"That's okay. I'll take the whole day off and we won't have to rush. Do you have the stuff you need to take before-hand?"

Dad was already familiar with this procedure. I had asked him at the time what he thought of the 'up periscope' diagnostic. "Felt right violated," he confided.

"Welcome to our world," I had told him then. I pointed to Mom and then back to myself, referring to physical exams that we females are subjected to.

"I hoped to not ever experience your world, actually." *Oh well.*

I pulled myself back to the present as Dad spoke again. "The doctor called the *GoLytely* stuff into the drug store. I'll need you to pick it up when you can."

I did as he instructed me and then I trusted Jim would do as the prescription instructed him. I picked up Mom and Dad at 6:45 a.m. on the day of the colonoscopy. They stood expectantly by the back door as if they thought the bus would leave them behind if it pulled up and they weren't ready. The hospital was only two miles away, closer than *Captain D*'s. Door-to-door delivery would take fifteen minutes, factoring in Dad's measured and deliberate gate. I had done the math. We would *not* be late.

I helped the eager-beavers into the car and, as predicted, we arrived right on time. After we got through the checking-in process, a nurse took Dad back to where the magic happens. She assured me they could handle things from there. I was relieved. I was determined to keep a bit of mystery between my dad and me as long as possible. Plus, my time was better spent tending to Mom as she wandered the waiting room offering assistance to complete strangers.

After a while, Mom and I settled in. I had brought magazines with photos of beautiful gardens and pulled them out of my backpack. I hoped this would keep her interest and make the time pass more quickly and pleasantly in the same way she had lured us into obedience with Little Golden Books on our trips to Minnesota. It worked because it seemed like we had looked at only a half dozen pictures when the doctor came out to talk to us. He sat down next to me with a serious expression on his face.

Oh God. This is it! My mind zoomed forward at warp speed to work out how I would begin to deal with Dad on chemotherapy. I'm not one to give in to optimistic thinking. It's much better to jump to the worst conclusions and then be pleasantly surprised when the results are better than hoped for.

"You're the daughter, right?"

"I'm *a* daughter." I told him, trying to use humor to gloss over my fear. "*The* daughter couldn't make it today. This is my mom.

She's *the* wife." I relied on snark to navigate any impending unpleasantness.

"I had to stop the procedure...," the doctor skipped right over my poor attempt to joke, as if it did not compute. I thought it was because he thought droll comments were inappropriate when he had such bad news for me.

"I couldn't see anything...," the doctor continued.

That far gone – oh Lord – I bet chemo won't help. My brain raced further ahead.

"He's not cleaned out," the doctor shook his head in wonder. "You'll have to bring him back again, maybe Monday or Tuesday..."

"WHAT?"

"Your dad must not have drunk all the *GoLytely*. His colon's not clean and I can't see anything. I'll give you another prescription but you'll have to make sure he takes it all this time. It's important."

I'll kill him! That's what I thought, but I kept my facial expression neutral so I wouldn't be the prime suspect.

"The nurse is getting him dressed – if you want to go ahead and get your car and pull up out front, we'll have him out there to you in a few minutes."

I did as he suggested. As I pulled up beside my dad sitting in the courtesy wheelchair, he adopted an innocent expression. I leered at him through the window debating whether I would pop the locks on the car door for him. With a deep self-righteous sigh of resignation, I let him in. He got in the front seat and I looked at him. Eye to eye. So he could tell I meant business.

"What happened, Jim?" I used his given name to give myself a psychological edge.

"I don't know. I guess that stuff didn't clean me out."

"The doctor said you didn't drink it all...and that's what the problem was."

"Ben Clark says you don't have to drink all of it."

"Ben Clark, what??"

Ben Clark was one of Dad's best friends. Ben Clark was not in the medical profession.

"Ben Clark says you don't have to drink all of the liquid they tell you to drink – they always give you more than you need..."

"Really? So, Jim, tell me... how did that advice work out for you today?"

Dad had enough sense to appear uncomfortable. I'm sure it was a ruse. I was relentless.

"You know I work, don't you? You know I'll have to take another day off from work to bring you back, don't you? Unless Ben Clark's free and can bring you…"

"He can't. He's in the mountains. But don't worry. I'll drink it all this time, if it'll make you happy."

"Yes, Dad. It will make me happy. My life will be complete if you'll just do that one thing for me."

"Good. By the way, I'm hungry. Let's get fish sandwiches before you take us home." Dad was not going to let a cranky daughter get in the way of his mid-day meal. He had his priorities.

The second trip for the colonoscopy went without a hitch, I'm happy to report. The doctor ran out to the waiting room after the procedure was completed with a 5 x 7 glossy colored print in his hands. He sat down beside me and held it for me to see. I couldn't tell at first what it was. It was abstract. Was it a Picasso? A Modigliani? Maybe. But was it art?

"Much better! Much better, this time," the doctor was enthusiastic toward his work. "And I remember your dad now. See here?" He indicated a little hair pin curve of a shiny pink tubular pipeline on the print. "Do you see this little crink in the colon right here? I remember it from last time…"

You don't remember my dad's face but you remember an interesting twist in his colon? I don't think I said that out loud. What I did say out loud was: "So… that's my dad's colon?"

"Yes, and it's clear. He did a great job this time with the laxative. Oh, and there are no polyps. But I *had* to show you this crink…"

"So, you're showing me a photograph of my dad's colon?" I was in shock. I had only moments before been looking at lovely gardens in a magazine with Mom. It was hard to switch gears that quickly.

"Yes and it's good news…"

"Can I have that?" I interrupted his good news.

"The photo? Sure. I can get more. I have a digital copy on the computer." He thought that I was excited because I shared his enthusiasm enough to want the photograph. He was wrong. I framed the photograph and hung it on the wall of the den next to

Dad's easy chair. When my sibs visited and asked what the photograph was of, this glistening pink shiny abstract piece of art, I told them crudely: "This is our dad's ass hole from the inside out. And it's one of those things that if I have to know it – YOU have to know it!" They didn't understand why I was snippy.

Another doctor's appointment with Jim. I took an extended lunch break from work to drive Dad to see his primary care physician. I flew into the driveway and jumped out of my truck to let him know that I had arrived. He moved slowly toward the back door with his coat on. Think *tortoise* of tortoise-and-the-hare fame here. He handed me the keys to his and Mom's car. We got in and I immediately backed it into the ditch. Of course the neighbor staying with Mom saw it and came to help. I didn't need help. I only needed to pull forward and try again, but instead we had to make a huge big deal out of it. After that, I had to pick up the pace to make up for lost time. Dad cautioned me in his wise and gentle way. "You know, there's no reason to be in such a hurry… we got plenty of time and…"

I took a deep breath. "Okay, you're right," I agreed. It crossed my mind that if I slowed down a little I could enjoy this time with Dad *and* prevent a possible speeding ticket which would only slow us down further. We arrived at the doctor's office with minutes to spare, but then we sat in the waiting room longer than usual. When we were escorted to the examining room, Dad took the comfortable side chair, and I climbed up on the examining table to wait for the doctor. We sat there longer than usual too. I didn't mind. I had taken Dad's advice and I was groovin' on the moment, enjoying the time with my daddy. Just Jim and me. Feeling pretty lucky. After another quarter of an hour passed, and we had not seen the doctor, Dad started looking at his watch in an agitated manner and sighing exasperatingly.

"What's up Jim? Got a date?" I teased him.

"We need to get this show on the road," he answered. He was serious.

"Why?"

"I got things to do."

"What kinds of things?" I mean, what did he *have* to do? And what happened to 'we got plenty of time'?

"It's almost time for *Matlock*."

"Matlock? You can hurry for Matlock, but not for me to get

back to work?"

In addition to taking Mom and Dad to doctors' appointments, I also had the pleasure of helping them get ready for Christmas. Mom loved decorating for Christmas. She always made Christmases and birthdays special. Always. But the various tasks required to prepare for holidays were now too complex for her to do alone. She didn't remember where the decorations were stored. Sitting down and writing a list of names and possible gift ideas was out of the question because it requires thinking ahead, and thinking into the future is an abstract notion. Not to worry. If there's a list involved, I'm your Huckleberry. I took Mom with me to the local department store so she could be involved in selecting presents for all. The colors and bright lights delighted her and I enjoyed seeing her face light up like a kid in a candy store. Back when Rusty was very much *the* mother, she took us children shopping uptown and made it an event. We dressed in our Sunday best and Mom treated us to lunch at the Mezzanine counter at Belk Department Stores. This was huge to children who usually ate a peanut butter and jelly sandwich for lunch at home. When we shopped in the main Sears store, Mom made the trip special by buying us freshly roasted cashews from the candy counter. In my memory, I can smell them, and it's enticing. I wished this store had cashews, because I would have bought us a bag full.

Since sewing was always a huge part of Mom's life, she naturally enjoyed touching the fabrics of the clothes, the shawls, the hats and gloves. She relished feeling the textures of the different material between her fingers. We selected the gifts on the list but before we checked out, I needed to run back over to the Christmas wrappings area and pick up a few supplies. I knew that to get across the store and back to the checkout counter with Mom in tow would turn a five-minute task into a thirty-minute chore. Her unhurried pace provided more opportunities to spy objects of interest - and, *every*thing she spotted was an object of interest which required her full attention. Wild horses could not pull her away from shiny, colorful objects. I understand this phenomenon, I have the same gene, but I needed to speed this project along. My plan was to leave her near awesomely attractive items (like the jewelry case) while I walked briskly to the gift wrap department, grabbed the items I needed, and returned to her side before she realized I had been away.

    I implemented the first stage of the plan as I guided her to the jewelry counter. I instructed her to stay right there. Simple. All she had to do was just-stay-there and I would be back in a flash. I implemented stage two and assembled my gift-wrapping kit. Stage three, which was return-to-the-jewelry-counter-and-meet-up-with-Mom, occurred in record time. Except for the *meet-up-with-Mom* part. She was gone. GONE. Oh lord. Why did I ever think I could get away with cutting corners and saving myself a few minutes in the process? I was frantic. The cart was gone too but I predicted she was attached to it. This comforted me. I thought it would be easier to spot the two of them and I hoped it slowed down her progress enough for me to catch up. I worried that Mom would be frightened when she realized she was in the store alone and couldn't find me. Would she know where she was? Would she feel abandoned? Would she be frightened? I was anxious that she might wheel the cart, full of unpaid inventory, out the door and set off the alarms. The thought suppressed my anxiety some as I considered that scenario to be a possible winner in the how-to-find-Mom contest. I briefly wondered if the store manager would believe my story, and then wished that there was an identifying Med-Alert bracelet for people with Alzheimer's disease. I understand they are now available.

    I walked up and down the aisles looking frantically right and left. At last I found her, looking at children's pajamas. "Look at these," she said when she saw me as if no time had passed and no change of venue had taken place. "They're like real pajamas but 'tiny'. Aren't they cute?" There she was, finding pure pleasure in the dinky little pajamas. How's that for a little miracle?

    Little miracles weren't always enough. Mom's condition deteriorated, in spite of the Aricept. We needed more specialized professional help. Mom's GP referred us to a neurologist whose specialty was patients with Alzheimer's. Andy and I accompanied Mom to the consultation. The neurologist sat down opposite Mom. Andy and I were not offered seats so we looked on from the sidelines.

    "Draw these objects," the man instructed her without much preamble.

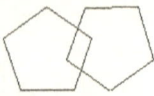

Mom sketched the design skillfully.

"Count up from 7 by adding 7 to each sum." She did this brilliantly. The doctor spoke encouragingly to her. And I thought to myself, *Wow! I can't do this in my own head.*

"Now, identify the present month, date, year, day of the week and time of day." Mom hesitated and then guessed wrongly.

"Oops, got that one wrong," the doctor said. "No problem. I get that one wrong myself. And it happens a lot if you're retired."

I was no longer inspired with confidence in this man who was not able to remember today's date. Nevertheless, the evaluation continued, and I wondered how one can get an accurate assessment of someone's mental capacity if you cheat for them.

"Where are we?" the doctor read off a printed card that had the Alzheimer's questions on it. I was thinking in terms of in which country, state, county or town we currently resided and was sure that any of those would be acceptable answers. Mom's answer: "your office". Duh.

"Take this paper, fold it in half and place it on the floor."

She did what she was told. *Good job, Rusty.* Mom still followed short and simple instructions at this point, but it would have been more revealing to request that she "Take this paper, fold it in half and place it on the floor – *after* you leave the office, walk down the hall, enter the elevator, and then return."

"Now, write a sentence," he continued.

Mom was in the *fake-it* stage of the disease and she faked a healthy cognitive state. If she could fake it here, why couldn't she fake it at home as well? All her responses were appropriate. Andy and I noticed the doctor looking at us as if we were nuts. The implied question on the doctor's mind was, *why would you do this to your poor sweet delightful mother?* He conveyed his displeasure to us with a sneer.

I was afraid Mom's sentence would read: "Save me from these conniving, deceitful children of mine." It was not. She wrote a simple yet acceptable declarative sentence.

Andy and I described how Mom had begun misplacing items and forgetting to bathe. "These things happen as we get older," he said. "And besides, the older we get the less often we need to bathe. It dries out the skin."

"She's not exactly forgetting *to* bathe," I stuttered, feeling intimidated. "She's forgetting *how* to bathe."

"Then help her." He was dismissive and displayed no inclination to take mine and Andy's complaints seriously. "OK, well… um… she has trouble…um… finding the right… um… *words* for a given situation or remembering people's names," I stammered, having trouble finding the right words.

"Well, really!" the doctor glared at me accusingly. "Who among us doesn't do *that*?"

"She gets lost easily and can't find her way home when she's out driving."

"But does she eventually find her way home?"

I can't speak for Andy, but I felt a little defensive.

"Yes," we answered in unison, "so far."

"She asks the same questions over and over," I told him.

Mom looked at us. She was hurt and her expression said, *go ahead, rat me out… but this man is on my side even when my own children conspire against me.*

The doctor shrugged his shoulders. "There's nothing more to be done," he stated without emotion. "She does need assistance with her personal care. I assume you can provide that." His body language indicated that if we took a little time out of our busy lives and mustered up a little patience, all would be fine. "If things become worse, feel free to come back in and see me."

What if we let her move in with you for a few days and then let's talk, I thought. Mom drew herself tall and erect in her 'at least I still have my dignity' posture. I felt like a creep. My secret wish was that Mom could either find it in her heart to forgive us for dragging her through this public scrutiny or the Alzheimer's would obliterate this ordeal from her memory. I got my wish, on both accounts.

CHAPTER SIX

Not on my watch

I wanted to stop time. Mom's memory blips that were caused by Alzheimer's disease meant that the spunky bits that made up Rusty's personality leaked slowly out of her like air from a worn tire. If I was able to patch even one leak, I knew another one would pop up somewhere else. All I could do was slap a band-aid on my own sadness and carry on. I realize now how remarkable it was that Mom retained much of her original character even while she became unsure of herself - an obvious departure from the vital woman of our childhood. She adapted to her new world and I compensated the best way I knew by becoming more involved in her day-to-day activities. Donna and I re-worked schedules, making Mom and Dad our top priority. This included mowing their half-acre of lawn as well as our own and assuming responsibilities for Jim and Rusty's finances. Having their Power of Attorney eased the way for me to pay their bills and deal with their bank. Because of their extenuating circumstances Connie J. Vetter, Mom and Dad's attorney, met with them at their house to describe the legal implications of this decision. She talked to them candidly with me out of the room so they wouldn't feel pressure to sign the document and could express any reservations they had. This document allowed me to legally act on their behalf on any matter. They signed their lives over to me. Two adults, who had done a pretty good job of conducting their own affairs all their lives, gave me *carte blanche* for all future decisions concerning them. The significance of the transference of power was not lost on me. It was not lost on them either.

A minor miracle dropped from the heavens when Mom accepted that her 'little memory problem' contributed to her forgetting to pay some bills. I was afraid that her natural streak of independence would make her stubbornly hold onto the bill-paying job with disastrous results. Effects of the Alzheimer's disease made Mom question herself and her decision-making capabilities, and every step into this new self-questioning phase made her become more reliant on me and even welcome the help. So, for me to *help,* I had to have their Power of Attorney. The bank wouldn't talk to me. The phone company, the electric company – no one would talk to me without this legal document. So Mom and Dad signed the papers. On my next visit to see them, Dad told me, "the day after Connie's visit, Rusty heard some loud hammering in the neighborhood and came into the den to ask me what I thought it was. I told her... 'Oh, that's just Marsha nailing up a *For Sale* sign in the front yard,'" he teased me and I smiled. I had been afraid that his biggest fear would be that I might start making them do things they didn't want to do. I would do that very thing eventually – but not yet. And I believe Dad was letting me know that the thought had passed through his mind. He knew in his heart that I would only ever do what was best for them, as they had always done for me and my brothers and sister.

When possible, Mom continued to participate in various activities even though it was at a reduced capacity. She went to church, and the grocery store. But the grocery store trips began to yield more cookies than cucumbers. This newly developed sweet tooth was yet another departure from Mom's old ways. She never allowed us to 'fill up on junk' when we were growing up and the dessert tray held little attraction for her. Instead, she was a devotee of fresh vegetables, meat, and fruit (mostly home grown). "Fill up on your meal and you won't want sweets," she would tell us when we were children. She practiced what she preached until now. Now, I caught her *filling up* on cookies and other sweets. She used the automatic dishwasher as a secret hiding place to stash the packs of cookies she held in reserve for a rainy day. She often forgot they were there, though, and built up a sizeable inventory.

The disproportionate quantity of snack foods was not the only cause of Mom and Dad's disintegrating nutrition. As Andy had noticed, food was forgotten in the refrigerator so long that it was in danger of becoming a penicillin manufacturing facility, and Mom continued to leave food to burn on the stove. Mom's cholesterol levels, which had been naturally low until now, became elevated. Two incidents hastened my decision to take on meal-planning and grocery-shopping duties because of health and safety reasons.

The first incident occurred one day when Mom had driven to the grocery store alone. Dad had promised to accompany her on these excursions but couldn't go on this one. The store was two miles from the house with only a few turns between them. One particular shopping day, the parking lot was being repaved and the exit Mom usually took was blocked. The pavers routed traffic to another outlet on a different side of the lot. You and I would follow the arrows out of the parking lot then re-trace our path back home without giving it a second thought. For Mom, whose knowledge and problem-solving skills were ebbing, the one route she knew to the store and back home was no longer available to her, and it threw her for a spin because it forced her into territory she no longer recognized. Mom didn't have the capacity to *see* or imagine in her mind a suitable alternate route home. Trying to retrace her steps back home was, for Mom, like turning a blindfolded person round and round in a game of Pin the Tail on the Donkey, disorienting and confusing.

A friend of Mom's, who was also at the grocery store, saw Mom's confounded expression as she got to the car. She encouraged Mom to follow her out of the parking lot and then led Mom home. The friend, who had known Mom for years, realized that this was alien behavior for Rusty and called me to relate the story to me. From the quaver in her voice, I realized it was difficult for her to do this and she admitted that it hurt her to see Mom in that state of mind. I appreciated her calling me and sharing her kind, thoughtful concern. I assured her that Mom's state of mind hurt me, too. I explained some of the things we were doing to assist Rusty and Jim. I also realized that when someone develops Alzheimer's, it affects the entire community, not just the sufferer and immediate family. Friends who had always relied on Mom's decisive solving of problems had to witness the descent of a once bright mind into a smaller and smaller world as it approached inevitable darkness.

Lest anyone accuse me of allowing Mom to drive longer than she should have, I assure you that I appealed to two higher authorities on this matter. When I consulted Mom's physician about whether she should be driving or not, he believed that short forays to familiar places close to home such as the grocery store, would be okay. He assured me that when the renewal for Mom's driver's license came due, there would be no decision for either one of us to make since he was confident that Mom would fail the test. When it was time to renew her license, Mom drove herself to the DMV office, without my knowledge. *How did she find it without Dad? Was he with her? Sneaky parents.* The examiner actually *helped* her identify the signs and commiserated with her that failing to remember the different categories in which various signs belonged happened to her all the time. I go to get my license renewed at the same highway patrol office. I have gone there for every renewal since I received my license at sixteen years old and I have never interacted with anyone helpful. Rusty makes friends everywhere.

Dad suspected I was working behind the scenes to get Mom off the road so he assured me again that he would ride with her wherever she needed to go. And to be sure, he was with her for the second incident. On that evening, I stood in front of my class, trying to lecture. I couldn't keep my attention focused on our subject. I couldn't form a coherent sentence, and I consistently lost my train of thought. I looked at my lecture notes and thought *I have never seen these notes before in my life!* I said to the class, "I feel a disturbance in the force tonight," a *Star Wars* movie reference which they understood. I dismissed class early. No one opposed the decision. I went home, wondering what was wrong with me. I knew I was running on empty, but this was different. I barely stepped inside the door when Donna told me that a friend of the family called and asked me to call him back pronto. I did and he told me that he had been with Mom and Dad several hours that evening, trying to handle their latest crisis. They had been involved in an automobile accident and the car was totaled.

After he told me what he knew I drove immediately over to Mom and Dad's house. I was upset. I was afraid. I was angry. I walked past Mom who was standing in the kitchen. She realized she was in trouble; it was written on her face. The *former* Rusty would have let me know in no uncertain terms that this was not my business and I was welcome to butt out at any time. But *this* Rusty stood there looking contrite. My heart went out to her. I knew she was doing the best she could. So I concentrated my wrath on Jim. I made a bee-line to the den where he stoically awaited my arrival.

"What happened?" I asked without preamble.

"We were just going to get a sandwich at Hardee's. A car hit us. We're okay, by the way. The driver of the other car wasn't injured either."

"Well, I'm glad of that," I conceded. "But tell me, who was at fault?"

"There was no fault. It was an accident. The police came but they didn't give anyone a ticket."

Dad sat silent, in his easy chair, gazing down at his gnarled up arthritic hands. He looked like he had been caught stealing the last cookie from the cookie jar. But not for himself - the last cookie was to be given to his beloved. Jim would never steal one for himself. I took a deep breath and started over.

"Daddy, you've got to be honest with me. I need you to tell me exactly what happened. I want to hear your side of the story."

He told me quite candidly how the accident happened, and then he instructed me on what to do to get the car repaired. I told him that I was not going to have the car repaired, and I was not going to help them buy a new one. He looked dejected. I was firm.

"Mom shouldn't be driving anymore, Dad. This is our opportunity to take the keys away." After a pause I asked, "Are you sure you're alright? You didn't get hurt at all?"

"No, I'm fine. But the steering wheel whipped around and banged up your mother's fingers pretty good. They're bruised."

I kissed and hugged the ol' guy then went to put some ice on Mom's fingers. I fixed some dinner for them since they never got to Hardee's.

A couple of days later, I got a call from Dad's best friend, Ben Clark, of colonoscopy advice fame. He told me that Dad had asked him to rent a car for him. Of course he knew the score concerning developments at the Burris household as well as anybody. He agreed that getting them another car wasn't such a wonderful idea but he didn't want to disappoint his buddy either. I told Ben I appreciated his call and that his instincts were right. I told him that I would handle the situation. I think he was relieved.

Next day, I went by Mom and Dad's house on my way home

from work to see how they were doing. The first words out of Dad's mouth were, "The insurance company will pay for another car. Will you call and work it out?"

"There aren't going to be any more cars, Dad."

"What do you mean? I want a car, and I'm going to have a car."

"Daddy, I believe *someone* was looking out for you two when this wreck happened. I've thought for a while that we should stop Mom from driving. Maybe this was the divine intervention we needed to help us do that. I probably should have put my foot down and taken the keys away from Mom before now, but it's hard for me to make these decisions for you. After this accident, though, I can't allow Mom to drive anymore, it would be irresponsible."

Put my foot down? Can't allow? Wow. Our roles had made a complete about-face!

"How are we supposed to get around? How are we supposed to live?" He pressed me.

Near-panic was in Jim's voice. I may as well have taken away his manhood while I was at it. I tried to assure him. "Daddy, I drive right by your house every day on my way in to work and on the way home. I pass the grocery store on the same route. *And* Hardee's. I take you and Mom to all your doctors' appointments. Your buddies come by and pick you up now when you go out to lunch. It's not going to be a real big adjustment. It'll be fine. Please don't worry. You know Andy and I will make sure you have everything you need. Please trust me on this."

"It's just that having a car makes us feel as if we still have some freedom." Jim shrugged, he knew he was defeated and it showed on his face. I couldn't have hated myself more than I did right then. This man had gone to war for our country. He had held important positions in his career. He had helped raise a family of four children. He had coached baseball teams. He bought me hiking boots, supporting gender equality way before it was cool. Now, he wasn't permitted to pick up a chicken sandwich for lunch without assistance.

In my new parental role, I provided Jim and Rusty with a variety of food from the grocery store. I got a payoff every time I drove up to unload the goods. They both met me at the back door, excited as little kids, wondering what surprises I had brought them. I liked this part a lot.

Dropping off food to Mom and Dad was not the only regular job I took on. Mom's personal hygiene needed more regular attendance. I knew from a friend whose mother had already gone through this nightmare that baths and showers would drop down the list of priorities. The bathroom is a scary place. And it's scarier if you're older, frailer, and unsure of your footing and ability to keep yourself upright on wet, slippery floors. If you *do* get yourself into the shower, and if you *can* get yourself back out again, well, it's COLD. And who likes being cold?

I encouraged Mom to have her showers during our leisurely Sunday visits. One Sunday while she was in the shower, Mom let out a blood-curdling scream. I rushed into the bathroom, pulled back the glass shower door and found her backed up to the wall opposite the shower spray. The water was scorching hot. I turned the single-handled faucet quickly to the off position and climbed into the shower to calm Mom down. She said she didn't know what to do to stop the hot water. Her reaction did not embrace the concept of simply getting out of the tub. She was trapped with no exit strategy. This woman who had figured out how to repair lawnmowers and sewing machines no longer had the problem-solving capability to regulate water temperatures in the shower. Although the hot water was painful, it didn't blister her skin, but the ordeal frightened me as much as it did her. I had not foreseen this particular scenario in my crystal ball to prevent it. Andy had thought to install a grab-bar on the wall beside the tub for safety and to assist her getting in and out. After the scalding incident, he turned down the thermostat on the hot water heater to prevent a repeat of this performance.

A couple of days after this episode, I was at work and walking across campus when I met my friend, Frances, who was the secretary of the history department. She also happened to be the best friend of Ben Clark's wife. (I marvel at the interconnected web of people in my life). She's a little older than I am and much wiser. She had recently taken care of her own parents and, knowing I was doing the same, offered me insights on the changing of roles that I was experiencing. Her suggestions helped me tremendously. When we met on this day, I must have looked haggard. With boundless sympathy for my position, she asked how I was doing.

"Frances, I can't keep even a step ahead of them. They're killing me. I'm scared to death something bad is going to happen to them. They can get themselves into trouble, but they can't get back out on their own."

I mistakenly believed that I could stay a step ahead of Mom and Dad and keep them safe. I literally laid awake nights trying to conjure up potential difficulties and dangers they might get into so I could thwart them. Frances read my thoughts.

"Oh dahlin'," she shook her head in sympathy, as her Richmond, Virginia accent dripped like honey. Comforting. Soothing. "You can't save them from everything. You can try, and you can do your best, but at some point something's going to get them. In the end, you know you'll have to let them go… it's inevitable."

Not on my watch, I thought defiantly, heroically, naïvely.

Her words stuck, though, and would become some of the best advice I received concerning my responsibilities for Mom and Dad. It settled me down enough to understand that the events unfolding before me were not entirely under my control. The direction my parents' lives were taking was bigger than anything I could command. Much bigger. Her message helped me through the next few years of bumps and scrapes and tragedies.

Frances offered another suggestion. "Turn the chores of caring for your Mom and Dad into a labor of love," she said. She had done that with her own parents with no regrets. I had considered my involvement in Mom and Dad's life as a chore but I determined to do as Frances suggested. My first labor of love was to take a more active role in Mom's hygiene. After our Sunday lunches, I settled Mom into a nice warm bubble bath. I was surprised she agreed to this scheme because it was something she had rarely, if ever, done for herself. According to her philosophy, soaky-baths consumed time that could be better spent doing important things like 'work'. That old way of thinking dissolved as soon as she found herself spoiled rotten among a mountain of luxurious bubbles. Eventually, I would rinse her off, towel her dry, and slather her skinny little body with Neutrogena. She oooh'd and ahhh'd while exhibiting little modesty. Apparently Alzheimer's strips away pesky, petty, self-conscious behaviors that stand between us and pure pleasure which I recognized as a small compensation of the disease.

Instead of being uncomfortable that her daughter found it necessary to give her a bath, Mom delighted in the pampering.

With more adaptations necessary to insure Mom and Dad's welfare, I scoured bookstores to find information on this and on dealing with Alzheimer's. The literature was scarce then, but I found some helpful resources, especially from the Alzheimer's Association. I felt I had a clear picture of what to expect (*I was wrong*) but at the time I was amazed that Mom was able to still do so much for herself and for Dad - a testament to Rusty's fortitude and drive. All the same, I began to think ahead for when they could no longer manage their own basic needs. I was uncertain what form the plan should take. Should I move them into my house? Should we sell each of our houses and buy a larger one to accommodate both households? Should I find a live-in companion for them? I couldn't fathom moving them out of the home they loved and into an assisted living facility. Assisted living accommodations can be quite inviting these days, but in the end, it's not home. I redoubled my efforts to adapt their home environment.

Events worked against me at times. Since Jim was of sound mind, I relied on him to keep an eye on Rusty and update me regularly on their state of affairs. Mom had done a great job with her smoking cessation program. We continued our walks at lunchtime, and Mom's physical health improved. Occasionally though, and unknown to me because somehow this tidbit of information slipped Dad's mind, Mom forgot that she'd quit smoking and walked to the store to buy herself a fresh pack of Camels. No filters. (That part she remembered). As her autonomous spirit emerged on these occasions Mom hiked to the local convenience store, a mile away, on foot, along a curvy country road. The curvy country road had been nicknamed 'Jackass Avenue' almost a century earlier. The Newell family, for which the community was named, had raised mules for farm work. The road by their house leading up to the highway has many sharp and dangerous curves in it. It was said that only mules could navigate that particular stretch of road safely. And if you call for emergency assistance, be prepared to tell the dispatcher that you're on the Jackass Avenue side of the two Rocky River Roads. As renowned as this road is, it has no sidewalks and no shoulder to speak of either. There's road. Then there's ditch. But these things did not deter Mom - as we learned later from friends who saw her walking, stopped, and gave her rides to and from the store. I could have throttled Dad.

As I look back now, I can cut the ol' guy some slack; perhaps Rusty waited until his nap time to make her get-away. And anyway, Dad had other redeeming moments. For instance, when I decided that my classroom lectures and my own research interests would benefit from poking about in the Oxford University archives of the Bodleian Library, Dad became an enthusiastic supporter. For several weeks I was able to put worries for Mom and Dad out of my mind and enjoy a break from those cares.

When I returned to *real life*, there was more to do to get Mom and Dad's legal affairs in order. I had their Power of Attorney, but other issues needed to be addressed - issues such as what if intensive round-the-clock medical care was required? What provisions did we need to make concerning their home? We consulted an attorney who specialized in Elder Law and she developed a plan for our family. I highly recommend this avenue for anyone in a similar situation; it's better to do it sooner rather than later. Have a trusted friend or family member accompany you to the appointments. Our attorney provided us with written documents spelling out the plan of action which I could refer to at my leisure. But it helped to have Donna and Andy there to ask questions and we could discuss later what we thought we heard in the meeting. With this knowledge, we invented various scenarios for some of the inevitable occasions we feared would materialize.

A shadow appeared on Mom's annual mammogram about this time. Further investigation revealed the need for surgery. Mom had had a lump removed several years before, but with this event I was afraid she would not completely understand the nuanced information concerning the surgery. But she did. She marched fearlessly into this potential threat as always, but she relied on me to deal with the details. I picked Mom up the morning of her surgery and we drove together to the outpatient clinic where Dad had his colonoscopy. The surgeon performing Mom's surgery was the same woman who performed my gall bladder surgery a couple of years before. She fell immediately under the *Rusty-spell* and made an instant loving connection to her. This pleased me. I prefer that the person cutting into me or one of my loved ones feels emotionally driven to succeed. I felt confident in her abilities and she had an easy-going, light, bedside manner. She was upbeat when she met with us before Mom was sedated and optimistic that the procedure would be textbook and little more than a formality. After the procedure was completed, the surgeon came out to the waiting room to discuss the results of the surgery with me. Her facial expression had changed. The spunky tone in her voice when she greeted us earlier had vanished.

"We had no complications during surgery," she said. She kept her eyes on Mom's chart and did not look at me. "She'll be in recovery for a little while longer, then she can go home. Here are the post-op instructions. Call us if anything out of the ordinary happens, or if you have any questions. My office will contact you to make a follow-up appointment."

Warning bells. I asked her point-blank if everything looked okay when she cut the lump out. Not precise professional medical terminology, I know, but I was freaking out after this apparent 180-degree turn in her demeanor.

"The procedure is to send everything off for a biopsy. It's always best to get those results before making any pronouncements. We'll have those results back in time for your Mom's follow-up appointment."

Vague. I tried to pin her down. She did not budge.

So we waited for the follow-up appointment.

I didn't tell any of this to Mom. In the back of my mind – well, not *too* far back – was the thought that Mom's only sister had died from breast cancer. Yet, if Mom didn't mention the connection, neither would I. She had little pain, she said, and she did a good job following the post-op self-care. When Mom and I went to her next appointment, the surgeon fairly bounced into the examining room with the results.

"Wow! *You* look different than you did on Mom's surgery day!" I said this out loud before I could stop myself.

"Great news! The tumor was benign." She examined Mom and bragged on her for healing rapidly. I couldn't let the discrepancy in her behavior go. I was sure it wasn't my imagination.

"Why were you so vague and distant the day of her surgery?" I asked her. "You were completely different than how you seemed before surgery and today."

"When I looked at the tumor on the day of surgery, I observed that the edges were not clearly defined. The consistency of the mass was what upset me and frankly, I was scared that it was cancerous after all. It upset me. I'm sorry."

"No problem," I reassured her. "I'm glad surgeons can get upset that a patient might have cancer. Thanks for telling me."

Another telephone call at work. Friday. Five o'clock in the afternoon. Mom sounded worried. "Honey, your father's having some problems. The doctor wants to see him at the urgent care office as soon as possible."

Urgent Care. At least it's NOT the Emergency Room at the hospital, I thought. *This is not too bad, then.* I asked her what sort of problems Dad was having and where the urgent care office was located. She said Dad would explain when I got there. I hung up and sped over to their house. On the way, I called Andy's cell phone and told him that I was taking Dad to the urgent care office and I'd let him know where as soon as I could. I didn't have any other information about Dad's medical crisis.

Dad gave me the destination, then he and Mom belted themselves in and we headed out. Since we were driving to a medical plaza in town, in rush-hour traffic, on a Friday, I was anxious about getting caught in the congestion causing Dad's condition to worsen as we sat at a stand-still. It's good to think up problems before they happen. Valuable worry-time is lost otherwise.

"By the way, what *is* your medical condition, Dad?" As I asked the question, I darted from one lane to another, trying to leap-frog my way to the front of the traffic line. Dad cut his eyes at me. His telepathic message was clear: *calm yourself down and drive safely*. Mom was in the back seat chattering away. I don't know what the topic was, but her tone had a jovial nature.

Out loud Dad said, "I can't go to the bathroom."

"You can't go… um…" In the back of my mind, I calculated the intake, output ratio that constituted good bowel regularity in humans. Not that I'm an expert, but I thought that maybe a heads up would have been forthcoming before five o'clock on a Friday afternoon. Like, say, three o'clock, or maybe even a day before.

"How quickly does something like this come on, Jim?" I

wasn't sure if this medical matter had an actual urgency associated with it but I wanted his side of the story.

"Several days," he said nonchalantly. "That's why the doctor insisted on seeing me now. It could be worse than mere constipation. I might be impacted, and that's serious."

I know I'm being impacted by this, and it is serious, I thought.

"Several days! Why are you calling me now? I mean come on Dad, it's five o'clock ON A FRIDAY." This was symbolically important to me for some unfathomable reason. Maybe I was secretly disappointed that we would miss out on our Captain D meal. I continued the tirade. "Couldn't we have done something before now?"

Upon our arrival, the receptionist knew who we were and why we were there and sent us to the waiting room, 'urgent care' being in name only. We chose our chairs and averted our eyes from one another, waiting for the awkwardness to subside. Which it did the minute Andy arrived. He rushed in, spied us and took a seat beside Dad.

"What's going on Jim? You okay?"

"Can't go to the bathroom." Poor Dad.

"You can't *what*?"

"Can't go to the bathroom." I bet he never got tired of going over that piece of news.

"It's serious in older people," I explained. Now I was Dad's protector.

"Jim!" Andy shook his head. Dad smiled, he knew what was coming.

"I already had my funeral suit picked out. I thought you were having a heart attack or something. Now you're telling me that the emergency here is an inability to poop."

Dad broke down and laughed. Tee hee hee. His shoulders bobbed up and down – the spitting image of his mother when she laughed at herself. Andy's gift is that he can say anything, *any*thing, and it sounds fun. He's a kidder and Dad welcomed his kidding good naturedly.

After a forty-five minute wait, Dad was called back to the examining room. Mom wanted to go too. But if Mom went with Dad to this unfamiliar space, I was afraid that she would become disoriented. I felt compelled to be by her side, and I also felt compelled to hear whatever the doctor had to say. So we all went together. Except for Andy. He had enough sense to remain in the waiting room. When the medical personnel indicated that an actual physical examination would commence in the general area where poop is or is not released from the human body, I offered my regrets and returned rather hastily to the waiting room. On the way out I had the presence of mind to tell the doctor, "As Dad's Health Care Power of Attorney, I need you to discuss your findings with me when the exam is completed."

Only a few minutes after I had returned to the waiting room, I saw Mom wander in from another entrance, looking lost. I went to her.

"There you are!" she said, relief clearly evident in her voice.

"I thought you were with Dad. How'd you get here?"

"I don't know. I've been wandering back here for ages." Three minutes is an eon in Mom's world.

She sat down beside Andy and when the doctor came out to find us, I followed him back to the examining room. I noticed there was another door that led from the examining room to an interior corridor that in my panic-driven escape I had not noticed before. The doctor prescribed some medication to get things going again for Dad and packed us off with an optimistic outlook for his prognosis.

This incident proved to be only the beginning of Dad's problem with regularity. But this predicament took a back seat to a more exciting development. This one, quite pleasant. Andy was to get married.

When Andy gave Andrea a Bluetick Coonhound as a gift, we knew the courtship was serious. They set the wedding date for late November. Andrea, Barbara, Donna, Peggy, our Minnesota cousins, and I began planning what we would wear for this formal evening affair. The bridal showers, the tea, the rehearsal dinner, and the actual wedding, all required Mom's presence, of course, as mother of the groom. She looked forward to being a part of the festivities, but getting her there was my responsibility and getting her there in appropriate attire was a huge undertaking for someone who loathes shopping. I had to get creative. Of course, the old Rusty would have designed her outfits, found the perfect fabric and completed the project in record time. She would probably have done the same for each of her daughters and offered to make the wedding gown and bridesmaids' dresses, too. She had done it before. This is how I know what she would have done. However, reality dictated that we purchase her clothing from a store for the wedding.

Taking Mom shopping was out of the question. She didn't have the attention span to make a decision between one dress or another and she didn't have the stamina for the task of trying on the various garments for any length of time since being in unfamiliar territory was becoming more and more stressful for her. Even more important, *I* didn't have the patience to dress Mom for a shopping outing, *and* get her in-to and out-of the various iterations of wedding-wear. I related my dilemma to a salesperson at one of the department stores and she suggested we choose a selection of suitable outfits for Mom to try on in the comfort of her own home. We could return what we didn't want. A wonderfully helpful suggestion!

Dad needed only one outfit for the wedding itself. He wouldn't be required to attend any of the other affairs but he believed any one of the suits he already owned would be adequate. Barbara was adamant - Jim was to have a new suit. She took him to get fitted. He balked at spending money on himself. "I don't know why we're spending this much money on something I'll wear only once," he complained.

"Oh, you'll wear it twice," Barbara remarked. "Once to the wedding and at least once more after that." Barbara's dry wit was inherited from her dad. Dad understood the hidden meaning of her quip and as quick as ever he replied, "oh yeah, I guess so." His eyes twinkled. He then picked out the best suit money could buy off the rack, especially since it would be the one worn for his final send-off. It was a handsome dark blue pinstriped single breasted style that had no trace of polyester in its composition. And, as long as he was choosing a strikingly gorgeous suit, Jim decided that he also wanted a classy shirt, a fine silk necktie, and a bright and flashy red silk handkerchief for the breast pocket. He did not entertain the notion of having one of those pre-folded pocket square thingies. He could certainly fold and place the handkerchief himself and did not need to take short-cuts. The necktie had to be perfect in color and contrast. He championed the Double Windsor Knot and I believe he already had an image of himself gracing the cover of GQ magazine. Dad, at that moment, became single-minded and unwavering in his determination to look his handsomest, and I believe he would have put to shame any peacock trying to rival him.

Regretfully, Dad's gastro-issues had not resolved themselves as we approached the wedding day. His doctor persisted in trying to figure out how to coax Jim's bowels into behaving more gentlemanly. We all went to the appointments – Mom and Dad and me. It had developed into our family togetherness time since we no longer left Mom at home alone. During one of these more memorable appointments, the doctor asked Dad to provide him with a *sample*, for testing purposes. Dad wanted to make the deposit there and then, before we went home. I was for it. Mom insisted that she needed to accompany Dad into the bathroom to assist him with the procedure and he agreed. I maintained my entitlement to ignorance. But then Mom locked them inside the bathroom and couldn't figure out how to get them out. Dad was indisposed and unable to do door duty. He was probably relieved for the moment that the door couldn't be opened. But even if he were ambulatory enough to make his way to the door, he couldn't see because of the macular degeneration, and he had little dexterity for opening door knobs because of the rheumatoid arthritis in his hands.

After an uncomfortable amount of time passed, and since I appeared to be lurking in the laboratory without purpose, I confessed to one of the nurses the probable situation with my parents in the restroom. I asked her to rescue my mother and father from what I believed at that point to be certain doom because by now, it was getting dangerously close to lunch time *and* Matlock.

Rescued at last, Mom and Dad had enough sense to be chagrined at their obvious failure to produce a suitable sample for the lab. We were instructed to march back up to see the doctor for new instructions. He explained how this process could be accomplished at home, after which the results could be brought back to the lab. *Oh goodie.*

He also explained that Dad probably needed to have another colonoscopy. My look of despair prompted him to ask why that would be a problem. I told him briefly the domestic situation and he assured me that the colonoscopy could be performed in the hospital and Dad could be admitted the day before and assisted with the prep by professional medical staff there. I wanted to hug and kiss this man, but to maintain decorum, I promised him a specimen from Dad ASAP instead. He seemed happy with that bargain. I took Mom and Dad home and we awaited *the blessed event*. News travels fast in Newell. The encouragement he received was touching.

The following Saturday morning greeted me with a ringing telephone. I learned to hate Saturday morning calls.

"Honey, your father wants you to take the bag over to the lab today. It needs to be there before noon. Can you come on over?"

I knew which *bag* Mom referred to, however vague she attempted to be. I was relieved but Dad's success meant a decree would need to be sent across the land to those who had expressed concern for Dad's well-being. Hearty congratulations were exchanged. Donna and I put our Saturday chores on hold and drove over to Mom and Dad's house to pick up *the bag* for delivery. Mom grabbed it out of the refrigerator and handed it to me. My stomach lurched. Mom noticed.

"It's okay. It's in a bag inside the bag, so it's really sanitary. Don't worry."

Rusty's intuition was still tuned into the meanings of not-so-subtle body language. That realization buoyed my spirits. Dad came thumping out from his TV room, proud as can be. His pride was short-lived when the results of the lab test came back inconclusive. For the time being, Dad would have to tolerate the current state of affairs until the doctor could get the colonoscopy scheduled and he could delve deeper into the cause of Dad's predicament.

For the moment, the Burris family confronted a more compelling affair. Andy and Andrea's big day! They planned every aspect of the wedding themselves; we had only to show up. Friends and family gathered from Charlotte, Minnesota, London and Albemarle for the event! Our sincere wish was for Andy and Andrea to have a long, loving and happy life together. But our immediate concern was focused on how good we looked. No detail was too small to go unnoticed. If Dad could look debonair in his dual-purpose suit, then we could spiff up a bit too. Mom, Donna and I had manicures and pedicures. Our cousins were gorgeous. Robert was handsome in his navy suit. Aunt Ruth, recently widowed, made a valiant effort to join in the merriment. Our friends, Paula and Susie, were *très chic*. Barbara, Peggy,

Donna and I had never looked more elegant. Mom was absolutely stunning. Her gown, a deep forest green with sequined accents, glittered and sparkled. The color suited her perfectly.

Andy and Andrea exchanged vows. The photographer earned his pay. And then it was time to party. We formed a procession from the church to the banquet hall a few miles away for the reception. The facility had a ballroom dance floor, tables laden with food and wine, tables and chairs for everyone, and a DJ to manage the music for our listening and dancing pleasure.

This was a celebration - of life, of love. And it was pure fun. Andy danced with his bride. Then he danced with his mother. After that, the floor was opened to all. Mom didn't sit down for more than two minutes before one friend and then another asked her out onto the dance floor. That woman loved to dance! Dad was not able to dance but, looking dapper in his brand new suit, complete with folded handkerchief, he never took his eyes off his own beautiful bride as she shined brightly under the mirrored disco ball. On the drive over from the church, Barbara told Mom and Dad that one of their friends complimented her on how much she, Barbara, favored Mom, and how she always thought Mom was so beautiful. Dad cut into the story. "She's right," he affirmed. What a romantic guy.

Andy's entourage of women - sisters, cousins, friends, and Mom - made a circle and danced with him as the DJ played *We are family, I've got all my sisters with me...* a song made popular by Sister Sledge.

Andy and Andrea's wedding wins an award for being the most fun the Burris family had enjoyed together for ages. We didn't know that we would never experience such carefree times together again.

CHAPTER SEVEN

Just ride it out

Andy and Andrea began their honeymoon and the rest of us returned to our daily routines. Mom needed a follow-up appointment with her dentist but since he had closed his practice due to his own health problems I transferred her records to my dentist and accepted the first available appointment. It happened to fall on my birthday. I sat in the examining room with her as I reflected on how we got to this point. Then, without thinking I said, "You know what, Mom?"

"What?" She smiled at me.

"It's my birthday today…"

"It is?" I caught her off guard and her smile changed instantly to a frown.

"Yes." I immediately regretted this selfish declaration. We had celebrated her birthday only three days earlier. A recollection of the gift she gave me on my last birthday popped into my head. The gift was fabric, accompanied with a promise of making me an outfit of my choice from it. The box of beautiful folded wool and good intentions sat untouched in my hall closet.

"Oh." The tone of her voice was tinged with sorrow that she did not have access to this information. "I'm sorry, I didn't know. Happy Birthday, honey."

It was a close contest as to who was most miserable at that precise moment, and who was the most heartbroken. *Good job, Marsha.*

Looking after Mom and Dad became more intense, but I made Saturday nights a sacred restorative time. I took that night to be off the grid, to relax, watch TV, and enjoy a glass of wine. One Saturday night, the telephone rang. I picked up the receiver.

"Marsha, this is your mother." *As if I wouldn't recognize her voice.*
"Hi Mom! What's up?"
"Well...," she hesitated, then sighed.
"What is it?" I froze as I heard the serious tone in her voice.
"Well, honey, the worst thing that *can* happen *has* happened."

My knees went weak. I sank into the closest chair. Silence on both ends of the phone line. She didn't elaborate. I needed more information. I began to panic and mentally formed a list of people I would need to notify. I chastised myself for not having the list created already. When nothing more came from the other end of the line I thought, *poor Mom must be in shock.*

"Ok, Mom." I pulled myself together and entered into meet-the-crisis-head-on mode. "It's ok. Tell me what happened."

"I don't know how to tell you, but we're totally out of toilet paper. I can't think how it happened." She was truly vexed. "We usually keep extra in the laundry room. But your Dad's in the bathroom and..."

I went from devastation to euphoria with the speed of sound - the sound of Mom's confession of toilet tissue miscalculations.

"Say no more, Mom." *I could fix this.* "I've got extra paper here," I assured her. "I'll bring it right over. Tell Dad to just sit tight." *Giggle.*

"Thank you, Sweetie. You don't know what a life-saver you are!"

Boy, how things had changed. This was strong praise from a woman who previously saw potential for improvement in almost everything we did as children, from housecleaning to the thickness of potato peelings. Now I saved the day by merely bringing toilet paper into her house. I did question my own part in allowing the incident to transpire at all since I was the one who supplied them with the essentials of daily life. I had miscalculated this one, but they sure did use a lot of toilet paper. After I hung up the telephone, I realized that I had subconsciously been waiting for *the call*.

I recognized that I was becoming a parent to my parents. In that position I renewed my commitment to keeping Jim and Rusty in their home as long as possible although I continued to expect help from them in making important decisions on their behalf. I looked to them (in vain it turned out) for suggestions about the direction their needs were taking. They were beginning to require more assistance than I was able to give them, and their financial resources were not sufficient to cover extended home-health visits indefinitely. One problem that needed to be tackled immediately was Dad's inability to physically get himself into and out of the bathtub. He lacked the dexterity to apply a soapy wash cloth to the appropriate places and I was not willing to offer Jim and Rusty a two-for-one Sunday afternoon bath deal. Nor do I believe Jim would agree to that deal under any circumstances. I insisted we hire a home health care professional to come in during the week to give him a proper bath. He surrendered.

On one of my visits to see Mom and Dad after work, the next door neighbor told me he saw Mom topple into the flower bed by the front porch one morning. Depth perception is a problem for individuals with Alzheimer's. The ground or floor may appear closer or farther than it actually is, causing missteps, stumbles and falls. A dark rug may look like a hole in the middle of the floor and they will walk around it rather than over it. Mashed potatoes on a white dinner plate literally disappear in the perception of the Alzheimer's sufferer. Mom's face-first dive into the soil didn't injure her, the neighbor assured me, as he had rushed over to help her up, but the fact that it happened at all upset him and alarmed me.

Other evidence of Mom's decline became apparent. Her inability to prepare meals was one, so Donna arranged for Friendship Trays from Meals on Wheels to begin delivering mid-day meals for Mom and Dad. The meal was hearty enough to provide a substantial hot lunch with enough left over for a light supper. Donna and I would continue to make casseroles for them as well and we would keep their freezer stocked with Stouffers, but here was an opportunity to have a dependable hot meal available to them every week day. I popped in to see Mom and Dad on the second day of the meal delivery program. As we sat at the dining room table chatting, I noticed a few dishes in the sink and walked over to wash them. Over my shoulder I asked them how they liked the delivered meals.

"We want you to cancel it," Dad said without preamble.

"What?" I was confused. I thought I heard him wrong. I thought he said: *We want you to cancel it*. Friendship Trays were a god-send to me. Food. Nutritious. Hot. Delivered-to-your-door.

"We don't want it anymore." He was clear.

"Why not?" I stopped washing the dishes and turned to look at them. Dad's hands were resting on the table in front of him, clasped as if in prayer. His eyes were cast down upon them.

"We just don't."

Jim had spoken. I knew the tone. It happened infrequently, but when it happened, his word was law. Defeated, I turned back to the sink and said resignedly, "Fine."

Fine. That's all I said. I didn't say it hatefully. I didn't say it shrilly. It was swift capitulation on my part, because I recognized I was defeated. But when I turned back to look at them again, they both were sitting there with tears in their eyes. No lie. I made my parents cry. With one unskillfully uttered monosyllabic word I had brought both my parents to this point. *What the hell?* is what I thought. *What are these people trying to do to me? What's the big deal about having food brought to you?*

I had emphasized to them before we started the service that they would be paying for it – it wouldn't be charity. Why wouldn't you want to have food delivered to your door step? But, maybe, just maybe, the little bit of dignity and self-respect they had left resided in that place where food does not have to be delivered in an aluminum container by strangers to your back door. Mom and Dad worked hard their entire lives to earn their living, to pay their bills. They did *not* live beyond their means. Now clearly, they could not endure one more attack against their pride. This was one step too far and Dad stood his ground. I regret that I brought him to this point, but at the time, the only thought in my mind was, *you are killing me!*

That was the frame of mind I was in when I drove Dad to his next doctor's appointment. With so many facets of their care on my mind, I was at my wits end and I didn't know what to do or what *should* be done. I wanted help from Mom and Dad before I made any more decisions concerning them. If Jim could assert himself regarding Friendship Trays, then he could take a position on one or two other considerations related to their lives. While Donna sat with Mom at home, I took the opportunity of my one-on-one status with Dad in the car to confront him with this topic. The drive would take thirty minutes and I had a captive audience. I had to shout, of course, because of Dad's hearing impairment. If we'd had this conversation at the house, Mom would be sure to hear it and know we were conspiring against her. I didn't want her to hear me point out that their living arrangements were becoming dangerous.

"Dad, I won't be able to live with myself if you and Mom die from food poisoning or if the house burns down. It would be horrible if Mom fell out in the yard and seriously hurt herself. What are we going to do? Mom's not going to get better, you know. It's only going to get worse."

"I know." Dad slumped. His posture reflected defeat.

Great. Real subtle. And sensitive, too. But I didn't care. I was nearing the end of my rope and Dad needed to be an active participant in his and Mom's welfare. I was desperate. I needed help. It was time for Jim to step up and help me out.

No response. Nothing.

"So what do you want to do?" I was relentless.

"I don't know. I thought I would just ride it out…"

RIDE IT OUT? RIDE IT OUT?!?

My brain searched its database for a definition that matched *ride-it-out* and it found: Your Dad has no inclination to do anything pro-active in making decisions on his or Mom's behalf. It means *let's wait and see* (or) *let Marsha figure out a solution and handle it all.*

Of course, Dad's phrase could have meant, when confronted by a storm the magnitude of that which was heading our way, make for open sea, wait for the storm to pass and live to fight another day. That interpretation never crossed my mind because I knew this storm would not pass. We needed to face the inevitable.

"Dad, I don't know what that means. What do you mean *ride it out?* I mean, that's nothing. That's not even helpful. I need more."

I couldn't prevent those harsh words from pouring out of my mouth. I had never talked to Jim in this way before. I guess he tapped into my dissatisfaction. He responded, "That's all I have. I don't know what else to do except ride this thing out."

I was livid. I felt Jim had let me down. I wanted to walk away from the quandary we were all in. If Jim's plan was to ride it out, I'd let him work that plan on his own, *without* me. That sentiment lasted three and a half minutes when a speck of compassion returned to me.

Looking back on this exchange, I'm able to have a vague

indication of what Dad was going through. It must have been devastating to him to recognize the predicament that he and Mom were facing. For Dad alone, his naturally athletic body was deteriorating and failing him on a daily basis. His eyes were failing him. He couldn't hear well. And his digestive system was a wreck. His wife and best friend, on whom he had always relied to make decisions and take action on their behalf slipped away at an accelerated pace. His independence and autonomy were being stripped. How frightening it must have been for him to no longer be able to conduct his own affairs. He was completely dependent on his daughter. What a nightmare. I couldn't see it, though. How damned sad is that?

I can see now, though. Dad couldn't bear to bring himself to think about where they were heading. He was losing his lover, his wife, his life. Jim had no practice with sharing his feelings that I'm aware of - not with me, not with any of his children. Why in the world did I think that he would acknowledge his feelings now? No doubt, he saw this entire thing as a private matter and none of my business. On one hand, I believe he was relieved to have me manage the details of his and Mom's life. On the other hand, he must have loathed having me interfere at all.

I would not let them down, despite the increased frequency of calls for assistance. One Sunday afternoon, Mom called Donna and me to see if we could come over and repair an electrical socket in the kitchen. I know Dad put her up to calling us. She was not able to make those sorts of decisions at this point but she was still able to dial our telephone number. That she could remember my telephone number at home and at work was itself a tiny miracle.

Although Sunday is traditionally a day of rest, some of us use it to catch up on chores when every other minute of the week is full. I had planned to mow my lawn, but we went over to see to the problem. Donna, the electricity whiz kid of the family, started troubleshooting the problem. Since the circuit breaker trip switches were not properly labeled, she had to turn each of them off in turn to figure out which one killed the power to that particular wall outlet in the kitchen. The outlet worked only intermittently, but with a lamp plugged into it, we were able to locate the right one. Unknown to us amateur electricians, as Donna flipped the power on and off at the breaker box, one of the breakers cut the power to Dad's television.

With macular degeneration, Dad couldn't read the newspaper any longer or thumb through an American Sportsman Journal, but he could certainly change channels on the television. Pitted against any other channel surfer on earth, my money's on Jim. He was so skillful that he could punch any button he desired on the remote control without looking. He had memorized every command which was handy since his sight was shot *and* he had worn all the printing off the device.

Donna continued her task, confident that poking around the electrical wires in the socket would not send a voltage of current through her body. She loosened the screws to remove the outlet box and replaced it. Mom and I stood in the middle of the kitchen floor ready to assist Donna at her command. Then we heard Dad stomping down the hall, heading toward the kitchen faster than he had moved in five years.

"TV's off," he reported briskly.

A fuse shorted out in my own personal electrical system. My face flushed red and in a blind rage I geared up to lay into Jim. Donna saw that I was going to blow. Horrified at the prospects of the explosion about to escape my lips, she said to me, "Go home."

Between clenched teeth I said, "What?"

She said, "Go home. Go home, now."

She had hopped down from the kitchen counter where she was perched making the repairs and grabbed my shoulders. She physically turned me toward the door. I resisted. She was stronger. "Get in the car and go home. I'll call you when I'm done and you can come back for me."

I did as I was told. On the way home random thoughts echoed in my head and I sputtered and spewed words that did not make sense but would look a whole lot like *%*^!$#@!! if written and roughly translates to:

I swear to heaven, I have never seen the likes of this before in my life. I give up my Sunday to go take care of some stupid problem in their house and put off my own work at my own house and go take care of their stuff and what thanks do I get? If I get a half-minute alone with that man... I'll... I mean, really!?! The TV is off?

I generally follow the Biblical commandment to 'honor your father and mother', but I could not do it at that moment. My tirade lasted until I entered the shed in my backyard. It continued as I pulled out the lawn mower, and mowed my yard. But, on the bright side, I mowed my lawn in half the normal time. When I drove over to pick up Donna, who was waiting in the driveway for me, I thanked her for getting me out of there. I cringe now when I think of the damage I would have done if I had been allowed to give in to my reactionary impulse.

Things calmed down a little after that ordeal. Christmas was a quiet affair contrasted with the merriment we enjoyed at Andy and Andrea's wedding. Robert brought Aunt Ruth with him for an afternoon visit with Mom and Dad. He gave me a navy blue wool blanket and Mom a red fleece blanket. I gave him a coffee table book of military history. We sat in the living room of Mom and Dad's house and caught up on the news with each other. I don't recall anything exceptional in connection to this, our last Christmas together as a family.

With a flip of the calendar, the New Year greeted us with an ice storm. The storm wiped out electrical service in Mom and Dad's neighborhood, but miraculously not mine. Since our power remained online, Andy brought Mom and Dad to my house so they would have warmth, food and water. Water for their house came from a well and the pump was electric. No electricity meant no water. No water meant no toilet flushing. No toilet flushing would be a problem. Even if we lost electrical service, we would continue to have city water service. We also had a fireplace for warmth and a Coleman stove for cooking if we needed it. Mom and Dad preferred to stay in their own home for better or worse, but my imagination already pictured them dead from frostbite, lying in each others' arms under Mom's little red fleece blanket. I was pretty sure friends and family, and possibly the entire law enforcement community would hold me responsible for negligence in their care. So they stayed with me. They were not pleased.

Dad was surly, Mom was nervous. But why? My house was warm. We had supper cooking. And more important than that, my television worked. What else could they ask for? It seems the issue for them was the extent of Dad's diarrhea problem, the full extent of which was unknown to me at the time. They preferred to handle this state of affairs in their own way without interference from a well-meaning daughter. Like an ostrich, I buried my head deep in the sand of denial and realized none of this.

After supper, we settled Dad down in front of *Touched by an Angel*. Mom wanted to wander. I had an idea, a crazy idea. I fetched my guitar and led her to the guest room to be entertained. I strummed and sang off-key as Mom leaned against the double bed, clapping her hands. "That's such beautiful music!" She praised me.

After being fed and entertained, Mom and Dad were ready for bed. Donna and I thought they were down for the count so we relaxed and flipped through the channels hoping to find something of interest. Before long, we heard Dad thumping into the bathroom for a few minutes, then come out, then go back in, then come back out. On the third rotation of going-in and coming-out, I got up to see if assistance was required. To my surprise, it was Mom in the bathroom at this point and she was washing out Dad's boxers in the sink. She looked as if she'd been caught out behind the gymnasium smoking cigarettes with the bad girls.

"It's okay," she preempted my question. "I'm just rinsing these out for your father."

I could see that they had been soiled and I know for certain that it had to have been an accident and therefore nothing to be ashamed of, but Mom gave me the impression that she was uncomfortable being discovered *in flagrante delicto*. I had a sense that Dad's gastric upheavals had become routine for them, and that Mom and Dad dealt with it in the privacy of their own home, and that it was *no*body else's business. I was an intruder. I felt nothing but empathy for Mom and Dad, but I also did not want my mother hand-washing Dad's dirty underwear. I wanted to cry.

"Mom, I can throw those into the washing machine."

She hesitated, but I prevailed. It broke my heart to realize that she felt like she needed to hide this delicate situation from me. After giving the situation some thought, I realized that predicament was not only embarrassing, but perhaps they thought that if their children cottoned on to these domestic difficulties, somebody might insist on bringing in unwanted help from strangers, or worse... send them to a nursing home.

Everyone finally settled down enough to get some sleep. I woke up early and went to the kitchen to start breakfast. Mom and Dad were already up, sitting in the living room, dressed, bags packed and perched at their feet.

"Where ya going there, Jim?" I was, frankly, surprised at their blatant attempt to effect an escape.

"Home. Andy's coming to pick us up," he said.

So they could still dial Andy's number too. I filed this information for later use.

"Is the electricity back on at your house, then?" I could have been a prosecutorial attorney.

"No, but we called our neighbor and he thought it'd be back on by lunch time. We'll be fine until then. It's what we want to do."

Crafty duo. When Dad wants to move mountains, he finds a way. It is not likely to be the same mountains I think need to be moved, but never mind. Jim got his way. I'm glad. It was one of the last times he was able to do so.

After only one night of cohabitation with my parents, I was a complete nervous wreck. My state of mind answered the question I had been mulling over, and that was the possibility of merging our households. That course of action was not a valid solution to Mom and Dad's domestic circumstances – a fact that was established in less than twenty-four hours. Sanity would not be maintained if we lived together. It made me sad but now my eyes were wide open to what Mom was doing for Dad and how much Dad was covering for Mom. But I now had even more concern for their safety. I had no idea what I could do for them. Fear, dread, anger, apprehension, alarm, panic – rolled up together it made me feel sick. I thought of them all day long and I lay awake at night desperate for divine inspiration. None came.

On a Friday night, shortly after the ice storm, I met friends for dinner and a movie. They were aware of my parents' health problems and asked how I was doing.

"You know, I can't even explain how I feel right now," I said. "I think I want to ignore the whole situation for the moment and just have fun."

After the movie, on my way home in the privacy of my own vehicle, neurons in my cerebral cortex exploded like particles accelerated in the Large Hadron Collider. A lightening flash of clear insight into where we were and where we were heading seized my consciousness. It terrified me. I pulled over and stopped. I had literally reached the limit of my mental capacity. I was aware of watching myself, as I had done years earlier when Robert had hid under my bed. Outside my body, looking down on a frightened little girl who had no idea what she was supposed to do, I screamed at God.

"What am I suppose to do?" I shrieked. I had kept much of my rage inside and like a pressure cooker the steam had built up. Now I was out of control. "Where the hell do we go from here?!? And where are YOU? I need help!" The violence of my screams damaged my vocal chords.

I begged and pleaded but I received no answer. I was abandoned, alone. Exhausted and spent, I had no hope. Insurmountable problems loomed before me. Mom and Dad didn't want any outside help, we couldn't consolidate our homes, and I didn't believe it was quite time to move them into a nursing home. It would have been devastating for them at this point, but living on their own was becoming unreasonable. A yawning chasm stretched endlessly below me. I needed answers. I needed solutions.

Eventually my body and my spirit reunited and I found my way home. I slipped into an exhausted sleep which is why I was in bed when the phone startled me awake at eight o'clock on Saturday morning. I was up and had the telephone to my ear before my eyes were opened.

"Hello," my voice raspy and hoarse.

"Honey, I need you to come over here. I can't get your father to talk to me."

"Okay, I'll be right there. Give us two minutes."

The reader may think that a husband refusing to speak to his wife is no cause for alarm but some intuitive sixth sense in me understood that the problem wasn't that Dad wouldn't speak to Mom, but that he *couldn't* speak to her. Somehow I knew that the probable cause of Dad's inability to speak was a stroke. I went into auto-pilot.

I pulled on some clothes. Donna saw the determined expression on my face and did the same. She drove us over to Mom and Dad's house. Mom met us at the back door.

"He's on the bed. I can't get him up. I was trying to get his clothes on him. He won't talk to me."

"It's okay, Mom. I'll see what I can do."

Donna stayed with Mom and comforted her. I went to the bedroom but I wasn't prepared for what I saw. Dad lay half-dressed on the bed, paralyzed, as if he had been sitting on the edge while pulling on his trousers, then fell backwards with his legs dangling toward the floor. His eyes stared up at the ceiling, not focusing on anything. His mouth gaped open. He looked confused, frightened. I had never seen a stroke in progress but I knew that I was witnessing one at this moment. His eyes lighted on me briefly and I felt he was slightly aware of his surroundings. I placed a pillow under his head.

"Dad, it's me, Marsha." I was in crisis mode, my tone was soothing. I didn't consciously force it to be. It just happened.

"Do you feel any pain?" Nothing.

"Don't worry, it's going to be alright," I lied to him. It's a mystery to me how we can become amazingly calm once confronted with the actual disaster we anticipate for so long. I stepped into the hallway and told Donna what I thought had happened. She called *911*. I asked her to try to get more information from Mom, to see if he had been feeling ill before now. I went back to sit with Dad. I held his hand and spoke quietly to him. I assured him the ambulance was on its way and we would get him to the hospital to fix him up. He didn't appear to hear me or understand me.

I didn't leave Dad's side until the EMTs arrived and came into the bedroom to take his vital signs. Donna had discovered from Mom that Dad had slipped out of his easy chair the day before and they'd called Dad's friend, Ben Clark, to come over and help him up. I called Ben Clark. He corroborated Mom's account and said that Dad was alert and appropriately interactive when he was there. I told him Dad was in the ambulance and we were heading over to the hospital now.

Before breakfast on the last Saturday of February, Dad's stroke changed everything. All of the difficult decisions for my parents were taken out of my hands and placed in the hands of destiny. If God had answered my desperate appeal for help from the night before, I did not recognize it as such at the time. But forces beyond my control began to guide and direct us from then on as we moved along an invisible current where I was but a mere character in the story.

CHAPTER EIGHT

*I looked over Jordan, and what did I see, comin' for to carry me home,
A band of Angels comin' after me, comin' for to carry me home*
- Wallis Willis

A stroke killed my dad's father. Since that event, Jim feared he'd meet the same end some day so the fact that a stroke indeed dealt Dad a powerful blow was not lost on any of us. The massive hemorrhaging that seized the right hemisphere of Dad's brain served as a defining moment not unlike the moment of realization that, at sixty-two-years old, Mom had Alzheimer's. Our lives were radically altered as Dad's stroke split our world view in two.

Before-and-After. Significant turning points in our lives can be quantified using the tape measure of before-and-after. We all have these events. Nations have these events. Pearl Harbor, Kennedy's assassination, 9/11. Individual examples are marriage, the birth of a child, graduation. Illnesses and accidents that occur suddenly bring with them a seismic shock that is marked with the distinction of then and now. The current plot twist to our family story had not appeared in any of my what-if scenarios so I had no contingency plan. The rip in the fabric of our domestic lives was a colossal departure from our now familiar routine. Not a hint of comfort from our former family life was to survive and the wave of painful events that engulfed my family didn't let up for three and a half years.

The EMTs who responded to our call for assistance were confident and efficient. With them in charge, and except for deciding our destination hospital, I was not needed. I found this strangely desirable as I moved along in a fog. On the ride across town with the ambulance driver, I asked him about Dad's status. He responded evasively. The absence of conversation gave me time to reflect on my screaming match with God less than ten hours before. I entertained the possibility that I was somehow at fault for this turn of events.

At the hospital, I signed forms allowing the emergency room staff to endeavor to save my father's life while absolving them from all responsibility for anything problematic that might ensue while in pursuit of that goal. Donna drove her own car, bringing Mom with her after seeing to Mom's immediate needs: bathroom break, sweater, purse. They arrived in the emergency room waiting area only a few minutes after I found a seat there. Donna's calm and practical approach helped as we summoned reinforcements and circled the wagons. I called Andy first since he was geographically the closest sibling. I reached Andrea. She said Andy was out of town but she would find him, get him home, and meet us at the hospital. I called Barbara in Virginia to notify her of this serious turn of events so she could make arrangements to come home. I also called Robert and Ruth to bring them into the loop.

Then, the waiting began. It's odd that progress in emergency rooms is so deliberate and slow because the ER is precisely where I assume actions should transpire with haste. Instead, everyone moved at a snail's pace on Dad's behalf. I wanted to crack the whip, Rusty-style, to get the staff motivated. In her prime, my mother would have gotten results, by God, and then been thanked for her efforts afterwards. Things had changed. Rusty was no longer in charge of the world. Therefore, we waited.

We waited for the doctor. We waited for the MRI people. We waited for the results from the MRI people. We waited for the doctor's interpretation of the MRI results. We waited for a room to be assigned.

Andy and Andrea arrived first. Andrea brought with her a carry-all emergency kit full of magazines, tissues and snacks. Clearly, she had experience waiting in hospitals and she showed us how it was done. We milled around and found ways to kill some time. We distanced ourselves from the pain of reality with humor. Mom strayed from that usual pattern. She declined to participate in our banter and witty repartee. We stopped too, the moment the doctor summoned us to a small private family room located within the larger ER department. It's never a good sign when the doctor segregates a family from the general waiting room population. Fear shot through me, and not for the first time that day.

Providing a private room inside the very public environs of an emergency room setting, even if temporary, is truly a humane and kind policy that allows loved ones a quiet place to process bad news without feeling like they are on a stage, and we were grateful. After we seated ourselves comfortably among the love seats and arm chairs, the doctor told us that Dad had suffered a severe and massive stroke. He called it a 'significant cerebral event'. He swept the palm of his hand over the entire right side of his head as he said this. Then he announced that Dad was not likely to survive the week-end.

Not survive the week-end? What do you do with a prognosis such as that? Dad was seventy-nine years old. I don't consider that old in today's culture. I had just turned forty-six, and was not ready to live in a world without Jim. I couldn't conceive of such a silly idea. More importantly, if Dad died, how would it affect Mom?

A private room for Dad became available by early afternoon, and like pioneers moving west to stake our claim, we gathered our paltry possessions and followed Dad to the next encampment. No Conestoga wagon for us though, only a medical gurney to lead the way to unfamiliar territory. Dad's room became our home base and we were its latest squatters in an unending succession of families laying claim to it. This was the place we would gather to prepare for Dad's death.

Robert and Ruth arrived shortly after the room assignment. Ruth entered, repeating, "My brother, my brother." Robert was quiet. Dad's room barely had enough space for his bed, the IV tree and a side-chair so we sat on the floor, lined up against one wall like the See-No-Evil monkeys. Ruth nudged Mom out of the way as she approached the bed. I bristled. Dad was silent, unable to communicate. The left side of his face was slack and drooped a little from the nerve damage of the stroke. We looked on, assessing the change in his features, hovering and hoping to be able to do something to help him. Even on his death bed, we did not leave Dad to the tranquility of his own inner world. Donna took Mom out for a wander through the labyrinth of hospital hallways to keep her occupied. It was best to allow Ruth some time with her brother without competition.

In shock like the rest of us, Robert seemed numb. We

probably all looked bewildered. It's a recognizable expression for many visitors under similar circumstances at hospitals and nursing homes. When Barbara and Peggy arrived in the early evening after a six-hour drive from Virginia, they assumed care for Mom. It helped me greatly since I was called on, as Mom and Dad's representative, to discuss Dad's care plan with the medical staff and sign yet more papers. Mom wandered up and down the corridors nervously, in perpetual motion. She paced the paltry square-footage of Dad's tiny room when she wasn't straightening items lying near the sink. She did what she knew to do to feel as if she was doing 'something'. Interspersed with housecleaning, Mom patted Dad's leg or stroked his face. They exchanged loving gazes and loving touches. In their world, there was only the two of them and nothing else mattered. Mom's tender actions of love carried more healing than conventional medicine. Yet, there she was – a lost soul, in unfamiliar surroundings, whose husband wouldn't talk to her.

After a day spent surviving the shock of Dad's stroke and reacting like automatons to this unimagined turn of events, we all went home to get some rest. Except Andy. He would not leave Dad. He remained by his bedside the entire night. When we returned to the hospital on the following morning, Andy said he witnessed Dad doing some interesting things during the night.

"It was like he was acting out scenes from his life or something," he explained. "He made gestures that looked like that game Charades…"

Since the doctor had proclaimed Dad's death to be imminent, and since we had no reason to doubt his expertise in such matters, we settled in. Mom hovered over Dad's recumbent body between intervals of more housecleaning. At times, she seemed to think she was at home, tending to Dad there. It was obvious that the pressure was getting to her. Understandably. She rarely interacted with my sister, brother and me. She was focused on only one soul. Her husband.

We kept the room dark and quiet. We were reverent, for a change. Or maybe we were frightened and that was the best and only course of action we were able to come up with. By mid-morning, each of us independently, began to notice what Andy had explained to us about Dad's exceptional behavior. Although Dad was not coherent and ignored our presence at times, he seemed to be relating to someone or something we ourselves couldn't see. If we got in his face to attract his attention, he brushed us aside rather rudely, or responded only reluctantly. Taking him away from whatever he was doing annoyed him.

We found a recliner and dragged it into Dad's room which left us even less space to move around in. Occasionally, we took breaks and walked to the end of the hall where a small seating area gave us a change of scenery. To fight the intensity of Dad's death vigil and to alleviate the claustrophobic feelings the small room imposed on us, this little waiting room became our oasis. It was easier to talk more openly there. We discussed what we'd seen, and we knew that whatever it was, it was profound.

"I *cannot* be the only one who is witnessing this," Barbara told me. "Can you believe it? I think he's communicating with somebody on the other side…"

"I know. I wish Robert was here with us. It'd be good for him." Robert had told us during his goodbyes the day before that he would not come to Charlotte without Ruth and since she had church commitments on Sunday they wouldn't drive into town two days in a row. We were disappointed. He should have been there with us. Barbara agreed. "I hate he's missing out on this. It feels special. Maybe we're witnessing an interface with God."

"Yeah, like a portal," I added.

"What do you think his gestures mean?"

"I don't know, but he's not all that interested in us anymore, is he?"

"Doesn't matter. We have to tell him good-bye. We have to give him permission to go - I've always heard that's important."

"Okay, you go first." I was willing to take my sister's lead.

"I'll go first, but you have to go next."

"I will," I assured her. "I don't want to be the one who holds him up. I'll never hear the end of it. But, what will we do with Mom when Dad's gone?"

"Just stay in the moment, here."

We got back to the room. Dad moved his legs non-stop, like he was walking somewhere, somewhere pretty far away. And yet, according to the doctor, Dad was mostly paralyzed as a result of the stroke. Not only had Dad moved his legs consistently, but since the nurse had taken the deep vein thrombosis pneumatic compression leg cuffs (DVT cuffs) off, he had picked up the pace. It went on for hours. As he 'walked', he searched for bits and pieces of what? Treasure? Within the folds of the bedcovers, invisible to us, he plucked the precious things dexterously into his hands and then held them above his head as if he were offering them to somebody. He also pulled imaginary objects out of the pocket of his pajama shirt and made the same gesture. We didn't know if it was food he was offering, or money. Was it a gift or a payment of some sort? Maybe he was giving coins to Charon, the ferry boatman, so he could cross the River Stix. I was covering that very topic in my classroom lectures.

Whatever Dad was doing, it was clear to us that he was giving a valued thing to someone only he saw. At one point, Mom leaned over him to smooth the blanket and talk to him, and he literally pushed her aside because she was in his field of vision, between him and whatever was holding his attention. His facial expression was calm, serene and full of peace. Wonderment reflected on his face making him look young and ageless, and masking the facial paralysis at times. There were four distinct areas that held his interest. Three of them were in front of him, roughly to the left of his feet, at his feet and to the right. The fourth point of focus was behind him, over his right shoulder. He craned his head to the right as far as possible, looking past the IV tree. He frowned when he looked in that direction. He appeared worried about whatever was going on there. He tracked these four definite areas of interest throughout the course of the day. The same four, without variation. We each knew that what we were witnessing was important; we certainly didn't know what. When we asked the doctor to explain it, he said that it was common behavior for stroke victims to have hallucinations. We surveyed the nurses and although they were reluctant to share their points of view with us, they indicated rather nonchalantly, but respectfully, that they'd seen this phenomenon many times before. Apparently, Dad's behavior resembled an experience common among people drawing near to death. This explanation felt more accurate to us.

For someone who had just suffered a major stroke which would allegedly render him paralyzed for the rest of his short life, Dad was *active*. We didn't question the doctor's diagnosis. It didn't occur to us to question him or his vast knowledge and experience. But it was incredible that Dad, who had suffered a significant cerebral event, was able to move that much. Of course his muscles were too weak to hold him upright if he had attempted to walk and of course the aphasia affected his ability to speak clearly. But frankly, we hadn't seen Dad this active in a while.

Mom continued to make busy work which helped her maintain some influence on the situation at hand. Renegade drops of water that lingered on the sink couldn't escape annihilation from the absorbing qualities of the ever-present paper towel Rusty wielded with authority. Each time Mom took a moment for herself, to use the pocket-sized bathroom inside Dad's room, she mistakenly pulled the string attached to the emergency call button thinking it was the toilet flusher. She was barely out of the bathroom door, returning her attention to Dad, when a nurse showed up to see what we wanted. The nurse acted as if it was an emergency. At first we thought she was applaudingly attentive. Then she became increasingly exasperated with us. So, behind her back, we accused her of being a tad anxious and high-strung. When we figured out that she was being summoned by the emergency cord in the bathroom, we realized who the guilty party was and we laughed like hyenas.

As Sunday evening approached, Donna and I volunteered to stay with Dad so the others could go home and get some rest. We settled in. During the day, Dad seemed to recognize us and interact with us a little more. I'm not sure the recognition was from face-recognition because his responses seemed to be on a deeper level, on a heart connection level. I would witness the same thing from Mom when she was no longer able to relate to us in the physical world. Into the night, Dad continued his activities and I looked at Donna and asked, "What do you think he's doing?" In a brilliant stroke of pure genius Donna said, "Ask him." *Duh.*

I bent over Dad and put my mouth near his right ear and said, "Daddy, who's here?"

"People," he said.

Jim was always thrifty with his words. I would have to probe for more information.

"How many people?" I asked him.

"Lots of people."

"Who are they?" I investigated further.

He pointed directly in front of him, roughly over his legs, and said, "That's Mom and Dad." Then he gestured slightly to the left and said, "I don't know them."

Donna and I believed he was favorably disposed to those three groups and I imagined them being the band of Angels making their way across the Jordan River *'comin' for to carry my daddy home'* and I was pleased to know that they existed. Donna and I bobbed our heads up and down in their direction indicating that it was fine by us if they were present. I had grave concerns regarding whoever was stationed behind Dad, over his right shoulder. Dad's face always changed to a frown when he looked in that direction.

"Who are they, Daddy?" I indicated surreptitiously with my thumb, hoping they wouldn't see me pointing rudely at them. I doubted they would thank me for demanding an accounting of their presence and purpose.

"I don't know." He frowned again.

"Do you like them, Daddy? Do you trust them?" I asked.

"No."

"What do they want from you?" I pushed.

"They want me to go with them."

"Do you want to go with them?"

"No. Not with them."

"Good, then wait for a better crowd to go with. You don't have to go with them if you don't want to." I wasn't sure if I was allowed to defy emissaries of the spirit world but if Dad wished to shun these visitors then I would move heaven and earth and confront inhabitants in both realms, to grant him that wish.

"Do you want to go with Grandma and Grandpa now?" I asked hesitantly and without sincerity.

"No, not yet."

"Okay, good. Can you tell me why?"

"I've still got things to do here."

"We'll be glad to have you as long as you can stay, Daddy."

Wasn't I magnanimous? I felt relieved knowing that Jim had some fight in him yet.

Donna and I kept looking at each other in awe, our eyes as big as saucers. We couldn't believe that he described what he was seeing. He continued to extend his arm and reach his hand out. Donna whispered for me to ask him what he was doing.

"Daddy, what're you doing there? Can you touch them?"

He smiled when he said, "Yes."

In a blinding flash of brilliance of my own, I asked, "Can they touch you back?"

With a tone of exasperation in his voice, as if the answer should be as obvious as the air we breathe, he said, "No." He looked disappointed.

When he reached out to touch them, he looked like the kid who just won a big red lollipop. There was no better prize and his face lit up radiantly. I thought then, and I think now, "Wow. I can't wait to do that."

He eventually fell asleep. Donna and I hoped Dad's decision to stay would bear out. And it did.

Dad's doctor was impressed with ol' Jim's resolve to hold onto life. Physical therapy and speech therapy were ordered for him. Dad began to eat some food and take a little interest in his family here, in the flesh. Since it appeared that Dad was going to survive the stroke and stick around a while, I had to get busy and make preparations for more long-term care. The hospital had no obligation to keep him there for convalescence or rehabilitation, so residential arrangements for Dad had to be made quickly. Preparations for Mom to follow him promptly had to be included as well. Regretfully, we couldn't afford constant medical attention for the two of them at home. The only way care could be acquired for them both was to qualify them for Medicaid and have Medicaid supplement their small income to pay for long-term care in a nursing home facility.

Stress from Dad's stroke and the fear she must have felt for his welfare, hit Mom hard. Barbara had been staying at Mom and Dad's house while she was in town. Like school girls having a sleepover, Mom slept on the sofa in the living room, and Barbara slept curled up on the adjacent love seat. Fun, when you're twelve. Not so much when you're an adult. But it's where Mom felt safest, and Barbara stayed by her side. Mom would awaken during the night and wander in and out of the other rooms in the house looking for Dad.

"I can't find your father," she informed Barbara as she woke her from a sound sleep. Mom was frantic. Barbara calmed her down and explained that Dad was in the hospital and they would go visit him in the morning. She explained that, first they would sleep, then have some breakfast, then drive over to the hospital to see Dad. Mom said she was grateful that the arrangements had been made then she patted Barbara on the hand and thanked her with lavish praise. Barbara then silently cried herself back to sleep.

Mom became increasingly confused and disoriented. Barbara observed firsthand the extent to which Mom needed care from the time she woke up in the morning until she went to bed and completely agreed that Mom was a candidate for twenty-four-hour care. We found no reason to hope that the ground Mom lost in her coping capabilities would or could ever be regained. Whatever we decided to do ultimately, I wanted to begin laying the foundation immediately. The social worker assigned to us at the hospital helped me tremendously in this respect by giving me guidance and information and advice on next-step-possibilities to be taken for Dad, and for Mom as well.

Dad would never go home again, and in his incapacitated condition, we got the paperwork and recommendations we needed to qualify him for long-term nursing care. Medicare covered post-hospital expenses at a nursing home for a certain number of days which gave us a little time to play with as we made arrangements for him. Our social worker instructed us to get a physician's order or FL-2 form filled out on Mom's behalf to make her eligible for admittance to a skilled nursing home facility. This form verified that Mom, along with Dad, required the high level of medical attention offered by such a facility. Assisted Living arrangements would not suffice. After getting the documentation we needed, we would be able to move Mom into the same nursing home with Dad. They wouldn't be in their own home, but they'd be together. It was the only way we knew to play the next step.

In one of my conferences with the social worker, she suggested that I call the neurologist who had examined Mom when Andy and I had taken her for the Alzheimer's assessment. She was confident he could fill out the required forms on Mom's behalf. I telephoned the doctor's office and when he returned my call his response took my breath away.

"This is Doctor Smith *[not his real name]*. What do you need?" He got to the point abruptly but I appreciated that we would not have to waste valuable time on idle chitchat.

"Yes, doctor. You examined my mother about a year ago. We've had some changes in our family since then. My dad has had a stroke and my mother's condition has worsened because of it…"

"Why in the world are you calling me? I can't fix your family problems." *Huh?*

"Your family's problems are your responsibility, not mine. I don't see why you're calling me."

"I don't need you to fix my family problems," I told him. "What I need is for you to complete the forms that will allow my mother to be moved into a nursing home. She can't be at home alone to look after herself."

"I can't do that from your word alone."

"Of course you can't, but it's not *just* my word alone. She has been a patient of yours. You examined her. Surely you have a file on her and your own notes concerning your assessment of her condition. You should be able to recommend this level of care for her."

"I'm not comfortable with your request. I'll have to examine her again."

At that point, sticking a flaming hot poker in my eyes was preferable to seeing this disagreeable person ever again. I answered with a brisk, "Thank you for calling me back, but no, we won't be making an appointment. We'll make other arrangements."

I called Mom and Dad's GP, which I suppose I should have done to begin with, and explained the recent turn of events.

"I'm sorry about your dad," he told me. "And, I love your mother. I'll have the forms to you tomorrow. A nursing home will be the safest place for your mother and it's good that she and your dad will be together."

Before I hung up the phone he added, "Marsha, this is the right thing to do." *Now, was that so blasted difficult?*

Dad was in the hospital for a week. Long enough to get the hospital smells inside your nostrils without being able to get them back out again. Dad improved slightly and the physical and speech therapists worked with him until the hospital determined nothing more could be done for him and he was to be discharged. I had never seen Dad so motivated. I had never seen him work as hard at anything as he did in speech therapy and physical therapy. He was just plain showing off.

On the day of Dad's departure from the hospital, we were not told by any of the hospital staff exactly when his discharge would take place. It was a closely guarded secret. We had been warned that the decision, when made, meant a quick and sudden exit. The social worker got busy rounding up possible vacancies at suitable facilities for us to consider and we decided on one that was near their home. When the hospital administrators deemed it time for Dad to depart, we were expected to vacate his room in five minutes. Five minutes. From the time I was told of Dad's discharge, and that transportation had been ordered for him, we literally had five minutes to pack his bags and scoot. I was unaccustomed to speedy actions within these walls. It was a surprise.

Attendants came to transfer Dad from the hospital bed to the stretcher that would take him to the non-emergency medical transport service vehicle. They asked us to leave the room while they completed the strategically delicate move. The room was too small for all of us, and if moving Dad from the bed to the stretcher made Dad uncomfortable or if it caused him pain in any way, I'm sure they did not want us to witness it. And in truth, I did not want to see ol' Jim in distress. I grabbed his hand before I left and assured him that we would see each other at the next port of call. Mom and I linked arms and headed down to the parking deck together. I wanted to get a head start to the nursing home where we could greet Dad when he arrived on that end. I explained the plan to Mom as we exited Dad's room but by the time we reached the ground floor and preceded to the parking deck, Mom had totally forgotten the plan. Well, that's not correct. Something forgotten is something that is remembered when reminded. To Mom, information related to this plan had never been communicated to her at all. As we walked to the car, carrying Dad's belongings in two small plastic bags between us, Mom stopped briefly and looked through her bag. She recognized Dad's personal effects.

"These are your dad's things," she said. A pained look surfaced in her eyes as tears welled up. She looked at me. "Did he die?"

"Oh, no, Momma. No." I grabbed her and hugged her. "He didn't die. We're only moving him to another place. He's actually better so he doesn't have to be in the hospital any longer. We'll drive over to his new room and see him there."

"Oh," she said. "I didn't know…"

CHAPTER NINE

Miracles all around me

I drove unhurriedly from the hospital to the nursing home that would be the first stop for Dad's long-term, acute care. Mom sat quietly beside me and in that silence peace washed over me. I was driftwood gliding on ocean waves; not the violent ones that previously dashed me against rocks, but gentle ones, carrying me towards shore on an in-coming tide. Until Dad's stroke, I was terrified of the outcome of his and Mom's fate. I wanted to control the circumstances of their daily lives so there would be a storybook ending which made me miserable because I knew that in reality there is no such thing as happily-ever-after. I was not in control, nor had I ever been. I influenced minor decisions, yes, but I wielded very little power in the ultimate fate of my parents' lives.

Accepting this reality and consciously giving up the pointless craving for control helped me ride the waves of fate more gracefully. I was still apprehensive, certainly, and I questioned whether or not I possessed the strength to provide for Mom and Dad's health, welfare and happiness. In fact, it didn't look promising at all where their happiness was concerned. And contrary to Frances' advice to me an eon ago, I continued to try to save my parents from the grabby clutches of death and disease. Nevertheless, deep in my soul, I felt protected and encouraged as I had not felt before. My desperate, irreverent plea to God opened a door. I needed help. God sent help. I believed I had support from that point forward, held in the caring hands of something much larger than myself. Solutions for Mom and Dad's care were presenting themselves to me, now. From the moment the ambulance arrived at Mom and Dad's house until the day of their deaths, many of the major decisions for their care were guided by the hands of professionals. I had only to pick and choose from an array of options as from a buffet.

I wished the challenges that Mom and Dad faced could be anything other than this devastating string of heartaches. And even though I felt great sadness for them I experienced calm and a sort of reassurance that helped me comprehend, probably for the first time in my life, that wishing for things to be different was futile. I could only play the cards dealt to me. I would play this hand and do my best. I've heard it said that challenging times test our mettle, help us grow, and make us stronger. This is not always the case, I know. But I also know that we can choose to collapse in the face of our upsets, or we can discover a nugget of gold in the greatest tragedy. The choice is ours.

The silver-lining sentiment is not an instinctive part of my personality. And yet when I entertained the possibility that difficulties hold within them the seeds of reciprocal rewards, these rewards, or unexpected gifts, found their way to me and assisted me in executing the tough decisions that benefited Mom and Dad. I welcomed this change in outlook as a miracle. I found it nearly impossible to find a trace of joy in the next three years, but it became my desire to seek it in the darkness that followed.

At the nursing home where Mom and I waited for Dad's arrival from the hospital, I signed admittance forms and listened to the instructions presented by the administrator. Dad would be here temporarily while Andy and I searched for a permanent facility that better met our requirements. We wanted a combination of highly skilled nursing care, a special Alzheimer's unit, and an environment that embraced Mom and Dad as husband and wife rather than two separate individuals.

While Dad settled in, Donna contacted the American Red Cross Armed Forces Emergency Services to locate Tony who, as a Seabee, was on assignment with his Navy unit. Through Red Cross channels Donna got word to Tony about Dad's delicate condition and the Red Cross facilitated his homecoming to visit his grandfather. It was wonderful to see Tony; we had not seen him since he left Charlotte for basic training three years earlier. Tall and muscular from active service, Tony carried himself with a competent military bearing. Dad rallied when Tony appeared at his bedside. Pride in this mature and handsome grandson was a shot of Vitamin B12 and infused Dad with renewed vigor. Tony's visit was good for Mom too. The extra lift helped her with the adjustments rushing at her. Changes and unfamiliar environments are difficult for individuals with Alzheimer's to process. But in good old Rusty fashion, Mom did her damndest to fake mental health for Tony, and for the rest of us, too. His visit was brief. Too quickly a week had passed and Tony had to return to base. As we said our goodbyes, there was no foreshadowing that we would see him again very soon.

Our search for a nursing home suitable for Mom and Dad moved forward. While we waited for the details to be worked out, Barbara went back to her home in Virginia to tend to affairs there. In her absence, Mom stayed with Donna and me. I wanted to have Mom with me night and day. I wanted to protect her and provide for her every need. Tucking her into bed gave me that illusion. That feeling of satisfaction never lasted long, though. After we tucked Mom in for the night, and after we had gone to bed ourselves, Mom exhibited the typical Alzheimer's sundown syndrome behavior of waking and wandering. Luckily she did not leave the house, probably because she found new and uncharted territories to explore. In the wee hours, Mom sorted through the deep recesses of the closets. At three o'clock in the morning, after one such scavenger hunt, Mom threw open the bedroom door, flipped on the lights, and exclaimed with enthusiasm, "Look what I found!" *It was a blanket.* "I bet you were wondering where this was!" She said.

"Why yes, Mom. Yes, I was wondering just that." My response was glib. I was unable to muster enthusiasm and glee to match Mom's own. I praised her, though, as I would a two-year-old. I wanted to send her back to bed with a warning not to get up again because I needed sleep so I could work. But I couldn't bring myself to reprimand her. So Mom, like a spoiled child, was allowed to have the run of the place while she stayed with us.

On the Saturday following Dad's stroke, Robert and Ruth came to the nursing home to visit Dad. I asked Robert to find a way to visit Dad on his own, to be with us as we tackled this significant and pressing family emergency. I hoped for this to be a healing time for us since he and I had not had truly warm sibling exchanges since he was sent to prison for his driving while impaired offence. I know now that I did not understand the disease that is alcoholism because I just wanted my brother to stop drinking and hurting himself. I did not comprehend why he couldn't do that.

"Try to find a way to come visit alone, just once a week," I told him.

"I can't," he replied simply.

"Why not?"

"I don't have a car," he explained. "I only have Ruth's and she won't allow me to drive it without her. If I tell her where I'm going, she'll expect to come too."

I suggested that he sneak out under some other pretense. We had done that sort of thing when we were kids – right under Rusty's nose.

"I *can't*," he insisted. "There are other things going on that you wouldn't understand."

"Try me," I begged. "I might understand if I know what the problem is."

"No. You won't understand."

"Don't you think you owe it to yourself to come and visit Dad, and to be with us? We're having important spiritual experiences here. We want you with us. Just you. Just us. Is that so hard? Do this one thing for yourself!"

He was resolute. I was angry. We had words. Indeed, I knew nothing about Robert's world. I had no choice but to accept his decision.

After a few more days at this nursing home, Andy and I found a long-term skilled care facility for Dad. We talked to the administrator there about accepting Mom too. She understood the situation as we presented it to her and assured us that Willow Lake could provide for Mom and Dad's current and long-term needs. She told us Dad would be in a separate room from Mom at first because the rooms were dedicated to residents by method of payment and Dad's first thirty days were paid by Medicare.

"When they are both switched over to private pay we'll make arrangements for them to share a room," she told us.

I imagined their room to be warm and cozy, a delight to visit. In my mind, the room was filled with knick-knacks and mementos from home. I went from reality to fantasy in 3.2 seconds. Returning to reality bites.

I'm sure only a few individuals actually want to move a parent out of his or her own home and into a less comfortable environment – let alone two parents. But I had researched possible resolutions for Mom and Dad's situation and there was no alternative for us. Emotionally, I agonized over the necessity of transferring them to a nursing home environment. This decision, although I was convinced it was the right one, was distressing. Here was the very thing that I never wanted to do to my parents. I had postponed this moment as long as humanly possible. When I took my heart out of the equation, I recognized that in practical ways, a nursing home was the safest place for them. They would have 24-hour supervision and nutritious food available throughout the day. But I found it impossible to extract my emotional feelings from the decision concerning these beloved parents of ours.

We moved Dad to Willow Lake first. Barbara was back in town and rode the short distance over to the new place with him in the medical transport van. Having her by his side gave him comfort and we looked for every opportunity to reduce the distress of uprooting Mom and Dad from their familiar life while it disappeared in the rear view mirror. The plan was to get him established in the new environment and then work out a gentle way to move Mom in soon afterwards. Until then, Mom was able to stay with Dad during the day while I attempted to get some work done at the university and prepare lectures for my evening history course. I was mostly on auto-pilot while I was on campus since my attention and energy were focused on Mom and Dad. At the nursing home, Rusty hovered and fussed over Jim. Her contributions to Dad's care made a difference. That she could be there with him for much of the day was priceless. They could be together – the two of them – without interference from offspring directing their every move, and Mom was free to horde food and drinks for Dad. She and I share the hunting and gathering gene. Whereas I was the one who shopped and brought food to them while they were at home, now Mom had access to food herself and provided once again for Jim. Perhaps she didn't trust that the dining room staff would provide meals to Room 221. So she did it. It's possible that Mom was only acting at a gut level but it's nice to know that our gut continues to work in survival mode even when Alzheimer's steals our power to reason.

In the course of tending to Dad's dietary needs, Mom often sneaked sodas to him. Sodas were contraband. And Dad knew it.

He understood that he was restricted to thickened liquids only. Liquids were to have a thickening powder added to them because viscous fluids tend to make someone with swallowing issues choke which can cause them to aspirate liquid into the lungs. This is a common problem for stroke victims that can lead to pneumonia. Throughout Dad's infirmary, his intelligence never diminished; his keenly observing eyes didn't miss a trick. His difficulty in communicating was only because he slurred his words. He stayed sharp and had a clear comprehension of the events surrounding him and Mom. Therefore, I am confident that Dad asked Mom for the sodas because he knew there was no other way to get them, and he knew Rusty would not fail him.

The nurses asked me to keep Mom away from Dad as he moved through the rehabilitation phase of his stay. "Absolutely not!" I told them. "Let them have this time together without so many rules." If Mom and Dad had the illusion of choice in their lives, even at this microscopic level, maybe they wouldn't mind that I was yanking their home right out from under their very noses. I did not want my dad to get pneumonia, but I truly believed that the damage of managing each facet of their lives as they were being forced to give up every other bit of their freedom was not worth the damage to their pride.

Various solutions presented themselves so we could move Mom into the nursing home as a resident, too. Much more preparation was required for this to happen than for Dad. Their financial circumstances did not permit them both to live at Willow Lake indefinitely and provisions had to be made to accommodate them financially. Mom and Dad were children of the depression. Their needs were simple and few and they were frugal. They paid their bills in full, and on time. Their retirement nest egg covered the essentials as long as they lived in their home that was paid for. But their savings and investments were not enough to provide them a monthly outlay of cash necessary to cover the exorbitant nursing home expenses for the two of them indefinitely. I consulted a Social Services counselor who advised us to rent Mom and Dad's house to create income that would supplement Medicaid coverage of their living expenses when their finances dwindled to poverty levels. I literally impoverished Jim and Rusty so they would have a place to live. I never told them this bit of information. Mom and Dad had worked their entire lives and always paid their own way. They were independent and self-sufficient, and they would not want to know that they would soon be dependent on state assistance. Allowing my parents to remain in their home with the help of home health care was not an option available to us at the time of their need. I believe it would have been less traumatizing for us if they could have remained at home. We took the only choice available to us and began the process of getting the house ready to lease.

First, we cleared out Mom and Dad's belongings including every stick of furniture, every thread of clothing, all dishes and kitchenware. This was no nostalgic stroll down memory lane. It was a rushed job of doing something with everything Jim and Rusty had accumulated throughout their life together. Pieces of their lives and pieces of our childhood had to be purged. Mom's entire collection of garden tools and sewing things were dispersed along with generations of photos, and everything in between. Everything. Every. Thing. We sorted through a lifetime of possessions and memories and culled and reduced to only what fit into a two-foot by four-foot closet and a bedside table.

As daunting as this task was, we recognized that in some ways we were pretty fortunate. After the close call at the hospital when we thought Dad would not make it through the first week-end because of the stroke, we became sensitive to how suddenly a loved one can be taken from us by death. We were grateful that Mom and Dad were here, with us. We could hug them and kiss them. We could gaze at the faces of the two loving souls who gave us life. The difficulty that I foresaw, and the problem I did not want to face, was how in the name of all that is good, do I explain to my mother that I was going to move her out of her cherished home and into half a room in a nursing home?

The move-in-day deadline drew nearer. I lay awake at night trying to work out how to approach the subject. How do I tell Mom the plans we made for her without her knowledge? How do I tell her she will no longer have access to the life she loves? I was going to rip the familiar environment out from under her. Her house. Her beloved garden. Friends nearby. Access to food of her choice. Her own dishes. Television programs she selects. Her own bed. Her own bed time. Sweet and delicious peace and quiet.

Postponing the moment of confrontation on the issue of

moving Mom to the nursing home became more torturous than just doing it. So one day, when Mom and I were running errands, I pulled into the parking lot of a department store. I switched off the ignition but made no move to get out. We sat together in the cab of my small truck for a few moments as I gathered my courage. The time was right. I struck.

"Mom," I began. "You know Dad is going to have to live at the nursing home from now on. He's very sick and he won't be able to come home again, ever."

"I know," she said as sadness settled into beautiful olive green eyes.

I counseled myself to not cry; I didn't want to upset Mom. *Don't cry*, I repeated silently. *Don't you dare cry!* I swallowed the stupid lump in my throat a hundred times before I continued.

Out loud I said, "Mom, I need to know something. Do you want to go live with Dad at the nursing home or do you want to stay in the house?"

"I want to be with your father."

"If you decide to live where Dad is, I'm going to have to rent out your house in order to get money to pay for the nursing home. If I do that, you can't go back there to live anymore. Mom, do you understand what I'm saying?"

She took my hand, looked me the eyes, and said, "I don't care about that house. It's just a house. I'd rather be with your father." She was clear and she was lucid. The tone in Mom's voice held the strong conviction of her decision that I dared not hope for, yet it was exactly what I needed to hear her say. It was a miracle and I knew it.

"OK, then. I'll make it happen."

"I know you will."

And I did.

Seventeen days after Dad's stroke, Donna and I took Mom and a few of her things to Willow Lake and left her there. I just left her. All alone. In alien surroundings. I may as well have dropped her on the moon. And yet this place had one thing of importance to Rusty Burris, and that was Jim Burris.

Mom stood by Dad's bedside as Donna and I initiated our exit. The staff, having been through this situation countless times before, assured me it was best to leave Mom in Dad's room when we told her goodbye. They promised to see that she was tucked safe and sound into bed. They had provided this service for sons and daughters since their doors were open for business. I was merely one more in the endless line of broken-hearted offspring.

Before leaving I told Mom, "You'll sleep here tonight, okay?" I used a fake cheery tone. I hugged her to add a pinch of sincerity. She didn't seem to understand the concept. "Stay with Dad now and I'll see you tomorrow. I'll come over to visit you and Dad right after work, in time for dinner, okay?"

"No, I can go on with you now," she said, innocently. She believed I would never abandon her. She had done her best for Dad and was ready to go home with me to relax.

"Not now," I told her. "Stay here tonight. You'll have more time with Dad if you spend the night here. Dad needs you."

Mom couldn't reason out why I would do this. She knew there was no other way for her to get back home where her surroundings were familiar if I didn't take her. We turned and walked away from her. My heart broke into pieces. My body seized with the wrenching sadness of how vulnerable Rusty had become. How could I leave her with strangers? As we walked to the car on that Tuesday afternoon, Donna was by my side. She supported me in every sense of the word throughout the years of caring for Mom and Dad, and at this moment she physically held me up to prevent me from crumpling to the sidewalk. In the car, she buckled my seat belt for me and I dropped my head into my hands, sobbing the whole way home.

I know Mom understood what I asked her in the parking lot, but days had passed since then and her capacity to grasp this new development did not quite register. She didn't comprehend that she would not be going home again, and in fact did not have a home to go to. She didn't grasp how the current upheaval in her life affected her future. I personally had no difficulty comprehending the turn of affairs. I clearly understood that she would never work in the soil of her garden again. She would not enjoy the bluebirds that nested outside her kitchen window. I knew she would not sit in the cool shade of her big front porch. I knew that we would never have another family gathering in her dining room for Christmas or Thanksgiving or to celebrate our birthdays. And I knew I'd never go grocery shopping for them again and have them meet me at the back door like kids, waiting to see what I'd brought them.

On that chilly March evening, as I left Mom behind at the nursing home, all of the traditions that made up our family history vanished. Once upon a time, we were children at home, eating Mom's made-from-scratch biscuits and blackberry cobblers, complaining about weeding a stupid bed of iris. Rusty had been strong and competent. Jim had been athletic and capable. Now, here we were leaving these two beautiful, frail people in a nursing home. Where did the time go? How did we get here so quickly? This was the hardest thing I was ever called to do. I could think of nothing worse.

Jim and Rusty were not abandoned. We did not warehouse them in a nursing home to relieve us of the burden of their care. I felt like wearing a sign board to this effect. Instead of a sign, I visited frequently and regularly. The message: *Do you see me? I am here. I am a caring daughter so don't try any funny business with* MY *parents!*

Getting Mom settled into a routine came with ups and downs, and visits were a test of our grit. I lived in fear that Jim and Rusty would find out what we were doing to them behind their backs and that we had no intention of ever taking them home again. Dad continued to harbor dreams of going home eventually, even though I hinted it was not likely. Would it have been kinder to say, *read my lips – you are never going home again.* I don't know. But I did know that hope of going home motivated Dad to work extra hard in his physical therapy sessions and the physical therapy helped in Dad's recovery. I did not want to impede his progress in any way so I chose not to confront the matter directly. I took a page out of the Jim Burris playbook to just 'ride it out'. Dad, on the other hand, slammed the playbook closed and decided to meet the matter head on.

"I saw the doctor today," Dad told me one evening. "I asked him when he thought your mother and I could go home."

"Oh? And what did he say to that?"

"He said we can go home whenever my daughter said so."

Intense brown eyes stared right through me.

"Dad, you need to be here where you can have nurses looking after you."

Thanks a lot, Doc! I thought. I could have used a little back-up at this point. He got paid big bucks to do his job. Would it have been so difficult for him to tell Dad that he needed more medical assistance than he could receive at home? I felt like the villain of the story.

I avoided being alone with Dad for days after that, then one Sunday afternoon his old friend Ben Clark stopped in for a visit. It was a welcomed surprise since Ben's wife had told me a few days after Dad's stroke that we shouldn't expect a visit from Ben. Dad's welfare mattered to Ben but he could not make himself go into a nursing home. I totally understood and assured her that we honored Ben's decision. Then, out of the blue, Ben appeared. In a nursing home. To visit ol' Jim. Now, that's true love. The room was crowded since Dad shared the room with another resident. The two beds were accompanied by a side chair each which filled most of the floor space. I hopped up onto the built-in desk while Ben took the visitor's seat beside Dad. I have no recollection where anyone else was. I suspect they were out having fun somewhere. No matter. I was riveted by this turn of events and the miracle that was Ben's visit. They chatted sporadically, then Dad turned to Ben with a serious expression on his face and asked him point blank, "Ben, reckon when Rusty and I can go home?"

Oh lord. There it was again, the burning question of the century. I squirmed. Poor Ben. I felt sorry for him. Here he was visiting Dad in a nursing home against his policy and now he was being put on the spot. I averted my eyes and hummed a tuneless song under my breath. I needn't have worried. Ben paused a moment, taking a respectful amount of time to consider Dad's question. Then he replied without preamble. And without relevance. "Jim, what kind of chance do you think the Braves will have for the championship this year?"

That's it? That's it? Hell, yeah! Classic evasive action. And it was a thing of beauty. I was to adopt this strategy myself a time or two henceforth whenever confronted with a topic I did not want to face. Just change the subject. Easy as pie. And it worked. It got Dad off his original question and on to an area of interest that was equally important to him. Baseball. Thank you, Ben Clark! This strategy would have never occurred to me on my own. Growing up with Jim and Rusty as parents, we were never allowed to be evasive.

Mom continued to be content enough at Dad's side during the day but she mentioned, artfully, that it would suit her much better if she could go home to sleep at night. We had set up her room there at the nursing home with only a few personal things since it was temporary until we moved her in with Dad, then everything would be agreeable. I secretly willed for Mom to realize that her greatest wish in the whole wide world was to spend the night there. Mom and Dad were together, soon they would share a room, and all would be right with the world. It's what mattered. To me. Until that day came, we improvised ways for Mom and Dad to be together as much as possible. The certified nursing assistants (CNAs) got Dad up, dressed him, settled him into a wheelchair, and then wheeled him down to Mom's room as frequently as possible. On occasion, the CNAs persuaded the dining staff to deliver dinner trays to Mom and Dad in Mom's room so the two of them had an opportunity to enjoy a nice quiet and intimate meal together. Willow Lake's dining room was attractive but it was noisy and filled with commotion. Sometimes it's the small things that make a difference and the CNAs pulled many *small things* out of their bag of tricks during our stay with them.

Sundays were the best days for visiting because we could have Mom and Dad together and to ourselves in a more relaxed atmosphere. Usually, week-day visits after work were conducted around dinner and other duties. On Sundays, if we arrived at noon, we could work in the mechanics of a meal with our visit, then at nap time, we quietly scooted out the door. Mom was a little clingy at times, with good reason. At times, as we were leaving she looked lost and abandoned. I told myself that after I was out of sight, Mom was probably like a kindergartner and returned to her playmates with lighthearted merriment. I told myself what was necessary in order to survive.

One particular Sunday, Andy and I had completed a most satisfying visit. Mom and Dad were in Mom's room where we sat and chatted and cut up, and as time drew near for our departure, they both wished us well and sent us on our way. It felt borderline normal. Most visits ended with, "Can't you stay a little longer?" This was pure heaven for Andy and me.

As we walked down the hallway to leave, Andy said, "That went well."

I noticed it too but was afraid to say anything for fear I had been hallucinating and didn't want to call attention to it.

"Yeah," I agreed. "Too well. Kinda makes me want to run."

"I know," Andy smiled. We didn't break into a full sprint, but we did pick up the pace.

Mom, ever resourceful in spite of diminishing mental resources at her disposal, found ways to make herself feel more at home in her new environment. She visited residents who were bedridden. Many of them looked forward to the attention she showered on them. A few were more reserved and protective of their privacy, which is understandable. But to be the focus of someone's interest who clearly likes to be with people was a tonic for the residents and they commented on it to me.

Mom made friends with her fellow residents, but the nurses and CNAs also became allies. They were moths to her flame. Some things never change. Several times Mom asked one of them to telephone me. The nurses were sensitive to when and how often they allowed residents to contact family members at work and at home. When they called me they were apologetic. I assured them that they could call me anytime. They could call me day or night. I promised I would never be too busy to talk to my mother. In a conversation with Mom, only a few words needed to be exchanged to reassure her. I think she just wanted to hear my voice to know I was real. When I pledged to see her as soon as I got off work, she relaxed and I heard in her voice a sense of relief that she had not been fabricating a fantasy of life outside the walls of Willow Lake. When I arrived for my visit and walked into the hallway where Dad's room was located, I was met by various staff members who gave me accounts of Mom's day.

"You won't believe what your mother did today…"

"I've never known anybody like your mother…"

One particular CNA took Mom with her to the designated staff smoking area outside the kitchen door each evening before readying her for bed. Mom forgot that she had quit smoking, so without reservation she joined the smokers and fit right in. I was grateful that caring people took a personal interest in Mom. On the cigarette pack is the label: *Cigarette Smoking is Dangerous to Your Health.* The irony of that warning did not escape me. I was not troubled by the fact that puffing on a cigarette subtracts ten minutes from the smoker's life if some of those minutes were enjoyable to her. While they sat on their milk crates, Mom described her beautiful house to her audience and gave a detailed account of her flower garden and how she would be moving back there soon. They asked me if this was true.

"Yes, to the first part. No, to the second."

Rusty would never step foot in her own home again because we were busy clearing it of all evidence from her life there. In the evenings when I was not in class or at the nursing home, Andy, Donna and I met at Mom and Dad's house to figure out what to do with their things. A lot of beer was consumed. Friends dropped by to witness our progress and commiserate. We loved being commiserated with. It helped. Barbara and Peggy came to town on week-ends when possible and that is when we made the big decisions. Once again, Robert was invited to participate but he said there was nothing he wanted from the house. I think he felt like we were vultures circling and waiting for the right time to swoop down and snack on the carrion leftovers of the ill-fated former residents. Trust me. It was not like that. The point was to disperse Mom and Dad's worldly possessions in order to prepare the house to rent before their money ran out. Even if Robert was not inclined to claim ownership of dining room furniture or hunting gear, we could have used his help in making decisions. At the very least, we needed to retrieve personal possessions stored at Mom's over the decades - report cards, high school letter jackets, Little Golden books. We collected various objects into piles that we each laid claim to. A pile was created and dedicated to Robert in spite of his absence.

Much of our time inside the house was spent looking through this box of photographs or that stack of books. We laughed at our school pictures and reminisced as old memories were triggered by the last item we grouped into arcane categories. "*Remember when...,*" started every conversation. Robert should have been there for that, damn it! And quite frankly, we needed the help. Going through Mom and Dad's belongings was a herculean task. And truthfully? Beer was not strong enough medicine to dull the psychic pain. But we did it anyway thanks to the discipline running through our veins compliments of Rusty Almighty.

As we sorted through papers and documents we found greeting cards sent to Mom and Dad from us to commemorate birthdays, Mothers Days, Fathers Days, and anniversaries. In one stack of documents, I found familiar-looking Social Services application forms. Mom already suffered many of the limiting manifestations of Alzheimer's when her brother, Jack, was diagnosed with liver cancer and yet here was evidence that she somehow found a way to get him enrolled for benefits *and* help him handle other medical issues. I was amazed because I found negotiating that same system especially complicated. I admired Mom for her inner strength, fortitude and willpower. Was there *nothing* this woman couldn't do? Even with Alzheimer's eating away at her brain?

Days passed and Mom and Dad settled into their new residence - more or less. Changing their address continued to be an emotional sore point for me but I began to justify the rightness of the decision. I can't imagine how Mom and Dad felt about it. I didn't ask them. In some ways, the move was actually easier on me and positive aspects of Mom and Dad living in the nursing home emerged. Caring for Mom and Dad at their house had become increasingly stressful for me. Being their landlord, nurse, caregiver, and electrician, took time which was scarce after a full day's work. I was willing to provide them with lawn service, groceries and taxi service but in reality, it took its toll on me. Now, with them at Willow Lake I felt a little relief and the freedom to resume my role as a daughter. As their Power of Attorney, I signed legal documents on their behalf and took responsibility for decisions that related to them medically. But if the light bulb had to be changed, somebody else changed it. If food was to be prepared, somebody else cooked it. Meds? Handled. Laundry? Endless supplies of clean linens and towels appeared daily like magic. With countless details seen to by the professionals, I began to feel a little insulation between me and the severe turmoil in our daily lives. Gradually, I resigned myself to make the best of these new domestic arrangements and I began to accept the inevitable path set before us. Apparently, we can get use to almost anything.

We became acquainted with many residents at Willow Lake. Connecting with individuals, and recognizing we were in the same boat, made a difference. I still hated the place, but if this was to be where Mom and Dad lived, then I was going to have to consider it 'home' even though the idea was abhorrent to me.

There was nothing inherently wrong with the facility but I loathed it anyway - until a dear friend demonstrated a slightly different point of view. When Susie came to visit us from England soon after we moved Mom and Dad, she plopped herself up on Mom's bed, took in the room, and declared with enthusiasm, "Sign me up!"

"Are you crazy? Nobody *chooses* to be in a place like this." I was incredulous.

"A place like this? Why wouldn't you choose to live here? Look how nice and colorful the bedroom is, and it has an *en suite* bathroom."

The interior was done in shades of mauve. Tasteful, not jarring. Susie relocated to the side chair.

"This arm chair is comfortable. And what's this? A lamp for reading?" This woman should be in sales. She continued. "Savory food is prepared and served three times a day, right? And additional snacks in between? Bingo games are scheduled weekly. Everywhere I look, I see interesting people to talk to. On-site medical attention is available for any ailment. I repeat, *Sign me up!*"

In her opinion, this place was a dream-come-true. What a difference perspective makes. It certainly was counter to the one I held and it did me a world of good to see things through her eyes. Susie saw only the positive points and I admit that I found it easier to visit Mom and Dad after she shared these observations. I slept a little better at night knowing they had continuous assistance throughout the day including readily available nutritious food. Now, when I came to visit, I enjoyed Mom and Dad's company. Having them in a nursing home brought different problems, but they were problems that were in many ways, preferable to the ones I had been dealing with.

One challenge was impossible to overcome and that was my inability to find a way to ignore the nagging sadness that seeped into my soul when I witnessed the heartaches inside the nursing home. I knew Mom and Dad would die here. Most everyone who lived here would die here. Seeing what the other families confronted hurt as much as what we were going through. How pitiful the human body can become. We come into this world wetting ourselves and drooling and by god, there's a good chance some of us will go out the same way. Paradoxically, I found many unanticipated blessings at the nursing home. I had no impulse to look for them on my own, but they appeared nonetheless. In a place of overwhelming suffering, I found love, affection, help, compassion, and caring, the depths of which I'd never known before. And Angels? They were everywhere. If Angels are messengers of a divine being, if they are a gift from God sent to help us through trying times in our lives, then I was surrounded by them as they were manifested in the individuals I met along this path. From them I received pure love and their wishes of wanting only the very best for us mortals.

In the nursing home, I found that the more help I needed, the more help I received. After my temper tantrum with God on the Friday night before Dad's stroke, I began to recognize there were miracles all around me. I didn't even believe in miracles. Okay, that's not an accurate statement. I did believe in miracles, but I believed they were for other people in other times. Here at the worst period of my life, one miracle after another transpired to help me bear this painful journey. One Angel after another came along to assist me along the way. CNAs went far beyond the call of duty to help with Mom and Dad. Nurses and other staff knew what my parents needed before I knew it myself. The woman at the Social Services Department walked me through each phase of the process to get Mom and Dad qualified for assistance. Other residents at Willow Lake were watchful and helpful where my parents were concerned, as were family members of the residents. We made alliances which supported me through three and a half extremely trying years. I was blessed to have them in my life. I hope they know that. I will forever be in their debt. We laughed together and cried together and ate together and grumbled together. Having these people in my life was definitely a bright spot in an otherwise dull and unrelentingly dreary daily routine. In addition to this new community of friends, another bright spot that made a decided difference in my quality of life came to me each night after I dragged myself home. There, our two husky-mix dogs, Phantom and Dickens, sensed my heartache and ministered to my ailing spirit. A simple nudge from their cold wet noses was quite a tonic. I began to trust the benevolence of the universe again.

CHAPTER TEN

It's a very small club you belong to now.

Dining rooms are a source of much amusement in nursing homes. Dad missed out on the fun because his meals were brought to his room where he could be fed more comfortably. There, he ate food that was softened and puréed, and drank iced tea that was thickened. He was in no way allowed by the dietitian to be tempted by actual appetizing meals or beverages. Mom seemed content enough to eat within the social environment of the communal dining room and if I was there during lunch or dinner time, I joined her. It's where we became acquainted with other residents and their families.

With a room full of my elders, most of whom were grumpy because they did not feel well and were not likely to be in the nursing home of their own volition, I noticed that tempers flared at times. Each resident wanted to be served first. This one wanted his meal precisely at the moment hunger began to gnaw at his belly. That one wanted sugar in her iced tea and assumed that her food preferences were already known to the nursing assistants who distributed the meals. Some residents relished repeating themselves and flung their echoing cries for condiments across the dining room as haphazardly as any fledgling newsboy delivers the morning paper.

A perceptive sociologist would find the social organization within nursing homes as interesting as the *Yąnomamös* of South America. Social standings within the nursing home culture emerged most notably in the dining room group setting. Residents at Willow Lake shared similar economic backgrounds for the most part, but at times a monkey wrench got thrown into this well-oiled social machine. For example, it was generally accepted that gentlemen, if it was in their power, wheeled themselves into the dining room using manually operated wheelchairs. On Sundays they were dressed in their Sunday best polyester slacks and sported a nice respectable pair of Dr. Scholl's velcro-closured shoes. At the dinner table, they conversed amiably with the pretty ladies as they waited for their chicken, green beans and mashed potato meals. When a newcomer shows up from out of the blue in supple leather opera bedroom slippers and a silk robe over a freshly-pressed pair of pajamas while he gently and dexterously guides his motorized wheelchair to the same table, dynamics among the dinner companions shift. Abruptly. This is rare, but when it happens, there is an instant recognition that the usual and customary table etiquette has been breached!

I looked on with curiosity as the two men to whom I am referring engaged in fisticuffs. A duel to the death. If they had been mounted on fiery steeds rather than four-wheeled mobility devices there would have been no difference. Egos required defending. As did the ladies' honor. Although, the ladies did sit up straighter and pat their perms when the fancy guy showed up. Fickle, every last one of them. But not Rusty. She had eyes only for Jim and her efforts were spent industriously squirreling away contraband packs of cellophane-wrapped Saltines for her sweetheart.

When I was not at the nursing home observing the men competing for attention from the ladies, I was at Mom's house engaged in the clandestine clearing-out project. We continued to protect information related to this endeavor like it was top secret government information, which meant it was pretty much public knowledge. But we tried to stifle the flow of information as much as we could. It meant getting to the nursing home on Sundays before church friends showed up to visit when they might innocently inquire about the progress of the dismantling of Mom and Dad's home. If we were there during the typical visitors' hours, we directed the conversation. It would have been more complicated to go to all of Mom and Dad's friends and suggest they don't bring up the subject, under penalty of death.

One Sunday, I arrived at the nursing home at lunchtime and couldn't find Mom and Dad in any of their usual haunts. I tracked them down in the front parlor where they sat, their attention on the front parking lot visible through the picture window. Both of them were dressed as if they were going on a lengthy excursion. I became immediately suspicious.

"What are you two doing here? I thought you'd be having your lunch."

"Already did." Speech therapy improved the clarity of Jim's uttered words but did not increase the quantity of them.

"Looks like you're expecting somebody important to arrive." I had already guessed it wasn't me. They did not take their eyes off the parking lot.

"We are."

"Who?" I looked at Mom. She looked at Dad. These two were in cahoots.

"Taxi."

"Taxi? What taxi?"

"We called a taxi to come take us home."

My stomach lurched but I feigned nonchalance. "Well, what will you use for money to pay for a taxi ride all the way out to Newell?"

"I have money."

"No, you don't!" I snapped back, a little too hastily.

"Yes, I do." Dad pulled a roll of one dollar bills from his shirt pocket. You don't want to know where my mind went on that.

"How did you get that? You been gambling?" I had suspected that more went on at this place after hours than meets the eye. Now, I had evidence.

"I asked for it. Whenever somebody comes into the room, I say, 'you got a dollar?' and they usually do and they give it to me and I save it for things I need, like a taxi ride home."

Whoa. This was the exact same tactic Dad used with me at home when I stopped in to visit. 'You got any change?' he would ask me. And without thinking, I dug automatically into my jeans pockets for the quarters, nickels and dimes jangling there. 'Yeah, I got some…,' I would answer him. 'Good. Put it in that jar there.'

I always fell for Dad's ploy. Most of the change in Dad's change-jar was mine and it's why I took possession of it during our homestead clearance project. But here in the nursing home, he extended the scam to gullible employees and casual visitors, and expanded it to include folding money.

"Daddy," I sat down in front of him and put my serious face on. "I'm afraid you can't go home." My voice cracked. "You need the extra care they can give you here. Mom can't look after you. I have to work. I'm sorry. You have to stay here."

He hung his head. I made Jim hang his head in defeat. This did not make me happy. I saw in his eyes the recognition of his failed attempt at the great escape from this prison. He shook his head soundlessly then looked up as if to say to the spirits above, *Oh well, it was worth a try.* I know the disappointment stung him. I left him there with Mom who patted his arm to comfort him. I think I saw a look exchanged between them that said, *we'll try again when* she's *not around*. I went to find the nurse on duty. I asked her to call and cancel the cab. In my attempt to supervise Mom and Dad's day-to-day life, I had not anticipated them to be a flight risk. Once again, these two were miles ahead of me.

Robert and Ruth visited on Sunday afternoons, and occasionally drove up for a week-day visit, too. During his visits Robert became Dad's valet. He shaved Dad's face, brought him clothes he'd washed for him, and changed his socks. The socks always confused me a little since Dad couldn't walk and his feet never touched the floor. It must have been a father-son thing.

Andy's visits took on grooming characteristics too as he searched through Dad's bedside table drawer to find the hairbrush. "Jim, you need currying," Andy told his dad. Then he'd brush his hair more capably than any barber, wash his face with a warm, soapy washcloth, and clip his fingernails. Robert and Andy took good care of Dad. Much love and tenderness was exchanged between these men. It made tears well up in my eyes and then I pretended to be needed somewhere else.

Mrs. Annas was a great ally. Her room was directly across the hall from Dad. She had seen a hundred springs come and go, only the last few of which were spent here. And she was a baseball fan. But not just any fan. An Atlanta Braves fan! The only fan who rivaled her was Jim Burris. Mrs. Annas was wheelchair-bound because her knees gave out on her at age ninety-seven, but her mind was as sharp as ever. She kept me informed when baseball games were scheduled and told me what channel I should have Dad's television tuned to for the broadcast. Mrs. Annas, a self-declared Jeopardy Game Show expert, would ultimately be the recipient of three centennial birthday cards from two presidents. She tacked the one sent to her by Clinton on the bulletin board in her bedroom. The subsequent two found their way to the trash basket - thus was her politics.

Just as thoughtful as Mrs. Annas was Lucy Gladden. Her room was next door to Mrs. Annas and if she sat in the doorway of her room, which she did often, she could get an angled view to Dad's bedside. From there she monitored the comings and goings of medical staff and friends and family members alike. She brought me up to date with this information as soon as I arrived each evening with a conspiratorial nod of the head and a come-here waggle of her index finger. She was as sweet as my Grandma Susie, and even resembled her too. Her loving nature coupled with her surveillance on Dad's room endeared her to me and I looked forward to receiving a report of the day's happenings at every visit. If Mom wandered into her room, Mrs. Gladden offered her a banana or other nutritious snack and invited her to sit and visit. I liked sitting in her room to visit too. She liked my mother. To be honest, she needed no other qualifications to recommend her. Mrs. Gladden held a special place in my heart.

Four weeks had come and gone since we moved Dad and Mom to Willow Lake. In that time, we began to settle into a routine. Mom relaxed a little as she began to trust that she'd be with Dad each day as much as she wanted and also see us as often as before her move, maybe more. It was nothing close to being able to see them both in their home, but on the bright side, they were safe here. And knowing they were safe helped me get on with my work-a-day world and the business of earning a living. I was sitting at my desk at work reviewing my weekly calendar and taking note of the date, Friday, April the 14th, when my telephone rang. I picked up the receiver and identified myself to the caller. It was Robert.

"I just saw Dad," he told me

"Okay, I know he probably enjoyed that," was all I could think of to say.

"Yes, well, I brought him the clothes I washed for him. Bought him new socks, too."

"That's good. Thanks."

"I wanted you to know I was there today."

"I appreciate it."

"Well, talk to you later."

"Alright. Talk to you later."

That was the entire conversation. I was baffled but I let it go. Maybe Robert was trying to make an effort to be agreeable and it pleased me that he called.

I went to see Mom and Dad after work. Dad had been confused over his whereabouts a couple of times that week and I wanted to check in with him before the week-end. Sometimes he'd get days of the week mixed up, which is understandable and typical when living in a structured institutional setting. But it also meant that I took some of what Dad told me with a grain of salt, like the following exchange.

"Robert came by to see me today," Dad told me.

"I know. He called me at work and said he came by here. Gave you a shave, too. You look good." Dad ignored the compliment.

"He said he was taking a job out of town and we wouldn't see him for a while."

"Oh, really? He didn't mention that part to me." I thought maybe Dad was a little confused so I played along. "I hope it's a good job. I hope he likes it."

"He didn't seem that happy about it, but he said it was something he had to do." *Okay.*

The next morning started off with coffee in bed for me. I took Saturdays as my day, to do my own chores and run personal errands, and I rarely rushed into the day. Doing laundry or vacuuming gave me the illusion of normalcy. This Saturday was tax day - April 15th. Seven weeks to the day since Dad's stroke. Although he required a great deal of assistance, Dad had progressed far beyond the hopes of the original prognosis given to him by the emergency room physician. Donna and I had been bragging on ol' Jim for that progress and we patted ourselves on the back for having our tax forms completed and in the mail to the IRS with days to spare. We were feeling quite content, until the phone call. Andy identified himself.

"I just got a call from Ruth. You're not going to believe this, but Robert shot himself. He killed himself. The police are there now, we have to drive to Albemarle."

I had no response to that. I had no words. I detached, as if it was happening to someone else. It was like being underwater and the words were garbled. Then, slowly, the meaning of Andy's words began to unscramble inside my brain. Disbelief. I didn't believe the message that was coming through the telephone line. Then a hint of the reality of what Andy was telling me began to seep in and I began to comprehend. The room rotated as I stood frozen at its center. Then, I was swirling with the room, looking back at the person with the telephone receiver against her ear and I heard these words being spoken, "Okay, I'll get a shower. Come pick me up."

Andy told me he would pick up his friend, Devrin, and that Andrea would be coming too. "But Marsha, Barbara has to be called. I don't know what else has to be done."

"I'll call her, don't worry. We'll figure the rest out."

Donna looked at me oddly. She knew something terrible had happened. I repeated Andy's words to her. She was speechless. What do you say to that? I dialed Barbara's telephone number. No answer. They had already started their day. Barbara and Peggy are early risers and hard workers. They were not lounging and drinking coffee. I left a message for her to call back. Donna would be the one to tell her the news.

Somehow my legs took me to the bathroom and I stepped into the shower. The water beat down on my back and then I began to cry. I couldn't catch my breath. I gasped for air but there was no oxygen to draw into my lungs. I was vacuum-sealed and separated from the world as I had known it only moments before.

I slammed my fists against the shower wall. "Why?" I screamed. "Why would you do this? Why would you do this to us? Why would you leave us?" I demanded. "Why would you leave us with this mess? What about Mom and Dad?" I was angry. Robert had skipped out on us and I was appalled.

Why… why… why… I wanted answers. I naïvely thought answers would help me process this unthinkable thing in some way. I stood in the shower and contemplated how we had saved his things at Mom's house and how we had made a pile of the prized possessions she had kept for him over the years. It seemed like he was ungrateful for our consideration of him. What? Was I losing my mind? I don't remember getting out of the shower, or dressing, but only a few minutes after Andy's telephone call, he and Andrea and Devrin drove up my driveway. I went out to meet them. I had the perception that I had pulled myself together. I didn't want to fall apart in front of my little brother.

Donna stayed at home to direct communications. I knew I would be braver if she was not with me as I delved into the unknown sphere of suicide aftereffects. I needed to access every ounce of inner strength I could muster – her comfort would weaken my resolve to face the day. She asked me to keep her informed of our discoveries and I promised to do that.

We drove to Albemarle, taking the same route Dad always took for our Sunday dinners with Grandma and Grandpa after church. It's a forty-five minute drive from my doorstep, due east. On the way, we passed the house that Robert and his family had lived in before... before alcoholism consumed him, before he lost the house to foreclosure, before his DWI conviction, before Tony came to live with us, before a lot of things. It's the house where we celebrated Christmas dinner only a couple of years before. I caught a glimpse of the Lombardy Poplars Mom planted for him as a house-warming gift.

During the drive, Andy and I tried to figure out what happened. There was precious little information to go on and we hoped to learn more after our talk with the police and Ruth. But as we drove down the highway toward Albemarle, we couldn't make any sense of it. To this day, we try to figure it out and make sense of it. And to this day we innocently believe that sense can be made out of something like Robert leaving us so abruptly.

Andy drove directly to the police department to get the official report. Ruth would be inconsolable and we wanted to check other sources available to us before talking to her. We didn't need a map - our grandparents lived in Albemarle all our lives; a Burris lives on virtually every corner there. Growing up, we spent many summer days playing with the neighborhood children and roaming the town on our bicycles.

Andy introduced himself to the officer on duty. Instead of being helpful and sympathetic, this law enforcement officer was annoyed by having to respond to the scene of Robert's death. We were dumbfounded by his attitude. The officer's facial expression showed resentment toward us for not keeping our family troubles private which caused him and his men to have to see the results of it. Clearly, he was disgusted and wanted to expedite the paperwork to get us out of his sight. Undeterred, Andy asked him what he could tell us about our brother. The policeman stated the facts frankly and offered details:

- caliber of the gun
- who it was registered to
- why they will keep the gun in custody for a while
- position of the body when they arrived
- the fact that he was sitting in a chair in his bedroom
- position of the gun as it fell from his right hand
- nature of the wound
- vodka bottles found around that chair
- impending court case…

What impending Court Case? From another DWI? This was news to us. We filed it away.

"We talked to your aunt when we were called out there this morning," the officer said. "She's the one what found him, but we don't think she capped him. We're sure he did it hisself. The liquor, the positioning…"

CAPPED HIM? CAPPED HIM?

Surely I did NOT hear this man refer to the manner of my brother's death as being "capped". When we got back into the car after the officer suggested we go to the hospital next, I asked Andy, Andrea and Devrin if they heard what I heard. They did.

We went to the hospital as instructed. Again, we knew the way without having to ask directions. We entered through the emergency room entrance and told the receptionist our story. Albemarle is small. She knew the story. We were preparing ourselves for more ill-treatment but she responded to us with compassion. Then she walked us over to a private consultation room. Another private consultation room - the second private hospital consultation room in less than two months. Not good. The emergency room physician came in to talk to us a few minutes later. If my mother could fake mental health then so could I. I was probably as transparently bad at it as she was.

The doctor explained the details of the situation to us. She told us the time that Robert's body was brought in and the condition of the body. She used professional medical terms which made the 'cause of death' seem less offensive. She chose her words thoughtfully, sympathetically, compassionately. It made a difference.

"There's no doubt that he took his own life." Her voice was soothing. "We can tell there was alcohol in his system, but not the level. We can do an autopsy, but only if you want one."

I looked at Andy for answers. He gestured 'no' with a slight shake of his head and the look in his eyes told me he was confident in that decision. I agreed with him.

"No," I told her. "That won't be necessary."

"We'll release the body to whichever funeral home you choose. You'll have to call them yourselves, then they'll call us, and we'll set a time for the release of your brother's body to them. Will it be Hartsell's?"

"No, we're from Charlotte. We'll have McEwen's handle everything."

"Ok, no problem. I do need someone to sign this."

I signed the papers she handed me. I have no idea what they were. We asked few questions. She was thorough. Before she left us, I asked to see him. It was an afterthought, really. I held out one last ounce of hope that this whole thing was a huge mistake. I would look at the body, it won't be Robert, and we'll go home. A stupid mix-up. How we will laugh about this one day. Andy looked at me like I was being ghoulish but the doctor understood. She discouraged me from seeing Robert and offered this alternative confirmation of Robert's identity instead. "His wallet was in his trouser pocket. Would you like to have that?"

I replied 'yes' as all optimism vanished.

We departed with the assurance that the hospital staff would treat our brother with respect. As we drove to Ruth's house, my stomach muscles tightened with the fear of what we were going to find there. It sure would have been nice to detach and jump outside of my body right about then. Robert had a way of scaring me out of my skin.

We found Ruth crying on the sofa in her living room. Of course she was crying. She found her nephew dead from a gunshot wound to the head. We consoled her with a few unoriginal stock phrases then Andy asked her the obvious question. "What happened, Ruth?"

"I don't know. I didn't know he was even feeling down in the dumps. I went to my hairdresser's at ten. He's usually up by the time I get back. When he wasn't, I thought he might be sick so I knocked on the door. When he didn't answer, I opened it and found him. He was sitting in the chair. I thought he was asleep at first."

"Where'd he get the gun?" Andy continued. My mind was moving in slow motion and I couldn't keep up. There was a time-lag between the point at which the thing was said and when it hit my brain as information.

"It was Ben's," Ruth said. "Robert asked for it and I didn't see any reason not to give it to him."

"Well, what about this court case? We didn't know anything about a court case, but the police said he was due in court on Monday."

"That's true. He got another DWI. When his boss found out, he fired him. Robert knew he'd have to go back to jail again – he didn't want the rest of you to know. I think he was ashamed. But I didn't know he would kill himself."

She cried more tears then told us she wanted us to clean out Robert's room. Andrea stayed with Ruth. Andy, Devrin and I headed down the hallway. Robert's bedroom looked trashed. It hadn't been, but it was a small room and all Robert's worldly possessions were in it. After Robert completed the DART program (Drug Alcohol Recovery Treatment), he moved in with Ruth and Ben during the probationary period. Everything he owned, excluding only the few items saved back for him at Mom and Dad's house, was in this room. Some of it was packed up in cardboard boxes which took up much of the floor space in the bedroom and were stacked haphazardly along with an unruly mess of other personal articles. We took in every detail as we surveyed the room. What we were actually looking for was a *note* - an explanation of what drove Robert to this action. We did not find one. We threw the legal and financial papers we found into an empty box and hoped to piece the puzzle together later to make sense of what happened in this room. Andy picked through a pile of Robert's things on the bed. I stood there like a lump and stared at it all. I was in shock and I knew it. Shock is anesthesia. Like a toothache that has been temporarily numbed with Novocain, I knew it would wear off eventually. In this protective daze I wandered into the kitchen and found a box of plastic trash bags. We collected garbage in one, clothes in others, and personal items in yet another one.

Ruth looked in on us through the doorway of the bedroom to check our progress. Andy asked her why the boxes were packed with clothes and things.

"He was packing up his things to move to the basement while he was in jail so I could rent out his room." *Oh.*

Andrea fetched Ruth back to the living room and poured her a glass of iced tea. I cherished the gesture and I would treasure her help even more before the day was over.

I called and talked to a friend who knew Robert and was better acquainted with his personal life than his family was. I told her what happened and she filled in more details of the upcoming court case and his job and how he got fired.

"But he intended to do the time, Marsha. He knew what to take with him this time, he was getting those things together, he knew to get a pre-paid phone card, and to get stamps… I don't understand."

We cleaned the entire bedroom out. We loaded the boxes and bags into Andy's car. Ruth seemed pleased with our efforts and since she had calmed down, we drove back to Charlotte. We felt an urgency to talk to Mom and Dad before news reached them prematurely from well-meaning sympathy-wishers at home. First, we needed food. None of us had eaten a bite all day. I called Donna and asked her to meet us.

Before we reached the restaurant, reality burst through my delicately woven protective blanket of numbing shock. *Oh dear god,* I thought. *I have to tell Mom and Dad that their son has died. By his own hand.* Cleaning up Robert's room was not nearly as difficult as the prospect of telling my parents that Robert shot himself dead. Up to this point in my life, the most difficult thing I had ever done was to leave my mother at the nursing home. On that day, I could not have imagined anything sadder. Now I could.

I leaned forward from the back seat. "Geez, Andy," I said. "I can't do it. It'll kill them. What do I say?" My mind feverishly sought a solution. Panic gripped my gut.

Andrea offered an alternative. "Tell them he had a heart attack."

"What?"

"Don't tell them the whole truth. Just tell them he had a heart attack." The *impossible* suddenly became doable.

From the restaurant I called the funeral home. The woman who answered my call was a friend of Mom's. I was not surprised. She knew precisely what to say and do. She told me to wait for a call back from an associate and we'd take things one step at a time from there.

Eating a meal was impossible. Why in the world did I think I needed food? And yet, when we got to the nursing home, I insisted Mom and Dad eat some food before our talk with them. We arrived at supper time and we waited patiently until after our parents were done to lead them to the conference room where we would have privacy. In the conference room, they gave me their full attention as they sat side-by-side. I took a seat directly across from them. Andy, Donna, and Andrea were with me.

"I've got some bad news." I looked at them. I took a deep breath. "Robert has died. He died from a heart attack. I'm so sorry."

They just stared at me. No movement from either of them. The meaning of my words didn't register. I understood. I understood that you can hear words being spoken to you but the words make no sense. They are words you never expect to hear in a lifetime. Dad comprehended the message first. After a few moments, Mom realized what I was saying to them. The memory of this conversation is a fog to me now so I cannot be any more precise about what followed.

Barbara and Peggy arrived in town the next day, Sunday. They accompanied Andy, Donna and me to the funeral home where we met with the youngest director we had ever seen. Jeff discussed details of the arrangements that required decisions on our part. We chose a casket, the site of Robert's interment, the words to be written in his obituary.

"How do you do this?" I asked Jeff. He looked no older than twenty five. What could anyone this young say to aid us in our grief? "Especially, how do you deal with suicides, or the deaths of little children?"

"That's where I can help the most," he told us with complete sincerity. "You see, although we may not understand these things we must take it on faith that it's part of a grander plan than we're privileged to know. There are no mistakes. God does not make mistakes."

That's what he said. What I heard was: *It's not your fault that your brother is dead. You think you could have stopped this catastrophic event from happening, but there was nothing you could have done. It's bigger than you.* It was exactly what I needed to hear. Jeff's confidence helped. His simple faith inoculated me with a vaccine that helped me survive the tricky days and weeks and years ahead and provided me the ability to remain attentive to Mom and Dad as they mourned the loss of their son.

After leaving the funeral home, we met with the minister of Andy's church to plan the service. Mom and Dad's church was between ministers and we needed to bring in a ringer. We laid out what had taken place, how we lied to Mom and Dad – everything.

"Do you think you can preach a funeral knowing that?"

"Absolutely."

The minister realized our dilemma and was able to give Robert a proper farewell service at Mom and Dad's church. The Burris family will be forever grateful to him for that.

Once again, the American Red Cross tracked down Tony to come home for his father's funeral. The night before Robert's service, we took Tony to see his dad. Jeff had gone home for the evening but the CEO, Paul Helton, met us. Mr. Helton knew Mom and Dad and made a special point to be there for us. We followed him to the private room designated to Robert. We needed to know if Mom and Dad could be allowed to view the body of their son. We wanted them to have time with Robert to have some closure. It was also our hope that by virtue of not concealing Robert from them, our heart attack story would be substantiated. Dad was skeptical of Robert's manner of death, and inquisitive. He asked pointed questions and frankly looked unconvinced that our story held any veracity at all. We needed evidence, no matter how scanty, to back up our story and to perpetuate the myth that this man's son died from a heart attack.

We looked down at Robert as he lay in the box that would hold his physical remains for eternity. At forty-four, there was little grey in his hair. *He'll never grow old*, I thought. *But he will miss so much.* We agreed that Mom and Dad would be able to say their good-byes to Robert in person. Dad's eyesight was hindered greatly by macular degeneration. Mom's Alzheimer's dulled her grief-stricken state of mind even further. Tony requested a closed-casket service for everyone else. Before we left, I asked for

Robert's hair to be re-arranged. It had been combed straight back and he never wore it that way. I wondered briefly where the miracles had got to, and then I looked at Mr. Helton, this kind man who showed us compassion at a horrible moment in our family's life. Angels show up in funeral homes, too. And a bit of kindness makes a huge difference when plodding through a life that has been rent to pieces by the sudden and violent death of a loved one.

On the afternoon of Robert's funeral, we organized time for Mom and Dad to be alone with Robert in the sanctuary of our church before the visitation began. The visitation would take place in the parlor that sat off to the side of the church foyer. Until then, Mom and Dad were able to have their time with Robert. We asked for the overhead lights to be dimmed, then Donna and Peggy made sure that no one else was admitted into the sanctuary.

Mom couldn't keep her hands off Robert. She stood at the head of the casket and cupped her palms on either side of his face. Her hands shook as she stroked his cheeks, without uttering a sound. She got make-up smudges on her hands, but she didn't realize it. Parents are unable to absorb anything so trivial when confronted with burying a child. She ran her fingers through his hair. She patted his chest. She did not want to leave his side, but she did. And she kissed his forehead for the last time.

Dad stared at the brass handles of the casket that were at eye-level as he sat in his wheelchair. His shoulders shook as he cried silently. I walked up the center aisle and turned away from them. I could bear to observe their grief no longer. It was not my business. It was a private moment between a mother, a father, and their son. They were consumed by their sadness and took no notice of their surroundings. It wouldn't have mattered if the room was full of people because they were incapable of focusing on anything other than this lifeless body that had been their child.

After Mom and Dad had their time with Robert, we directed them to the parlor to greet their friends. Having the visitation the same day as the service was easier. We had only to get Mom and Dad fed and dressed and ready for one event, rather than two.

In the sanctuary, during Robert's service, Mom and Dad's strength and dignity showed what they were made of in spite of their frail state. Dad sat in his wheelchair in the aisle, in his best suit - the suit he bought for Andy's wedding - the suit he had laughed about wearing twice. The irony and the necessity of wearing it three times was in no way funny. Mom was dressed in a silk pantsuit the color of a sandy beach. God that woman was gorgeous. Even in ill-health, she was calm and composed. I sat beside her on the pew with my arms around her, trying with all my heart to protect her. She patted my hand as if to let me know that she was able to comfort me as well. Donna sat next to me, and the rest of the family sat in the row in front of us.

The church was packed. Many friends were there. The first grade teacher that Andy, Robert and I had at Newell Elementary School was there. Several of Robert's friends since childhood were there too. Grown men now, who looked as if their hearts were breaking, sat in the church, wearing their Sunday best. I hurt for them. Each of them wishing Robert had reached out for help. I hurt for Mom and Dad, and for Barbara and Andy. I hurt for Tony. I didn't stop to hurt for myself. I was afraid to. I was afraid of the pain. To be able to deal with my brother's death, with moving Mom and Dad out of their home, and to tend to their health issues, I felt it was safer to disconnect from my own feelings. As we sat in church to honor Robert's brief life, full of turmoil, I longed for the whole thing to be over. How much sadness can a human heart endure? I was at my capacity. My whole family was.

The service moved to the family grave site in the church yard. It was a pretty day, the week before Easter. As Robert's casket was dropped slowly into the ground, I was reminded of the time I dropped him in the creek as we attempted to cross over to our tiny island by way of a rope. I let him down then. I had the impression I'd done it again. But many times when we were kids, we covered for each other so we wouldn't get into trouble with Mom and Dad. We covered for Robert one last time.

After the sod was replaced on the freshly disturbed red clay over Robert's grave Barbara took Mom and Dad back to the nursing home where they would mourn the loss of their son in that public place.

Robert's death was tragic. With his action, we had no opportunity to say, *Wait. Let's try to work through this.* Because of his death I was angry and hurt and even offended. I was angry because Robert got the last word in. I was hurt because he didn't ask for help from his family. I was offended that he took the life that Mom and Dad gave him and threw it away.

According to Elisabeth Kübler-Ross, the esteemed psychiatrist and expert on 'death and dying', we go through the following stages of grief: denial, anger, bargaining, depression, and finally acceptance. But the typical grieving process does not apply to families mourning a loss through a sudden, violent act - whether or not the death is intentional. Grief associated with this kind of death is complicated. Grief is, by definition, painful mental anguish caused by loss. It is the significant reaction to losing a loved one, but reactions to a suicide are more complex than Kübler-Ross' stepping stone stages of mourning. My own unscientific list looks like this (not in any particular order): shock, disorientation, disbelief, guilt, revulsion, sadness, anger, resentment, shame, more guilt, isolation, irrationality, and grasping unsuccessfully the reality that your loved one's absence is final. Regret and resignation follow. I have not reached the acceptance part of the process yet, so I can't add it to the list.

As a suicide survivor, I alternated between near paralysis created by the severe sadness which permeated my life, and moving through the motions of life with a soul that ached inconsolably. Shock, which is a sort of numbness or dazed feeling that was, no doubt, brought on by the overwhelming emotions associated with a tragic event, was actually helpful. If its purpose is to insulate us from the experience, then it is most welcome and it would be helpful if that insulation lasted a little longer. When the protective coating of shock began to peel off, I was raw, skinned alive. When the most tender part of my soul was bared and exposed to the world, I was as vulnerable as a flounder staring at a filet knife.

Robert's death disoriented me and knocked me off balance. I was shattered. We were all shattered. His death drained fragments of life from us all. While I wandered inside this wasteland of confusion, I couldn't believe that Robert was dead. In fact, I thought that if I ran the events that led up to his death on a never-ending loop in my imagination, I could conjure up a different and better outcome. Also, I was riddled with guilt. Because of the avoidability of suicides, survivors may feel culpability that they did not prevent the event from happening.

Already present in the back of my mind the moment Andy told me about Robert's death were the questions, 'Should I have seen this coming? Was the telephone call at work a cry for help that I missed? Could I have stopped it?' I failed Robert as a sister.

I felt physical revulsion toward the image of what Robert had done to himself. In killing himself Robert became both perpetrator and victim. I hated the one while I mourned the other. Robert's death left a huge hole in our family and while his absence brought me deep sorrow, I was angry at him for failing to find a better way through the problems in his life. I was even angrier at myself for not seeing or anticipating this disaster before it happened. I just did not see Robert's freight train of despair veering off track.

There's little privacy in death, in fact death and dying is a ritual opened up to the public by mutual consent. From an obituary published in the local newspaper to the gathering of friends and family at the funeral service, deaths are shared. And yet, when a loved one chooses to die, it will turn the process of mourning inward. *It's a very small club you belong to now*, a friend told me one week after Robert killed himself. She knew how I felt because her sister had died from suicide. I was sympathetic when she had told me about it. I thought I had been sensitive and understanding toward her loss. I was wrong. I have a better understanding now. Now, I'm a member of the club.

I irrationally believed I could somehow go back in time and recreate the events leading up to Robert's death thereby giving me the opportunity to take steps to prevent it. This is what cognitive scientists call 'magical thinking'. One problem with this perception, besides the actual inability to time-travel, is that there is often no clear answer, no *one* thing that caused the death. That truth is difficult to accept. So is the fact that, even if I had suspected Robert might take his own life, it is unlikely I could have prevented it. It's also possible that Robert had not planned his death in advance but took the action only after drinking excessively to dull his pain. Perhaps he didn't want to die, just stop the pain. Either way, Robert chose to not share with us the problems he was confronting in his personal life. Whatever he needed, he felt it could not be found.

My feelings were typical reactions to a suicide. I've sorted through them after much time has passed and considerable consideration has been given to them so I can present them here. Only after many of these irrational notions took their course did I begin to accept the reality and the finality of Robert's death. And only then was I able to abandon expectations that my brother's death was anything other than exactly what it appeared to be – Robert had taken his last breath on earth. At the time, though, soon after all of this took place, each of these feelings melded into a jumbled mess and competed for dominance. Perhaps I should have joined a grief therapy group, but I resolved to research information related to suicide on my own. Did any of my findings pertain to Robert? I do not know. I did discover that the need to eliminate psychological pain, coupled with having ready access to alcohol and firearms is a deadly cocktail that contributes to the likelihood of completing a suicide.

As a member of the club, I do have suggestions for professionals whose vocation brings them into contact with those of us who must carry on after a suicide has taken place. It is imperative for survivors of suicide to have a safe place to vent emotions of anger, pain, rage and heart-wrenching sadness. It is a necessity to be assured that it is alright to feel shame and guilt and any other emotion. We must be able to tell the whole story as many times as we feel we need to tell it. Using friends and family members as sounding boards may not be the wisest choice for this venting because they will be processing their own reactions to the death.

Time passed agonizingly slowly. If the old saying, *time flies when you're having fun* is true, then the flip side is true as well when you are in pain. I was living inside a nightmare. I waded through each hour like it was molasses. I was amazed that I functioned at all. Actions and conversations unfolded in slow motion. Friends, co-workers and acquaintances spoke to me, but the sound reached my ears only after a time-delay. I walked around as if inside a clear plastic bubble where others peered in at me but sights and sounds reaching me were distorted. I believed I would never know normalcy again.

I tell myself to dwell on Robert's life and the good times. But I rarely look at photographs where Robert is present because I know the ending. I know how it turns out. This is the legacy my brother left his family.

CHAPTER ELEVEN

We have to find a way to let your father go...

Particulars of my brother's suicide will claim squatters' rights inside my brain until my own last breath. Memory. The thing that my mother was running out of, I still had in great abundance and I wished for a little Alzheimer's to rub off on me. The sadness of Robert's death permeated every cell of my body, but I wasn't the only one - we all felt it. I watched sorrow errode the fight Mom and Dad had previously used to face the massive disruptions in their lives. Dad's stroke. Mom's Alzheimer's. Being moved out of their home and into a nursing home. Any one of these events would have been devastating; all three were a monumental challenge. Add losing a child to that list and no words in any lexicon can describe Mom and Dad's state of affairs. Seeing the pain etched in their faces after Robert's death stung like alcohol on an open wound.

I cannot imagine the devastation caused by the death of a child. I have only the first-hand knowledge of how it feels to be a sister of the child who has died. My parents' grief shaped each thought I had from the moment I told them about Robert. Moving through normal grief takes time. Moving through grief associated with the death of a child takes an eternity. No matter what age, parents don't live long enough for those wounds to scab over.

Dad carried Robert's obituary in the chest pocket of his pajama top. It was neatly clipped from the newspaper and laminated in protective plastic for him by a well-meaning friend. He took it out often to show nursing assistants, technicians and visitors who crossed his path during the course of the day. Never before had Jim displayed his inner thoughts and emotions so publically. But on this occasion and on this subject, he shared.

"Wonder what caused a heart attack in a forty-four year old man...," Dad asked his physical therapist.

He had worked steadily and conscientiously at PT since his move into Willow Lake. He was determined to prove the doctors and me wrong about not being strong enough to go home again. He would improve. He would show us. Although I admired his grit, I didn't share his optimism toward the ultimate outcome. The physical therapist caught me as I walked past her office one afternoon. She discussed Dad's care plan with me, his level of physical recovery, and she described how his momentum slowed considerably after Robert's death.

"It has knocked the stuffing out of him," she told me. "And he questions the probability of your brother dying from heart trouble. I know the story and I told him that if his son had abused alcohol and if there were health issues related to that, then it was possible for his heart to give out. I don't think he bought it though."

I didn't know what to do for Dad. There's no band-aid for this kind of wound. Our lie about Robert's cause of death was not the palliative we had hoped for. The truth would be even less so. Having questions about how Robert died, in my mind, was not as horrible as knowing for a fact that your son had died from a bullet to the head by his own hand. I could be wrong. I'll never know.

Mom suffered physically and emotionally too. She may not have remembered her address or that we had visited her the previous day, but she surely retained the information that her son was dead. Before Robert's death, Dad was her focus and purpose and the project kept her engaged. Now, she was more unsteady on her feet, wandering aimlessly up and down the hallway. She was lost and at loose ends. To mitigate some of these issues, Donna and I stepped up our efforts to get her out of the nursing home and into the land of the living as often as possible.

Sundays continued to be the best days for unhurried visits with Mom and Dad. At times, after joining Mom for lunch, we would sign her out and then drive over to the mall nearby. There were two fundamental yet essential attractions there. Ice cream and babies. We ordered our scoops of frozen chocolate delight then sat down to watch young families doing the same. The babies captured Mom's attention. Each one was a precious Angel to her and she was not shy in telling its parents. I was afraid at first that they would take offense at a stranger commenting on their family members and yet without exception they greeted Mom with smiles and gracious *Thank Yous*. Social filters limit how much love we allow ourselves to share for fear our actions will be misunderstood. Mom no longer had such constraints on her behavior.

Occasionally, we sprang Mom from the nursing home dining room before the traditional Sunday chicken dinner arrived and took her out to have lunch. The restaurant of choice became the local Burger King since having Mom in public without benefit of social contracts was becoming a challenge. Her attempts to engage in other families' dining experiences in a more upscale restaurant were not welcome since having a trespasser join your family at a table there was not nearly as endearing as having someone at the ice cream shop tell you your baby is precious. In the casual atmosphere of the BK, guiding Mom back to her own table caused us all less anxiety. Although once, when Mom was determined to insinuate herself into the family dynamics of the table next to ours, I was compelled to suggest that she sit back down. Mom reminded me that our role reversals had not fully taken place and clearly remembered that I was *her* child and not the other way around. Nevertheless, I would not allow a precocious five-year-old child of mine to run unchecked in public the way Mom was doing, so something had to be done. Enter Donna. She is not just my friend; she was Rusty's friend. An equal. Unlike me.

"Rusty, come sit with us. Don't wander to other tables right now. You can visit people later." Donna looked Mom dead in the eyes and said these things in clear but kind terms. Mom was not pleased to be called out but she returned to our table as she rolled her eyes. I observed this exchange with great admiration for Donna's courage. Didn't she know the penalty for her impertinence was an afternoon of weeding a bed of iris?

Being in public with Mom brought other challenges, too, like taking her to the restroom which was a test of patience. She maintained the ability to maneuver through the steps required of this personal activity, but there were hiccups. For instance, most of us take for granted that toilet tissue is now provided to us in mega rolls enclosed in a dispenser that is usually made with an opaque plastic cover. In Rusty's day, the tissue was displayed clearly and spun freely on spindles in a visible and convenient manner. It is now a high-tech mystery. For Mom, whose brain told her that if she does not see it, it-does-not-exist, it was problematic. Of course once I understood the problem I could engage in preemptive actions and make sure paper was available to her before she needed it.

If we did not have enough time to take Mom to the mall, Donna and I could at least stroll the nursing home grounds with her, looking at and admiring the flowering trees and the colorful landscaping. We met other families doing the same thing and often they would be dragging a canine friend with them on a leash. Mom's attention would immediately be drawn to it. Nothing topped that except babies, of course. Occasionally, we engaged in good old fashioned Sunday afternoon visits. Several of Mom and Dad's friends from church lived in the assisted living apartments next to the nursing home and we often walked over to see who was at home. We stopped in to see Golda Robinson on one such Sunday afternoon. Golda was a favorite friend of Dad's because of her famous homemade chicken and dumplings which she made in abundance and shared with him when they all still lived in Newell. Mom and I knocked on the door of her apartment for this particular Sunday visit and she welcomed us warmly. Mom had a hazy recollection that she knew this person from a long ago and distant past. Gratefully, Mom's vague uncertainty didn't matter to Golda. We talked about old times as Mom took in her surroundings and the decorations in Golda's living room. I told Golda how quickly things were changing in our lives. She assured me this is the way things are. Mom's eyes lit up when she saw a tiny white porcelain Angel and walked over to pick it up. Golda encouraged Mom to take it with her back to her own room. A beautiful gift and a thoughtful gesture. It perched on Mom's bedside table looking over her for the remainder of her days. It sits on my own bookcase now.

My world revolved around Mom and Dad although other responsibilities loomed in the background. In addition to my research duties at the university and the history course, Donna, Andy and I worked overtime to prepare Mom and Dad's house to rent. Their Medicaid qualification depended on completing that step. Furniture, washer-dryer, boxes and boxes of personal effects, clothes, dishes, all that they owned had to be removed from the house in anticipation of potential renters. Add *landlord* to the many hats I was wearing. I was no more cut out to be a landlord than I was suited to be a caregiver. Donna, steady as a rock, has great business sense and the ability to step back from any situation and perceive it as a rational enterprise rather than worrying how strangers who moved into Mom and Dad's home would *not* appreciate it as much as they should.

Coping with the daily routine of my life was difficult. I couldn't rest, I couldn't relax. Getting on with the business of seeing to the care of Mom and Dad was a challenge. I existed on adrenaline alone since I was always in emergency-response mode. My body was tired. My brain was tired. I was emotionally spent. I slept little, when I slept at all. I resisted falling asleep because memories of the recent events flooded back to me the moment I woke up. I experienced only a moment of blissful amnesia before I remembered how out-of-kilter life was for me and my family, that my brother was dead, that Alzheimer's was stealing my mother's memories of her life, that a debilitating stroke bludgeoned my father's brain like a club, and that I had packed my parents off to a nursing home. Robert's death continued to sit inside the 'Disbelief Folder' of my brain - I literally could not *believe* that the event had actually taken place. Rationally, I knew it had. There was documented evidence that I could consult if I needed to. When I woke up each morning, I would contemplate the possibility that I had somehow, ghoulishly, dreamed up the story of Robert's death. I just could not hold the idea in my head that something like that could ever happen in our family.

To mitigate my inability to sleep, I made up a bed on the sofa and napped with the television running all night long for background noise. When I woke up, as I did frequently, my mind could immediately focus on the broadcast rather than the first thoughts that would rush to my mind in a continuous loop. Phantom and Dickens, our faithful four-legged canine friends, lay contentedly on the floor by my side and watched over me. When I stirred they came over to me, anticipating my emotional needs before I was aware of them myself. *Just pat my head and you'll be okay,* they prodded me gently with their noses. Stroking their luxuriously thick fur coats made me feel better. It was exactly what I needed. How did they know? They were incapable of worry themselves and they showed me that at least for that precise moment in time I was warm and fed and loved.

The lesson Phantom and Dickens shared with me was not enough, sadly. I'm not as evolved as canines. It took great effort for me to get up each morning, to go to work and to see to my other responsibilities. I would have gladly grabbed at any quick fix to staunch the grief process strangling my body. Grasping at the minutia of daily life during grief actually gave me something normal to hold on to. We can ignore grief for a while but there is no shortcut to the other side. I built myself a protective shell to fend off any more pain; I was afraid I wouldn't survive otherwise. In this compromised state, I couldn't catch my breath. I was physically incapable of inhaling a full cleansing breath. My body could only sip oxygen through halfhearted sighs. The shock and the stress of the preceding three months pitched me into instant menopause. I resigned myself to view this as a twisted sort of compensation that at forty-six-years old I would never have to contend with the inconvenience of menstruation again. I changed my diet and became a vegetarian. I could no longer tolerate having meat in my belly. The new diet helped relieve some of the sluggishness that was paralyzing me.

I drifted along in a fog and then three weeks after Robert's death, we were tugged back into action. Barbara was in town for a visit. She discovered Dad unresponsive in his bed, staring into space. It looked to her as if he had had another stroke. The nursing home staff maintained that he was only sleeping late. Barbara demanded a medical response, so he was transported to the hospital. He was running a fever of 102 degrees, but the hospital diagnostics showed his lungs to be clear and his white blood cell count was good, meaning the fever was not the result of an infection. A massive subdural hematoma was in evidence from his initial stroke in February and may have masked a smaller stroke on this date because the doctors could not tell us for sure that he had suffered a more recent one. They suggested that his symptoms could indicate that he was dehydrated. Severe dehydration can increase body temperature, cause confusion and delirium and may lead to unconsciousness and finally death. It's not unreasonable to believe this was the culprit since Dad was restricted to drinking only thickened liquids because of the possibility of aspirating fluids into his lungs after the stroke. Dehydration could have been prevented and the nursing home staff should have known to take precautionary measures. Mom, always an advocate of drinking more water, would never have allowed this state of affairs if she had been in charge. I reproached myself for not being more vigilant. My friend, Frances Glenn's cautionary advice, *Oh dahlin', you can't save them from everything* rang through my head.

Dad rebounded quicker this time than he did from his previous hospital stay. Rehydration therapy improved his outlook and he was able to sit up and interact with us again. I was relieved that we were able to move him back to his bed at Willow Lake only five days later because I had been warned that if he was absent any longer, the facility could rightfully give his bed away to someone else if it came to that. If that had happened and if there had been no further openings when Dad was released from the hospital, we would be back to square-one in finding a suitable place for Mom and Dad to be together, still our highest priority.

The day we brought Dad back to his room was a busy day. I took Mom to a dental appointment in the afternoon. The denture made for her less than two years earlier was ill-fitting and needed to be replaced. Replacing the denture with a more comfortable one meant Mom could eat better. Anything to maintain a healthy diet makes a huge difference in someone whose existence is so precarious. It was not pleasant to have to do this – for either of us – but Mom was good as gold, compliant without question, and she trusted me that this thing that she didn't quite understand had to be done if I said so.

In our haste to return Dad to the nursing home, we had forgotten his electric shaver in the hospital room. I bought him another one while I was out with Mom for her dental appointment. Good thing, too, because the next time I saw Dad, he looked at me beseechingly and rubbed his hand across his chin, raking the stubble back and forth. A subtle hint.

"Dad, come on. I don't know how to shave a man's face."

He looked like I had licked the red off his lollypop. I had seen Andy shave him with loving care, and much skill. I know Robert had used a razor to give Dad a professional and close shave. But Dad sported a mustache which added an extra facet to shaving proficiency that I felt I did not possess. How could I tell Jim no? I gave in, then I patted myself on the back for having the forethought to buy another electric shaver already.

"Okay, I'll do it, but I can't promise the outcome." His face brightened up. I'm glad I did it.

Dad's health began to decline once more the following week. Mom was always at his side. The nursing assistants got Mom up, dressed, breakfasted and into Dad's room before the sun came up every morning. One CNA in particular, Jama, was especially attentive to Mom and Dad's needs. Another CNA's young nephew came by the nursing home almost every day after school and made a point to stop in to see *Mr. Leroy* on his rounds. At times he would merely stand by Dad's bedside and be present. Other times, he would read verses of scripture from the Bible he carried. Mom thought he was an absolute Angel. So did I.

Dad started having hallucinations again. In some ways it was upsetting, and in other ways, I was happy for him to have experiences, real or imagined, that were more engaging and qualitatively better than the ones he was having in the nursing home. On one occasion, Dad told Barbara that he had been out with a Ford Motor Company executive, someone he had known when he worked at the dealership in Charlotte. In Dad's imagination, they had ridden throughout Charlotte in the executive's car, inspecting local Ford franchises as they had done together years earlier. Dad had enjoyed the sights and sounds of the city, he told her, and he'd had a good day but was tired. I guess so. A few days later, Dad instructed Donna and me to meet the train as it arrived the next day to receive a shipment of fur coats. We assured him we would. Lying to my father was coming easier and easier to me.

Dad became more lethargic and soon did not have the energy to sit up in bed even with help. He had not regained an appetite since the stroke but now he was eating next to nothing. He was taking in less liquid than before his second hospital visit too, making dehydration a huge problem. The staff doctor called us in for a family consultation to discuss decisions that needed to be made on Dad's behalf.

"I don't care what you have to do. Do whatever's necessary, but keep my daddy alive," Andy told him.

Barbara and I agreed with Andy. We were not prepared to let Dad go and we were concerned how his death would affect Mom. What would happen to Rusty emotionally when Jim was gone? How could she possibly withstand the force of that blow? She didn't have the resources to shore herself up after two devastating deaths. Even someone without Alzheimer's disease would find these exceptional turns of events difficult to survive. Would she want to return home? Her job of looking after Dad would be complete and she might get it into her head that she'd be better off back in her own house. That option was out of the question, of course. Even if she was able to reconcile herself to living in the nursing home until the end of her days, how would she spend the time? She was in and out of Dad's room a hundred times a day, beside him, to love on him, to tuck the blanket up under his chin. She patted him and comforted him. She was being *useful*. Some of our fears were on behalf of Mom. Some of them were our own.

"We'll have to start an IV right away, then," the doctor told us. "It may work. It may not. But you have to ask yourself what you're saving him for and what sort of quality of life he will have. He has a healthcare directive on file and it states that he wants no heroic measures. And I assure you that a death that comes as a result of dehydration is peaceful, euphoric even."

Retelling the doctor's response here makes him sound clinical and cold. But he wasn't. He was direct and honest with us. He shared with us some of the difficult decisions he and his own family had made in similar circumstances. I appreciated his candor.

"Do the IV," Andy insisted. "Let's at least try to do something. We cannot lose our father so soon after losing our brother. It's only been a little over a month. What would that do to Momma? If there's a chance to save him, we have to do it."

Even after starting the IV drip, Dad slept more than he was awake. When he was awake, he was seldom capable of focusing on any of us. He appeared to be in no pain and the doctor had assured us that at the first indication of discomfort he would prescribe something to manage it. Mom, always present, caressed his forehead and stroked his hands. If I was a betting woman, I would bet that this was more soothing than drugs even though we observed no improvement in Dad's condition.

One Sunday afternoon, Mom refused to leave the nursing home for an outing with Donna and me. She wanted to be at Dad's bedside. We stayed with her and Dad for the entire visit. The room was quiet and Dad barely roused himself for any length of time while we were there. We had hoped the IV needle taped to his hand would re-animate him through the miracle of fluids but it made no real difference in his recovery. In fact, his hand was swollen grotesquely because his fragile veins were collapsing. The process is known as infiltration; Dad's body was rejecting this last-ditch effort that we imposed on it.

Donna and I stayed with Mom and Dad longer than our normal Sunday visit before we edged our way toward the door and made our getting-ready-to-go moves. In the South, we don't just unceremoniously get up and leave the people we are visiting. We must first do the good-bye-dance. The initial step is to announce that we are thinking about leaving, giving our host the opportunity to protest. It's considered good manners to accuse your visitors of being foolish for harboring such a notion as leaving so soon. The proper response to this accusation is to agree, reconsider, and stay a bit longer. Only then can we insist that we have out-stayed our welcome and it's time to get on home. It's appropriate at this point to offer an excuse to the host; maybe use the pretext that the dog needs to be fed and how responsibilities like that are totally out of our hands. Follow up with how we would otherwise stay a spell longer. In the end, after promising to come back real soon, we're allowed to keep a hint of dignity and self-respect intact as we make an exit. It's how we do things here.

Mom didn't hold up her end of the dance, but I got the message. She did not want us to leave her. She stood by the bed and held Dad's untethered hand. She looked sad. She said no words, but her eyes spoke volumes. It was the expression in her eyes that implored me to stay a while longer. I came back into the room and sat down on the chair beside Dad's bed. I pulled Mom over to sit on my lap. She weighed less than a hundred pounds and was no burden at all. I slipped my arms around her middle and held her tight and secure.

"What is it Mom? What's wrong?" Perhaps our role reversal was accelerating.

"We have to find a way to let your father go," she said quietly.

Mom was clear and cogent. She was on target with her assessment of Dad's situation. Dad had held on for so long, through the critical days of his stroke, and through losing Robert. Just his being with us and with Mom was a gift I never dreamed was possible. Because he had stayed with us, we were able to move Mom into the nursing home more smoothly than if she had been forced to move in on her own. What a great job Jim had done. His philosophy of *Just Ride It Out*, which had infuriated me, was the precise course of action needed in this case. But now Dad's condition was deteriorating to the point where he could no longer muster the strength to stay with us. Plucking up the courage to let Dad go was preferable to pumping him full of liquids, and here was Mom being the voice of reason.

"How do we do that, Mom?" I wanted to know. I hoped Rusty had the magical formula for us to follow.

"I don't know," she said simply. "But we have to find a way to do it. It's time."

"Okay," I agreed.

If Mom could be reasonable, then so could her children. Barbara, Andy and I had another family powwow and we agreed to honor the choice Mom and Dad had made much earlier when they still had control over their lives. Dad's doctor assured us that this was the right decision - difficult, yes - but the best thing for Dad. Nothing had to be done. No active steps had to be taken except to remove the glucose from his veins. Then, there was nothing to do but wait. It made us feel helpless. As humans, our first reaction to a problem is to do *something*. We want to come to the aid of someone in trouble. If there is nothing else we can do to help a person in need, we can at least offer them food and water. We had to go against this inclination, as Dad could no longer eat or drink by mouth, and his body was rejecting the IV too. I signed the DNR order (Do Not Resuscitate) presented to me by the administrator although Dad's Living Will was on file with them. I didn't care. I'd rather the staff make triple-dog-sure of the family's wishes before they mounted a sign over Dad's bed that basically means: *just let the ol' guy go in peace when the time comes*. Signing that document though, made me feel like I had issued a decree to starve my father to death.

I had two goals to accomplish before Jim left us. Get Barbara down to Charlotte in time to say her good-byes, and complete the

Medicaid benefits process. I was determined to get Mom and Dad qualified and I had worked to that end since we moved them both into the nursing home. I wondered if I would have time to accomplish this feat. Renters were successfully in the house, all the T's were crossed, and I had been instructed on how to direct Mom and Dad's finances in accordance with the Medicaid rules. At last I was successful on Thursday, the first day of June. Two days ahead of what would become the final deadline. I was relieved to know that Mom and Dad's nursing home bills would be covered.

Barbara drove to Charlotte and had some time to sit with Dad. Andy was at Dad's side frequently. He and Andrea had announced a couple of weeks earlier that they were going to have a baby. Dad was alert then and took in the information with joy. Although Dad was already a grandfather, he seemed pleased that he would have that honor bestowed upon him again - the joyful gleam in his eyes when he heard the news attests to that.

At four o'clock in the morning on Saturday June 3rd, the nursing home called me at home to come over immediately. At this point, I really was beginning to dread Saturday mornings. We called Andy, and then we took off to the nursing home. Barbara drove the eight miles that usually took twenty minutes, in about half the time. The streets of Charlotte are much easier to navigate at that hour of the morning. We jumped out of the car when we arrived and someone met us at the front door to unlock it and let us in. We ran down the corridor toward Dad's room. Jama, the CNA who took such a special interest in Mom's care, was squatting on her haunches in the hallway just outside Dad's door. She held her head in her hands and cried. She had become an ally. Burris hearts weren't the only ones breaking under pain of loss.

"What is it?" I asked her. "What's wrong? Where's Momma?"

"I got her up an hour ago and into the bed with your dad. They're together. He's gone. Just now, maybe five minutes ago. You can go on in." She nodded her head in the direction of Dad's room.

We walked into Dad's room. Mom was in the bed with Dad, both of them lying on their left sides. Jama had gotten Mom up out of her own bed in the room across the hall and helped her into bed with Dad when she realized his death would be soon.

Rusty had her arms encircling Jim, holding him from behind. They both looked as if they were sleeping peacefully. What a precious gift. If Mom and Dad had been at home, we would not have known to do this. If Dad had been at the hospital when he died, we would not have been allowed to do this. I was grateful for the thoughtfulness that these special people bestowed on Mom and Dad.

We thought we were being quiet as we came into the room, but our voices woke Mom up. She lifted her head and looked at us. She was groggy and a little bewildered.

"Hey Mom," I whispered.

"Your father is gone," she told us.

"Okay. That's okay."

"Did I do it?"

"No, Mom. You helped him. It's good. You helped him over to the other side."

"I did?"

Precisely seven weeks after her son died, Mom lost her husband of fifty-three years.

We had all wanted to be with Dad for his last breath but if we were meant to be there at the moment of his death, we would have been. Obviously this was an experience to be shared only between sweethearts. We accepted it as such. Mom wanted to get up, so we helped her and I took her to the bathroom. When I came back into the room, Andy had arrived. He joined us in marveling how young and serene Dad looked. Lying on his side, he looked like he was sleeping. Not a care in the world. A sweet and contented smile graced his face. There was no doubt that he embarked on this last adventure without fear and with a sense of leaving no unfinished business.

"Looks as sweet as a baby, doesn't he?" Andy reflected.

"Yeah. I want to go wherever he's gone when it's time," I replied. "If we get to choose where our destination is at death, sign me up for that place right there."

The nurse on duty came in and told us we could have as much time as we wanted with Mr. Burris, but it would be helpful if they could have a few minutes to wash him and put fresh pajamas on him. "You'll have to make the call to the funeral home yourself," she reminded me. "Do you want me to get the phone book for you?"

"No," I told her as we vacated the room. "It's on speed dial."

We went back into Dad's room after the nursing staff was done. They had, borrowing the words of my grandmother, *laid him out*. There are reasons that this is done as soon as possible which I'll not describe here, but it is important in the long run, I'm told. The problem for us was that Dad no longer looked like he was in peaceful repose. He looked wooden, like a lifeless statue. His jaw had dropped and his mouth gaped open. To be blunt - he looked dead. During times like these, I guess we deceive ourselves with any means possible to save us from an unpleasant experience and we much preferred the illusion of him being asleep to this reality.

I called the funeral home and they arrived quickly. I was determined to stand watch over Dad while Andy and Barbara walked Mom down to the parlor. The CNAs closed all the residents' doors up and down the hall. It was the policy of the facility to do this whenever a resident passed away. Whatever the reasoning was, it surely was not to disguise the fact that someone had just died and was on the verge of being rolled out the door on a stretcher to a hearse because as soon as the population realized they were room-bound, they knew someone was leaving for the last time. The only question to be answered was who. I suspected there was back-room betting going on with odds in favor of this resident or that. And it was probably one of the ways Dad got taxi money for his big escape attempt a few weeks earlier. He needed no currency for his getaway this time.

The funeral home attendants asked me to step into the hall while they performed their duties in Dad's room. I had no interest in observing them move the lifeless body of my father out of the bed he had occupied for the previous three months so I complied quite willingly. However, it did not mean that my vigil was over. What in the world I thought I could *do* is a mystery to me, yet I was on stand-by until they brought ol' Jim out in a red velvet body bag. I appreciated that they used something to transport Dad to the funeral home that matched the official Burris family color rather than the more impersonal and common black vinyl carrier. The only way they could have been more accommodating was if they used a red and black plaid flannel model that matched Jim's favorite hunting shirt.

I watched the men roll Dad's down the hall to the back door

where the hearse waited for them. Then I refocused my attention on Mom. Our plan was to get Mom showered and dressed, go get some breakfast, and meet with the funeral director by lunchtime. As we were doing all this, Mom looked me straight in the eye and said, "I do not want to hear anybody say that 'this is for the best'." I agreed with her and I knew I wasn't inclined to suggest such a thing. Barbara put some finishing touches on Mom's hair then we all went to eat.

At the funeral home, we made arrangements for Dad's service. We contacted the interim minister at Mom and Dad's church and settled on a date and time. We chose Dad's casket, wrote the obituary, and selected his pallbearers. I remember only now a conversation I had with Dad a year or so before their move to the nursing home. After he and Mom had finalized their pre-funeral arrangements, Dad told me outright that he wanted his children to act as his pallbearers. I was honored. But I had absolutely no recollection of that conversation on the day of Dad's death. I'd like to think he will forgive me for this breach of promise.

We handed over Dad's fancy suit, the one he bought for Andy's wedding, the one he splurged on because he knew he'd get double duty out of it, the one with the hand-folded red handkerchief. Then we were done. Back at my house, we fixed some sandwiches and Barbara began making the necessary telephone calls. We encouraged Mom to lie down for a nap. I took her into the guest bedroom and closed the blinds.

"Just lie down for a few minutes, Mom. You're tired and you'll feel better if you rest."

"Oh, I can't do that," she insisted. "I've got to get back and fix lunch for your father."

"You don't have to, Mom. He's gone. Dad passed away this morning."

It was the first she had heard this news. She had witnessed Dad's death, and she had understood the reality of it at the time, but that was hours earlier and she had been to two or three unfamiliar places since then. It's possible that Rusty had relied on her trusty fake-it tactics while we were making the funeral arrangements, and that strategy enabled her to appear mentally competent. Perhaps the stress prevented her from being able to hold on to the experience of Dad's death that morning. Whatever had taken place, Mom had maintained control of her emotions and her pain had remained bottled up inside of her without an opportunity to vent it until now. Upon hearing the words that Dad had died, she was devastated. The anguish of her loss burst to the surface and issued forth as she wailed. A long, loud, pitiful, cry came from her like a violent thunderstorm erupting on the horizon. The sound of her grief pierced the closed bedroom door. Then the sound of her distress became less like a scream of shock and more like that of an innocent child who had just had her favorite thing in the world snatched away from her without a good or fair reason. After a few minutes, we calmed her down a little. Before dark, Barbara took her back to the nursing home. We believed that it was important for her to maintain a routine and return to the people she had become comfortable with at bedtime. Thank you, dear sister. I was incapable of saying any more goodbyes. Also, to be completely truthful, we felt that tucking Mom into her bed at the nursing home instead of my house would give us some much-needed time for ourselves to regroup and prepare for the next two days ahead of us.

We held the visitation the following evening. Mom had rested some and was back in control of her emotions. Jim looked good, as we say in the South. I guess it means we can cast our eyes upon our loved one without flinching. Dad's casket was set up in the adjoining room beyond where we were all standing to greet family and friends as they came in. We arranged for a chair to be brought in for Mom in case she got tired, and we handled other last minute details before the appointed hour. We hovered over Mom, protective, wanting her to be as comfortable as possible, afraid she would feel overwhelmed because of the circumstances and having to see so many people. We needn't have feared for her at all. Alzheimer's had been stealing Rusty from us for seven years but she plumbed the depths of her soul to deal with Dad's death, to perform the duties of a widow. By some miracle, by some grace of God, Mom knew precisely where she was and why. She was fragile, but her courage and dignity radiated strength and it filled the room. She told us in no uncertain terms, "Do not ask me to go in that room and see your father. That's not him. He's not here and that body he left behind is not the Jim I knew." She shook her head in polite but firm refusal. We respected her wishes. We knew not to push Mom when she took that stance.

Many friends came to be with us. Dad's cousins from out of town, whom we hadn't seen in ages, came too. We need not have worried at all that Mom's stamina would be tested. Being with people energizes this woman and she held up like the Amazon warrior she had been when we were growing up. I had harbored a suspicion, when I was younger, that Mom's portrayal of a hearty, larger-than-life character was phony. Who could be that strong after all? But it was genuinely who she was all along. Passing this latest test of her will was proof of it.

Mom couldn't recall names as individuals came up to greet her (many of us have difficulty with name-recall) but she recognized faces and she knew who they were. She was pleased to see each person who paid a visit. One friend stepped up to Mom and took her hand. She remembered him as the son of her friend who owned the fabric shop that Mom frequented in her sewing heyday.

"How is your mother?" Mom asked Tommy.

Tommy's mother had passed away many years before but he responded with tenderness, "She's just fine, Rusty. Thank you for thinking of her."

The noise level crescendoed as the group grew larger. When I was much younger and I attended similar events, I resented that these gatherings turned into reunions and people seemed to enjoy themselves and have a jolly good time. Someone's death was serious stuff, so my thinking went, and it was just good form to act sad. On this Sunday night, I understood that the visitation wasn't related to Dad's death at all. It was about his life. That's why we were all there, to celebrate his life. Dad was one of the good guys. He had touched many lives, in positive ways. These fine folks took the time to come and tell us their stories and I loved hearing them. If Barbara, Andy or I heard a tale that the others had not heard, we couldn't wait to share. Although I felt great sorrow for losing my dad, and even more sadness for Mom's loss, I enjoyed the assembly of friends and family on Dad's behalf. Not a bad legacy, Jim. Thank you.

We held Dad's service the next morning. Peggy, who had been caring for her own dad in Virginia, flew down in time to be with us. It was not necessary for us to be devious for this funeral. We could be honest concerning the circumstances of Dad's death unlike Robert's. We much preferred this way to the deception we manufactured for Robert's service. The Burris family gathered and we filled the first two pews of the church. The scriptures we chose for Dad instructed us to look to the hills to find the help we needed to get us through this moment in time, to accept the promise Jesus makes that we will have everlasting life in spirit, even after the earthly body dies. The last scripture assured us that Jesus has prepared a heavenly place for us to dwell in for all time. Promises of a better world were meant to soothe and comfort but our hearts were laden with sorrow, no matter what the scriptures promised. An image floated through my mind of two days earlier when Rusty had held Jim until he took his final brave breath. Her parting gift to him was her embrace. With the faith of a child, Rusty pushed Jim into eternity and into God's everlasting arms.

Despite the despair, we felt certain that Dad believed the hopeful message recorded in the Holy Bible. It was written on his smile that lingered at his death and it was just like Jim to leave a gift this precious to his family without fanfare. To honor Dad's deep faith, we sang the Hymn, "How Great Thou Art". We had witnessed for ourselves evidence of what is reflected in the last verse:

> *When Christ shall come, with shouts of acclamation,*
> *And take me home, what joy shall fill my heart.*
> *Then I shall bow, in humble adoration,*
> *And then proclaim: "My God, how great Thou art!"*

When the service was done, the congregation stood, the pallbearers assembled, and the rest of us organized ourselves to follow Dad's casket as it was rolled down the aisle. The quiet was pierced by the faint low drone of the lone bagpipe standing at the door. The bellows filled with the piper's breath readying it for the lament. The Presbyterian Church has its origin in Scotland, and Celtic legend has it that bagpipes are considered a call to arms on the battlefield. The last warrior standing, usually the piper, would play the pipes as a matter of honor after the battle was ended to guide the souls of those who had fallen to the place where they can rest in peace. It is believed that, above all other musical instruments, bagpipes can be heard in the *Otherworld* by the departed, and in hearing the pipes, they know that their passing is mourned. To me, it's the sound our grief would make if we could give that grief a voice. The volume increased and filled the church with the powerful and familiar refrain of Amazing Grace.

It had been just shy of two months since members of the congregation had gathered for this man and his family. Now they followed their old friend along the same route to the sod which would shortly be shared by father and son. I wondered how Mom would get through it. How in God's name would she meet this trial? Surely Angels held her gently in their arms because she never wavered, even though the loss of a son and a husband must have demanded all her strength.

It was a warm but drizzly spring day. We walked the soggy steps to the gravesite for the interment ceremony. As we approached, a ready salute from the Navy Honor Guard greeted us against the backdrop of Taps being played for Jim. They stood at attention by the red clay as it yawned in readiness to receive Dad's mortal remains. I sat down on a seat in the front row. Dad's sister, Ruth, was on my left and Mom sat on my right. Ruth was visibly and audibly bereft with grief over losing her brother. Mom sat with quiet dignity, enduring this last rite. The minister uttered the time-honored words, *Ashes to ashes and dust to dust...* Then, with perfect economy and crispness of action, the sailors folded the United States flag that draped Dad's casket. They presented it to Ruth, who they thought was the grief-stricken widow. I indicated with a surreptitious move of my head that the widow was the quiet one on my right. They glided past me and kneeled at Mom's feet to present the colors with these words: *Accept this flag on behalf of a grateful nation, to one who fought valiantly for his country...*

We went back to my house afterwards. Food had been brought to us by the Women of the Church. We ate and we rested from the morning's demands. Mom had been amazing, but I could see that she was getting restless. She searched for her handbag which indicated that she was ready to go somewhere. Mom had demonstrated no mental confusion throughout the day. The cobwebs of Alzheimer's had given her a reprieve and I expected her to say to me, "*Okay, now that your father is gone, I want to move back into my house, thank you very much. Today will be as good as any...*" What the hell would I say to that? How would I tell her that she had no home to go to, that she was destined to live the remainder of her days in that place where she would never have another moment of freedom or personal privacy ever again? What she said to me in fact was simply, "I guess I better get on back now…"

Another miracle. Willow Lake had become the place Mom associated with safety and comfort. It had become her home. She had grown comfortable with the people there, she relied on them, and it's where she chose to return to begin the new era in this story.

My sister and me posing for one 'cowboy' Christmas and a rare moment as Rusty is caught off guard during another 'cowboy' Christmas.

Jim and Rusty at a cocktail party. The infamous telescoping cigarette holder is probably hidden inside the elbow-length gloves.

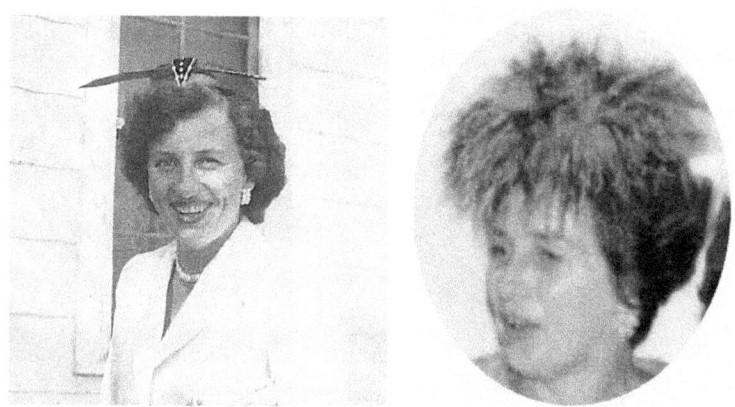

Rusty's bold Sunday hats hint that flight is imminent.

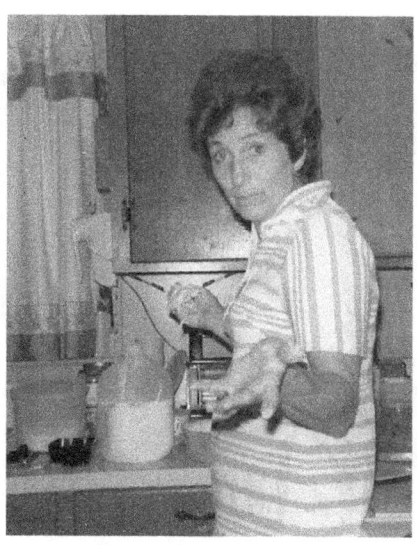

Mom' homemade biscuits were the best and she rarely permitted distractions from the task.

Rusty and grandson Tony (l) and Tony as a Navy Seabee.

Rusty (l) putting finishing touches on Aunt Virginia's (r) shiny gold lamé turban.

Rusty and Jim on their wedding day (l) and still kicking a few decades later.

Rusty and Jim as newlyweds and after fifty years together.

Andy and Andrea's Wedding
(l-r) Robert, Marsha, Barbara, Andrea, Andy, Rusty, and Jim.

Rusty dancing with her first born, Barbara.

Rusty and Josh enjoying a stroll at the nursing home.

Donna and Rusty exchange smiles.

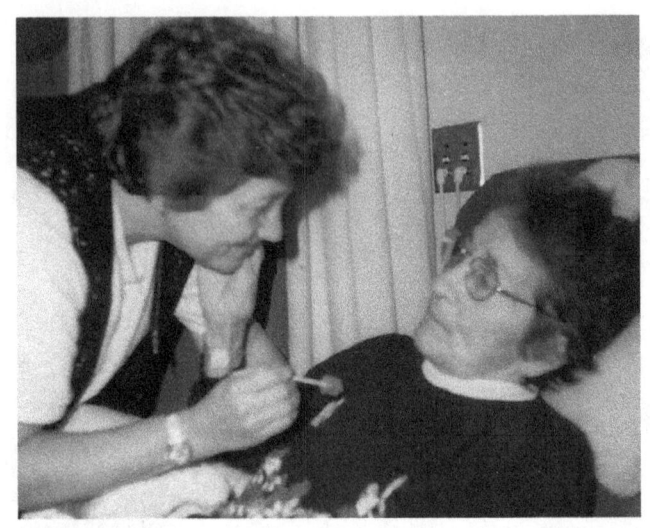

The author enjoys a pat on the face from Rusty.

Forever in our hearts…

CHAPTER TWELVE

Thank God, even for the lice...

Rusty never needed a lot of sleep, not when she was healthy and the mistress of her own home – there was too much to accomplish. In bed by midnight and up before sunrise fueled her chore-driven mornings. A brief nap after lunch recharged her batteries. In the nursing home, Mom continued her habit of early afternoon naps but she maintained no regular sleeping habits otherwise. Night time wanderings took her in and out of the rooms inhabited by her fellow residents at odd hours. For those facing lonely, sleepless nights, Mom's visits were a welcome break. Despair occupies the eternity before daybreak and accompanies acute, long-term medical care. Mom stood by the bedside of new friends, held their hands and offered words of support while she kept them company. Rusty was good-hearted and generous naturally, but now she was incapable of being anything other than agreeable, sweet and helpful because the disease tempered the ego's need to be protective or seek a return on investment.

Most recipients of Mom's attention took great pleasure in the pre-dawn ministrations on their behalf. The exception was Mrs. Annas (she who rivaled Dad as most loyal Atlanta Braves fan) who was *not* a fan of interrupted sleep. To insure a restful snooze, Mrs. Annas was allowed a splash of Jim Beam before bedtime every night. She bought it, but the nurses kept it locked in their med cart and it was dispensed like a prescription. If I, like Mrs. Annas, achieve centenarian status, I intend to remember this trick. Still, Jim Beam didn't protect her from Rusty's dead of night drop-ins. Mrs. Annas informed the authorities that Mom woke her with insistent taps to the shoulder to ask if there was anything at all she needed and demanded action be taken to prevent further transgressions. I hold no ill will toward Mrs.

Annas. In fact, because I have sleep issues myself I totally empathize with her and would not relish being awakened at the whim of another resident. As a deterrent to Mom's wandering ways, a detachable cloth band was velcroed across the doorway to Mrs. Annas' bedroom and displayed the words:

WARNING - DO NOT ENTER

The message was too subtle for Mom. And Velcro, quite frankly, is a feeble obstacle for keeping Rusty out of forbidden spaces. A more effective solution to this problem was needed. Perhaps cloistered within the confines of the Alzheimer section? The locked door to the *400 Club*, the euphemistic name of the Alzheimer's unit in the rear wing of the facility, taunted me each time I passed it. I glanced at the sign out of the corner of my eye as if it were a snake-haired gorgon that would turn me to stone if I dared to regard it boldly. I often sensed the icy hand of fate clutching at me, beckoning me through its portal into another world. A code pad, positioned shoulder-height on the wall beside the electronic doors, stood between anyone wanting to get in *to* or out *of* that world. I had no desire to have this particular combination of numbers at my command even though our decision to move Mom and Dad into Willow Lake was based on this particular specialized service. Whatever lay beyond those doors terrified me so I swatted the notion away like a pesky fly.

Mom kept the residents on their toes, and also gave the staff a run for their money. Literally. Mom was wily when she decided she wanted something. I thought Alzheimer's would have diminished her advanced level of cunning strategy, but perhaps her actions were more instinctive than premeditated. However it was conceived, when Mom wanted to have a wander outside on her own she found a way to do it. Attempts to escape were successful when Mom accompanied visitors – completely unknown to her – as they exited the building, mixing with them, making small talk with them, and walking away from the nursing home with them until an official tracked her down and returned her to safety. Wandering is a real problem for individuals who have Alzheimer's; sufferers can be gone in a flash without the ability to retrace their steps back home again. This is because Alzheimer's robs the brain of the ability to place objects, buildings and places into context with the larger world or to understand relationships and connections. You may recognize that you are either in Neiman Marcus or your daughter's home but not be capable of conceiving in your mind that her house is a half mile from your own with two left turns and two right turns between them. A person with Alzheimer's disease can no longer think abstractly to connect-the-dots. I call it the out-of-sight out-of-mind phenomenon. It's similar to an infant brain that is not yet capable at that developmental level to understand 'Object Permanence'. When a two-year-old child watches a ball roll under the sofa, to the child the ball no longer exists. If the child witnesses a toy train enter a tunnel, he is surprised to see another train materialize at the other end because to him, the train going in and the train coming out are different entities. What takes place in the gap when the train is out of sight, cannot yet be imagined and therefore does not exist. The same was true for Mom. If she did not see it, it did not exist. We were lucky that Rusty never ventured very far from the nursing home. The beauty of the landscaped grounds held her attention and kept her close. Nevertheless, responsible parties running the facility suggested that Mom be fitted with an ankle device that tripped an aggravating alarm when she walked through the door so she could be fetched back safely. I didn't fault Rusty for wanting to escape this place, but we agreed to have her 'tagged' anyway.

Mom displayed great depths of sadness over losing Dad but it never impeded her desire to be helpful within her new world. Being useful while in great emotional pain was not new behavior for Rusty even before this disease exercised its power grab. She had lost two parents before celebrating her twentieth birthday. She outlived her only sister and only brother, her first born son and her husband. She had lost her home, her freedom, and was losing her mind. Some small miracle allowed Mom to survive great personal loss and continue to minister to others. I envied her inner strength and fortitude but the sadness reflected in her eyes broke my heart. I saw the spark that made Rusty's heart tick being snuffed out. I watched Mom run down like an old pendulum clock that someone neglected to wind. I hated how quiet she had become and how she didn't have access to words to describe her feelings. Her grief was most apparent to me when I was with her at dinnertime. Often, she forgot that Dad was gone and went in search of him to make sure he had eaten his supper. She still saved packs of crackers for him. But she couldn't find him... my poor Momma. What could I do to help her at this stage? Not long before (*it had been less than four months since Dad's stroke*) I desperately wanted to shrug off the caregiver role as a burdensome yoke. I now moved into a new phase to find a way forward in this epic journey. I was doing nothing different but my outlook changed. Caring for Mom became my calling and my purpose.

I was not alone in my dedication to Mom. The CNAs who worked the night shift fell in love with Rusty, as did the day shift employees, but the night shift folks had more flexibility in the time they were able to shower on Mom particularly. June, who was assigned to Mom during second shift, continued including Mom in her cigarette breaks each night before changing her into pajamas and getting her ready for bed. The extra attention Mom received from the nursing assistants pleased me, their personal touch made a difference in the institutional setting. The connection Mom had with her caregivers and the depth of the loving care they returned to her in this sterile environment provided Mom a small island of pleasure in a sea of heartache.

When I was free after work, I drove faithfully to the nursing home. I had no energy for extracurricular activities so most of my evenings were indeed free. As I walked through the front entrance and down the hallway to find Mom, there was nothing finer than seeing my mother's face brighten when she caught sight of me. Her greeting never varied. *"There you are!"* she exclaimed as if she had just won an epic game of hide-and-seek. It was a reward of no small value.

On my own time, I was incapable of holding a significant thought in my head. My attention span could only have been measured using the precision of nanotechnology. Reading was out of the question. I couldn't focus. I could, however, look at pretty pictures. Magazines with colorful photographs of delightful gardens became a staple in my literary diet. I took the magazines to share with Mom. I thought it was important to engage her mind. I had taken a fairly simple jigsaw puzzle in with me previously as entertainment for us to enjoy together because she had enjoyed solving them once.

Quiz time. What is the word we associate with putting puzzle pieces together? *Solve.*

And what capacity was Mom losing rather rapidly? *The capacity to* solve. Did I make this connection? *Why no, I didn't.* And yet looking at beautiful renderings of flowery vistas would be appealing, right? *Wrong!* Mom wanted nothing to do with the intrinsically passive nature of gawking at a photographed thing that merely represents something else. It's also possible that since Alzheimer's distorts the individual's depth perception, Mom was prevented from fully experiencing the colorful photographs as reproductions of blossoms and flower gardens. Whatever the reasons for her disinterest, Mom also lacked the capacity to engage in the social convention of pretending to look at the magazine illustrations solely for the purpose of appeasing me. She wanted nothing more or less than to be active and participating in the here-and-now of her life. Grief be damned! Mom lived in the moment and she was interested in people - people who were living and breathing and animated with molecules and cells and personalities.

While carrying the accumulated sadness of so much pain, Rusty somehow remained interested in life. I, on the other hand, was interested in escaping from life. I wanted to participate in her Zen-like emersion of each moment but I couldn't stop myself from wallowing in my own emotional pain. My brain dwelled in the past (*what has happened*) while also thinking forward (*what may happen in the future*). I held both of these notions in my head as I tried to process what was going on in the present. I was exhausted from the enormity of such self-manufactured anxiety. If I could have adopted Mom's outlook, the same outlook that Phantom and Dickens tried diligently to teach me from their doggie world, perhaps I would have realized that what truly mattered was right in front of me. I was with Rusty, and Rusty was safe.

I was incapable of adopting a Zen practice of that scale. Instead, I grappled with the circumstances as I perceived them. Namely, my brother was dead, my father was dead, and I despised having Mom in a nursing home. I couldn't sort it all out or place these events into any kind of larger perspective. My heart ached with every beat as it was being ripped from my chest. It didn't occur to me then that coming to terms with these changes in my life was possible.

At work and at home, I felt isolated and I continued to exist inside that plastic bubble of insulation which distorted the rest of the world. Life outside the bubble moved at light-speed; I couldn't keep up. Not physically. Not mentally. *They* were lively and quick. I wasn't. There is no detergent strong enough to scrub off the stain of suicide. If anyone touched me or my world, the world where suicides take place and fathers die and mothers have Alzheimer's, they too may become infected with this disease I carried - the disease we dodge as long as we can - *sorrow*.

From my new vantage point, I observed two worlds separated by a thin thread. In one world humans believed the odds are with them and that nothing bad can happen to them if they are careful. In this world, tragedy only happens to other people. In the other world, the one that I now inhabited, evidence proved otherwise. Only after being introduced to this other world did I comprehend the anguish of loss. A select few brave friends entered this garbled, mixed-up world of mine and walked the daunting path with me. I found that a couple of supportive family members and a handful of good friends are the essential keys to surviving an epic emotional blow-out like I was having. Patience and love make the best medicine for whatever wretched conditions we find ourselves in. Patience, because recovery takes a long time. Love, because it heals us.

Even though I wished to reconnect with normal life, it is probably a kindness to the one who is wandering through the wilderness of misery that the two worlds intersect rarely because when they do, it is not pretty. For instance, one morning, as I walked past the university library on the way to my office, I crossed paths with a colleague from the history department. She was congenial and asked me how I was doing.

"Pretty well," I said. "Losing Dad so soon after my brother is difficult for my family and me but we're doing the best we can."

"Your dad?!?" she challenged me. She looked confused. "I thought it was your mother who died."

"No, it was my father."

"Oh, I thought it was your mother."

"I'm sorry. It was my father."

Why I believed I needed to apologize for the inaccuracy of this person's information is something I cannot begin to grasp.

"Well, I thought it was your mother."

I was afraid our *pas de deux* would continue indefinitely and I had no intention of being late for work because of it so I said my goodbyes. I had no doubts about who had and had not died in my family and quite frankly didn't relish being questioned about it. I left her there, looking perplexed. Two worlds colliding.

Merely surviving the death of a loved one is not enough. Several mandatory duties must be seen to on behalf of the departed one. One task in particular is filing the Last Will and Testament. Mom and Dad had few remaining assets but Dad's Will had to be probated and I was the Executor. I took a day off from work and drove into town to Government Center. Donna met me at the Clerk of Court office, Division of Estates and Special Proceedings. Her presence helped neutralize the anxiety I always feel when dealing with authority. The sign on the door read: *First Come, First Served.* Fair enough. I wrote my name on the sign-up sheet and was called in due time by a gentleman who tagged *Esquire* onto the end of his name. He wasn't a lawyer by profession as one might assume. I asked. But he occupied a position in an online Knighthood organization that extended him the right and privilege to use Esquire on his name plate. I was intrigued. I secretly wondered if there was a group for failed or thwarted Mad Scientists who had been cut down in their prime, and what that title would be.

As he read Dad's Will (and he read every word, from beginning to end) the Esquire unsheathed a rather wicked looking fountain pen from an official-looking receptacle and brandished it as if it were Excalibur itself. He advised me that the next step was to place a notice in the newspaper. The point of this is to notify anyone to whom Mr. Burris owed money to come forward, thus allowing me 'to resolve all claims that may reside against his estate'. Last thing, the Esquire asked me to place my hand on the Holy Bible and swear that I would fulfill the Executor's responsibilities to the letter, so help me God. I personally have no moral conflict with swearing to God on a Bible promising that I really and truly mean to stand by my word, but I believed I should question the unspoken consequences that befall any of us who renege on the promises for which we take this oath.

"Or else?" I asked him.

"Sorry?"

"I promise to execute my father's Will to the letter of the law, so help me God... or else what? What will happen to me if I say I will, and then I don't?"

"Yes, you promise to carry out your father's wishes as expressed in his Last Will and Testament."

"And, what if I don't?"

"You have to."

"But, what if I don't?" I sat up straighter and continued. "What is the penalty if I don't do what I say I'm going to do? Are you going to send me to jail? Because, frankly, life has taken a belt to my behind for so long that any penalty you impose on me cannot be worse than what I've lived through or will hurt me more than I've already been hurt."

"Ma'am, I'm sorry but-but-but... "

My deviation from the script frightened him. An Esquire Knight should be bolder. Since I was incapable of shutting up, I butted in to halt his timid and hesitant reply.

"You are asking me to swear to something. And I'm asking you, 'What's the point if there are no consequences? I'm asking you what these consequences are. What will *you* do to *me* if I don't fulfill the thing I'm swearing to? My dad has no worldly goods. He has no debts. There's nothing for me to abscond with. What can you do to me that can scare me?' "

Donna touched my arm to calm me down and bring me back to the real world. She indicated telepathically to the Esquire that I was essentially harmless and not normally aggressively hostile. And besides, in my defense, there was no real need for him to be alarmed because a huge desk stood between us. And let's not forget that he was a guy. In fact, a fairly large guy. I stand five-foot three-inches with loafers on. He had youth and vigor on his side. *And*, he wielded that medieval fountain pen rather threateningly. It looked pretty sharp and dangerous if he took a notion to poke it in my eye. I don't know why I terrified him so. Surely he met unhinged clients and deranged heiresses every day in his line of work.

"It's the law," he squeaked. "By law, you, as the Executor, have to execute your father's will according to that law. You agreed to be the Executor, right?"

I was baffled by my combative behavior. I stood to gain

nothing whether I followed the letter of the law or not. But I was receiving some intangible payoff by provoking this innocent adversary who played a reluctant role in my impromptu dramatic scene. So I persisted. I wanted the truth and I meant to get it.

"I understand that part. But what if I don't? What will happen to me? What does the law say is the penalty? Will you send me to jail? Because I'm okay with that. In fact, jail looks real good to me right now. I don't look bad in orange, and sitting around in flip-flops watching Oprah sounds like a delightful way to spend my days. No decisions will be expected from me and if I act out and get solitary confinement, well, I have to admit that I would welcome the peace and quiet in my life at the moment. Do you have anything worse you can threaten me with?"

"I don't think you would get jail time. I think there's only a fine..." He finally addressed my burning need to know my punishment if I failed to carry out my duties.

A fine? How absurd. And, disappointing. Paying a fine was worse than jail time. I swore the oath. He breathed a sigh of relief.

The next point on my list of duties on Dad's behalf was to notify the Social Security office of Dad's death and apply for the *one-time-lump-sum-death-benefit* of $255 for Mom, the beneficiary of that bounty. I went on my own to this appointment, having purged my impulse to make a scene with perfect strangers. The interview went smoothly. Although the death benefit is, by any standard, outrageously low, the $255 would help defray the costs of Mom's few and simple needs.

When that deed was accomplished, it was time to get Mom qualified for Dad's veteran's benefits to which she was entitled as his widow. I had been working with the Veterans Administration since my first discussion with the Department of Social Services right after Dad's stroke. The Social Worker assigned to Mom and Dad's case suggested that since Dad was a Navy veteran of World War II, he qualified for VA assistance and the assistance received from the VA is considered separate from DSS qualifications. In other words, any benefits he was entitled to from the VA (an amount that would be approximately $200 per month) would not reduce his Medicaid benefits. The monthly VA benefit would be available to pay for services not covered by Medicaid; services such as dental care, podiatry care, haircuts, pajamas, toothpaste, or a sweater. I applied to the VA on Dad's behalf in early March – three months before his death. It was now the middle of June. The VA dragged its feet so long that it was too late to help Dad at all. Mom was entitled to widow's benefits, though, and I meant to get them for her, one way or another.

I nudged and prodded the VA to make a decision but with no favorable outcome. I called or wrote to them weekly to request an update on the status of Mom's application. I assured the individuals at the VA that if more documents were vital to their decision, I would expedite their delivery. As days and weeks and months ticked by, I began to suspect that the Veterans Administration not only hated our nation's veterans but also supported the policy of simply out-waiting its applicants in hopes that they will die before a payout need ever be issued. It worked in Dad's case. Would there be enough time for the benefits to help Mom? I was upset and I was angry. I wrote to our Senator, who was Jesse Helms at that time. Surely to God his staff knew how to nudge the VA toward a resolution of this application on a constituent's behalf. I never heard back from the man. Or from anyone in his office.

After one of my prodding telephone calls to the VA office, followed by yet another attempt to talk to Jesse Helms or an associate of his, and hitting yet another dead-end, I hung up the receiver and did the only sensible thing. I cried. I was angry. I was frustrated. And I was exhausted. I honestly had never been so tired in my entire life. The only rational thing to do in that situation is to cry. So I did. Precisely at that same moment, after receiving a subconscious psychic message, my sister called me. She detected the sniffling tone in my voice and immediately demanded an explanation. I told her the dilemma I faced and she said, "Let me call him. I'll get back to you."

I knew at once that all would work out in our favor. My sister does not take 'no' for an answer. Our nickname for her is Bubba. On this day she was promoted several levels above Bubba to the distinguished title of the *Bubbanator*. Before the week was out, a VA representative contacted me and made an appointment to come to my office at my convenience to complete the application process. I called Barbara at home that night.

"What did you *do*?" I asked her. I'm always in awe of my

sister's efficiency.

"Simple," she said. "I tried to talk to someone in Jesse Helms and John Edwards offices - I got nowhere fast - then I talked to my representative, Jo Anne Davis. She tracked down Jesse Helms in person and told him,

> *I understand one of your constituents came to you for help and you haven't been able to come through for her. I want to offer my assistance to you because it appears that you have not been able to inspire the folks at the VA office to help this woman acquire the benefits earned by her father who fought bravely in the Second World War and which is due to her widowed mother. I would be delighted to extend to you the resources of my office and those of the Great Commonwealth of Virginia and place them at your disposal on this family's behalf. Please let me know what we can do to help you out.*

Mom began receiving her widow's benefit the following month. It made a difference.

Another important duty that must be dispatched after the death of a loved one is selecting the headstone for marking the site of their burial. For Robert, we made efficient use of the polished faceted surface on the hunk of granite we chose for him. On it we had his name, birth and death dates carved. Below that, we borrowed the last stanza of Robert Louis Stevenson's poem "Requiem": *Home is the sailor, home from sea, and the hunter home from the hill.* These words were appropriate for our own Robert, both a sailor and a hunter. The bronze plaque at his feet informs passers-by of his Navy affiliation.

The historian in me enjoys a quiet amble through cemeteries, whether it's looking at family plots at local churches or visiting renowned monuments in Père Lachaise or Highgate. Looking at the markers and reading the epitaphs engraved upon them connect us to the past. Their messages tell us a little bit about that person's life and for those of us who make the time and effort to give them attention we are rewarded by that connection. The Burris family wanted to do its part in leaving a sentiment on which future generations could ponder. After some consideration, Barbara, Andy and I agreed on the engraving for Dad's headstone: *Nothing's So Sacred As Honor And Nothing's So Loyal As Love.*

The verse was borrowed from a beautiful poem by Alice Cary called "Nobility" and had been made famous by its appearance on the stone that now marks Wyatt Earp's grave. The phrase was fitting for Jim and mirrored his own philosophy of life. Dad made a habit of listening to his conscience when making decisions rather than selling out to the highest bidder or taking a popularity poll. If we had considered an epitaph for Mom alone, it would read: People Don't Drink Enough Water. Jim went first, so he got first dibs. Since he believed that his greatest accomplishment in life was his family and the love he had for us, we paid homage to that achievement on the reverse side of the headstone by having the date of his and Mom's wedding engraved on it, followed by the names of their four children.

During the days and weeks following Dad's death, he was in my thoughts constantly and I indulged in some good old fashioned reminiscing as memories effervesced to the surface of my consciousness like delightful little champagne bubbles. The first Father's Day I celebrated without my father appeared two weeks after his death. In his lifetime, Dad rarely said the words, *I love you*, but I appreciated the many benevolent and generous acts of kindness he showered on me. Actions do speak louder than words. Dad was dependable and he provided for his family. Without pause, Dad accepted me and my siblings as we were. It never crossed his mind to shape us or change us from anything other than exactly who we grew to be.

What Dad lacked in demonstrative words, he more than made up for in deeds and while my grandmother sat in her parlor hoping for me to take to lace and crinolines, the foundations of little-girl fashion in my early years, Dad took me to the Army-Navy surplus store to buy me those hiking boots vital to my Girl Scout adventures. He bought me a pair of baseball cleats that I wore proudly to my softball games when I was a teenager and an awesome softball glove that he also bought for me before providing its replacement when the original glove was stolen. As I write this, it sounds as if my relationship with my father was a material one but nothing is farther from the truth. Other than their mortgage, Mom and Dad bought only what they could afford to pay for. There was no piling up of credit card debt for these two survivors of the Great Depression. What touched my heart was that these items were not usual purchases for a young girl in the 1950s and 1960s but that never mattered to my dad. He saw my interests and he honored them as elements of who I am – not what I ought to be.

Rarely were we reprimanded by Dad. He didn't try to teach us lessons, although he encouraged each of us to learn lessons from our experiences; teaching and learning being different only in who is engaged in the action. On this fatherless Father's Day, I strolled down memory lane even while I was aware that Mom was unable to do this very thing herself. A host of dinnertime conversations floated through my cache of childhood memories. For example, whenever the topic of hunting wild game came up as an issue to be discussed, as it often did, Dad defended his love of the sport that yielded our family many meals by proclaiming, *something must die so something may live*. It's not easy to argue with that logic. Although many times, after ammunition was purchased, licenses acquired, and travel time and expenses accounted for, the hunting of deer or quail yielded little in the way of providing economical meals for a family of six. Nevertheless, Dad was unapologetic toward his inefficient supply of meals. Often, when Dad, Robert and Andy were out on a hunt, Dad was caught red-handed by one of my brothers, leaning against a pine tree, snacking on a Kit-Kat candy bar as deer, within ear-shot of Dad's noisy wrapper-wrangling, skittered off into the forest - safely out of range.

Once I asked Dad what attracted him to hunting animals and he told me, "It's not just the *hunting* I like, I like being outside, in nature."

"You could be outside in nature without a loaded gun," I replied. "Maybe take a camera, shoot photographs instead of Bambi or Thumper," I suggested helpfully.

"Can't eat a photograph," he stated firmly.

"No, it's not as edible as a Kit-Kat, that's for sure."

My dad and brothers brought home a great deal of wild game over the years and our family enjoyed Mom's culinary proficiency in preparing tasty dishes because of their accomplishments. But that fact never stopped us from poking fun at Dad and claiming that animals are never safer than when ol' Jim is in the forest with his firearm and a two-day supply of Kit-Kats.

Our dinner table topics ran the gamut from religion to politics to social issues of the day. Many times Dad quizzed us on the capitals of the states, but he was always comfortable introducing controversial topics to his children for debate as well. Some of the things he came out with made me cock my head in wonderment. He posed questions like: *If Cain murdered his brother Able (sons of Adam and Eve - the first two people God created on earth according to Genesis) and then went off to the land of Nod to marry, who did he marry?* He tossed out riddles to exercise our brains and test our logical reasoning skills. I remember the classic riddle: *As I was going to St. Ives I met a man with seven wives. Each wife had seven sacks, each sack had seven cats, and each cat had seven kits. Kits, cats, sacks and wives - how many were going to St. Ives?*

Jim countered any frivolous complaint we made by responding with the old Persian adage, *I cried because I had no shoes, then I met a man who had no feet.* That one made us sit up and appreciate what we had. I would have heeded Jim's philosophy for counting my blessings now if I could have identified them, or if I felt blessed. Blessings are not absent because we cannot recognize them – I know that now.

I doubt I was the only member of our family clinging to the consoling nature of nostalgic daydreams of Jim in his robust years but Mom could not tread in those soothing waters. To her, the simple fact was, her husband was gone. And it hurt. His absence created a huge void in her life. Dad was her focus, her purpose, and no amount of caring for other residents filled that emptiness in her. I justified Dad's departure with a few well-placed stand-by clichés like: *he's in a better place now,* or *it was his time to go,* or *at least he had a long and full life.* I did not want other people to parrot these platitudes to me, but I sure didn't mind wrapping myself in them like a warm blanket. Mom didn't possess the ability to deceive herself. *I do not want to hear anybody say that 'this is for the best',* is what Mom said to me on the morning of Dad's death. Her words rattled inside my head reminding me that the same trite suggestions I clung to were useless to allay her suffering.

There were days I dreaded going to visit Mom. As much as I rationalized the necessity of having her live in a nursing home, it was distressing to see where she would live out her life. I was not naive, I knew that Mom's condition would only get worse and then she would die. This is what we had to look forward to. As

Peggy Lee had sung when I was in the ninth grade, *Is That All There Is?* If so, I had to find a way to enjoy what Mom still had to give us. I was at a loss for how to accomplish this feat, though. After each visit, I gave her a heart-breaking 'good-bye' knowing that in a few hours (or even minutes) she wouldn't remember that I had been there with her. She was not able to retain the comfort and assurances I offered her when we were together. And I did give her comfort. I saw it in her eyes as I sat with her, held her hand, rubbed her shoulders and hugged her. It was a comfort to me too, just to be with her. The only difference – I took the feeling with me and recalled it at will. In Mom's world, the exchange never took place. In her world, she was alone and abandoned and wondered where I had been for such a long time. She couldn't hold on to any of that comfort or pull it out later to use when darkness descended and sleep was elusive. The burden of so much sadness hastened the rate of her forgetfulness.

Alzheimer's disease hungrily devours the memory of even our most precious experiences. Because the disease savaged Mom's mental capacity I struggled to devise a plan to ease the heartache that bashed Mom's senses each time she had a flash of awareness that Robert and Dad were dead. When my sister came to town for a visit, Mom sat her down, grasped her hands and said, "I've got very bad news I need to tell you, honey. Your father has died."

I began to wonder if it would be kinder to Mom if we discontinued the Aricept dosage and let the disease have its way with her. If the nature of the disease is to steal memories, then having it steal the memory of these great losses was a small compensation for having this stupid illness in the first place. Like Dad, Mom fought hard to 'stay' with us but the battle was taking its toll on her and it was absurd to perpetuate the pain.

I didn't want to let her go. I did not want to lose what remained of the personality that was my mother. I would have done anything, agreed to any task, if it arrested this disease from exacting further penalties on Mom's faculties. If I had the power, I would have moved heaven and earth to turn the calendar back four months. But whereas keeping Mom in limbo would comfort me, it was cruel to force her to dwell in a never-ending time-loop of Groundhog Day repeats as she hunted for Dad, only to find out he had died. Every day.

Alzheimer's was getting the upper hand. Mom had no freedom, no autonomy. She was observed, every hour of every day, and watched for any odd behavior that might require helpful responses. Barbara, Andy and I discussed the benefits and drawbacks of taking Mom off the Aricept. Once Mom was no longer taking the prescription, her cognitive decline would accelerate. There was no going back if we decided later that we had made a mistake. The benefits were in Mom's favor. The sacrifice would be ours. I told Mom's physician. He assured us this was the best path. Once again we were in accord as we moved to shorten the *Long Goodbye* to our mother.

At night, before going to sleep, I tried to pray. But that well of comfort was bone dry. What was I supposed to pray for anyway? In the dark, I groped for something to be thankful for. Of course I appreciated the love and friendships in my life. I had a job and my supervisor granted me the flexibility to see to Rusty's needs with no fear of losing my position with the university. Although I did little in the way of giving my body nutrition and exercise, it rewarded me with generally good health anyway. I had the desire to count my blessings, but not the power to do so even though Mom and Dad taught us the importance of a glass-half-full point of view, but the previous few months presented the greatest challenge of my life. I was not sure that I was strong enough to endure what was happening here. I sought examples of everyday citizens who had overcome great odds to give me strength to carry on.

One story I recalled from my young adulthood stood out and inspired me. Corrie Ten Boom described the events that resulted from her family's involvement with the Dutch underground during the Nazi invasion of the Netherlands in her book and the movie made from that book entitled, *The Hiding Place*. The Ten Boom family's Christian faith led them to hide Jewish refugees in their home to facilitate their escape from deportation and the almost certain death in Hitler's ovens. The Ten Boom family was ultimately captured and the sisters were sent to Ravensbrück as punishment for their part in aiding the Jews. In Corrie's story, one exchange that takes place between her and her sister, Betsie, stuck with me all the years since I first saw the film. Betsie maintained the convictions of her faith and found it in her heart to thank God for everything in her life. She found ways to value her experiences, while Corrie found it impossible to thank a God who allows such injustices to happen. Corrie's faith faltered as she was tested to her limits and she regretted that she couldn't maintain the same positive spirit as Betsie. The scene depicted in the film that was indelibly written into my brain portrayed a poignant exchange between the sisters. They and their bunkmates had brought their dinner back to the barracks to eat after standing in a long line for it and after a grueling day of hard physical labor in extremely cold temperatures. As they sat on their lice-infested beds to eat the bowl of watery soup, Betsie gave quiet thanks to God for it.

"He doesn't expect thanks for this!" Corrie responded.

"It's warm," Betsie insisted. "And I'm thankful for every moment we can be together. We can at least lie down tonight and rest."

Corrie refused to be drawn into the atmosphere of appreciation that Betsie tried to create. She had seen too many brutal acts committed against the other prisoners by the guards and unfair treatment of innocent individuals who shared the sisters' fate in the camp.

"I won't be grateful for the lice," Corrie snapped back.

"God doesn't make mistakes," Betsie answered with unquestioning faith.

Just then, another prisoner addressed the group. She was the woman who was savvy in how to work the camp system in hopes of increasing the odds of survival. As she cut the hair of one of the other inmates to help combat the effects of the lice infestation she said, "Lice, you'll learn to love the little darlings. The guards won't step foot in *this* lice pit. Past this door, we can do anything!"

Betsie leaned over and whispered in Corrie's ear, "Even the lice."

Because of this disgusting parasite, the guards did not come into the women's barracks to molest them. And because they were safe behind their door, the women had the freedom to create supportive communal groups in their barracks where they interacted, discussed topics of interest to them, and held Bible readings. These freedoms kept their morale up more than otherwise would have been possible for them. In time, Corrie recognized and accepted that suffering does not mean that God does not love us, but at times we have to accept circumstances we do not understand. And because of Betsie's guidance, she realized that "God didn't make this place. Men did."

I honestly do not compare the challenges my family faced to the ordeal confronted by the Ten Boom family that I describe here, but I was not reluctant to use the inspiration of their actions to encourage me as I attempted to meet my own challenges with a bit of grace and courage as they had done. The lesson I learned from Corrie Ten Boom's story is important. I personally failed to find much to be grateful for at this precise time in my life, but Corrie and Betsie's bravery emboldened me to search for a way to *thank God, even for the lice.*

CHAPTER THIRTEEN

They come to see me in my dreams...

The Administrator for Willow Lake Healthcare Center stopped me in the hallway as I walked toward the dining room to have supper with Mom.

"I'd like you to start thinking about moving Lottie to the 400 Club." Beth used the common nickname for the Alzheimer's unit. The various halls were uninspiringly otherwise named 100, 200, and so forth. She did not use Mom's own nickname, Rusty. The facility's policy was to call residents by their legal first name. At Willow Lake, signs with first and last name of each occupant were posted outside the bedroom doors. For my parents, who never went by their first names, this policy could be a little confusing. The staff called Mom, *Lottie* and Dad, *Leroy*. Mom and Dad often failed to respond because they had no idea who was being addressed.

In Mom's case, using different names for various stages and distinctive personalities of her life, made *Lottie* appropriate at this time. Lottie was her mother's given name so the family called Mom LaVern to make a distinction. Mom's friends used Rusty and that's the name I most associate with Mom. This latest moniker, applied to Mom's newest persona, was the person we were now getting to know and was rather fitting after all.

I did not readily welcome Beth's suggestion to move *Lottie* to the Alzheimer's unit but she offered the words with such compassion that the stark reality of her meaning hurt less. I hoped I had misunderstood her words but when I needed to lean against the wall for support, I knew I comprehended precisely what her suggestion meant.

"Why in the world would I want to think about that?" My attempt at humor was pitiful.

"It'll be a better environment for her."

The sympathy reflected in her eyes and the gentle tone in her voice soothed me but also gave me the impression that hordes of residents were lining up in front of my mother for a coveted place in this *better environment*. If I dallied, would we lose out?

"How so?" I channeled Jim as I sprinted straight to the point.

"Out here, your mother wanders in and out of residents' bedrooms. Most everyone welcomes her and they love her visits but some aren't happy and that's understandable."

I had to agree. The focus of my suspicions for Mom's impending eviction fell squarely onto the shoulders of Mrs. Annas.

"It's hard on your mother," she continued. "It's hard on her when we have to tell her that she cannot do something or we have to stop her from going wherever she wants."

I bet it is, I thought. The robust Rusty never liked being told what to do - neither did her mother, the original Lottie. And neither one of them liked to be told 'no'. But I suspected that in all honesty, the difficulties lay within the CNA population whose job it was to herd Mom away from un-friendly fire.

"Mary Ann already takes Lottie with her to the Alzheimer's unit during the day," Beth continued. "She asks her to *help* her, which your mother enthusiastically agrees to do."

Mary Ann was one of our favorite CNAs. She had been attentive to Dad and was now as dedicated to Mom. *Mary Ann's a genius,* I reflected.

"She gets along well with the residents in there. And, believe it or not, Lottie will actually have more freedom in the 400 Club. Even though the door is kept locked, she will be free to come and go as she pleases behind those doors without restrictions. Also, we have a nice range of activities for our residents with Alzheimer's that keep them engaged and interested and active."

"Okay," I began to yield, reluctantly. "What else?"

"You can continue to visit her any time of the day or night, of course, and you can still have dinner with her as you do now. The residents have their own dining room and their diets are monitored more there than in the main dining room where your mom has no supervision over her meals. You can take your mother with you on excursions anytime you want, you'll just have to sign her out. One thing that makes a big difference between being in the 400 Club and being on this hall is that there is a higher ratio of staff to residents there, so Lottie will get more attention." Beth paused, choosing her words carefully. "She'll be safe, Marsha. She'll be safer than wandering out here on her own. The rooms are nice back there. I can take you in to see them now before you make your decision."

I nibbled at the bait grudgingly, not yet ready to swallow the hook. I declined the invitation. Beth was good at her job though and before I knew what hit me she reeled me in with, "Your mom loves gardening and helping with chores. We'll see to it that she has some garden soil and plants she can tend to. She can help fold freshly laundered clothes and we can even give her a broom."

Work! Nothing engaged Rusty Burris more completely than having chores to do. One month after Dad died, Mom was an official card-carrying member of the 400 Club.

I memorized the digits to decode the keypad located at the entrance to the Alzheimer's unit – an ability the residents on the other side of the door no longer possessed. Mary Ann handled the moving arrangements, transferring Mom's belongings to the new room and settling her in. All I had to do was learn the code since knowing the precise combination and sequence of numbers was the only means for unlocking the passageway. Only then could I pass through those mysterious double doors to visit my mother who was now concealed and isolated from the general population. Locked in or locked out - what's the difference? Relocating Mom was for her own good, and for her own safety. I held tight to this notion like a tick on a hound dog.

The image of Mom's kind and loving face was with me always. She was never far from the forefront of my thoughts. Was she comfortable? Was she eating enough? Was she resting? Was she lonely? With Rusty in new living quarters, I stepped up surveillance and monitored her every move until I became more familiar with the 'club' culture. I could not have been more protective of Rusty if she had been a fragile and delicate hot house orchid - which she had *never* been. A hardy hybrid tea rose, maybe. Complete with thorns. But Mom's steady descent into the Alzheimer's prison-of-hell left me with few choices. To allay my reservations about the move, I put a positive spin on it. In this, the latest chapter of our nursing home odyssey, I convinced myself that the new bedroom, although no different to the untrained eye from the previous one, was infinitely more inviting. It occupied one corner of the large space that encompassed the Alzheimer's area. Mom's bed was by the window which overlooked a patch of grass. Truly a positive sign. Chi flowed through the room unfettered bringing invisible yet vital life energy in a Feng Shui way. I got good vibes - or so I believed. A bedside table held toiletries such as hairbrushes and hand lotion. These are the items valued by the residents that are taken and guarded jealously as their own if not kept locked inside the drawers. A three-foot square closet, built out into the room just inside the doorway, held Mom's summer wardrobe and a weeks-worth of undies. An *en suite* toilet and sink proved convenient for residents like Rusty who were somewhat continent still and could be encouraged to brush their teeth. Members of the 400 Club were assisted with their personal hygiene in a centrally-located bath and shower room, so individual shower stalls were unnecessary.

Mom shared this room with Karen, a lovely woman close to Mom's age. Karen's husband, Hunter, had dashing good looks, a healthy shock of white hair and a jovial disposition. He visited his wife at lunchtime since the funeral home where he worked was nearby. He arrived many times for supper too, which is how we got to know him. He was a breath of fresh air.

My visits were as frequent as before but Donna came with me more often, as she had done in the early days of our arrival. After four months in the nursing home habitat, we had adapted and we had acclimatized. In the long-term-care-hall population where we spent those months, we were veterans and with our tenure came a certain amount of familiarity and comfort with the environment, and with the residents and staff there. Now, we were the new kids on the block again; wet behind the ears and wearing the same shell-shock mask we sported upon our initial arrival. Without question, I needed Donna's moral support, and at times I needed physical assistance as well to keep me steady on my feet. As we left Mom each evening before her bedtime, we encountered the inevitable worst part of every visit - the part where we said good-bye. Farewells were unpleasant before our move and their nature assumed greater significance after it. The ugly truth was that our loved ones believed they would never see us again. Since Mom could not remember that I had been there the night before - essentially abandoning her for all eternity - she was afraid I would never visit again. It was distressing. Past and future. These were abstract concepts that could not be employed to explain that, since I visited on this particular day and the day before, it was a good bet that I would be there the next day as well. This population had only the present available to them.

One evening, before entering the code into the door pad, Donna and I contemplated that magical obstacle that stood between the normal world and the abnormal one. Just then the son of one of the residents broke through the door and rushed carelessly past us. Before the doors closed behind him, his mother attempted to follow him out. Mrs. Lambe's arms reached out to him, clawing at him, imploring him to stay with her. We stepped in front of her, responding quickly without thinking, and we guided her back inside. The busy staff then took the situation in hand and since Rusty's attentions were mercifully focused elsewhere, Donna and I slipped back out to the hallway to check on the young man. Mrs. Lambe's son was slumped to the floor of the corridor outside those damnable doors where he buried his head in his hands and wept inconsolably. We paused by his side, at a loss for what to do. We asked him if we could help in any way. He shook his head, slowly rose from his squatting position, and then ran out of the building to his car. Witnessing this man's grief haunts me. It was the outward expression of what I was feeling deep inside myself and had yet to confront.

So yes, good-byes were emotional and stressful. But the nursing assistants often found clever ways to divert our loved ones' attention without being asked to, as good kindergarten teachers do on the first day of school. It meant an easier departure and it helped greatly. The alternative was pulling away from your mother or wife or sister as she pleaded desperately to not be left alone in that place as you swear pointlessly to come back soon. *But why do you have to go? Can't you stay with me?* Tomorrow, Momma. I promise, I'll see you tomorrow at dinner.

Mom couldn't remember that I would be with her at suppertime, but she remembered that Dad and Robert had died. Not consistently, but often. So at her request, I drove her over to the cemetery one gorgeous sunny summer Saturday because she wanted to pay her respects. She was composed and serene as we loitered on our family plot. I told her the headstone for Dad was ordered and would be delivered in another week or two. She looked down at the two rectangles of red clay, not yet disguised with a healthy green comb-over of crabgrass like the older gravesites wore. Then she looked up at me, total clarity in her eyes. All her former intelligence and understanding charged to the surface of her awareness. She pulled me to her chest and wrapped her arms tightly around me. Surprised by the resurgence of a classic Rusty mannerism, familiar and yet long lost to me from lack of use, I could only stammer, "What is it Mom?"

Sadness dripped from her voice in place of the tears she seemed incapable of shedding. "Oh goodness," she said. "I've just left you with all of this to deal with, haven't I?" Rusty Burris had been a can-do person. It was not in her personality to shun responsibility or farm out unsavory tasks to anyone else.

"Don't worry, Mom. I don't mind." I absorbed her validation. That she recognized and acknowledged, even briefly, all the details that I had been handling was huge. Then I leaned on her shoulder and drank in the comfort we crave from our mothers. Another miracle. The Alzheimer's that made many sufferers fretful, suspicious and unpleasant, allowed Mom to be free and agreeable and trusting. And it *was* okay. I hated that my father and brother had passed away but I certainly did not mind taking charge of the associated arrangements for them. It was a burden I gladly shouldered for Rusty. I assured her that I had lots of help, that everybody was chipping in to do their part and that she was not to worry.

"Alright, then," she stroked my hair gently. "But it seems like so much to do."

When feeling the tug of grief as acutely as we did at that moment, there was only one course of action open to us. Food.

"Are you hungry?" I asked Mom.

"I could eat something... "

"Where do you want to have lunch, then?"

"I want to go to that restaurant where your friend from childhood works. What's her name? You've known her all your life."

"Joy."

Not the emotion. My favorite childhood friend's name is Joy.

"Yes! Joy!"

I called Donna and she met us at the sports bar in Newell. When we arrived, Joy rushed over to Mom for a happy reunion. Only a few weeks had passed since we sat at the same table and the fact that Mom recalled Joy being there and wanted to see her again meant we were having a very lucid day indeed.

Mom's random coherent moments did not prevent me from worrying about her. Dad's absence in her life meant she no longer had him to look after as part of her daily routine. Without him Mom was lonely and the move to a new environment did little to allay those feelings. I voiced this concern to Donna one evening and she told me, "Jim is now a Guardian Angel for Rusty. He'll watch over her while she's here and then come for her when it's time."

I liked the idea of Dad keeping watch over Mom. I found the suggestion comforting. And then, as if to punctuate the belief that Dad continued to be present in our lives, two things happened immediately.

First, Donna received a visit from Dad within the context of a dream and held the following short conversation with him. "Jim," she told him, "you looked so peaceful when you died... ." In his characteristic application of brevity Dad responded, "It was."

And second, since I apparently needed another nudge to convince me that Jim was still very much connected to his family, Mom validated the notion during my next visit to see her. We entered the 400 Club at dinnertime as usual and instead of finding Mom seated at a table waiting for her meal, we saw her sitting off by herself. Her face reflected the desolation that recent circumstances had thrust at her. I embraced her tenderly then stooped down at her feet to look directly into her eyes.

"What is it, Mom?" I asked her.

"I miss your father. And your brother." She said this as she looked down at her shoes.

"I know you do. I'm so sorry."

"But they visit me." She looked up at me just then. A spark of life returned.

"They do?" I was surprised. I was not aware that Mom should be subject to hallucinations yet.

"Yes," she smiled. "They come to see me in my dreams."

As Mom said these words I got goose bumps, which is the

universal sign that a curiously strange truth has resonated with us. The scientific term is *Cutis Anserina* (I had to look this up) and it's where bumps pop up on our arms or legs involuntarily as a reaction to being cold or feeling the strong emotions of fear and awe. May I interject here that I have never experienced the sensation of being cold inside of a nursing home. And I was certainly not frightened by my mother's words. That leaves awe. As the hair on my arms stood on end, I knew Mom had not *dreamed* of Robert and Dad. I knew that her description was precise and accurate: Dad and Robert visit her in her dreams....

The value of dreams has great importance for us. Generally speaking, dreams are a series of conceptions that we experience in our minds while sleeping. Within these impressions we may see, hear, touch, and smell with such tangible realism that we feel as though we have actually had the experience. There are several hypotheses concerning where exactly in the brain dreams originate but it is commonly accepted that dreams occur within the unconscious mind – the part of the mind where we are not aware of thoughts, opinions and ideas. It is believed that ninety-five percent of our dreams are forgotten after we wake up. Therefore, the ones we remember must be pretty important. For the most part dreams come to us spontaneously and can be generally classified into three groups: daily dramas being played out during REM sleep; a symbolic treatment of problems which when examined can help us heal wounds inflicted on us by circumstances; or an experience of paranormal events. As John A. Sanford states in his book, *Dreams: God's Forgotten Language*, perhaps dreams provide the best condition for messages to be exchanged between the spirit world and the physical world.

I favor clear objective evidence concerning matters of interest to me, but that's not entirely possible in the case of explaining dreams. So trying to figure out why we have dreams and for what purpose is subjective. I acknowledge that. However we choose to categorize dreams, though, my family and I were dreaming a lot during this time. One important example is a dream of mine where we (my family and I) had a chance to save Robert. In the dream we were aware that he was in emotional turmoil and we were able to reach out to him, talk to him, and change his mind from taking his own life. Then we encouraged him to seek professional help which turned his life around. In the dream I was tremendously relieved at the success with which our efforts were met. But when I woke up, I wasn't confident that, in real life, we could have saved him. The dream may have been a fulfillment of wishful thinking and it was certainly a response to my refusal to deal openly with the issue as it affected me personally. But having the dream and contemplating its significance meant I was forced to confront some of the facts. Alienated and alone, Robert must have felt drawn to the grave because there seemed to be no better place to go. My brother had an unrequited love affair with life which made staying alive a challenge for him. He was loved by his family and by his friends but he was unable to feel the love. He couldn't absorb love and hold onto it to get him through the times when he was suffering. It was like his heart was made of Teflon - love slid right off without leaving a trace. Until this dream, my thoughts were caught up in a perpetual cycle of what-ifs: *What if I had done just this one thing, would it have saved Robert's life? What if I had said just this one thing, would it have made Robert want to live?*

Having the dream forced me to look at various aspects associated with my brother's death and to understand a little more clearly how it came to pass. The dream did not diminish my sadness but it facilitated movement toward an acceptance of the reality of Robert's death rather than living the fantasy that I could somehow rewind the clock and stop that fatal event. I began to heal then, if only a little. It was the first step in the right direction on the road to reclaiming some equilibrium for myself and the dream was responsible for that. Afterwards I was able to hope for Robert to find in death the peace he sought in life. Feeling a bit of hope contributed to my being able to get up each morning.

One night, less than a week after Mom told me that Dad and Robert visit her, Dad came to see me too. In my dream, Jim looked to be in his mid-thirties. Tall and trim with dark wavy hair; handsome and debonair. The setting for our meeting was outside the nursing home, behind the kitchen where the nursing assistants took Mom for her pre-bedtime cigarette. In the dream there was an outdoor shower like people install at their beach cottages to rinse the sand off before going inside. My dad and I stood side by side and watched as a stream of water poured over Mom's body. A look of sheer delight was reflected on her face as she ran her fingers through her wet hair. Dad and I enjoyed seeing her take pleasure in that cool and refreshing moment. But, I was aware in the dream that Dad had died and was no longer living at the nursing home so I was perplexed at his presence. My question of why he was here floated directly from my thoughts to his. His answer came back to me the same way. "I'm here to take care of your mother. I'll be with her and watch over her here."

I knew he would, too. I also knew at that moment that death was not the end of our existence. Our souls survive the bodies' last breath. I was raised to believe this concept but I *believed* it with reservations. Now I knew, without a doubt in my mind, that we are connected to our loved ones for all eternity.

When I woke up I knew ol' Jim was on the job and I could relax my vigilance over Mom's welfare a little bit. I told Donna about the dream and she smiled knowingly. Her *I told you so* was not the least bit smug but she did look satisfied with herself.

Why do our loved ones not communicate with us in the light of day? I think it's because the dream state is a perfect environment for us to meet since our pre-conceived sense of *what-is* and *what-is-not* possible is suspended then. While asleep, we are able to get out of our own way and allow *impossible* things to happen. One way to know whether or not the experience is a visitation is by how the person in the dream communicates. If the message is complete and instantaneous, and passes from mind to mind without vocalizing words while the information that was exchanged is understood clearly, then it is assumed that the information was imparted telepathically. The experience is interpreted as a 'visit' (in a spiritual sense) by your loved one. If the experience can be described as vague, murky or 'dream-like', in all likelihood that is a dream *about* the person. In a visit, a perfect understanding is produced. The message is crystal clear and there is no doubt what the message means. You 'just know' that the information rings true and does not have a fantastical quality to it that other dreams may have. And quite frankly, memory of the experience will stay longer than a more typical dream, maybe for the rest of your life. For many of us who can recall our dreams upon waking, we find that those dreams and our memory of them fade considerably by the time we hop into the shower or have that first cup of coffee. After a visitation we typically feel comforted, more peaceful, and enlightened with a sense of relief knowing this person who is special to us is all right.

We may bring the joy of the reunion with us into our conscious life, even while continuing to feel the bitter longing for their return.

Being with our loved one again feels like being in the presence of pure unconditional love. Through this experience we get a peek at how expansive we are as souls. There are no limits as to how we can communicate. And for me it's important to know that we have a connection to our loved ones. The experience is magical and I was pleased that Rusty enjoyed such magical moments with her husband and son.

Moving Mom to the Alzheimer's unit meant another upheaval in her life and while I tried to limit the chaos, I couldn't insure that she would have only peace and calm. While we were in the relocation process Mom was wobbly and physically unsteady from the effects of the grief she felt. She was so unsteady in fact that one afternoon she tripped and fell. She landed hard on her left side and an angry bruise rose immediately on her hip. Mom, unlike me, was blessed with a high tolerance for pain, but clearly the injury to her hip, elbow and wrist affected the slightest movement she made, and walking was especially difficult for her. She was mobile enough for me to take her to the University Hospital for a CT scan to determine the amount of damage. On the twenty minute drive from the nursing home to the hospital Mom got weepy. It seemed to me to be out of the blue and I was puzzled.

"What is it, Mom? Why are you sad?"

"I miss your father and brother," she said. Then she started crying.

Mom's answer caught me off guard. That she remembered losing Dad and Robert, even though we had taken her off the Aricept prescription allowing her memory functions to decline fairly rapidly, was surprising. In sympathy, I joined her. Through tears I agreed that I missed them too and it made me sad as well. Then she looked out the window and saw a couple of signs that caught her attention. She started reading the words out loud:

PANDA'S-DEN-CHINESE-FOOD
HICKORY-GROVE-PRESBYTERIAN-CHURCH

She was extremely pleased with herself for maintaining this skill of recognizing the written word as she scooted out of grief mode and into 'Aren't I smart to be able to read these signs' mode without so much as a Mother-may-I. The wave of sadness that grabbed her so completely only a moment earlier disappeared just as quickly, leaving no trace. Mom was now perfectly calm and content as she moved speedily and effortlessly into the present moment where all was right with the world. I, on the other hand, was not able to jump out of the tearful mode as deftly as Rusty Burris. I refocused my attention on the road in front of me as I cried. *Alone.* I was unable to switch off the pain the way Mom was blessedly able to do. Emotional whiplash jerked me off balance but Mom was fine. I flicked my own tears away and laughed. Was this a little miracle? It was certainly a benefit of the disease. Alzheimer's would not allow Mom to dwell too long on any topic, even the topic of recent deaths.

Trying to keep apace, I changed our topic of conversation. "Do you remember your mom, Mom?" I asked her out of the clear blue.

"Yes," she answered me. "I do." She didn't appear to think this was a weird question and she didn't require any segue as we hopped from topic to topic as our whims took us.

"Do you think that if your mom had lived long enough to know us..., well..., do you think she would have liked us? Because I wish I had known her," I confessed.

I was surprised at my statement because after the stories we heard growing up about Lottie Senior, how strict she was with my mom and aunt and uncle, and especially the tale that she carried *Brass Knuckles* and a .38 when she drove the jitney service in Memphis during the 1930s, I harbored a healthy level of fear of what she might do to defenseless little grandchildren if we had stepped out of line in her presence. As a child, I thought that it was probably a blessing that we didn't know her. It was hard enough surviving the Wrath of Rusty, I was certain that we would have perished under the harsh qualities Grandma Lottie was famous for. But today, I wanted to know. I wondered if her grandchildren could have mellowed her out. Never mind. I was an adult now. I had stood in front of my parents and announced the death of their son. I would never wear the mantle of coward again in this lifetime. In my newfound courage, I thought I could bear up to a strict grandmother.

Mom paused only briefly as she gave my question due consideration.

"Oh, yes," she assured me. "She would have loved you all very much."

Her response pleased me greatly. But after this exchange I knew that I needed to either adapt to quick changes on the rollercoaster ride of 'emotions' or I would have to adapt to chronic neck pain.

At the radiology department reception window, I handed over the paperwork needed to check Mom in. Afterwards, a nurse injected dye into her blood stream and advised us to go kill a couple of hours before coming back for the scan. We ate some lunch, but had time to spare before we were due back at the hospital. I was afraid that Mom would recognize that we were prowling around Newell and familiar stomping grounds and demand to go 'home'. But she didn't, which made me comfortable in suggesting a visit with Emily McClellan.

Emily and her family had been members of the Newell community, and the church my family attended, since the beginning of time. Or so it seemed to me. Her family home sat on the main road that slices Newell down the middle. The deep front porch ran the full width of the house and faced the railroad tracks that ran prominently forty paces away along the other side of the road.

Mom and Emily had been friends for decades in dedicated service to our church. Emily was a good bit older than Rusty, but age differences were never an issue for Mom in either direction. Emily was suffering from a type of dementia herself. Hers was mild yet, and since it was not as aggressive as Mom's, Emily remained in her home with the assistance of family members who lived close-by. If Rusty had been clicking on all cylinders, she would have made a point to visit Emily frequently since grocery store errands took her past Emily's house on a near-daily basis in the good old days. So, in the spirit of trying to walk in my mother's footsteps I asked - WWRD (*What would Rusty do*)? The obvious answer was - stop in to visit Emily. What a great idea, I thought as I patted myself on the back.

Emily was sitting on the porch looking expectant when we drove up. She was tall and slim. She sported a hairstyle known as

'The Bob' like my Grandma Susie wore as soon as shorn chignons became fashionable after The Great War. Emily hadn't changed since I first met her when I was in the third grade. She was not the frilly type but for every encounter I can recall having with her as a child or an adult, she was as sweet as her name.

Emily watched us with interest as we walked up her sidewalk. She welcomed us cheerfully in spite of having no idea who we were; her gracious southern greeting was a testament to her true nature. Rusty was cordial too, even though as far as she was concerned, she had never met this woman before in her life. Emily's Meals-on-Wheels lunch sat on the floor beside her chair. She offered to share it with us. We politely declined. We had, after all, eaten only five minutes before. With sweet and loving exchanges, these two old friends, who were complete strangers to each other, chatted like two old friends. I witnessed this phenomenon as if I was having some sort of psychedelic trip. Mom complimented Emily on the lush iris blooms that flanked the walkway to the house. Emily complimented Mom on her summer outfit. In fact, Mom's trim figure looked as fresh as an iris bloom in her turquoise slacks and striped top.

There was no shortage of topics from which Mom and Emily tapped for discussion - usually at the same time, and usually not the same topic. I sat between them trying to keep up. I attempted to grasp and follow the various and assorted threads of conversation. I couldn't do it. It couldn't be done. I asked myself, *what* were *you thinking?* I vowed to never be that quick with self-congratulations again.

Both Mom and Emily operated within their own realities. At no time did their reality share any overlap with my own. But the truth is, they were happy and content. They enjoyed each other's company. And in their world, everything was satisfactory. I was the odd person out. In my world, I was confused and filled with anxiety. It occurred to me that I preferred to be where *they* were rather than where I was.

Mom and I went back to the hospital to complete the CT scan process which revealed that her pelvic bone was fractured and would take six to eight weeks to heal, but she had no other broken bones. I was relieved. She could be ambulatory with assistance. The most important thing was for Mom to stay as active as possible. Walking kept her leg muscles strong. Even a few days of immobility would risk losing muscle tone or worse, the ability of her brain to tell her legs what to do. Mom's physician at the nursing home was concerned when he got the report because, as he told us, "broken bones can be the beginning of the end for someone in a compromised state of health." He attempted to prevent further injuries from a fall by prescribing a hip protection girdle – not too different from hip protection equipment used in the NFL. She was to wear it during the day but it was bulky and uncomfortable for a tiny little 100-pound, 70 year old woman. And it made Mom's walking more awkward and unsteady. A quick internet search confirmed my decision to decline the device for Mom. The studies I found concluded that hip protectors were not necessarily indicated for the nursing home population since they are bulky, can be hard to fit properly, and they irritate the thin fragile skin of the elderly. The words that my friend Frances told me an age before rang in my ears: *Oh, dahlin', you cannot protect her from everything.* So, I did not insist on Mom wearing the thing. I placed Mom's safety firmly within the realm of Divine Providence. That trust would not be rewarded.

CHAPTER FOURTEEN

It's a poor sort of memory that only works backwards.
 -Alice Through the Looking Glass by Lewis Carroll

Like Alice, who stepped through the mirror in her drawing room, I too entered a strange reality when I walked through the code-protected portal into Mom's new world. I felt that, like Alice in that fantasy story, my mother and I were pawns in the great chess game of life.

In the 400 Club setting, Alzheimer's disease was still as hateful as ever and yet it was also fascinating to observe. Admittedly, examining *Alzheimer-behavior* as if it was fixed on a slide under a microscope is less vexing if the observer can maintain objectivity. But that's damned near impossible to do when a beloved family member is the one being observed. Nevertheless, it was worth a try. To understand this curious new world, I climbed up onto the metaphorical fireplace mantle willingly, as Alice did, and stepped through the looking glass to the other side. What I discovered was intriguing.

For many sufferers, Alzheimer's disease forces their personalities to regress. In Alice's journey, she too encountered a place where time runs backwards. Victims of Alzheimer's do not choose to step into this disorienting world - they stumble upon the phenomenon involuntarily. Developmentally speaking, Rusty's brain was becoming a confusing mass of tangles because of Alzheimer's, stripping away inhibitions. The absence of inhibitors can lead to unconventional behavior, that's true, yet Mom was able to behave appropriately for the most part. Her behavior became unfiltered, almost naïve, as a child's is before becoming self-aware and self-conscious. Self-consciousness is the mechanism that keeps us socially responsible. Being self-conscious promotes harmony by reinforcing social norms. It prevents us from showing up at the work place stark naked. And it reduces the occurrence of shoving matches at buffet luncheons. An overabundance of self-consciousness may prohibit the amount of fun we have at parties or other social gatherings which is why some folks will drink alcohol to enhance sociability. After a drink or two, the resulting loss of inhibitions may not increase the number of desirable traits of sociability, but it certainly makes those traits no longer important.

An actual benefit of having self-consciousness stripped away, at least in some cases, is that it leaves in its wake pure love - the kind of love the Bible describes in 1 Corinthians 13. Fear of not having that love reciprocated is absent, so it's freely offered. Mom and many of her fellow residents gave us unconditional love. Not just once, but consistently. They loved us without fear that it may not be returned. No strings attached. Individuals in this new world loved us without judgment because their egos were incapable of suffering the bugaboo of rejection that many of us dread. I am glad that I witnessed the lemonade qualities of this new behavior. Another unintended, yet arguably positive, consequence of Alzheimer's disease is the elimination of intense fear of being judged and evaluated by other people. Absence of the destructive qualities of self-consciousness means that feelings of inadequacy and embarrassment are removed.

Being able to recognize some positive points related to our move to the 400 Club helped us settle into Club life. We arrived most evenings before the dinner cart was rolled in. Donna and I chipped in and helped the residents find seats. We brought them iced tea, for which they seemed incredibly grateful as if no kinder gesture had ever been offered. Before their plates were in place, we snapped terrycloth bibs around each of their necks. We family members were cautioned to *not* call them bibs, however. They were clothing protectors. We were also directed to refer to the use of *Depends* as adult briefs. The staff corrected us gently whenever we slipped and used these inconsiderate expressions. We didn't mind. Substituting politically-correct terms help to preserve the dignity of the individuals in the nursing home.

We also learned acceptable seating arrangements. That is, we actively managed who sat with whom. Personalities clashed in some cases and we attempted to reduce strife in the Club by breaking up potential mischief makers. We did not want a replay of the hand-to-hand combat incident that took place in the main dining room. One of the biggest challenges we faced each evening was finding a way to persuade club members to eat their meat and veggies before dessert - they subscribed to the adage 'eat dessert first for life is uncertain', and they lived it. Alzheimer's disease increases the craving of sweets for many individuals and does nothing at all to decrease the lengths to which they will go to get their hands on a cookie.

It was one fellow's habit to appear out the blue, behaving rather nonchalantly as he made a pre-prandial stroll around the room. Passing by a table located strategically on the outer edge of the dining room area, he swerved in close then quickly palmed a nice hunk of cake that sat unprotected on the dinner tray of a poor unwary diner before any effective defense could be mounted. He ducked into a bedroom to devour the cake undetected then he repeated his stealthy mission until caught red-handed and instructed to return to his seat.

My own mother was an offender - she was as guilty of dessert-snatching as the next resident. She was less subtle in her approach than the drive-by guy and one night I caught her in the act. We were sitting at a nice table for four. I was on Mom's left-hand side and Donna sat on her right. This was a practical seating arrangement because we could corral Mom into a focused eating zone. We had her bibbed up and ready to dig in. Trays in place and iced tea tumblers within reach. Then Mom casually extendeded her left hand past me and picked up the square of chocolate cake right off Rebecca's plate. I took immediate action. I looked Mom dead in the eye and said politely, "Mom, you have your own dessert. This one is Rebecca's so let's put it back on her tray, okay?"

I was not harsh or critical. I didn't scold. I simply stated a fact. I did however want to prevent a ruckus. Rebecca was bigger than me and probably stronger, and I was within easy striking distance. Mom put the cake back reluctantly then turned her head slowly away from me in a classic Royal Snub. Pretentious snobs use this ploy when they want you to know that they are refusing to acknowledge your presence. It's clearly intentional because what good is having a disdain for someone if they don't know they are being disdained? Therefore a demonstration of contempt clearly must be displayed openly, with obvious intent. Mom's message was clear: *You no longer exist in my world.* This was not her usual

M.O. Mom was a confronter and met conflicts head on. But this - this was childish behavior.

Mom's use of the gesture made me laugh. She didn't know I was laughing because her head was turned so far away from me, it couldn't have gone any further if she'd been a hoot owl. She kept her gaze on Donna as if to say, *I will acknowledge* your *presence because* you *have not been unkind to me.*

Mom's displeasure with me was funny only because, compared to other residents who showed their anger in much more fundamentally basic ways, Rusty employed a sophisticatedly coy response by comparison. Even so, I couldn't let Mom's cake pilfering incident slide. This was too good to pass up so I tapped Mom's shoulder to get her attention. She refused.

"Momma!" I continued anyway. I called her loud enough that the ladies at the next table gave me their attention. But not my own mother. I was cut out of her world.

"Momma!" I tried again. "Are you mad at me?"

She turned her head woodenly back towards me, her back was ram-rod straight. With agonizing slowness she finally condescended to glance in my direction. Then she gazed down her nose at me to let me know she heard me, then she turned her head back toward Donna again, this time with her nose even higher in the air.

"Nooooo...," she sang. "I'm not maaaaaad... ." She held onto the word 'mad' for four beats.

I giggled again at the sight of Rusty's out-of-character response. (Although now that I think of it, I remember a similar response from her when we took our last road trip to Minnesota.) Then, and now, I saw a glimmer of Mom's inner petulant teenager. Then I realized that what was *in* character for Mom was the fact that she knew *she* was still the parent. This was her way of holding on to a tiny morsel of control in her darkening and restrictive world. Rusty Almighty emerged, ever so briefly, and she did not take kindly to a daughter of hers giving her instructions on how to behave. She had little personal power at her disposal to voice that displeasure so she snubbed me. Then she refused to eat for me, and she refused to acknowledge my presence at the table. I decided to have an early night.

"Fine." I told her with immaturity that matched hers but with no valid excuse for mine. "I'm going home, then. I'll see you tomorrow."

Mom hugged Donna good-bye; her rejection of me complete. My only consolation was that I knew the code to get out of her world and back into my own. I knew that the incident would be forgotten by bedtime and we would start fresh on my next visit. She was incapable of holding a grudge against me - grudges require memory.

On the next evening, as I walked into the Club, Mom spotted me immediately. "There you are!" A smile broke across her face as she spoke the words to my all-time favorite greeting from Rusty. It meant she expected me. It meant she remembered me. It meant she was glad to see me. A miracle. She had no recall of snubbing me the night before. Dinner was eaten only after gentle encouragement that it must come before dessert. No tantrums were pitched in response. It was a good night.

Donna and I brought a cache of cassettes from Mom's personal music collection into the Club to share. Patsy Cline, Andrew Sisters, Tennessee Ernie Ford and a few Big Band compilations accompanied dinnertime meals from that night on. Many of the residents got caught up in the tunes from yesteryear and I noticed a few toes tapping time to the beat. After dinner, Donna, Mom and I linked our arms and promenaded the perimeter of the room. Unable to resist our fun, first one new friend then another got into the spirit of the moment and joined us. Soon we walked in boogie-woogie time, singing *beat me Daddy, eight to the bar.*

To be eligible to stay in the Alzheimer's unit, residents must be fairly mobile and be able to sit at the table for meals. Exercise and food are basic components for maintaining any level of fitness so to keep Mom in-shape we made strolling to music a habit each night after dinner. When others joined us in an impromptu Conga Line, it felt as natural as breathing. No self-conscious fears of looking uncoordinated were valid in this environment. Alzheimer's disease grants its sufferers the freedom from having to justify their actions or worry what other people think of them. I joined them and quickly lost myself in the music and in the movement and in the connection we made to each other as we danced, holding hands and laughing. As our line morphed into the Bunny Hop and then transitioned into the

Hokey Pokey, it dawned on me that *IS* what it's all about!

Our nightly circuit was already a well-traveled route, before my mother's entry, favored by many of the inhabitants who needed to walk and pace and were no strangers to perpetual motion. Several individuals in the Alzheimer's unit were prone to pacing. This activity may communicate that the pacer is experiencing confusion or that they are bored and need to be more active. They may be afraid of something or in pain and unable to describe or express their feelings in any other way. Those who pace may not sit down long enough to have a meal and it's possible that pacing can burn more calories than the individual takes in, so it's important to encourage them to eat even if it's food-to-go; peanut butter crackers for instance, or dried fruits or a protein shake.

There are other reasons that cause those who have Alzheimer's to not eat and the problems relate directly to memory and the sensory impairment qualities of the disease. Your loved one may lose the ability to comprehend when he or she is hungry or full, or may decline food when it has been many hours since the previous meal. Some individuals claim to be hungry on the heels of the previous meal. Alzheimer's influences the sense of taste and smell which is why someone may turn up his nose to food that was appealing only a week earlier. It's possible that a person has an appetite for the meal but is confused over what the fork or spoon or knife is used for without suggestions or guidance. The staff in the 400 Club was aware of these risks and made every effort to encourage their charges to eat and drink as much and as nutritiously as humanly possible to prevent, or rather, to *delay* malnutrition and dehydration. These were the major sources of concern I had for Mom. At the top of the list of my fear list was, of course, a serious and debilitating fall.

One night, when the time came for Donna and me to tell Mom goodbye, she seemed to accept it with good humor. This was amazing good luck, I thought, and always a morale booster when it happened. As I turned to walk toward the door, Mom called out, "Marsha! Wait."

Uh oh... I turned to look back at her, dreading the inevitable but worthless reassurance I gave her every night that I'd be back the following day.

"I've got something for you!" She was in high spirits.

"What do you have for me, Mom?"

I couldn't imagine what she was referring to. I didn't see anything she could give me. When Mom and Dad were at home, they often gave me a parting gift before I could take my leave. "Wait," they would say to stop my exit. "Take some of these with you." And they gathered a couple of freshly harvested tomatoes or a bag of cookies to make a care-package for me. It didn't matter what the item was, it was the gesture that was endearing. I I never refused such generous offerings. I looked at Mom on this evening and recognized a former behavior but couldn't imagine what in the world she had access to that she could give me.

"Wait a minute. I've got it right here in my pocket."

"But you haven't got pockets in those pants, Mom."

"Yes, I do," she corrected me patiently.

It looked to me as if she was wearing plain light-weight cotton slacks. But I was wrong. Mom proceeded to reach deep into the right hand pocket. She pulled out what appeared from a distance to be a silver coin the size of a quarter. She held it out to me.

"I found this today and wanted you to have it. It's a nickel!"

It wasn't a nickel. It was a knockout plug from an electrical outlet box that had been installed recently. And it was infinitely more valuable to me than its weight in gold. Mom had seen it discarded on the floor, I suppose, picked it up and thought to save it back for me. And, she remembered that she had done so. That 'plug nickel' is now my good luck piece; I never leave home without it. It even traveled to Egypt with me.

Before Dad's stroke, our friend Sue, Donna and Donna's brother, Charles and I cooked up plans to travel to Egypt. We shared a lifetime wish to see the Pyramids of Giza, the Sphinx, the temples of Luxor and Karnak, and to take a cruise down the Nile. I would use the experience to spice up my lectures of ancient Egypt in the history course I taught. The scheme seemed like a great idea the previous year. Now, as the deadline for finalizing the plans was upon us, I needed to make a decision to go or beg off. With the events that had taken place since our original plan, I was reluctant to leave Mom for three weeks. I wanted to go on this trip of a lifetime, but I had no way of knowing what condition Mom would be in when it was time to me to leave.

Barbara and Andy assured me they would take care of Mom while I was away. They promised that Mom would not have time to miss me and they guaranteed that life would go on even if I was seven time zones away. My brother and sister could handle whatever popped up and I had complete confidence in their abilities. That was not the problem. The nursing staff was supportive and I knew they doted on Mom. Mom slept intermittently during the night and wandered throughout the Alzheimer facility like a lost child at times. The third shift CNAs discovered that if they made a bed for Mom on the sofa in the center of the sitting room she would settle down and nap for them, feeling safer in their midst than 'locked' away in her bedroom where, I can only imagine, the darkness and seclusion brought loneliness. Mom had made a practice of sleeping on the sofa in her own home, choosing to be in the middle of things and although the CNAs did not know this routine of Rusty's, they worked out that sleeping on the sofa was the best solution for her. If they made these special arrangements for my mother without being asked to, I knew Mom would be in good hands during my absence. So that was not the problem either.

What was I afraid of then? I was afraid that when I was no longer a part of Mom's daily life, she would forget me. In spite of that fear, I paid my final installment to the tour company and booked my November getaway.

Although Mom remembered to miss Dad and Robert more times than she forgot, and their loss made her sad, she in no way lost her zest for life. Even with the hardships she had known in her seventy years of life, Rusty found ways to enjoy herself. One particular pleasure was interacting with staff and residents alike. She sat patiently and lovingly with a fellow resident who was upset - listening to her, holding her hands, and speaking words of reassurance to her. Mom straightened dining room chairs and arranged pencil holders on the nurses' counter. I asked her once where she was and she answered, "This is the church fellowship hall, honey. Everyone will be here for the meal soon and we have to get things ready for them." *Naturally.*

Mom's service to her church and community was a part of her

- it wasn't just something she did. And this something was still inside of her, and motivated her choice of activities. The physical environment of the 400 Club was, as promised, better for Mom. She needed her days to be calm and predictable. She had never *ever* needed calm or predictability in her life before, but the disease demanded it, and this environment provided it. The planned activities accommodated her special needs, her progressively changing outlook, and increasingly unique perceptions of her surroundings.

During our dinner-time visits, Donna and I became better acquainted with the members of the Club and built camaraderie with the other families whose visits overlapped our own. Mealtimes evolved essentially into a social gathering for us all. In the real world I found it awkward at times to be with people who were not going through anything similar to this. For one thing, I envied them - not a good basis for a social outing. So while we fellow-travelers were together, this bizarre world seemed sane. Inside this world we knew the inhabitants and their personalities as they were at that moment in time. None of us knew each other before this disease altered our loved ones to the point where they had to be isolated and shut away for their own good. There's less emotional pain involved when you don't have a comparison and you don't have the inner dialog that runs like this: "What a shame. I remember ol' Danny when his barbecued wings made him the grill master of the neighborhood." Here, we got to know each resident as they were in that moment in time. Of course we learned about their lives before Alzheimer's claimed their brain, but it's different hearing stories of their lives and having the first hand experience to draw from.

At times the former life of the resident bled through into his or her current life. For example, Mrs. Lambe, the resident whose son we met running out of the door of the unit when we first moved Mom to the 400 Club, had been the organist for one of the large churches in Charlotte. She occasionally sat down at the piano and played a number of pieces from memory and she played them quite skillfully. Perhaps saying that she played from memory is the wrong way to phrase it. Music seemed to live inside of her and she accessed it at will, but she rarely played when requested - it typically had to be her own idea. But Mrs. Lambe considered Donna a trusted and safe friend. Whenever we arrived, Mrs. Lambe greeted Donna sweetly, grasped her hands and sometimes even kissed her fingers lightly. Mrs. Lambe greeted others in this way at times as well, but she accorded only Donna with a song on the piano when requested.

Miss Nell had been a school teacher. She brooked no dissent in the classroom, which is where she believed herself to be. It was easy to imagine that she had been rather strict in her day. As supper was being served, Miss Nell often clapped her hands sharply to get everyone's attention (unsuccessfully, I might add) then announced: *Your meal is here and you all need to come over and find your seats*. After she was done with her own meal, she repeated the gesture and dismissed the group with: *I've enjoyed having you here today, but it's late and now you must go on back to your own homes*. None of the other residents paid her a bit of attention really, but she was relieved that her duties were now completed and seemed pleased with herself that she still had control of the classroom.

Rita Trundle was a walker. Each time I saw her she was walking tirelessly around the large 400 Club room. She would rather walk than eat. Her son told us that the two of them enjoyed hiking before Rita was moved to Willow Lake and together they logged countless miles along the Appalachian Trail before Alzheimer's made it impossible for mother and son to continue the activity safely.

I saw the determined look in Rita's eyes each time a lap brought her by our table at dinner time. She clasped her hands behind her back, leaning forward with unwavering resolve to reach her destination. Rita had a serious way and I bet she accomplished a lot in her lifetime. One night, as we sat at the table with Mom, waiting for the dinner trays to arrive, Rita deviated from her path and walked directly over to our table. She leaned in close, conspiratorially, in order that what she was going to tell us could be heard only by those of us at the table. The message was confidential, no telling when *they* might be listening. And a good thing she was careful because what she told us in whispered tones was: *We're breaking out of here tonight*. My heart skipped a beat. I was actually excited with anticipation of this nocturnal caper. I secretly hoped that Rita's gang, of which I was proud to be included, would be successful.

A few residents were unable to interact with Donna and me in the conventional sense, but there are other ways to communicate.

Holding hands or exchanging a smile can convey affection between two people, maybe even more than the spoken word. Sometimes a resident only wanted to be near another human being. Donna and I welcomed invitations to sit beside a resident and occasionally we would relate to the residents through each other's loved ones. Elliot Stanton's wife, Eve, told us stories of their life together. Elliot never joined in, but his angelic smile hinted at his devilish playful nature. Eve's wit was dryer than the Mojave and she entertained us often with rather risqué jokes. Never a dull moment in the Club.

We loved the Rebeccas. One was tall and lean, with a gleam in her eye like she knew a great secret and was anxious to share it with us. I was quite fond of this Rebecca. The other Rebecca was tall too, but a little more solidly built. This Rebecca was not interested in interacting with any of us. For the most part, she didn't want people to talk to her or touch her or kid with her. So we didn't. This is also the same Rebecca from whom Mom swiped the hunk of cake right before her very eyes without showing one whit of remorse. At times, this Rebecca showed a gentler side and seemed to enjoy having Donna sit near her. Donna's presence is quiet, calm and peaceful. Rebecca didn't mind having that kind of person close by.

Mom's roommate Karen Brown, perplexed at her current circumstances, brightened whenever Hunter arrived. So did we. He usually made his regular visits at lunch time so when he came in the evening we deliberately engineered the table seating such that we could sit with him to have our meals. How does one work in the funeral home business and maintain such a rosy disposition? Hunter worked at being healthy, too. He ate sensibly, swam at the YMCA daily, and stayed connected to friends and family socially. I want to be just like him when I grow up.

Earnest Rowling was a fix-it man. He walked from bedroom to bedroom looking for things that needed repair. He squirreled away a fork or spoon from lunch then used them to restore dangling drawer pulls, silence squeaky door hinges, mend wobbly chair legs, and free sticky window casings. He was a man of few words, usually uttering, *Move!* or, *You're in the way!* He wasn't unkind. But he had no time to mess around because there was so much to do. Oh, how I wished he could have his own personal toolbox available and onsite. It must have been frustrating for him to have to improvise with a three-piece set of stainless steel flatware instead of proper gear. Earnest's wife and son and daughter were frequent visitors and they brought their children often. We came to know and care for each other in the Club. A few years later, it brought me great joy to work with the young man who married Earnest's granddaughter. I love it that the world is this small.

Being with the members of the 400 Club and their families was meaningful because having the support of a close community of loving people, as we did, made survival possible. Each one of them was special to me and I hope to God I never have the disease that makes me forget them, but one woman and her family had the greatest personal influence on me during our tenure at Willow Lake and that was Willie Poythress. Willie's residency had extended back a decade by the time we met her. Her daughters and son worked out a schedule where one of them came by each evening in time to feed Willie supper and to get her ready for bed. This schedule meant that a family member was available to be with Willie every day but no one was overextended. The family had gained much experience during their time there and they had already worked out the kinks of institutional life through trial and error when we met them. There are no words to express my appreciation for their love and concern as they took Donna and me under their wings and provided us with much-needed guidance.

Marie, Jean, Patsy and Vern taught us the first rule of survival; use humor as an essential element for dealing with the double whammy of Alzheimer's and nursing home life. Willie's children were not happy with the current state of affairs - far from it. They hated the disease and its effects as we all did. But they made the best of their circumstances and pulled me along with them on our shared pothole-riddled path. Misery loves company but when I was in the company of Willie and her family, Misery was left on the doorstep like a poor relation. It was empowering and took great courage to do it. Marie led the way.

Marie, Willie's eldest, had a playful side to her efficient, no-nonsense manner. When it was Marie's night for duty she approached Willie's ablutions with an organized and well thought-out technique. She had done this for so long she employed a time-saving system with a heapin' helpin' of gentle kindness that should have been trademarked. We felt Marie's love to the core but don't even think about wallowing in self-pity.

Jean was serious with a professional bearing. She always dressed fashionably and was attentive and vigilant. The idea of excellence may be old fashioned in our world today, but Jean's insistence on high standards and the ethical treatment of her mother and every resident at Willow Lake puts PETA to shame. Jean was a patient advocate in the purist sense of the word.

Patsy was the baby of the family - by six minutes. She and Jean are twins and they complement each other like yin and yang. As a dedicated hospice nurse, Patsy's impish playful spirit must bring comfort and joy to her patients. Patsy quickly cut through any barriers or pretentions the rest of us might be inclined to drag in from the outside world. In this place, Alzheimer's was the great equalizer. You cannot be touched by this disease and not be humbled.

Vernon. Dear Brother Vernon. What was it like for him to grow up with this bevy of brave and bold women? He was the strong, silent type but it was fun to watch him kid with his mother. From their interactions, we had a peek into their lives before Alzheimer's. And we saw that Willie was a remarkable character.

When we joined Willie for dinner we'd say, "Hey, Willie!" In southern-speak, 'hey' is not an exclamation to get your attention and it's no simple greeting either. *Hello, How are you*, and *Good to see you* are all rolled into that one little word. She would answer our 'hey' with a 'hey' of her own, accompanied with a huge smile. It was not possible to see that smile without responding with one of your own. She had been a waitress at a diner in her previous life. She provided for her children because customers returned time and time again to see that smile.

"How are you?" We would ask.

"Oh, I'm alright," she'd tell us without fail. She never complained.

Many times, as we sat with our Moms, keeping a steady stream of food moving from the plate to their mouths, Willie talked right through the entire process.

"I said, 'Daddy, where you goin'?'"

"Daddy said, 'I'm goin' down to the creek.'"

"I said, 'Well come back in time for dinner.'"

"Daddy said, 'I will, honey. What we havin'?'"

"I said, 'I don't know. Fried chicken and mashed potatoes and gravy, I guess.'"

It wasn't confusing if you were there. But basically Willie gave us both parts of the conversation, a running commentary of a scenario looping through her head based on a past experience. She played both parts herself as she recited verbatim the exchange she was having with her father. Willie sure loved her mother and father. And they sure ate some good meals if these conversations that we were privy to are any indication. Wherever Willie was during her reveries, it looked to me to be a pretty fine place.

Willie's family, Earnest's family, and so many others, embodied the concept of 'my brother's keeper'. When they were at the nursing home and I wasn't, they took a special interest in Mom. They called her *Rusty*, making a point to use the name Mom would recognize. They were not fooled by any rigid institutional policy. I'd like to think I reciprocated in some small way. I know this - I loved these people and their family members. I still do. I could not have endured the emotional strain of daily relentless poundings of grief and loss without them.

As I grew more comfortable in the 400 Club, I was growing more fatigued, physically and emotionally. The constant stress of taking care of my parents over the years and the critical turn of more recent events were taking a toll on me. I didn't yet have the tools that a meditation practice gives us to calm body, mind and spirit and which reduces the chronic distress that pounded me constantly. I attempted to apply myself at work but a decreased attention span required extra energy to do my job. I looked for ways to increase the joy factor in my personal life. I failed. I was sad, and the sadness made me unenthusiastic in any endeavor I attempted. Depression meant I had little interest in reading or watching television. I was unsettled, waiting for the next crisis to clobber me and my family. I was hyper-sensitive to the point that, if you said hello to me I harbored a suspicion that you may have a deceitful ulterior motive for doing it. I was clumsy. I washed dishes and broke many of them. We seriously considered using paper plates for a while. I wanted to disconnect and hide from the world. In the words of Jim Burris, I wanted to just *ride it out*. Maybe I could rejoin the human race after the hardest parts of walking through my sorrow was done. Donna advised to me to go outside, get fresh air, exercise. That would have been Rusty's advice as well - *do something active.*

Donna and Rusty won. I dug out my trusty bicycle from the clutter of the garage, dusted it off, and added air to its saggy tires. I loaded it onto the bike rack on my truck and drove it and me to the Greenway. I chose the Greenway for safety reasons. I had the good sense to not put myself at risk by mingling with automobile traffic. I live in Charlotte. There's a good reason we have the NASCAR Museum located in our fair city. Our drivers are not known for their benevolence toward those who choose a two-wheeled mode of transportation.

I didn't wear Lycra bicycle shorts on this brief, but vigorous Tour de Greenway; I had no need for the protective saddle pad that's sewn into its seat because the route I chose was a short one and the protection from potential saddle sores wasn't needed. I had ridden no more than a half-mile when I stopped for a drink of water. Why court disaster by allowing myself to get dehydrated? I returned the water bottle to its cage on the down-tube and stood up on the left pedal that was at the top of its revolution. I turned the handlebars to steer back to the main path, then *THUD*! I was on the ground instantly with the full force and momentum of my weight converging onto one boney little knee as it hit the pavement.

The handle bar caught the hem of the blousy shorts I was wearing. Simultaneously, the left-side pedal jumped forward because the derailleur skipped a gear. I lost my balance, plunged to the bottom of the revolution, and could not recover - mass and velocity worked against me. I knew having the full weight of my body directed to just the one knee had done damage. I examined the point of injury and watched helplessly as massive swelling welled up angrily. I had only one thing on my mind. Get home. I made it back to the parking lot and threw the bike into the back of my truck and drove home. I called the house on my way. Donna was at the grocery store but Josh was there and picked up the telephone.

"Sweetie, I fell off my bike and hurt my knee," I told him calmly. "Would you get some ice, crush it and put it in a plastic bag? Oh, and find the aspirins for me, too. I'll be there in five minutes."

Josh is the most capable individual I know. He had the emergency response items available and waiting upon my arrival. I lay down on the sofa, propped my left leg up on a cushion, and placed the ice pack on my savagely damaged knee. Then I had a bright idea. Disclaimer: *On hindsight, I cannot recommend the following course of action.* My bright idea was to chase the aspirins with a Miller Lite thus dulling the pain all the quicker. Time was of the essence in squelching the sharp throbbing sensation that was bringing tears to my eyes. Josh handed me the frosty bottle of beer and I took a couple of healthy gulps as Donna came in the front door with groceries. She asked what was going on and we filled her in. She took one look at the injury and declared, "You have to go to the ER and get that X-rayed!"

I had seen enough of hospitals to last a lifetime and was not overjoyed at the prospect of going again but I had to agree. I hobbled out to the car and she drove me to our familiar old friend, University Hospital. Two minutes from our destination a thought occurred to me.

"Oh no!" I exclaimed.

"What is it?" She countered.

"Do you have any chewing gum or a mint or a potato chip handy?"

"No. Why?"

"I guzzled a half a beer back at the house and I don't want to have alcohol on my breath when I tell the receptionist that I fell off my bike."

"Too late now," she said helpfully. Optimistic as always, she added, "I wouldn't worry about it, though, I'm sure the aroma will wear off before we get there." *Clearly, this woman doesn't drink.*

At the hospital, I limped over to window marked Emergency Room Admittance.

"What can we help you with?" The nice lady asked.

"I fell off my bike." I told her, putting on my innocent face.

"Fell off your bike?"

"Yes."

"How old are you?"

"Here's my insurance card. All the information is there." I didn't like her tone. I started to worry that this woman had a prejudice against adult bicycle riders. Then she must have caught a whiff of Miller.

"How did you fall off?"

"Well, I had stopped to get a drink of water and then the handle bar caught the hem of these shorts because I should have been wearing my bike shorts but I didn't think it was important because it was going to be a short ride and then as I pressed down on the left-side pedal, the derailleur skipped a gear and..., anyway I lost my balance and fell."

"Have you been drinking?"

"Oh that. No, I mean I took only a sip or two with aspirins..."

"Okay. Go wait over there." She pointed to the farthest corner of the waiting room away from the other patients who had arrived before me.

"It's not what you think."

"I have all the information I need. Somebody will be with you shortly but I need you to go sit over there for now."

I started to protest again. I suspected that I was being treated like the cliché wino who had wandered in off the streets looking for warmth and a comfy sofa to nap on. I wanted to explain and convince her that one cannot become inebriated from 4.2 percent alcohol content in eight ounces of lite beer. The admittance lady looked over toward the security guard. He bulked up. Donna took my arm and guided me over to the hinterlands of the waiting room to where I had been exiled in shame and where I would do no harm to the other patients who had legitimate complaints.

The misunderstanding worked in my favor. I was called back quicker than I had ever seen action taken in an emergency room environment before or since. The young male attendant, who had probably been one of my students, pushed a wheelchair over to fetch me, barely able to hide a giggle at my expense. He shook his head and addressed me. "So, you've been drinking and fell off your bike?"

"Ha. Ha. It was the other way around, actually. After I fell, I needed a drink."

The X-ray showed no broken bones and I was advised to keep weight off that leg and take the prescribed medication, preferably without a beer chaser. So much for trying to incorporate healthy activities into my life. And so much for my feeble attempt to mix a cocktail of exercise and fresh air.

There was no rest for me, I couldn't relax and I slept poorly.

There was no place I could go in my mind which was not filled with heartache. Donna suggested that I imagine a safe and peaceful place before I tried to sleep each night, that it might help me get some shut-eye. But I found no such place. Nothing calm or idyllic existed in my world. Anything safe or serene or comfortable to draw from had been stripped from me. Nothing felt right. I was exhausted from having to think of and manage the many details of Mom's care. I was terrified that I would fail her and I was emotionally drained from watching helplessly as her condition deteriorated from one day to the next.

After eighteen weeks of intense care giving and putting out fires, Donna insisted that we go on a week-end retreat for some R&R. I had been on-duty with Mom and Dad, hyper-vigilant and in hyper-crisis mode for four and a half months. Since fresh air and exercise didn't work out for me, maybe lounging inside a well-appointed mountain cabin with a remote control in my hand would be the answer. Donna's proposal was brilliant. Insisting on this restful break in the mountains I love so much came at the perfect time. As we approached the tiny log cabin, the words from the first verse of Psalm 121 popped into my mind: *I will lift up mine eyes unto the hills, from whence cometh my help.* We had chosen these same words for Dad's funeral service. The sentiment was appropriate on this day too.

Donna remembered to bring all the things that made our stay special. Food, drinks, snacks, silly movies on video like *The Mummy, Stuart Little, A Bug's Life* - mindless entertainment. We hiked the more gentle trails which generated a robust appetite. We grilled kebabs over a charcoal fire. For lunch we made Panini's to go with tomato soup. Comfort food. I felt comforted.

Having a break and a change in environment, even for a week-end, was healthy. Removing myself physically from the overwhelming cares of everyday life gave me time and distance from those cares and from the source of my stress. I was in an atmosphere where I could sleep and rest and relax. What I couldn't do on my own with self-discipline was contrived here, a mere 120 miles from home. The two-day respite was a life-saver. The change in venue restored a little of my energy and fed my spirit. We would remember this remedy for the future.

I had despaired of leaving Rusty because I feared the world might quit turning on its axis if I was not on duty. But, miracle of miracles! The world did continue to turn without me at Mom's side. Perhaps going to Egypt would not be so difficult after all.

CHAPTER FIFTEEN

Mom has none of her faith left. When I asked if she wanted to pray or have a minister visit, she had no idea what I was talking about - it's too abstract. She doesn't understand the concept of God or religion or heaven. How does she get through the long day and the longer nights? — Author's journal entry

The journal entry above reveals my constant concerns for Mom's welfare. I had hoped her lifelong and steadfast faith would pull extra duty and offer her relief from the pain of losing her husband and son. Sadly, Alzheimer's destroyed the part of Mom's brain that allowed her to grasp such theoretical and abstract concepts. But a Zen-like state of grace and acceptance emerged instead. Something worked behind the scenes to give me and my family the help and strength we needed to bear the challenge of our circumstances. This was an unexpected gift of the disease, a gift wrapped in layers and layers of tissue paper.

The flip-side of perpetually living in the moment meant that Mom had no sense of time ticking by, only interminable, endless *nows*. She couldn't look forward to an event, a visit, a birthday. She was not able to reminisce about the good times of days gone by. I sympathized with her on this account because I could no longer bring to mind any good old days either. It's not that I was incapable of drawing from my own memory, but in order to be in the place where Mom existed, and to survive in that environment, I chose to leave the past behind. Remembering Mom as she had once been was painful. The strong and intelligent Rusty was on a first-name basis with every one of her roses (common names and Latin ones too). Once I overheard the following exchange between Mom and a favorite hybrid tea: "Good morning, Mr. Lincoln. Can I offer you some water?" Memories like that made my heart ache. I had to let go of that Rusty, at least for the duration. The vitally active Rusty who directed work days at the church and who choreographed the many details that facilitated voting in Newell on Election Day as election judge was dead and gone. It did no good to dwell on that Rusty and pine for her loss. The intellectual faculties of the woman I visited almost daily were being reduced considerably by the disease that choked the life out of her brain cells. But while it wiped her memory, it also transformed her by peeling away the layers of her public personality to reveal the essence and purity of her character. It was important to realize and accept that *this* new person was my mother now. I loved her more and more as I came to know her. She was very different from the mother who gave birth to me but if I suspended all recollection of that one, I saw that this new one was pretty damned special too. But only if I did no comparisons. Self-imposed amnesia. I got pretty good at it. It was preferable to wallowing in self-pity. I couldn't long for the old Rusty if I stopped thinking about her as she had been.

As I became accustomed to Rusty's newest personality - she changed again. Donna and I noticed a drastic difference in her behavior from one Thursday to the following Sunday. We planned to take her out to lunch but she babbled nonsense in response to our conversation with her and she couldn't follow simple directions like seating herself inside the car. When she did speak in words that we understood, she was grumpy and her outlook took a negative tone. She made petty remarks about other people's appearance and about their conduct. Where did this come from? Mom's manner became belligerent and she was almost hostile with Donna and me. And contrary. If we indicated a chair for her to sit in, she chose a different one. I was puzzled about what to do with this spoiled two-year-old. Maybe, like a two-year child, this was the only way for her to assert her independence. As a parent, Mom always followed the notion that children need boundaries and rules and routines. These conditions make children feel safe, she believed. I applied her philosophy to our current state of affairs, except for one tiny detail. No matter how child-like the residents in the Alzheimer's unit were, they were not children, they were adults. They were our parents. We maintained the illusion of freedom for them as we corralled them behind doors with tamper-proof locks. Then, as quickly as Mom entered into the new and unattractive personality phase, she returned to her previous tranquil manner.

Whiplash. Again.

At home, Phantom and Dickens lived in the moment as Mom did. Without fail, they greeted us with wagging tails and a joyful expectation that good things were on the horizon. They welcomed every hug, every head pat, and every treat as if they were essential to their survival. Maybe they were. We took one dog or the other with us occasionally to the nursing home when we were not going to visit during mealtime. We had permission from the administrators to bring the girls into the facility as long as shot records were in their files, and they exhibited no behavioral problems. Just having their sweet furry faces to look at and pet was calming. Mom felt it and so did many of the residents. It was a little thing to do, but having a doggy visit cheered up the sourest of dispositions. Even my own. While watching Mom stroke the thick fur coat of Phantom one evening, I realized that it was actually interesting to have a peek at what Mom must have been like when she was a child. Lord, what a live-wire and a handful she must have been!

We discovered that Mom's new world, located beyond the Looking Glass, was best approached by adopting a bit of whimsy upon entering. After lunch one rainy Sunday visit we took our stroll inside the room to avoid the foul weather. Willie's daughter, Marie, stopped us on one of our laps.

"Your mom is such fun," she told us. "I was sitting on the piano stool yesterday after feeding Mother her lunch and Rusty came over to sit beside me. I asked her if she was going to play a song for us on the piano and she said 'I can play anything you want but that doesn't mean it'll come out sounding like music.'"

Before our visit on the following Friday evening Donna and I took a rose out to place on Dad's gravesite. It would have been his eightieth birthday. We didn't bother to mention it to Mom. I was learning to leave well enough alone and deal with more immediate matters. The nursing assistants were good at this. They attended to these residents who had no cure for their disease by responding to their immediate needs. Mom's CNAs continued to make up a bed for her on the sofa in the middle of the seating area. There in the middle of the main room, Mom slept. I appreciated that the CNAs did this for her. When rested, Mom was brighter and more interactive which meant she related to us and to other residents more meaningfully.

One example of this is when Joan Cleister, a dear friend of Mom's from Newell, was admitted into the rehabilitation section of Willow Lake. The rehab part of the nursing home admitted patients directly from the hospital and most of those patients brought with them no expectations of becoming fulltime residents even though nursing homes are sometimes called God's Waiting Room. For many of the temporary patients, physical therapy is ordered to assist in becoming mobile again and to regain other skills so they can return home. The rooms are private and spacious enough for family members and friends to gather unlike the other smaller rooms which are shared and can become crowded quite quickly. At Willow Lake, the Rehab hall was the first hall encountered from the main entrance. This was, no doubt, deliberate. If Rehab patients and visitors saw the condition of residents on the long-term care hall first hand and witnessed the atmosphere where there was little hope of improvement for these folks, it would surely hamper their recovery. I appreciated the effort made to foster a positive outlook for these patients, but there was another reality. At times, a patient admitted into the Rehab section was not able to go directly home from the hospital for one reason or another. Perhaps there is no one available at home to provide the level of sustained and intensive care for the patient. Or perhaps the patient's health requirements are simply greater than what can reasonably be provided for them in their home. And then there are times when the individual admitted into the Rehab may not survive long enough to become a resident. The second scenario fit Joan.

When I heard Joan had been admitted, Mom and I walked down to visit her. I don't know if Mom recognized Joan any more than she had recognized Emily when we visited her a few weeks earlier but once again Mom's heart recognized a fellow human being in need and did no more and no less than be present with Joan. Mom stood by her bedside, patting her hand gently. Mom was *there* and she literally had nowhere else more important to be - physically or psychologically. Joan's heart condition sapped her energy, even sitting up was too fatiguing to attempt. But she was able to talk a little and she responded to her visitors. Joan knew Mom and enjoyed her presence. The two of them interacted at a deeper level than I was capable of. Through exchanges of knowing looks and holding each other's hands, they seemed to understand that each of their journeys, their life paths were diverging from the rest of us in their families. Although I did not fully understand what I witnessed I did appreciate it. It touched me to see the love expressed between these two friends. I learned that we do not always need to *do* for others. Perhaps at the most momentous times of our lives, just being with someone is the perfect gift. Rusty-the-doer was stripped of the ability to-do by Alzheimer's disease, and being was all that was left to her. She shared it with Joan. I would have given anything to have the old Rusty back, but seeing this small compensation emerge because of the disease was a miracle I valued highly.

Joan's husband, Ronald, had been a good friend of Dad's. They both were instrumental in building the youth baseball program in Newell. I thanked him for taking Dad for haircuts so many times before the stroke. He told me he had always liked and respected Jim. That was awfully sweet of him. Then he got choked up. So did I. It was difficult to maintain any composure as I thought of the many old friends losing each other now. When it was time for us to leave and I was saying goodbye to Joan, she grabbed my hand.

"I always thought the world of your mother," she told me. "I wish I could have done more for her. I'm sorry I didn't." Tender. Raw. Real. A confession?

A few of Mom's friends bravely stayed in touch with her, offering assistance at times in spite of the disease which changed her personality. Others were unable to maintain a relationship with this friend under new and difficult circumstances. Unfortunately, this is a common consequence of Alzheimer's disease.

"You were a good friend. It was enough, Joan. No one could ask for more than that."

She patted my hand in response.

Lying in bed with few distractions, Joan must have contemplated what lay ahead of her, and yet here she was, thinking of Rusty.

Joan died the next day. I didn't tell Mom. She never asked. That experience was long forgotten by her. Or rather (in Mom's world) the visit never took place.

The inconsolable pain etched on the faces of Joan's family

members at her service sucker punched my gut. The experience of loss was familiar to me by now but I had yet to experience this one. My mind skipped away from that reality like Brer Rabbit heading into the briar patch for protection.

Making nightly visits during the week, when Donna and I were already tired from a long day at work, meant we focused only on making sure Mom ate her dinner. We said our goodbyes after this task was done and then went home to get our own supper. We repeated the process Monday through Friday of every week. I continued to take Saturdays off, but we spent increasingly more time with Mom during the Sunday visits. None of these visits was a duty, nor did they feel like an obligation although that's how the description sounds. There was no pressure on me to micromanage Mom's care to this extent. It was a privilege to have this time with her and I did these things as much for myself as I did for Mom. I couldn't stay away. My heart, my soul, and practically every thought that crossed my mind were in one place - the 400 Club. And I have to admit that the Sunday visits were my favorite. Staff members had a knack for making the day special, making sure every willing resident was taken to the church service held in the main dining room. The cooks did an excellent job making the midday meal extra tasty for the residents. After the meal was over, church choirs often came by to perform. The Alzheimer's group loved this! Many of them sang along to the traditional hymns, pulling the words from somewhere deep down in their beings. Meanings of the words may have been lost within the scrambled connections of their misfiring synapses but the music resonated in the souls of these individuals and brought them comfort for a time.

This was true for most of the residents anyway, but not for George Nguyen who was Cambodian. He didn't share the same connections to these songs. George typically spoke French when addressed in that language and rarely used English unless asked to do so.

"Bonjour, George," I greeted him. He responded by rattling off a string of words making complex French sentences at a speed far more advanced than I understood.

"Speak English," Theresa, the evening nurse, instructed him. She knew George had English at his command whenever he was reminded of it. He switched effortlessly to English to accommodate us.

George loved gardening. The CNAs knew this and took him outside often. At times he sat on a chair on the patio accessed from the Alzheimer's unit through a sliding glass door off the dining room area, and it was enough. Usually, it was Jama, the CNA who orchestrated Mom and Dad's final moments together, who would find time in the afternoons to take George for a stroll on the grounds. We're told in Deuteronomy that *Man does not live on bread alone*, and in George's case this was definitely true. He needed sunshine to live. George's survival depended on touching the green grass, squinting into the sunlight, and crumbling the earth between his fingers much as my own mother. In Mom's case, though, she had long forgotten this personal need. It was still a mighty force in George's life, however.

When George was obliged to be inside, he often napped in Mom's room on her bed. Remember, the best Chi in the building flew through Mom's room. He must have sensed these vital properties coursing through the bedroom and needed to be in their presence. Often, when Donna and I arrived for dinner, we brought clothes or other items to put in Mom's room, and many times George was stretched out on top of her bedspread. Usually, his eyes were closed in a deep meditation so we snuck in and out unobserved. On occasion, he stared out the window, daydreaming. Of what? Days when he was free?

One particular Friday night, nearing a full moon (a time in which we had come to expect mischievous behavior) we opened the door to Mom's room and startled poor George. He jumped up.

"Bonjour, George," we greeted him.

"Bonjour! Bonjour! Comment ça va?"

"Ça va, George."

"Embrasse-moi!" he shouted. "Embrasse-moi!"

"Ha! I know that one, George," I told him as we backed away. "And the answer is no, you Casanova. No kissing! It's dinnertime."

We ducked out the door. He ran after us.

"What is it?" Theresa looked concerned.

"George is chasing us down for a kiss."

"You too? He's been doing that all day." Mary Ann cornered

George then guided him to the dinner table.

"Don't you *ever* think about napping in my momma's bed again, George," I said this as menacingly as I could. "Especially if she's in there! Do you understand me?" George didn't seem very afraid. I looked at Mary Ann and cocked a resolute eyebrow at her.

"We'll keep an eye on this one," she assured me.

"I should hope so!"

For George, being cooped up indoors was like receiving a life-sentence without parole and it killed his spirit. But not before he was able to make one last stand. On the next full moon, George escaped. He was agitated and unhappy at being kept inside on this particular bright sunshiny day. Jama was on duty second shift and she had been busy most of the day helping residents with their showers. George sensed that the coast was clear and made a break for freedom. Assisting a resident back to her room, Jama caught sight of George dashing into Mom and Karen's room. She rushed to the room to see why George was in such a hurry. As she slipped through the door, she saw only the soles of George's feet following his body as he hurtled himself out the window in a swan dive. Somehow he'd gotten the window opened wide enough to propelled his body through it head-first. Jama, acting on pure instinct, dove after him and chased him across the lawn. She finally collared him before he reached the edge of the property and coaxed him back indoors. When Jama related the story to us, I briefly entertained the notion that Rita was behind this escape attempt. Upon further reflection I realized my suspicions were wrong since the endeavor was too haphazard for her liking. George was simply compelled by a blind need to escape his imprisonment. He found a more successful way out only a few weeks later when he caught a flu bug and died. I was not sad for George. In fact, I rejoiced that he was free at last.

For those of us who remained, life in the 400 Club continued much as before. We never, ever, knew what we would encounter during a visit. There was always something new popping up to surprise us in the world beyond the Looking Glass. One night when Donna and I walked in, the same time as usual, we observed that each and every resident was already seated and eating supper. Quietly. In pajamas.

"What did ya'll do?" I asked the group. I knew they had

messed up. This was way out of the ordinary even for this bunch. Donna and I were intrigued.

"They-have-tried-my-patience-all-day," Theresa told us through clinched teeth. "They-are-having-their-dinner-and-then-they-are-going-to-bed."

Another full moon.

On our next visit, as we came through the doors, Earnest stood before us, hands on his hips, looking all the world as if he wanted to blame us for something.

"Where's your shirt, Earnest?" I asked.

I looked over at the nursing station to see who was on duty. Then I panned the room for Rusty if only to make sure everyone else was fully clothed. I was relieved when I established that the general population was properly dressed. Mary Ann popped out of one of the bedrooms just then and saw Earnest.

"Where's your shirt, Earnest?"

Same question. Same answer. Earnest looked at his questioners as if our inquisitiveness into his personal business disgusted him. He didn't need to report his every move to us. He spent his spare time repairing things and he made it clear that we didn't appreciate the things he did for us. What he did and did not do with his shirts was none of our business. That, and the huge possibility that he had no idea where that blasted shirt was since memory was in short supply here.

Donna and I spent the dinner hour with Mom, quizzical frowns leaving nasty wrinkles on our foreheads, asking the same questions over and over.

"Wonder where Earnest's shirt could be."

"What do you think happened to Earnest's shirt?"

"Why would Earnest take off his shirt?"

To hide the evidence? Earnest has a paramour? Somebody's making a calendar? Yes, we were quite intrigued and unable to move on and put the issue to rest.

After supper and after our nightly Conga Line dance we took Mom to her bathroom to start the bedtime routine. With assistance, Rusty still managed going to the toilet, a welcomed achievement. Not having to rely on incontinence pads or protective adult briefs meant fewer occurrences of urinary tract infections. Too soon the part of Mom's brain that signals the urge to go to the toilet would be destroyed by the disease. We were grateful for any small blessing. After Mom was done, I flushed the toilet but with no success. As the water in the bowl rose to a frightening level, I snatched the tank lid off to lift the float ball and hopefully avoid an overflow. As I did this, I saw it - a bright red and black plaid flannel shirt. It was wadded up and submerged inside the tank. I pulled it out and wrung the water out of it over the sink. Leaving Donna with Mom, I walked out into the main room with it in my hands and waved it in the air.

"Found Earnest's shirt," I announced.

"Where was it?" Three or four voices responded in unison because everyone enjoys when a good mystery is solved.

"Inside the tank of Mom's toilet," I told them, quite proud of myself.

"Must've been trying to fix it," someone replied quite matter of factly.

"Just what I thought." I agreed then returned to Mom's room.

On a visit not long after Earnest's missing shirt incident, we noticed the nurses and CNAs, who were usually upbeat and happy, looked as if they'd been crying.

"Did you hear?" Peggy, the night nurse on this particular evening, ask us.

"No. What?"

"Hunter died."

Mom's roommate Karen could depend on a lunchtime visit from her husband most days of the week and the rest of us saw him occasionally in the evenings as well. We looked forward to any visit that overlapped with Hunter's. News of his death was a shock.

"What happened?" I asked Peggy.

"He was swimming laps at the YMCA this morning, had a heart attack, and died." *Oh, God.*

Death comes for us all. In this setting it came often. But Hunter's death did make me stop and assess what it was that I was missing in my life and I was missing a lot. I missed my friends. I missed having free time. I missed *fun*. I called my friends Paula and Patrick and invited them over on Saturday night. No alcohol had passed these lips since the unfortunate cycling incident that resulted in my rather rude treatment at the emergency room. I looked forward to relaxing with them, eating a nice meal and indulging in a glass of wine or two as any sophisticated adult might do. Then the telephone rang.

"Your mother has fallen and hit her head. We're having her taken to the emergency room and we wanted to let you know so you can meet her there."

I would not go to the hospital with alcohol on my breath again. I brushed my teeth and stuffed enough Spearmint gum into my cheeks to pass for a close relative of Chip 'n Dale. Luckily Donna had not imbibed so she drove us to the hospital across town. I sent Paula and Patrick home with my apologies. They understood.

We arrived at the same emergency room where we took Dad when he had the stroke. Mom's ambulance arrived only moments ahead of us. We broke through the main doors and flew past the admittance nurse. It took us less than a minute to find Rusty. She was dazed and unsure why she was there but she knew us and responded to our soothing words. Dried blood, the rusty red color of her hair was camouflaged on the back of her head. Apparently, it's not the hospital's job to clean up its patients so I did it. Before a verdict could be rendered on the damage, the ER doctor wanted to make X-rays of Mom's skull. We were installed in a sterile examining room to wait for her to be taken to the radiology department.

"What happened, Mom?"

"What do you mean?"

"You hit your head, how did you do it?"

"I did?" She put her hand to her head and winced.

"I don't know how it happened, but it hurts."

I searched for a medical practitioner to ask for an aspirin or ibuprofen or something stronger to help alleviate Mom's pain. The nurse explained that they couldn't give her anything until she'd been examined. I encouraged her to get on with it as it looked to be a slow night to me. There was no overflow in the waiting room and several examination rooms sat empty. She assured me that they would see to her in good time. *Really?*

The X-ray technicians eventually came for Mom. I jumped up to go with them.

"You'll have to stay here. We won't be long," they told me.

"I need to go with her. She's got Alzheimer's and she'll be frightened if she thinks I've left her alone. She won't remember I'm waiting for her here."

"We'll take good care of her, don't worry."

I felt powerless to fight yet more bureaucratic rules. My sister, the Bubbanator, would not have sat still for this. When the techs wheeled Mom back, we were moved to a different examining room to wait for the doctor to interpret the results for us. There we waited.

"Do you want to sleep, Mom? We'll be right here. Don't worry."

"Oh, no, I'm not sleepy at all. I'm fine."

I wondered how we could while away the time. When we were here for Dad, Andrea brought us a hospital-kit. Magazines, tissues, water, crackers, cookies, etc. If I had been smart, I would have created one of these things for myself and placed it by the front door to grab for just such an emergency. My kit would include a travel-sized bottle of mouth wash and breath mints, of course. Since I didn't have a kit, I rummaged through the cabinets that lined the walls of the room, looking for anything of interest to use for entertainment purposes. I found a box of latex gloves, size medium. Ha!

I blew them up and tied them off in a number of configurations and staged a puppet show for Mom and Donna, playing the different parts like Willie did back in the 400 Club. I was sleep-deprived, slap-happy, and unabashed. Mom wouldn't remember my silly show and Donna is much too good-hearted to hold this sort of thing against me so I let loose. I considered Mom's previous fall and how the hip protecting girdle prescribed for her in the event of another fall, even if she had been wearing it, would not have protected her head in this case. Would this doctor suggest the use of a helmet? Francis was right. We can't protect our loved ones from everything.

When the doctor came in with the results, I sneaked the used gloves into the trash can behind his back. After looking at the CT scans of Mom's head and the X-Ray of her neck, he determined that there was no damage to her neck but fluid pooled on her brain, a subdural hematoma he called it. He wanted a follow-up appointment in a couple of weeks, but we were free to go for now. He made a note to call the staff physician and the nurse practitioner at Willow Lake to discuss Mom's unsteadiness. With assistance from Donna and me, Mom walked out to my truck and we drove her back to the nursing home. It was cramped with the three of us in the compact cab, but we were together and that was enough.

When we got back to the 400 Club I asked Theresa how she fell.

"She and another resident were interacting with each other. Your mom stepped back, became unsteady, fell and hit the back of her head on the floor," she told me.

Her explanation was rehearsed and vague but I didn't question her. The floor is concrete with a vinyl tile surface; my imagination of what the fall must have been like for Mom was vivid. I pushed the image down as quickly as it popped up and chose to not fish for more details. We got Mom settled in and went home. After I got some rest, I began to regret not getting more information on what exactly happened to make Mom fall. Then I got a telephone call from another family member we knew in the 400 Club.

"Marsha, I was there when your mother fell and I saw what happened. Do you want to know?" I assured her I did.

"Jane was in her bedroom across from Rusty's. She was holding a baby doll before getting ready to go to bed. Miss Nell went into the room and took the doll away from her. Jane cried bloody-murder and your mom tried to calm them both down. Miss Nell shoved her backwards. Rusty lost her footing and fell straight back onto the floor. It was a sickening sound to hear her head hit the floor. We rushed over to her right away. She was stunned at first, of course. And then she looked like she was in pain. The staff reacted quickly and called for an ambulance immediately but I don't know if they are allowed to tell you the whole story."

"I guess they didn't want to name names. But I appreciate knowing what happened. I'm glad you were there."

"It happened so fast, there was nothing I could do. I'm so sorry."

How could I blame Miss Nell? How could I hold her responsible when dementia prevented her from controlling her own actions? The scenario could easily have been reversed with Mom being the aggressor. What good would it have done to let anger and resentment add to the sadness I was already carrying inside of me? I don't recall making a decision to feel this way, perhaps my Guardian Angels were guiding me here. I was pretty saturated with the accumulated gloom of our past few months. There was no room for more.

Two weeks after the fall, I took Mom to the neurosurgeon for a follow-up CT scan. The fluid buildup was still there but not any more than originally detected. He suggested that we continue to watch it. He wanted to postpone any actual surgery until it was absolutely necessary. The CNAs gave Mom more special attention after her fall, if that was even possible. They brought her extra snacks, which she ate with gusto, earning her the nickname, Sweet Lips.

Meanwhile, I continued my quest for normalcy in life outside nursing home culture. I focused on finding a suitable pair of walking shoes to take to Egypt with me. Our departure date was near and I needed shoes - sturdy, comfortable hikers. These shoes would stride across the desert sands of the Pharaohs so they needed to be special. We accumulated our gear, packed it, and then paid Mom one last visit. There was no need to tell her we'd be out of the country for three weeks. She already thought eternity separated our visits. I left her sitting at the dining room table complaining of a headache. Theresa reassured me that she would give Mom some aspirins before bedtime and watch her closely.

Donna and I flew to London-Gatwick where we met up with her brother Charles who flew in from Atlanta. We took the train out to Susie's house in London then caught our Egypt-Air flight to Cairo the next morning. The trip was uneventful if you don't consider fresh cool, circulating air in the passenger compartment of the airplane necessary. We had researched, discussed and agreed on the rules of engagement before our actual arrival in Egypt. We believed that these rules, when followed, would reduce the effects of Mummy Tummy or Pharaoh's Revenge. This is the so-called attack of diarrhea experienced by travelers going to unfamiliar destinations. We understood that during the course of our tour, the question was not *if* we would be stricken but *when*. We intended to reduce the severity and length of time we would be out of commission by drinking only bottled water and eating food that has been cooked. Egyptians are heartier folks than we tourists are. Not only do they eat fruits and vegetables that are uncooked, they also throw caution to the wind when claiming luggage. Orderly queuing at the baggage carrousel had not yet caught on in the Cairo Airport. We were compelled to join the throng making a mad dash to claim our belongings or risk never seeing them again. I had Imodium in my suitcase. I was a force to be reckoned with.

I never dreamed that a world stranger than the 400 Club existed but Egypt was a more exotic place than this southern gal had ever experienced. Bird of Paradise flowers grew like our daisies did back home. Lotus and papyrus plants were their Kudzu. Donkeys and donkey-driven carts were a major form of transportation, doing the hauling our pickup trucks did back home when taking farm fresh produce to town. The Great Pyramid of Giza, accompanied by its smaller but no less impressive neighboring pyramids, was visible from our hotel in Cairo. Here, it is an ordinary occurrence for Cairo citizens to see this sight, as well as the stately Sphinx, every day.

Six thousand miles separated me from my mother. I was far away from my cares and woes and I allowed my exhaustion to swallow me up. While my traveling companions dressed warmly for the evening light show at the site of the Sphinx, I snuggled down under the covers to sleep. We toured the Museum of Egyptian Antiquities in Cairo the next day and then out to the pyramids for a closer look. I was afraid that I would be too tired to visit every site on our itinerary but a cruise on Lake Nasser and on the Nile River was a gentle and humane way to visit the attractions of Egypt.

We began the lake cruise at Abu Simbel. The Great Temple of Abu Simbel was built by Ramses the Great, who is believed to be the Pharaoh of the Exodus in the Old Testament. Four figures of Ramses seated on a throne are carved in stone and are over sixty-five feet tall, the size of a five-story building. Our boat, the M/S Nubian Sea, was small (only fifty cabins and suites) but well appointed. It pulled up to the beach in front of the temple and tethered itself to a shoreline boulder. The gang plank was extended for us to disembark at our convenience while the boat floated in the shallow water right in front of the colossal statues. We walked to the site of the temple as often as we pleased. Sitting on the deck of the boat under an awning and sipping cups of delicious lemongrass, hibiscus or mint tea, or maybe a rich espresso while gazing at and admiring the workmanship that went into carving such a massive structure, makes for a delicious memory.

From Abu Simbel we cruised to the Aswan Dam by connecting the dots in between with visits to many celebrated temples including a trek by camel through the hot desert sands to one of them. One night, as our boat chugged along the massive shoreline of Lake Nasser, we sat in deck chairs around the pool. In the darkness, with no civilization for hundreds of miles and with absolutely no light pollution, we gazed at the stars and the full moon above us. The backdrop was black velvet. The sparkling stellar diamonds punched through the pitch-dark night sky illuminating the rolling sand dunes of the Sahara Desert. Seeing these dazzling and brilliant stars was a spiritual moment for me. One of our new friends pointed out the Constellation Orion to us. Before this moment, I had only ever recognized the Big Dipper in our own bit of sky. Out in the dark void of this night, the stars looked close enough to touch, no longer merely pin points of light 'out there' somewhere far away. For the first time in my life, I understood why our ancient ancestors were attentive to and smitten by these celestial show-offs.

For the Nile River part of our cruise, the M/S Atlas became our home base. It was smaller than the previous boat but just as nice and I imagined myself a character in Agatha Christie's 'Death on the Nile'. If you find yourself traveling abroad, make friends with the Brits. They are delightful company and practiced in ferreting out and sharing information that will smooth out the bumps encountered in your expedition. I also encourage you to hang out with the Dutch when possible. They are good tempered, take themselves lightly, and know how to party.

I could write pages and pages about our trip to Egypt, it was that memorable. When I was a child and daydreamed of becoming a mad scientist or absent minded professor, I never considered the possibility of touching a pyramid with my own hands or peering at the noonday sun from the shadows of a colonnade at the Temple of Karnak. Walking along the desolate and barren rocky, dusty tombs in the Valley of the Kings never made my bucket list because I dared not dream as big as my friends who brought me along with them. I loved this trip and I loved sharing it with these gentle people. But I was never once able to take my mind entirely off Mom and her welfare. I was anxious to get back to her. We flew back to London, enjoyed an un-traditional Thanksgiving meal with our friends there, and then prepared to return home. We arrived in Charlotte on a Saturday afternoon. Josh picked us up at the airport and drove us directly to the nursing home. Would Mom remember me?

Mom recognized me as soon as I walked through the door. *Hallelujah!* But I didn't recognize her at all. Her head was half-shaved. Her denture was nowhere to be found, distorting her face. And she had lost down to 95 pounds. After I regained my composure I hugged her. In my proximity to her I got a better look at the industrial-sized staples holding the flaps of skin together on her head. Oh. My. God.

"What did ya'll do to my mother?" I asked Nurse Peggy.

"Haven't you talked to your brother or sister?"

"No. We came here straight from the airport."

"Call Andy," she said. "He's going to want to fill you in."

I whipped out my mobile phone and hit speed dial. He explained how two days after we left, Mom's headache became unbearable. Her speech was slurred and she didn't recognize Andy when he visited her. Emergency surgery resulted in two holes being drilled into Mom's right parietal bone to drain the fluid collecting there as a result of the subdural hematoma and to relieve the pressure it placed on her brain. Mom was in ICU for several days and in the hospital a total of ten days out of the twenty-one I was gone. Barbara had driven down to help out and together she and Andy saw Mom through the latest events.

Mom looked like a casualty of the London Blitz. Severe bruising on the right side of her face and the new hairstyle was not the least bit attractive. But she was here. And she knew me. My mother knew me. It mattered that Rusty recognized me. I already mourned her inability to remember our birthdays; I hated the thought of the time when she would no longer know us. Alzheimer's makes orphans of us all.

But for now she *did* know us. A miracle. And we had important events to attend to. Mom's birthday was coming up – seventy-one-years old. Christmas followed quickly on the heels of that. On Christmas Eve, I went to the nursing home to visit Mom while Donna stayed home to begin preparing the Christmas meal. We recognized that this was going to be another difficult Christmas – we missed the many family members who were no longer here with us. We planned to visit Mom on Christmas day, but I wanted to be with her on this night too. Just me. Hanging out with Mom. Enjoying each other's company. Mother and Daughter.

I arrived after supper and fully expected the residents to be in their pajamas, waiting quietly for the prancing and pawing of hooves. Instead, the room was alive with activity and it wasn't even a full moon. Rusty sat at a table near the door with Jama and two other residents.

"Come join us!" Jama greeted me as she dealt a hand of cards to everyone at the table.

"What's the game?"

I scanned the surface of the table but saw no chips or pennies. Probably not poker, I speculated.

"Rummy," she said.

"Deal me in."

Oh yeah! Here was normalcy at last in the Land of Bizarre. I could get used to this. Nice frosty short-cans of soda sat at our finger tips. Pringles, dumped out onto a paper towel in the middle of the table, sat within reach of us all. A party! I do love a party.

I fanned my cards out to get a better look at them. Then I sorted 'like' cards together to make a book out of them. Jama watched my intense earnestness with amusement and laughed. I laughed too. I was happy to be there. Miss Nell looked at the cards in her hands as if they were foreign objects dropped in from outer space. Rita laid her cards down on the table, face up, showing us her hand. If this had been a game of *Go Fish!*, her strategy would certainly have turned the odds of winning in my favor. Mom, as was her way, faked it. She looked at each card with pretend interest. She followed my lead and rearranged a card or two in the array.

Jama said, "Okay, everybody lay down your cards, like this, and we'll see who won."

I followed *her* lead and laid down my cards. She called out a winner (not me, it wasn't my turn yet). I thought the method she used to choose a winner was rather arbitrary but I applauded the champion like a good sport. Jama scooped up the cards and gave them to me.

"Your deal," she told me.

The deck felt odd. I couldn't quite put my finger on it. We

played another hand similar to the one before. Then Jama dealt. Then back to me. A light bulb went off in my head. I counted the cards in the deck. Forty three. We were literally playing without a full deck. I looked at Jama. She grinned. Then I understood why she laughed at my serious approach to the game. I laughed too.

"Do you have a complete deck of cards anywhere?" I asked her.

"Would it matter?" she winked.

CHAPTER SIXTEEN

Ava is born!

Happy news!! And, it arrived via the dreaded telephone which I had begun to associate only with information that made me cry. Ava was born to Andy and Andrea on a clear and chilly January day. Her advent was the best thing to happen to our family since Andy and Andrea's wedding. When Andy called with the news, I was already at my work desk. After he gave me the highlights, I hung up the receiver and shouted over my shoulder to my supervisor as I made for the door. "I'm an aunt again!" I announced. "And only twenty four years since it happened last time. I'll be back in a couple of hours."

Donna met me at the hospital. We couldn't believe a baby could be as gorgeous as this little dark-haired beauty. She melted our hearts. I understood then, the whole circle-of-life and life-goes-on adages. The sages are right.

Dad had lived long enough to know that another grandchild was expected to him and Mom. We were sad that he was not able to share our joy for his granddaughter's birth but our excitement for the new addition to our family sent some of that gloom packing. When Andy, Andrea and Ava were home and settled we brought Mom out to their house. There, she held this little Angel in her arms. Home movies bear evidence of this fact. Even with Mom's wonky haircut and bruising on her face from surgery still visible on the video, re-watching Mam-ma Rusty and Ava is a pleasure. A full head of hair is not what's important in life.

Andy and Andrea will have another daughter in less than two and a half years from this day. Mom will hold her too, if only briefly. But it's enough for bragging rights. Mom cradled every grandchild sent to her in her arms. A little miracle.

Renewed optimism for the future followed Ava into our world. Life had been cold and dark for a long time but now rays of sunlight warmed us. Also, our two dogs, Phantom and Dickens, brought us much delight. I relied on them more than ever for their healing touch. Seeing their sweet faces daily boosted my morale. Our pets (and dogs specifically) are tuned into our emotions and can anticipate our needs. I've mentioned this already and it bears repeating. Research presented by Nova in their program, *Dogs Decoded*, suggests that our attachment to our pets and the benefits we reap are not in our imagination. Dogs distinguish various facial expressions we make and detect from them when we feel we're in danger or when we're sad or happy. They know if we're angry or in distress and they can communicate with us on that level. Having pets in our lives reduces stress, lowers blood pressure and may even extend our life span. Dickens' easygoing personality was a model for me to emulate. Phantom was particularly skillful in understanding when I was feeling melancholy and she never tired of offering her thick, lush Husky fur coat for me to stroke. And it *was* a stress reducer. I didn't think to do it on my own, but she consistently insisted that it would do me good. And it did.

Only two months after our Ava was born, Donna and Josh and I came home one evening and found Phantom lying on her side, unable to stand up. Josh responded immediately and we helped him lift her in the car and drove over to the emergency veterinary office. The vet thought she had suffered a stroke and held out little hope that she would survive it. We stayed by Phantom's side for the next hour until she exhaled her final breath. She was seven years old. Telling her goodbye was a blow. We had counted on her more than we realized.

Contrasting the happiness of Ava's birth with this fresh assault of grief was overwhelming. I was reminded of the old Proverb, *fall down seven times, get up eight*. It provided a little boost to my spirits but I began to have a slight notion of what the Book of Job was all about. Resources to draw from in response to this new and sudden emotional strike were in short supply and I didn't know what to do with the pain. The Alchemist's formula transforms something common into something special but I had no idea how to turn tragedy into joy.

In our household, Phantom had *alpha-dog* status in her pack of two with Dickens following her lead. But Dickens stepped into *only-dog* role without difficulty. She mourned the passing of her sister in her own way, of course, and it looked to us that she missed her sister so we took her to the nursing home with us more frequently than before. Faces brightened when this huge loveable creature entered that well of lonely souls. The only drawback to bringing Dickens to the nursing home was that it took us longer to walk through the main corridor on our approach to the 400 Club. It was time well spent, though. As we weaved a path through the wheelchair-bound senior citizens along the way we watched their faces go from a slack-jawed stupor to bright and youthful smiles. They extended their hands to pat Dickens' head and gave her shoulders a good ruffle. Bringing a bit of joy *on-four-paws*, where there is none, was its own reward. An Alchemist's whisper echoed somewhere in the cobwebs of my consciousness, *You manufacture joy for yourself by bringing joy – no matter how large or small – to someone else.* The solution for making joy from tragedy was not lost on me. In fact, we believed we had discovered the recipe for the fabled Stone Soup. We added just one ingredient, Dickens, and the residents each added a little smile or a kind word and before we knew it a delicious recipe emerged magically. Our environment of scarcity transformed into a tasty stew and before long we noticed more visitors began bringing their doggie friends for visits with their loved ones, too.

    My spirit enjoyed a small rebound, but my body, compromised by long-term fatigue and stress, meant I couldn't fight off even a cold before it turned into something more severe. My immune system was already well suited to bronchitis and this became my resident interloper. I took swift action and I followed the treatment prescribed by my physician. Nothing worked. Nine months later, after several courses of prescriptions and a hospital visit for chest X-rays to see if I had pneumonia (I didn't), bronchitis was winning the battle. I agreed to take the synthetic corticosteroid drug that shall remain nameless so that I do not have a lawsuit on my hands. It was a little more helpful than the previous meds but even following the instructions to the letter, the side-effects kicked my gluteus maximus. One afternoon at work, three days after completing the doses, one of those side-effects listed in the small print popped up. Initially, I had the urge to run through plate glass windows then I quickly moved into the next phase which was wanting to run out into traffic. I called the doctor's office. The receptionist responded professionally but the spiel seemed rehearsed since I was not the first patient to have adverse reactions to the drug. Her advice: "You can go to the emergency room, but the only thing they can do is make you wait for the side-effects to wear off." *Great!* RIDE IT OUT. The Jim Burris philosophy of dealing with the realities of life.

"Or," she continued, "You can get yourself home and wait for the effects to wear off there. Don't drink alcohol. It will not help." *What was in my records to make her tell me this last part?*

My supervisor chose this precise moment to give me an assignment. The glimmer of hysteria in my eyes told her it could wait until morning and she returned to the safety of her office. I did get home. I lay on my sofa and waited it out. Jim would have beeen so proud. No harm was done to me or others. I credit my own highly-honed self-discipline for the good result.

Donna thought my recovery would benefit from another brief holiday and planned a week-end trip to a rustic cabin near Gatlinburg. I had ceased all visits to the nursing home in my current state of unhealthiness so I thought, why not? The change in latitude might give me an opportunity to rest and repair. A cozy fire in the fireplace, a Sue Grafton mystery, good food, and lots and lots of sleep fortified me and kick-started a more productive immune response. At last I began to feel better. Then, before I became accustomed to a renewed gusto for life I fell victim to an outbreak of Shingles. Oh, sweet petunia! That hurt! I hadn't seen my forty-seventh birthday and yet I had been thrown into instant menopause, had spent the better part of a year coughing up a lung with bronchitis, and now I had Shingles. God, I felt old.

At first I thought the rash on my back might be hives but it was so painful that I sought medical intervention forthwith. My physician made the diagnosis. If you've ever had chickenpox, you have the virus that can cause Shingles. If, like me, your immune system becomes compromised, it will increase the chances that Shingles will make itself quite at home along a random nerve axon in your body. As long as I had a rash I would be contagious, so of course I did not visit Mom during this latest disease outbreak either and I hated it. Every day of my absence threatened to wipe my existence from Mom's memory bank. I certainly did not want to risk that but an additional concern was that the rash on my back was extremely sensitive and I could not stand to have clothes touch it let alone foundation garments. So I stayed home. My only ventures out into the world were to the doctor's office. My physician, her staff and I were no longer using formal greetings during my appointments. We now embraced each other as BFFs.

"What exactly is going on in your life that's causing you to be so sick?" my doctor asked.

"Well," I told her. "My dad and brother passed away recently and my mother has Alzheimer's and is in a nursing home and my dog just died..."

She nodded her head in sympathy. "Yes, those are pretty big life events. Have you talked to anybody? A professional grief counselor, for example?"

I told her I had not.

"If you do not take time to grieve for yourself, if you only feel driven to take care of your mother, you will not regain your health," she told me gently. "You have not given yourself time to heal and apparently your body's reaction is to get sick. It does that to force you to slow down. Ignoring the grief won't make it disappear; it just transforms it into physical symptoms."

I must have looked skeptical. But she knew what she was talking about - her parents had been killed in an automobile accident two years before. She was thirty-six.

"Why don't you give therapy a try?" she continued. "It'll be helpful for you to develop coping skills to deal with these things in your life while getting yourself healthy again."

She was right. For years now, my entire life was work and tending to Mom and Dad. But I was no good to Mom while I was sick. I agreed to get some high quality professional counseling. I asked her for a referral. She gave me one. I made an appointment. Mom needed me more than ever and the best way to be available to her was to be healthy. But I was tired and weary and I was unable to work out how to balance the different areas of my life. I had not allowed myself the luxury (I didn't yet realize it was a necessity) of dealing with my grief that was a result of losing Dad and Robert, witnessing the effects of those deaths on Mom, and the gradual loss of the mother who raised me. I was overwhelmed with sadness. Taking proactive steps like going to grief counseling meant not letting that grief paralyze me. Maybe an objective point of view *was* indicated. I had been under the mistaken notion that getting up each morning, moving, and handling the countless details of each day, would provide me with a little bit of control over this crazy life of mine. Perhaps seeking the help of a professional would do for me what I couldn't seem to do for myself. And I now knew a more precise label for what I needed: *grief therapy (and) coping skills*. I was optimistic.

Although my raspy cough associated with bronchitis lingered with the residual burning sensations where my rash used to be, I went in for my first appointment. I assured the therapist that I was not infectious - I just sounded like it. She treated me as if I had the plague. Fair enough. I kept a respectable physical distance from her; I was here to learn grief therapy and coping skills, not to get a hug. I summarized the events my family and I had experienced in the last eighteen months. I covered only the highlights; this was after all an introductory appointment but it took up the fifty-minute hour. As she started wrapping up the session, I asked her point blank, "So, do you think you can help me?"

"Oh, yes." She responded with confidence. "I think we can work together. I have one reservation, though. I don't get the grief part." *Huh?* How much loss does one need to have within a year and a half to qualify for using the grief card?

"I don't understand why you're feeling so much grief," she repeated in response to my blank stare.

I didn't go back. I had no energy to spare. After carefully weighing the pros and cons of struggling to be understood, I chose to put no more effort into what I thought was an uphill battle. Handling this stuff myself (no matter how unqualified I was) was better than being misunderstood *and* paying good money for it. So I vowed to take more of life's bumps in stride. I would be a duck - water would roll off my back. I lifted my head high and stiffened my upper lip. That lasted a week.

Mom's nurse, Theresa, called me early one morning at work. Mom had a terrifying seizure at the breakfast table that morning, serious enough to request an EMT response. I called Donna who made a 180 degree turn as she approached her own office and we both converged on the ER parking lot as the ambulance arrived. The EMTs rolled the stretcher out of the van and we rushed to Mom's side. She looked at Donna and me, and I saw that she recognized us. She seemed to be grateful for our presence. Andy came a short while after us and she definitely perked up a bit for him. Nevertheless, her complexion was the color of bread dough. Exhaustion from the stress of the seizure on her body dulled her otherwise bright green eyes as they sat sunken in their sockets. CT scans showed no return or enlargement of the original pooling of blood on Mom's brain after she was pushed to the floor that night in the 400 Club. Blood work showed no indication of abnormal electrolytes. I didn't know what this meant but I assumed that if a thing is normal, it is good. I looked it up on the internet later and saw the words: peptide and hydrogen phosphate and my eyes glazed over. Whatever an electrolyte is, it was not the culprit that instigated Mom's seizure. I've been told that a seizure as severe as Mom's is no longer called a Grand mal seizure. The term, Tonic-Clonic seizure is now used. These seizures affect the entire brain and are typically preceded by crying out, or in Mom's case a blood-curdling scream, losing consciousness, falling to the ground, and then convulsing violently. A traumatic head injury as serious as Mom's often causes non-epileptic seizures like the one she had. Seizures cause additional damage to brains that may already be vulnerable because of a traumatic brain injury. For that reason, people with injuries like Mom's are typically given anticonvulsant medications as a precaution against seizures. I have no record that this was done for Mom. But at the hospital, Mom was given Dilantin intravenously and further doses were prescribed to be taken when Mom returned to the nursing home.

Non-emergency transport was ordered to take Mom back to Willow Lake. She could not sit up or support herself enough to be able to ride with one of us back to the nursing home so we tagged along behind the van in our own vehicles. Mom was not out of my sight the rest of the day. It's common for an individual who has had a Tonic-Clonic seizure to be totally exhausted and to sleep on and off for the next day or two. The assault wracked Mom's body and the damage weakened her. We hoped that some repairing took place as she slept. When she was awake, she responded only minimally to Donna and me as we sat by her side. The next day she ate a little breakfast then slept until evening. We stayed with her on this day too. While we were with her, we observed her eyes darting back and forth. She focused on something or someone we did not see or hear ourselves. This was the first (but not the last) time we witnessed the phenomenon of Mom interacting with *them*. She followed them with her eyes and engaged in riveting conversations. When she interacted with us, she babbled incoherently and yet she spoke intelligibly to them. Although she clearly favored them over us, we rose above the rebuff and did not discourage further encounters.

I visited Mom at lunchtime on the following day. She was more alert and much improved. As I sat by her side, I thought about how I regretted not having her at home with me but I knew that if it had been me with her when she had this seizure, I would not have known what to do. The staff's quick reaction likely reduced the injuries that accompany such a violent assault on an already fragile body. I appreciated it and I told them so.

Mom's brain was already compromised by the destructive effects of Alzheimer's disease. The head injury, the surgery, and the seizure were yet more fuel on the fire that was engulfing and destroying her intellect. And yet, the ol' gal hung on. She became more and more frail but she was still in the game and so was I.

During the summer after Mom's seizure and the general decline of her health as a result, Susie visited us from London. Donna and I were planning to travel to the coast of Maine with our friend Paula to visit her mother-in-law, and Susie would accompany us. Betty Pat lived in Georgetown on Five Islands. Donna and I had been there once before and we were eager to visit her and her home's idyllic setting again. Before leaving home, I buzzed like a bee lining up visitors for Mom and making sure everybody at the nursing home knew I was going away. Mom's nurses and CNAs were terrific as they assured me once again that everything would be fine in my absence. Donna, Susie and I made our final pilgrimage to visit Mom during lunchtime on Sunday then enjoyed an event-free week in Maine. A month after we returned home, Mom got pneumonia. A mobile X-ray machine was brought in to the nursing home to do the diagnostics. Taking Mom out of the facility for these tests would have been much too taxing on her and I was relieved that the service was available. Mom rebounded from the pneumonia in good time and then suffered from a urinary tract infection. A UTI will kick your butt even when you are otherwise in the best of health. Mom's constitution had always rivaled that of an ox but I saw that the cumulative effects of the last year and a half were taking a toll on my poor mother. As she became more frail, Mom could no longer walk without assistance and she was not able to feed herself. Her hands were not steady for that and as it turns out, scooping food onto a fork and directing it to one's mouth, chewing and swallowing, is a complex set of tasks that Alzheimer's disease will steal from its victims. Before we moved Mom to the 400 Club, we were told that there were two rules that must be adhered to by its residents. They had to be mobile and be able to feed themselves. Mom could do neither. Rumblings that Mom would soon need to leave Alice's Wonderland filtered down to us.

Until then, Donna and I coerced Mom to continue a semblance of dinner time walks. Together we pulled her to her feet. With much assistance, we got her to take a step or two - but it took both of us to hold her up for those few steps. Our efforts kept her walking, *technically*. We had succumbed to the charms of this environment and we desperately wanted to stay in Wonderland. It was a stretch to say Rusty was mobile, but it was true that she was not bedridden either. The staff encouraged us and covered for Mom whenever administrators inquired about changes in residents' habits. Mom's nurses were as invested in stretching the rules as we were. We pushed the limit as long as we could but Mom was able to do very little for herself now and she communicated less too, using pats on the hand or meaningful gazes in place of full sentences.

At the supper table one night, I lifted a spoonful of mashed potatoes to Mom's lips and she simply smiled at me. An enigmatic, beguiling smile that rivaled Mona Lisa's. I read volumes into that smile. She conveyed much love to me from that simple smile. That she felt like smiling at all was a miracle. But I couldn't escape the sadness that blanketed me. How did we get to this point? How strong this woman had always been - in body and in spirit. Where did the time go? There was much yet to say, to see, to share. I returned her gaze.

"You're my hero, you know." I blurted this out terrified that the time was fast upon us when it may be too late to tell her these things face-to-face.

Mom's strength was concentrated in her spirit now as her

brain failed her. It no longer told her feet and legs and hands what to do or how to do it. But the brain is like a radio, someone explained to me once, and our thoughts are radio waves that pass through the air. When a radio is broken, you may get only static, or you may not be able to receive broadcasts at all. It does not mean there are no broadcasts. But the broadcasts may be sent in code and cannot be directed through the instrument for clear translation. On this night, the radio transmitted in plain text. My words made sense to her and touched her. She reached her hand out to stroke my face. "You're my hero too," she whispered.

When she finished supper and I told her I needed to go, we both got teary at the same time. I asked her why. She said that she was afraid she'd never see me again. "I will always come to see you - always," I reassured her. But the tears continued.

"Why are you crying, Mom?"

She said, "I guess we have to accept things the way they are."

Tears streamed down my cheeks. Mom reached up and pulled my head down to her shoulder to cry on. It was wonderful.

"We have to trust...," I said but I don't really know why.

"I know. And you know I live right *there* all day long, right?" She pointed to my heart. I could endure the sorrow associated with this horrible disease - until her words made sense. Then it was too real and too sad to bear.

I met with the physician's assistant at the next care plan meeting. Cindy mentioned moving Mom to the long-term care hall, a.k.a. the 200 Hall, when a bed became free. I was already resigned to this next step and didn't bother to fight against its inevitability. Our friend Willie and her family had already blazed a trail to a room there. I asked Cindy if we could room with them. She said she would work it out.

Mom's physical health suffered. She was not eating enough to maintain her weight. Tests showed that low hemoglobin made her anemic. Taking multi-vitamins with iron didn't make a difference. As a result of the brain injury and seizure Mom developed some involuntary jerking in her hands and body. When we saw her at dinnertime now, she sat slumped in her Geri-chair, always to the left. Her left eye drifted lazily on its own. I don't know the significance of 'left' and didn't have the presence of mind to ask then, but it was enough of a concern that the neurologist continued to monitor Mom and declared that a *subdural hygroma* was the culprit. He described the hygroma as the pooling of mere brain fluid, not blood. Lucky for us it was not at the level that required another 'draining'. My knees went weak during the conversation and I clocked out for a little while. I asked him to send the report to the P.A. at Willow Lake to be incorporated in Mom's treatment plan.

Along with the noticeable deterioration of Mom's health, the health of Willow Lake was also in decline. The facility was bought by a new group of investors and by its very nature the corporation watched its bottom line closely. It was not the only time ownership changed hands on the open market during our tenure at Willow Lake but it seemed to be the one that made the biggest difference.

The staff was spread more thinly, although I personally witnessed no change in their attitude or the care offered to their charges. I did observe that, as their numbers were reduced, they were frustrated because less time was being allotted for essential activities such as feeding, clothing and bathing the residents. I was not alone in my concern over the downsizing of the number of CNAs in the 400 Club. A new policy that required the RNs to cover two halls meant they were often called away from their present duties to respond to more pressing situations. My biggest concern was Mom getting fed. Time spent with each resident was rationed and little extra time was available for the labor-intensive chore of feeding the vulnerable ones who could not feed themselves. I made sure my visits coincided with mealtime. I tempted Mom with the reward of a chocolate milkshake if she ate her meal. Rusty never used this sort of coercion with her children when, as youngsters, we didn't want to eat. Times change. I resorted to any means fair or foul to get calories into Rusty - *fair* usually worked better.

Many of the family members at the nursing home were unhappy with the new policies. We responded by resurrecting the family council. This action served several purposes: it gave us a more direct route to facility administrators; it gave us an illusion of having influence over the policies we disagreed with; and it was a means by which we educated ourselves. The third reason was more helpful than I had anticipated. I wanted to know what, by law, nursing home facilities were required to offer its residents.

We held monthly meetings where the new administrator updated us on news from corporate headquarters. We invited speakers from a variety of state agencies like the North Carolina Division of Aging and Adult Services especially the Services for Older and Disabled Adults. We learned about available Long Term Care Options and the Ombudsman Program. Laws and regulations may be different in each state, so check what is specific to yours.

Many family members embraced the concept enthusiastically as a way to be better informed on the treatment of their loved ones. Some family members couldn't spare even an extra hour for this additional commitment on top of everything else they were juggling in their lives - this was understandable and we pledged to do what we could on their behalf regardless of their attendance at the meetings. And there were a few family members who had been in the nursing home environment so long that they remembered previous family councils and believed the ratio of energy invested was inversely proportionate to the results produced. Hopeless, I think is the word they used, and I respected their opinions. But I threw my lot in with the hope*ful* no matter the outcome. Being a part of the active group made me a more informed consumer of this service we were purchasing on the market. Also, as an added bonus, I fed off the camaraderie of the other members and I liked the feeling of doing something. If I had been on the Titanic, I would have been the one, right next to Rusty, rearranging the deck chairs just before going into the drink. We worked to improve the quality of life for residents, to provide support to each other, we advocated for residents by addressing common concerns, and we planned social activities, especially at Christmas time. We did some good.

My sister drove down from Virginia for a visit and observed that Mom's left foot and ankle were swollen. Mom's ankles were slender and dainty. Although the disfigurement was noticeable, I had missed it. Having an additional pair of loving eyes is helpful for seeing important details that may otherwise be missed. I brought the issue to the attention of the P.A. but she considered it unimportant in the whole scheme of things. It's not that she didn't care but she was now doing the work load of a nurse and a physician and she was compelled to prioritize the importance of various health complaints. Mom's ankle, which was no longer useful for walking anyway, dropped pretty low down that list. She diagnosed the problem as phlebitis and prescribed baby aspirin, antibiotics and elevation. I still kept a medical diary for Mom at this point and when I look at it now, I'm shocked that I accepted the diagnosis without question. Today, I look up 'phlebitis' and I think *that's pretty dangerous!* I did have enough sense to press the point when the problem got no better so an appointment with the radiology people was ordered. These good folks had already seen every square centimeter inside Mom's body, except maybe her ankle. Non-emergency transport took her to the office and I met her there. Scans did not rule out clots in Mom's leg but the radiologist prescribed medication to relieve the pain and gave Mom an injection of *enoxaparin sodium* to help dissolve possible clots. Deep vein thrombosis can develop whenever a person is immobilized for any length of time, as in Mom's case. She was put on a course of Coumadin and taken off the baby aspirin and antibiotics. The swelling did not go away, but we stayed the course. After a few months, Mom's ankle returned to normal and never gave her any more trouble.

Another Christmas came and went. No card games with the inmates this year and glad tidings were in short supply. It was not a memorable holiday, merely one to be tolerated. When we turned the calendar to another new year, it would be time to return our Alice in Wonderland adventure to the bookshelf. Our stay in the 400 Club was not idyllic but it was certainly better than the real world that we must return to on the long-term care hall. We moved Mom back out to the 200 Hall and into the room we would share with Willie and her family until Mom's death. Having the love and friendship of this family made all the difference in the next and final phase of our time at Willow Lake.

CHAPTER SEVENTEEN

The blade that once was shiny, bright
Is rusty now, beyond repair
Yet still, sometimes, a shaft of light
Illuminates what once was there
Look close my child and you may see
That keen, sharp blade that once was me
- 'Dagger of the Mind' by Susan D Nutley

Our friend Susie wrote the poem quoted above for Mom. Over several visits she observed Alzheimer's jackhammer chipping away at Mom's abilities. We were only a few months into the New Year when Susie's own mother died after a battle with cancer. I wasn't able to travel to London to be there with her as she had been here for me and I regret it still. But as sad as I was for Susie and her loss, I also felt a pang of jealousy. Her family's struggle was over, not that the pain ends when our loved ones pass beyond our reach, far from it. But the 24-hour-a-day worry is over. I was surprised by an odd, irrepressible envy I felt toward her circumstances. I did not want to lose my mother but I was so sick and tired of my own life that I longed for the whole ordeal to be resolved.

We moved Mom from the 400 Club back to the 200 Hall as directed by nursing home policy. I pondered the paradox of Alzheimer's residents locked away having more freedom because of that confinement and their segregation from the general population and the short-term nature of residents on the long-term care hall. In many ways the 400 Club was a magical place where we were protected from the real world which had become chaotic, noisy and scary. While we were there we danced and sang and played. We held hands and smiled. In there, when words were spoken or actions such as dessert-stealing took place, it came from a place of innocence. The incidents were not remembered, there were no leftover resentments. Ulterior motives, no matter how cagey or sneaky the perpetrator appeared to be, did not exist. The offender was merely trying to get his or her needs met without having at their disposal the socially acceptable methods the rest of us still had access to. Frustrations followed visitors in this strange land who tried to drag their 'normal' ways into its environs. Pure unconditional love lived there and I soaked it up whenever I passed through that Looking Glass portal. It was difficult to leave and I knew I would miss it. I did not relish returning to the neighborhood where we started out after Dad's stroke two years earlier. This would be our last stop before saying the final goodbyes. In the Club, there was life. On the acute care hall, there was death - or waiting for death. I missed the Alice in Wonderland side of the mirror.

Mom now roomed with Willie and it was a welcomed reward for being uprooted. Willie continued to re-live the enjoyable family meals from her childhood. We had missed her and her commentary! Being with Willie and her family during the last act of our story helped us face the future and the ultimate outcome. During my nightly visits, I rolled Mom in her Geri-chair down to the dining room for a change of scenery and for some interaction with the residents and staff. When we returned to the bedroom after supper, Willie's girls and Rusty's girls were a sisterhood. We brushed our mothers' hair, massaged lotion into their hands and changed them into nightgowns and pajamas. Willie's son, Vernon, rarely made an appearance there, choosing neutral territory when taking his turn to feed his mother. Too bad for us, we enjoyed Vernon's light-hearted company.

We settled in fairly quickly and made our room cozy, more so than any other room we inhabited so far. We set up the radio-cassette player on Mom's bedside table. Patsy Cline and Roy Orbison serenaded us nightly. Mom's bed was once more on the window side of the room, so we left the blinds open for her to attract natural sunshine onto this place of artificially manufactured hope.

The room was located across the hall from Mrs. Annas who had celebrated her 102nd birthday by this time and thrown away her second card from President Bush. She was as bright and engaged as ever. "I knew you'd be back," she greeted us with full comprehension of how things worked in this place. "Where's your brother? Is he going to visit me?" Some things *are* constant in this world, after all and I took comfort wherever I found it.

Other residents in neighboring rooms became important to Donna and me on a daily basis, too. Miss Sadie and Grandma occupied the room next door to us. Mr. Brown (of fisticuffs-in-the-dining-room fame) lived across the hall from us, two doors down from Mrs. Annas. We would get to know and love others in this section of the nursing home, but this was the core group who, alert as Meerkat sentries, peered attentively into each others' rooms from wheelchairs perched in doorways.

We adapted quickly and although I was happy we were with Willie and her family, my mental state was doing a triple half twist dive and I was afraid, truly afraid, that I would not outlive my mother. Crisis mode, where I lived for the past two years, was doing real damage and I could not have felt sorrier for myself. One afternoon at work, my supervisor walked back to my office and caught me sniffling into a limp tissue. She stood at my desk and said cautiously, "I know you've been through a lot, and it's been stressful for you, but I want to tell you that my sister sees someone, a therapist, who is supportive and helpful. Would you like to talk to her?"

Although I had driven down this road before without success I was at my wits end. I was not okay. I was broken. I needed help. "I'm open to anything right now," I told her. "Who does she see?"

"Her name is Mary Bobis. She has an office over near Presbyterian Hospital..."

"I know her," I butted in. A glimmer of light pierced the darkness. "Mom saw her before she was diagnosed with Alzheimer's. I've seen her myself, but it's been over twenty-five years ago now."

I called her that afternoon. At my appointment on the following day Mary told me, "Of course, I remember your mother. And I remember you too."

She began with the basics to move me out of crisis mode. She understood that even one or two of the prior events I had experienced were stressful and coping takes a variety of tools in good working order to assemble an effective toolbox.

Most important tool? *Breathe.*

"Breathe?" I asked her. "You've got to be kidding me."

"No. Try it. When was the last time you took a good long cleansing breath?"

"1998"

"Exactly. Give it a try."

"I am not paying you to tell me to breathe."

"Okay. But breathe anyway."

I breathed. It was a tiny slice of heaven. And, as Mom had stated herself after her first encounter with Mary: *That woman is so smart!*

Mary addressed the stress I felt as a caregiver. "Everything happened so quickly," she said to me. "You've had no time to pause, to repair, or to reflect and process these enormous changes. I can see why you'd be overwhelmed by it all. One approach to dealing with caregiver burnout is to get present."

I thought she said, 'get presents' which caught my interest. She meant 'be present in the moment and deal with only that which is necessary right then.' I pretty much hated every waking moment of my life at that point and would have done anything to *not* be in the present. But what I said was, "I don't know what that means."

"Try, for just a moment, to not think about tomorrow, to not even think about the next hour. Be here. Right now. In this moment."

"Oh, it's a Zen thing."

"Yes, consider it a Zen exercise if it'll help."

"And what do I do in this moment right now."

"Breathe."

"Okay, what's next?" I was Grasshopper in the old Kung Fu series.

"Are you getting enough sleep?"

"No."

"Sleeping will be next, then."

My connection with Mary was a lifeline, a tether that connected me back to the human race. A renewed optimism emboldened to survive this ordeal. In working with Mary I learned to accept that we don't always have control over the external forces in our lives but we can direct the way we react to those forces and how we choose to respond to life's challenges. It's naive to expect we will have no difficulties in our lives.

Wishing for my circumstances to be different than they were was not only a waste of time but a waste of valuable energy that could be better employed in a productive way. I had to identify the things I could change and learn to be okay with those I could not.

This new outlook was empowering. I made an inventory of assets and liabilities and was pleasantly surprised by the length of my asset column. I had help and support from Donna, my friends, and my family. My supervisor accommodated me with a schedule that incorporated working from home which made me more available to Mom during the day. This change alone relieved a considerable amount of stress that contributed to my physical illnesses. I started feeling healthier and I slept better too. I benefited by having a qualified mental health professional listen skillfully to my narrative. Losing a parent or anyone close to us can shake us to the core and together we explored what it all meant. Placing meaning on various life events and understanding them is important to us humans. Having Mary walk this path with me provided a safety net while I explored new territory. I searched for answers to the 'why' of it all and if I failed to find any, Mary offered gentle guidance. Being the skeptically inclined person that I am, I tested her suggestions, chewed on them and at times I fought them. But it was always my decision in the end what course to take.

Mary was kind and empathetic but not sympathetic to the point of being an enabler of my poor mental health habits. She remained objective in her relationship with me and was consistently straightforward and honest. But not brutally so - kindness is much more healing. She never answered telephone calls during my time with her or used me as an audience for her own personal stories unless they were relevant to the discussion. If I misunderstood the intent of one of Mary's messages, I could bring it up for discussion at any point without repercussions. Mary was not defensive nor did she take any criticisms I voiced as a personal attack. I'd like to think that I did not attack her personally, but if I was unskillful in presenting my viewpoint, Mary responded with, "I can understand how you might think that. Maybe I can explain it a different way. Here is the message I was actually trying to convey." I felt heard. I felt understood. She took time to convince me that, not only would I survive this trial but I would come out of it a stronger person.

Meanwhile, back in Mom's room, the unspoken rule was to live and laugh. We were not at home to self-pity. Willie and her family were in this nursing home for the same reason we were, but they had seniority and they knew a thing or two about endurance. I followed their lead and tapped into their vast knowledge like NSA on a telephone line. As we became better acquainted, I enjoyed their personalities and gifts. Because of Jean's serious demeanor and business smarts, I witnessed her passion for doing the right thing and I learned to never settle for less than the best the facility could offer its residents. Patsy cared deeply for each of her hospice patients, but those feelings did not come close to the attention she showered on her mother. She became a hornet whenever she saw an injustice. Vernon and Donna connected through their shared quiet, dry wit. And if one individual in any family is the glue that holds it together, then we should have called Marie, *Elmer*. In a word, she was competent. Marie ran various projects for Andreas Bechtler, the Swiss born industrialist and art mogul in Charlotte - dealing with issues related to her mother came naturally to her.

After our move, I continued supporting our newly re-formed family council. Clearly Willie's family needed no such medium to get their grievances heard - they were a family council in their own right. However, I liked having that extra inside track to administrative decisions being made as much as I loved holding on to the coat tails of Marie, Jean, Patsy and Vernon.

We continued to bring Dickens with us on our visits, but she came less often. Her right side hind leg was hurting her to the extent that getting her in and out of the car was becoming difficult. We thought she had pulled a muscle and when it didn't heal Donna took her in for a veterinary visit. Dr. Mark Green told us cancer was in the bone. Poor girl. I could not believe that there was any part of my heart unbroken. But we can carry a lot of sadness in our little human bodies.

We were given two choices for Dickens. Have her leg amputated or have her put to sleep. In the first choice, amputation would eliminate the intense pain she experienced whenever she put her weight on the leg and give her another six to eight months with us. The second choice expedited her reunion with her sister in doggie heaven and she wouldn't have to go through the surgery. Dr. Green explained how dogs do not have the same psychological hang-ups associated with losing limbs as humans do, and with her leg no longer a source of intense pain, she would adapt quickly. Dogs immediately compensate in redistributing their weight to their remaining three healthy legs by doing what is called Tripoding. "She will get around better than you can imagine," Dr. Green assured us.

Donna saw to every detail of Dickens' surgery and the special attention she required afterwards. Dickens was up and ready for duty in only a couple of weeks. Having her greet me each morning and accompany me again to Willow Lake proved that our decision was the correct one. On our way to Mom's room, Donna, Dickens and I passed Miss Sadie's and Grandma's room where we were frequently treated to our own old-time Gospel Hour. Both Sadie and Grandma suffered from diabetes so severe that each of them underwent leg amputations to save their lives. Miss Sadie had lost both legs but zipped up and down the halls in a motorized wheelchair. Grandma was bedridden a good bit of the day, but she welcomed her visitors with a huge toothless smile. How in the world these two sweet women kept their spirits up in the face of their trials is a testament to the strong faith they shared with us through their hymns. I stuck my head in their doorway on my visits just to be in that loving circle. Dickens, my three-legged dog, loved them too and made herself at home in their company. Watching their love-fest cast my life and my perspective on that life, into a more positive light and I could see a miracle or two wend their way across my path. Unexpected gifts of grace found me often. Miracles were *all* around me. Divine intervention interceded on my behalf and the effects were amazing and most welcomed. By now, I should have known to anticipate their arrival.

When Donna and I took time to just sit with Rusty, we noticed that she continued to interact with someone (often many *someones*) standing around her bed. They followed her from the 400 Club and even if these were post-seizure hallucinations, the illusion of 'helpers' appeared to comfort Mom, so where was the harm? Mom interacted with them and with us, at times simultaneously, as if it were all the same to her. After acknowledging our arrival in the evening, Mom returned to her engagement with each of them. As she lay in bed, comfortable and relaxed, Mom looked first at whoever was at the foot of her bed, then she looked to the right, and finally back over her right shoulder – much as Dad had done in the hospital the weekend of his stroke. In her exchanges, she nodded in response to them, mumbling a word or two. When I asked her to repeat her sentence, she looked at me as if to say, *that was private and I don't appreciate you listening in*. She also motioned us to step aside if we came between her and them. Again, just as Jim had done.

"Technically speaking, I think you and your gang are the rude ones," I expressed tentatively. I knew I was sassing her and that had been a capital offense in the world where the former Rusty reigned. To be safe, though, I kept my car keys in my pants pocket for a swift get-away. My newfound advantage in our mother-daughter relationship emboldened me, so I continued. "Why don't you have this little gab-fest before or after my visits? I'm jealous that you have so much fun with them and then say barely two words to me."

Her eyes sparkled mischievously as she patted my hand. Donna and I took that as encouragement to pin down who else was sharing Mom's room. Pointing to the foot of the bed I said, "Who is that, Mom? Is that your mother?"

She shook her head no.

"Is it Daddy?" *No*.

"Is it Jim? Or Buzz?" Her eyes lit up. Bingo!

I indicated toward her right-hand side, "Is *that* your mother?" *No*.

"Is it your sister?" *No*.

Remembering to use names, I asked her if it was Virginia. *No*.

"Try *Ginny*," Donna suggested.

"Is it Ginny?"

A broad smile accompanied a nod in the affirmative. Bingo again.

"Who's back here, then?" I indicated toward the head of the bed over her right shoulder. "Who is that?" No response. We tried everyone we could think of and eventually dropped it.

Mom still used the occasional spoken word to communicate with me or any other flesh-and-blood individual with whom she came into contact, but it happened only when she chose. For example, when the CNAs came in to help her dress or to wheel her down to the dining room she interacted with them readily enough.

"Hello, Lottie," Karen addressed Mom per the sign posted outside the door. "How are we, today?"

"Fine, thank you," she responded with a smile. "How are you?"

More and more though, Mom used eye contact and a gentle pat on the hand or arm to get her message across to us.

I began taking this new taciturn Rusty for granted. That was a mistake. During one particular supper-time visit we had parked Mom at a table, facing her toward the wall where an artificial Weeping Fig tree stood, or to use the more formal taxonomic botanical Latin name Mom would use if she could, a *Ficus Benjamina* (if a plastic tree can have such a thing). We justified this positioning by claiming that she would enjoy having a little greenery to look at, assuming she wouldn't know that the plant was fake. Sitting across the table from her, Donna and I kept the entire dining room in our view and monitored potential action that we knew it was capable of. We especially kept an eye on Mr. Brown. We were loading food onto Mom's fork and tempting her to eat when Andy arrived. Brother Andy is fun. He tells a good story. As Donna and I became engrossed in the tale, we began moving mashed potatoes mechanically to somewhere in the vicinity of Mom's lips. Until...

Mom clamped her lips shut and turned her head away against further intrusion. She looked toward the vicinity of the *Ficus* and said, clear as day, to *them*: "Do you SEE what I have to put up with here?" *Quoi?*

"Momma, what did you just say?"

More lip-pursing.

"Did you just rat us out to *them*?"

She turned her eyes heavenward as a five-year-old child would do to indicate that she had nothing more to say, being innocent of the accused action.

"Oh, huh unh." I replied eruditely. "We are sitting right here. Right now. With you. And you are talking to *them* instead of us?"

"We kind of deserve it," Donna suggested. "We really weren't paying her any attention at all, were we?"

Donna was right. We were having a grand time, but our party didn't include Mom at all. We were going through the motions but we were not present. I never did that sort of thing again.

Until the *next* time.

Donna and I were sitting with Mom one evening after she was tucked into bed for the night. I was rubbing lotion into Mom's hands and Donna was straightening up the bedside table when our conversation skidded into the ditch. Donna had one point of view on the subject and I assured her that my point of view was, perhaps, the more correct one. Things heated up. Sharp words were exchanged. Mom tensed up, focused her gaze on me, and frowned. I understood the message immediately: *Take this stuff outside - there's no room for it here.* Our loved ones who have Alzheimer's may very well comprehend what's going on in their presence and feel the negative energy we bring in from the outside world. Words were not necessary for Mom to demonstrate that she did not want us to argue in her presence without a thought for her welfare. She still had feelings and opinions about her environment. She had clear boundaries for how to behave when we visited her in her home and she found an effective way to get her point of view across to us. Donna and I stopped being on automatic pilot and became more sensitive to how our presence affected the quality of our visits with Mom from then on.

A few months after our epiphany, Mom entered into another phase of decline. At the care plan meeting, the head nurse showed Mom's stats to me. She was losing weight and developing bed sores at various pressure points. Losing weight was an indicator that Mom was taking in fewer calories and the quality of her nutrition decreased as a result. We took action. Mom was given an extra 'health shake' (a drink similar to Ensure©) every day. And since bed sores can quickly turn nasty we looked for more ways to deal with that. From a catalog that specializes in adaptive equipment, we ordered a foam wedge cushion designed in the shape of a trapezoid to elevate Mom's legs now that she was in bed much of the day. We also bought a padded chair cushion to line the Geri-chair reducing pressure points under her bottom and elbows.

Then Mom had another seizure prompting further adjustments in her Dilantin levels. She was also having eye problems that required the attentions of an ophthalmologist. Dr. Baxter took one look at Mom's red and irritated eyes and diagnosed "Trichiasis", which is a condition where the eyelashes turn inwards and scratch the cornea causing an infection.

"What can you do to help her?" I asked him. "Will she need surgery?"

"No, all I have to do is pluck them out. I can do it right here in her room."

"Okay. Well, I'll step outside, then. Just let me know when you're done." I reached the hallway before my knees buckled. The doctor fetched me only a few minutes later as I clutched the hallway hand rail for support. Mom looked fine but my queasy feeling remained for the rest of the evening.

Shortly after Dr. Baxter's visit, the staff doctor asked to have a chat with me. He was looking at Mom's record and at her rather rapid physical decline. With the weight loss, the seizure, and losing other functionality, he wanted to order Hospice services for her. My initial thoughts were, *Oh God. I willed the end to come because I was exhausted and now it's my fault that my momma is going to die.* I discussed this fear with Mary and she assured me that I did not have that kind of power so I calmed down. I met with the Hospice representative and they explained how they would be Mom's personal advocates and medical liaisons with the nursing home staff as long as they were needed.

I alerted the sibs and the Newell community to Mom's new status. Then I started preparing myself for the end. You can't actually prepare for this profound event, but we go through the motions anyway. I started the 'letting go' process. But Mom didn't. She entered a holding pattern. After the initial deterioration of her health that triggered the need for Hospice her health didn't change further. In fact, Rusty did not seize her new hospice-status as an opportunity to approach the Pearly Gates. I should have known better.

I didn't want to hasten Mom's departure but I was curious to know what was going on behind the scenes, as it were. I asked her, "Whatcha waitin' on, Rusty? Dad's there, your son and parents and sister and brother are there." She looked at me quizzically.

I paused briefly but then continued sympathetically, tenderly, helpfully. "Mom, are you afraid? Are you frightened to die?"

Mom had always been brave and courageous - so like her own mother and her sister, who had been valiant and fearless to the end. But this was a big deal, the biggest deal of all and if Mom was hesitant to explore the next world, who could blame her?

In a quiet contemplative voice she answered, "No, I'm not afraid." She patted my face and looked me directly in the eyes so I would understand that she was on my wave-length.

Yes! Rusty was still fearless. I accepted that she would continue to do things her way and in her own time. No exceptions. Alzheimer's was consuming her brain, but her indomitable spirit remained in control. She would leave this world when she got good and ready and not one moment before. With a second wind to be envied by any marathon runner, Mom rallied. She ate better and she gained weight. Having Hospice in Mom's life and having them monitor her medicine and care plan improved her health. Individual attention and timely responses make a difference.

Now when I arrived at supper time, Mom appeared more alert and she responded to me and to my conversations with her. If she had said to me, *wait just a minute there, don't go spending the inheritance yet* (as if there was any) I would not have been surprised. But Medicare will pay for Hospice to be involved in your circumstances only if a physician certifies the patient is terminally ill with a life expectancy of six months or less. By all indicators, Mom's health was improving and she showed no readiness to vacate her place here on earth. So Hospice was cancelled.

Since Rusty was going to stick around, I changed my attitude back to being pro-active in her care. To accompany the foam wedge and the padded chair liner, we looked for other means to make her more comfortable. When lying in bed, Mom was unable to arrange herself, move, or turn over when her position became uncomfortable. The CNAs showed us how to place pillows under her head just so and under her arms, too, for maximum comfort and to get the weight off her delicate joints. Mom's head tended to droop at times when napping in the Geri-chair so we found a neck pillow that gave her better support whether she was awake or asleep.

I was intrigued by the two worlds Mom now inhabited. At times she seemed to be involved in the activities 'over there' and at other times she passively observed whatever was going on. After one session I asked her where she went. She raised her eyebrows at me as if to say, "You saw that?"

"Oh, yes. I saw you. Were you *over there*?"

She nodded her head rather sheepishly.

"Do you like it there?"

Another slight nod yes.

"Do you want to go there?"

A change of expression and a slight shake of her head indicating 'No, not yet.'

A few moments passed and I wondered if she understood what I was saying and what any of it meant. So as a lark, I asked her selfishly, "Do you love me?"

A great big animated smile burst upon her lips. I had to laugh.

The respite we enjoyed as a result of the hospice-effect was short-lived. After only a few months without them, we watched Mom decline again. Donna researched various methods of treatments to help make Mom more comfortable. She chose Reiki. Reiki is a Japanese healing practice which incorporates into its name the notion of universal life energy. It is used as a complement to modern medicine and not as an alternative to treatment plans prescribed by a physician. In Reiki, the practitioner places the palms of her hands at strategic points on the body, not unlike acupressure. Energy, in the form of *qi* or *chi*, or God's divine love, is transmitted to the person who is receiving the treatment through the hands. Our bodies hold the possibility of great healing powers within it and Reiki encourages that healing ability with what I think of as a jump start. It's safe and never harmful.

Donna found a teacher nearby and learned the hands-on healing technique. She subsequently attained Master Level and now teaches the technique to others, but the first time she used Reiki on Mom I was doubtful that we would see any genuine results. What I witnessed, however, was nothing short of amazing. We returned to Mom's room one evening after supper. Mom slumped uncomfortably in her Geri-chair, a grimace on her face. She didn't appear to be in pain, but she was definitely heading in that direction. There is no rest from the fatigue of sitting all day. Donna tilted the back of the chair into a reclining position and stood at Mom's head. She placed her warm hands gently over each of Mom's eyes. At first Mom tensed up as if playing Peep-Eye was not fun for her. Then Donna lovingly cradled Mom's face in her hands. Sensing that she was totally safe with Donna, a peaceful calm washed over Mom and relaxed her body making her more comfortable. Incredible. Indeed, we are capable of making a healing difference to our fellow humans. Even if we cannot cure the problem, we can bring comfort to the sufferer by making a loving physical connection.

Donna's use of Reiki was helpful for Mom and we searched for additional ways to put Mom at ease. Mom's hands were beginning to close and contract involuntarily and her fingernails bit into her palms painfully. To slow down that process we gave her soft stuffed animals or spongy rubber balls to grip instead. At night, we gave her a big stuffed tiger to hug to her chest. Because Mom no longer moved on her own, her knees began to draw up painfully too. Lack of movement causes tendons and muscles to shorten and become stiff making it a common problem among the nursing home population. Reiki helped relax Mom's legs when nothing else slowed the crippling effects of the condition.

When weather permitted, we took Mom outside for a roll around the grounds. Simply breathing in the fresh air seemed to lift her spirits even if flowers and clouds no longer caught her eye. Mom's attention was focused on a time and place we couldn't share. Wanting to know more about the other world that Mom inhabited at times, Donna and I asked Mary Beth Wrenn, a psychic medium we knew, to come and sit with Mom, and share her observations with us.

I can hear the naysayers: *Oh, lord; she's gone off the deep end.* I know! I'm a linear thinking analytical kind of gal myself. But what the heck? I had witnessed events happening outside my practical world and outside what I could see or touch for myself. What did I have to lose? Mary Beth dealt in the spiritual realm. Mom lived half her day in the spiritual realm. I was curious to know more, and frankly, I was open to anything I could learn. At least I thought my mind was open to metaphysical and supernatural things, but when the Saturday afternoon of our meeting arrived, I was dubious that she could give us any additional insight into the spirit world Mom was so taken with. We purposely gave her no information on Mom, her condition or her personality. This is what took place. I found it enlightening.

Mary Beth walked into the room, looked around her and started describing what she sensed about Mom.

"Your mom is asking to have rocks, roses and trees – things

from the earth, and living things. Living things will bring her energy. She loves flowers and plants and living things. Where are the roses? Bring her roses. They have to be pink. She knows when you bring her things. Your mother is a stone-talker. Do you know what a stone talker is?" She asked me.

'She talks to stones?" I hazarded.

"No, they talk to her. Does she ever talk to her plants and flowers? Does she pick up stones?"

'Yes, as if they are long-lost friends. We found loads of rocks at her house when we cleaned it out."

Mary Beth sat down next to Mom and listened to messages we couldn't hear.

"Meditate when you're here with her. Hold hands and form a protective circle around her. Recite the Lord's Prayer and visualize white light, then pink, then purple and lavender."

"She extends a heart to you. A flowery Victorian-like Valentine heart. She's showing me a ring with hearts. The ring is encrusted with diamonds. Where is that?"

"I have it in my jewelry box. She gave it to me when I was 16. It was my Sweet Sixteen birthday present from her."

"Diamonds are in it?"

"A diamond chip. Probably the smallest one on earth."

'She wants you to wear it. Why don't you wear it?"

'Because I think it looks youngish," I told her. "Something a teenager would wear. She's given me other rings I like better."

"She wants you to wear it as a symbol of her love for you." A brief pause, then Mary Beth continued.

"There's a two-year-old here. Your brother. Robert Alan."

Well, howdy. That's specific. I guess she could have looked up obituaries published for the Burris family and recalled recent deaths in our family so I stopped myself from getting overly excited about her psychic powers.

"Did you lose a brother when he was two? He has hair like you, only a little darker."

"No," I responded. "I mean, I did lose a brother, but he was 44 when he died."

"He's coming through like a two-year old. He's impatient. He wants things "now"! I get the sense that he is emotionally stunted somehow, like he never grew beyond two years old emotionally-speaking. And he's manipulative."

That seemed harsh. She sure didn't sugar coat her statements.

Why are you coming through like you're two years old? she asked him telepathically. And his answer was, *the best way to get attention is through tantrums.*

Mary Beth explained that he had no reason to lie and that he was owning his behavior.

"Did something traumatic happen to him at two?"

"I don't know, I would have been only four, but he did bang his head frequently when he was little."

"He wants your mom to come over. He's jealous and he wants to have her to himself. He's trying to pull her to him. He thinks you've had her long enough."

Mary Beth paused for a moment.

"But, she's resisting. She says she has more to do here."

"More to do? What else does she need to do?" I asked.

"She's waiting for the new baby to arrive."

Another pause.

"Robert is surrounded by unconditional love where he is now, but he also wants his mother to himself. Also, when things go missing in your mother's room, it's Robert. If her hairbrush goes missing and reappears without explanation, it's Robert. He's playing pranks. Have things gone missing from the room?" Mary Beth asked me.

"Things go missing every day," I told her. "It's true that Mom's hairbrush is frequently found in the next room over. Her blanket rarely makes its way back from the laundry room. And her wedding ring has disappeared. I'm not sure I can blame those things on Robert, though." She didn't mind if I challenged her statements.

She continued. "Did your Dad fly during the war at all?"

"No."

"I have an image of a man in uniform, three stripes, and a flying reference. And there is a Joe or Joseph who is standing between you and Donna. A Susan is connected to your mom - not grandma Susie – friend Susie. And a Peggy or Margaret – connected to your mom too. They are friends to her but like daughters too. Your mom claims a little sister, a twelve-year-old little girl. She's in church clothes, a white blouse and a skirt."

"I know the Susie and Peggy reference but I can't recall a *Joe* or *little sister*."

"Your mother is strong-willed and independent. She will do things her way without care for what others think."

She described Dad as he looked when he was younger, maybe thirties, tall and thin with dark wavy hair.

"He claims your mom is stubborn. A 'stubborn old coot' is how he says it." We laughed.

"Talk to her of current events, she wants to know what's going on so talk to her. She understands and wants to hear the news. For communication with her, watch her eyes." I could believe that.

"Your mother is not bored and she is not in pain. She's actually quite peaceful, content, and calm. She's learning a lot from the spirit world. Being with them is enlightening to her and she's having a ball living in both worlds." We had not told her we suspected this.

"She is refusing Robert for now. Robert is insistent and the others are encouraging her to come over too. But she's refusing. Someone named Thomas explained to your mother about Robert's death. Did you not tell her of his death?"

"We told her and Dad that Robert died, but we lied to them about the cause. He took his own life." Mary Beth looked as if it all made sense now.

"Your mother does feel anguish over his death. Oh, and she says that there will be a baby.., two babies. One will be a boy and in her world she is sewing, making clothes for him. She sewed for a small boy once and she says she will sew again for a small boy."

Mary Beth changed gears a little.

"Your mom is very wise, a healer, and as I said earlier, she is a Stone Talker. A strong, muscular Indian with long black hair is your mom's spirit guide. Your mom has strong Indian energy, Cherokee Indian energy (that was not in any obituary) and has lived many long lives; she has much spiritual energy, and healing energy. If you're interested in Past Lives at all," Mary Beth said, "I can follow her soul backwards."

I nodded my consent.

"One past life was in 1801. She was traveling somewhere out west on a stage coach... Oh, has she had problems with her left ankle recently?" Mary Beth asked me.

"Yes." My face registered surprise.

"It was a past life issue. Did it come and go without a

reasonable explanation?"

"Yes, she had an ultrasound to see if a blood clot was causing it. The results were not conclusive."

"It was swollen... the swelling was a result of a snake bite in a former life. A rope was tied around her ankle to prevent the venom from moving. Either the venom or the poison or the tourniquet caused the problem that led to her death. She chose death over having her leg amputated." I did not know what to say to that.

"You and your mom have been connected before, without a doubt." That pleased me but it didn't surprise me.

"Do you have any questions?" Mary Beth asked us.

I did. I asked her what else we should be doing for Mom.

"You're doing what's possible for now, but bring in the live plants and talk to her more. Share with her, pray with her, and meditate when you are with her. Protect her with your energy."

"Who else comes to see Mom?"

"Charlie is here with her some."

"Are her visitors *here* or is she *there* with them?"

At that moment, Mom cut her eyes at me and shook her head side to side as if to make the point that some of the things we were discussing were not for us to know. But Mary Beth was not intimidated by Rusty and continued. She explained that exchanges can happen either way that it doesn't matter about 'here' and 'there' because it's all the same place to our souls.

"Can she visit us in dreams or in meditations?"

"Yes, just open up and trust what you see and hear and feel."

"Does she know about her grandchildren? Ava and any others who are on their way?"

"Oh, yes. She knows them."

"I have one last question. When Mom dreams, does she dream with full mental capacity or is she hindered there too?"

"She has full capacity in her dreams."

After Mary Beth's visit and the information she shared with us, we bought Mom miniature pink roses, and a small Norfolk Island Pine Tree to sit on the window sill by her bed. I brought in a handful of the rocks that she had picked up when she was free to roam the earth unguarded. I wear my Sweet Sixteen ring now. Donna and I made it a practice to say prayers on Mom's behalf when we visited and we burned a candle for her often and held her purposefully in our thoughts. I was comforted that so many of Mom's loved ones were with her, including Donna's father, Charlie. As Mary Beth explained to us, Mom was in 'school' and her contacts on the other side were her teachers. Mom enjoyed learning from this support group and was in no hurry to leave us because she enjoyed the experience of living in both worlds. We assumed that the friends Mary Beth mentioned who Mom had a connection with were Susie, our dear friend in London, and of course Peggy who has been a part of our family for decades. After Mary Beth's visit, we felt reassured that Mom was not in pain, was content, and that we were doing everything in our power to care for her. We settled down and relaxed into just being with Mom. Showing up was good enough.

Early one morning, about a week after Mary Beth's visit, Dickens had a seizure. She had been fairly active and in good spirits so it came as a surprise. Dr. Green told us that we would know when it was time to let her go, that she would find a way to communicate this message to us. Donna and I agreed that the message had been delivered so we called the vet's office and made an appointment with death. We held this special dog in our arms as she took her final breath. Dickens' struggle was over. Ours began anew. It was not only Donna and I who suffered this loss. Josh felt it too. And it was a sad moment when I informed Miss Sadie and Grandma that Dickens had made her last visit to see them. Dickens' absence was another hole in our lives. It would be a while before we entertained the notion of bringing another dog into our family. Saying goodbye hurts. As Queen Elizabeth II so acutely observed, *grief is the price we pay for love*.

We paid our debt and we coasted along. Again. We looked for a sliver of silver in the lining of our storm clouds. And once again, we found it. Mom was with us still. And even though I would not have chosen the circumstances under which my family and I found ourselves, being with Mom and enjoying her warm sweet presence was a luxury I did not take for granted. I was keenly aware that our days together were numbered and I was determined to make the best of each one of them. But talk is cheap and when Christmas arrived again, and as Donna and I sat in the nursing home feeding Mom puréed turkey and dressing, my determination wavered. Considerably. I wanted to be with Mom more than I wanted to be anywhere else on earth and yet I didn't want this to be the place where we had our Christmas lunch. The CNAs, as always, made a brave attempt to be cheery and optimistic. I loved their spirit. The other family members there on that Christmas day carried on valiantly. We all did. But none of us *wanted* to be there. Who, in their right mind would?

In my pitiful and miserable state, I wanted company. I asked Mom if she wanted to talk to Andy. In response she nodded her head in the affirmative so I called him. The call interrupted the holiday dinner he was enjoying with his family but I asked him to say a few words to Mom anyway. I held the phone to her ear and I heard him speaking to her. Her facial expression lit up and I assumed that she recognized Andy's voice even if she didn't comprehend how that voice issued from a little plastic box the size of my palm.

It seemed to be a good idea at the time, but upon reflection I realize that carrying a one-sided conversation with a mother he wished could enjoy Christmas day with him, his wife and daughter was for Andy distressing. I thought only of my own pain at that point and no matter how many people I tried to pull into my pity party, it did not make me any happier. I slipped into a silent funk. Mom had not used the spoken word for communication purposes for several weeks, so why should I? Sensing my dark mood, Mom looked at me quizzically as if to ask, *what's wrong?* In my current fragile emotional state, I didn't have the capacity to explain or the ability to shove my feelings aside. I only wanted to get out of the room, out of the building. I thought it would calm me down. Donna followed me out, pushing Mom in the Geri-chair down the corridor and into the front parlor where we pitched camp. When I failed to regain my composure, I told Donna that I was going outside to get some air and to walk it off. Mom looked puzzled. Donna assured her that I would return shortly and they sat together companionably until my return a few minutes later. When I came back, I looked at Mom as she sat regally, dressed in a dusty mint-green sweater and matching slacks, I marveled at how amazingly beautiful she was although the ravages of the disease were stealing her muscle tone as well as her mind. She regarded me with concern.

"I'm okay, Mom," I reassured her untruthfully. "I was upset

but I'm better now."

I took a seat on the sofa facing her and massaged her legs. We had long stopped expecting Rusty to use words for communicating, employing only the occasional nod for her part of the conversation. A smile and a glint in her eye expressed when she was pleased. She cocked her head coquettishly when she was being funny and coy. I was surprised when she reached for my hand and drew me nearer to her. As I leaned in close to her, she said, clearly, "I love you."

I looked at Donna to make sure she witnessed this miracle. "Oh, my God," she said. "Did you hear that?" I did.

Fresh tears welled up in my eyes and Mom saw that I heard her declaration. She gave me the best Christmas gift ever. I embraced her and cried on her shoulder and murmured in her ear. *Thank you, Momma.* Against the odds, Mom once again found a way to comfort me. Instead of falling into a funk with me, Mom intuitively knew that what I needed was not more company in my misery but a little extra Rusty-love.

A photograph of Mom taken that day in the parlor reminds me how difficult it was for her to initiate that last full sentence to me. It took great effort on her part to accomplish that feat. As Susie's poem so aptly captures in its message, this is the road Alzheimer's victims must travel. This hateful disease dulled Mom's once-keen mind. It reduced her booming baritone voice to a mere whisper. But there were times when the old Rusty burst through the fog like a shaft of light illuminating a lonely black night. The pain I felt while caring for Mom under these horrible conditions was almost unbearable at times and that Christmas was one such day. I hoard every memory, good or bad. And like a school boy carrying his stack of valuable baseball cards wherever he goes, I take one out now and then to savor, knowing that once there was a woman called Rusty. She was my mother. And she loved me.

CHAPTER EIGHTEEN

I shall be telling this with a sigh
Somewhere ages and ages hence:
Two roads diverged in a wood and I,
I took the one less traveled by,
And that has made all the difference.
- Robert Frost

I missed Rusty long before she was gone. Alzheimer's eroded her cognitive faculties as devastatingly as rough surf on a sandy shoreline. Like grains of sand carried out to sea by steady changing tides, this disease left a virtually unrecognizable landscape in Mom's personality. The sweet warm physical presence of my mother was still with us but individual characteristics that made her unique were being dissolved after a decade of damage. I mourned those lost pieces. It had been an age since I was able to recall the woman who gave birth to me and my siblings – the woman who canned fresh vegetables and designed flower gardens; the woman who sewed gorgeous clothes for so many of us; the woman who taught Sunday school and directed election days at the Crab Orchard Precinct in Newell; and the woman who cocked her head in a saucy pose for every captured Kodak moment. I walked willingly by Mom's side as the disease strangled her neurons but in taking that path I placed myself firmly in the present, in the here and the now and I stopped thinking back to how Mom used to be.

We experience changes and transitions as we grow older and as we watch our parents grow older still, but I found it difficult to reconcile Mom's extreme changes with those I saw Dad go through. On the upright piano in our living room stood a photograph of Mom and Dad taken for the church directory when both enjoyed health and vitality. Dad's likeness was recognizable to me and I chuckled as I remembered things he had said in certain situations. One predictable statement Jim made whenever he heard a sad tale was, *well, I'm sorry as a pig.* When you received this figurative expression of sympathy, you knew instantly that he understood your troubles and sometimes that's all we need. When I looked at Mom's photograph, in the Beefy Rusty phase of her life, I could see the devilish gleam in her eyes that accompanied a smile that said simply, 'Aren't I the cat's meow?' But my reaction to this Rusty was as to a stranger: *I don't remember you*, I told the photograph. *I cannot remember* this *you.*

I can't explain it, but Mom's Alzheimer's nipped away at my own memories each time I tried to bring to mind the dazzling days of Rusty's life before Alzheimer's. I wondered how she viewed her long grueling descent, or if she was even able to make such judgments. For me, it was like watching a bright, illuminating light dim agonizingly slowly, as it became extinguished. Darkness crept in where radiance once shone. Grieving for how Mom used to be and recalling the mother of my childhood was painful when I attempted to make comparisons from then till now so I didn't do it often, when I could do it at all. I began to set that Rusty free and the more I let her go, the less able I was to recollect snippets of our lives together before Alzheimer's. Having one foot in the past and one in the present was a struggle and it was exhausting. To conserve precious energy that I needed to tend to Mom's needs I chose to be with her in real time. I finally accepted that Mom's condition would not improve - funny how long we hold on to a shred of hope no matter how unrealistic – and it became easier to dwell in the present. The cost of this decision was to sacrifice the capacity to recognize the woman in the photo. The reward was enjoying the person before me regardless of my relationship to her. I was just as sad toward our predicament as I adopted the new attitude, but my sorrow was more palatable because of what this spoonful-of-sugar granted me. Diverging onto this road less traveled rendered me incapable of conjuring a mental image of Rusty before Alzheimer's took root, but I would rather walk that path and take from my experience a multitude of meaningful moments than dwell on a collection of resentments I could nurse for the rest of my life. It was not an altruistic response on my part, it was self-preservation. But choosing that road made a huge difference.

I sat in a contented post-supper stupor with Mom one night

and reflected on our journey together. I would like to have forgotten some of the milestones of the past few years, but many of them were worth remembering. Also, I felt it was important to reclaim Rusty at some point when I was able, the old Rusty, the one who had disappeared before our very eyes.

"Shall I write a book about us?" I asked her. She agreed with a barely noticeable nod.

Most evenings, now, when I arrived at the nursing home to feed Mom supper, she was already in bed. Stretching out on a soft comfy mattress must have been sheer heaven after hours of sitting slumped in the Geri-chair with only artificial means to prop her upright. Her own musculoskeletal structure was too weak to do the job without assistance. To make sure Mom ate, I hauled in armloads of groceries to fill the drawers in her bedside table. I kept a stash of Ensures on hand. Not the regular ones with 250 calories and 9 grams of protein but Ensure PLUS©! The benefit of the *Plus* is that it comes with 31 grams of protein and 355 calories per serving along with a complement of vitamins and minerals. I made sure a variety of baby food, chosen specifically for Mom's taste and preference, was on hand. Pears, bananas and apple sauce, as well as rice cereal, carrots, squash and sweet potatoes were favorites. For dessert, she was partial to chocolate, vanilla or banana pudding. There was absolutely nothing wrong with the food provided by the kitchen staff but after a while, pulverized chicken and bland mashed potatoes didn't hold Mom's interest like the sweet food I provided. When choices are clear, always select balanced nutritious meals. That's just good sense. But Mom's brain no longer communicated hunger pangs to her and she had little desire for food. Encouraging her to eat anything at this point was better than nothing. For us, meals were now a numbers game and calories equaled weight in the equation. Mom's weight hovered at eighty pounds which prompted me to use every trick in the book to get calories into her since malnutrition and dehydration are deadly for someone in her compromised state of health. To help increase her appetite, Mom's doctor ordered a prescription of Remeron (Mirtazapine) which is technically an antidepressant but also acts as an appetite stimulant. Mom could not swallow tablets so the nurse ground it to powder and mixed it in with a spoonful of applesauce. We would employ every scheme available to us to provide Mom with nutrition and medication - except a feeding tube. She had made her wishes quite clear on this point years earlier and we felt no guilt in following her wishes. Often, I resorted to the foolproof calorie-delivery backup plan of last resort, a Junior Frosty from Wendy's. Rusty never refused a Frosty. I'm just sayin'...

After a tasty dinner comprised of a chocolate milkshake, Mom thanked me with a gentle caress of my face, a playful tweak of my hair, or a pat on the hand which is a reasonable, sensible and normal reaction to having slurpy chocolate ice cream rather than puréed turkey and green peas for dinner.

Along with the new mealtime practices I implemented other routines. During my visits I lit a candle for us to enjoy during dinnertime. The candle is a symbol of light in the darkness for anyone walking through the valley of the shadow of death. It is believed that the light from candles raise the vibration levels of our souls to a higher quality making our spiritual connections stronger, too. That sounded beneficial and it became an important ceremony that I observed frequently. I sought and received permission from the facility administrators to have an open flame in Mom's room after I demonstrated the safety of a votive candle in a glass holder and since neither Mom nor Willie used any oxygen therapy.

When supper was done, and the CNA changed Mom into her pajamas, I'd ask Mom if she wanted me to get in the bed with her. She readily agreed each time, so I crawled in beside her, slipped my arm under her head for support and cradled it in the crook of my elbow. She relaxed and snuggled into the safety of my embrace. With my free hand I stroked her hair or gently massaged her shoulders until she became drowsy and fell asleep. It's all I knew to do and comforting her with this gesture was balm for my aching heart. When Mom was in the Alzheimer's unit, leaving her was torture since she couldn't understand the concept of time and or comprehend that I'd be back the same as always the next night. All she knew was that when I was gone, she was alone. Now that Mom was in bed before dinner and sleeping soundly soon after, I tucked her in before I left, content that her physical needs were tended to for the day. A small benefit of this stage of the disease.

Many nights, with Mom as a captive audience, I sang a song to her that ran through my head constantly. It was a snappy little tune that I first heard sung in the movie 'Babe'. The melody of the song is borrowed from the main theme of Saint-Saëns' *Symphony No.3 in C minor for organ* which makes the hair stand up on the back of my neck whenever I hear it. But it was Jonathan Hodge's lyrics to the song and their sentiment that matched what I was thinking:

> *If I had words to make a day for you*
> *I'd sing you a morning, golden and new*
> *I would make this day last for all time*
> *Give you a night dipped in moon shine*

Now that I sensed our time with Mom was short, I realized I would have done anything, *anything*, in my power to keep her here with us longer. But how cruel of me to desire her life-sentence to be lengthened because of my reluctance to face the next step. Nevertheless, if I could have turned back time and made everything all shiny and new again, I would not have hesitated. Instead, I had the sensation that time was accelerating in fast forward. We were all young not so very long ago. And then, we were here. Now that I saw an ending, I believe I would have made a deal with the devil himself to prolong Mom's time here with us. I needed a healthy helping of courage to see Mom through the final chapter of her life. But then merely walking through the front doors of the nursing home took guts as anyone who has done it knows.

The monotony of nursing home life, with its unvarying routine, is preferred to any excitement which usually appears as a health crisis. Seeing our friends on the hall each night helped alleviate the mind-numbing sameness and was a comfort to me and to other visitors. Usually the first person we encountered upon our arrival was dear Mrs. Annas as she sat outside her room waiting for the dinner bell. On one particular visit, she sat regally in her wheelchair with a towel draped over her lap, covering her legs from knee to ankle.

"Are you cold?" I asked her. "I'll get a sweater for you, if you are."

"No. I'm not cold," she answered somewhat sharply. My eyebrows shot up in surprise so she clarified the reason for the towel. With her head bent conspiratorially, she flicked her thumb down towards Mr. Brown's room and said in a whisper, "He keeps looking at my legs."

The tone of disgust colored her words, evidence of her displeasure at such a forward and ungentlemanly gesture. Under the same circumstances, I would have been delighted if anyone was interested in my hundred-year-old legs. I was not even half her age and I feared I was already past the point where I could fetch such a glance, but here was Mrs. Annas fending off unwanted advances and horrified that she had to resort to placing a towel over her knees to protect her modesty. The difference in our reactions toward leg-gazing lay in the changes of social mores that had evolved between the dates of our births. Mrs. Annas may not have remembered McKinley who was president at the time of her birth, but she did recall Teddy Roosevelt who succeeded him; vastly different codes of conduct from then until now.

Seeing Grandma and Miss Sadie was always a pleasure, but one night as I looked in on them I caught Miss Sadie staring wistfully out the window near her bed.

"What's going on, Miss Sadie? Are you okay?"

"Oh, it's nothing... it's just that I get tired of the same old food everyday."

"Is there anything I can get for you?"

"Sometimes I want me a good ol' can of Vienna Sausages and some Saltines." She pronounced it vie-een-er as any proper southerner would.

"Well, put your shiny red scooter in gear and run up to the Harris-Teeter," I told her.

"I would but it's pretty far and I'm afraid the battery will lose juice before I can get there and back. I don't have *Triple-A* on it."

We snickered at the joke and a brief mental image popped into my head of Willow Lake's handyman towing Miss Sadie back to the facility behind his golf cart. It had an undignified quality to it.

"Besides," she added. "The hills are pretty steep between here and the store and you know it ain't no fo' by fo'." She laughed out loud. Some of my brother's 4x4 aficionado expertise had rubbed off on me over the years and I had to agree with her assessment.

"Okay," I told her. "Let me see what I can do for you."

I had no interest in implicating Miss Sadie in controversies over contraband substances so I checked with her nurse to make sure any change in her diet could be tolerated. The next night, Miss Sadie had a cache of Viennas and Saltines tucked away in her bedside table.

A challenger for Miss Sadie and Grandma's spotlight came from an additional vocalist who brought down the house with her gifted voice. Christie was a friend of Miss Willie's family and when she visited, she sang spirituals that clearly came from her heart and was a joy to witness. Other regulars included Barbara Whitt who tended to her mother-in-law in the evenings and looked in on us like clock-work. She was active in the family council and I relied on her to interpret policy changes and administrative decisions that affected us and our loved ones. Mr. Rowling had returned from the hospital and occupied a room near us before he returned to the 400 Club. We were delighted to see his family again on a more regular basis. Donna and I had become friendly with many of the CNAs on our hall. Andie Beale invited us to a house-warming party at her new apartment and we enjoyed meeting her family. Danielle, who came to us from the Democratic Republic of the Congo (formerly Zaire) where French was her first language, graciously allowed me to practice a few simple phrases during each visit.

As my world became smaller and more insulated, the people who populated it grew to be more important to me. And as Mom's strength ebbed, I began taking a sick day off from work every other week and spending it with her. I had hoarded them for this occasion and with an official day off I had no obligations or responsibilities and was free to be with Mom without constraints. I was not teaching during this semester but was assigned a class for the next term so I took advantage of my free time. This was also a good opportunity for our friend Susie to pay a visit to us from London. While she was in town we drove down to Disney World for a few days. We were silly and I pretended to have no commitments for a few days.

Mom's status had not changed when we returned home. Spring had arrived and with it, hope and a renewed optimism which made our lives a little brighter. Even a fraction of optimism is a tonic and coupled with the return of sunshine and warm days Donna was ready to consider adding a new dog to our family. After losing Dickens, I was reluctant to have any other living thing to love but Donna had other ideas. She believes having canine companions in our lives is well worth the emotional risk. Ultimately, I agreed. We had rescued all previous pets, but now was the perfect time for Donna to find the German Shepherd she'd dream of having since she was seven-years-old.

Shepherds are intelligent, majestic and loyal animals but above all, they are working dogs. Donna intended to have this dog accompany her everywhere, even to work. She and her employer, Katie Tyler, negotiated ground rules to accommodate the new employee, so Donna began her search. She researched breeders and found the perfect one who met all her criteria in a small town nearby. When we went to see the litter, we met the special little soul who literally chose Donna as her human. While the rest of the litter frolicked in the background, this pup sat at Donna's feet with a *Here I am!* expression.

Donna named her Gypsy Madelina and we introduced her to our nursing home family right away. Miss Sadie and Grandma were delighted, while expressing their sadness that getting a new dog was necessary since they missed Dickens so much. Gypsy took naturally to nursing home life just as Dickens had. On each visit, she curled up at the foot of Mom's bed and slept for the duration, or she lay on the cool linoleum floor and watched the movements of the individuals who passed our doorway. Gypsy and Donna have been inseparable soul mates since the moment they laid eyes on each other.

Some of Mom's friends continued to visit her although she no longer recognized them. That's true friendship. There were times when I wasn't aware of Mom's visits until one of the nurses mentioned it to me and I tried to guess the identity of the visitor from the description. I realized much too late the value of having a sheet of paper or white board available in Mom's room for visitors to leave a note on. Many of my own friends came to visit Mom and to show their support for me too. Some of them had not known Mom before, but they visited for my benefit - that's true friendship, too. Susie traveled across the Atlantic many times. Jen came to visit from Texas by way of Maryland. Ellen, a friend since childhood who had known Mom practically all her life, came by one night and sang hymns to her.

Of course my dear friend Paula, with whom I have walked many a rocky path since our graduate school days together, visited Mom. Mom had always admired Paula's gorgeous hair and commented often on how thick and full of natural body it was. They also shared a love of gardening. During one visit Paula observed Mom's attention moving from something otherworldly, to us, and then back again. I had mentioned to Paula how Mom split her time between *here* and *there* and now she saw the phenomenon for herself. When Mom returned her concentration to our world from *there* at one point, she focused it intently onto Paula and Paula had the sensation that Mom was looking directly into her soul, tapping into something invisible to the rest of us. If Mom had a sudden realization of a great truth given to her through unseen spirit connections, Paula would have been open to receiving them. But just as quickly, Mom's keen attentiveness was gone.

On a bright, warm Saturday afternoon, Mary Bobis visited Mom. In one of our discussions we hit on the topic of Mom's current health status. I told her how I had taken Mom outside the previous Sunday afternoon for a ride in her Geri-chair past a showy flowering tulip tree that was on the property.

"Did she seem to enjoy it?" she asked me.

"Of course she did!" I answered. "I'm not doing it for my own pleasure."

As I said it, I realized I was lying to myself. Truthfully, Mom didn't notice whether she was inside or outside. We were thoughtful enough to place sunglasses on her nose so she wouldn't have to squint against the sun, but it was I who had wanted Mom to experience the fresh air, the sounds of birds singing, the brightly colored flowers - all the things she once loved. I wanted to give that to her again. Apparently I was not yet totally successful in accepting Mom's final phase of her illness but when I recently examined the medical diary where I chronicled her health issues, there were no entries during this period. Perhaps I recognized that being proactive in my responsibilities for her was no longer necessary. I had moved into passive, palliative, monitoring mode for her care at that point.

When I recognized these conflicting emotions, I was able to

talk them over with Mary. Mary encouraged me to confront truths I was reluctant to face. I only wanted to prove her wrong. I wanted her to see the spark of life in Mom that I saw. I challenged her to come see for herself. And she came. It was generous of her to follow up on this former client and it meant a lot to me. While she was there by Mom's bedside, she made a few observations and asked some questions. She asked if Mom ever recognized songs and I admitted that she did not acknowledge any of the tunes I played from her cassette collection. Mary asked what her favorite song was. None came to mind so she sang *Twinkle, Twinkle, Little Star* to her.

Mom was not alert or very responsive for Mary's sake and she did not allow herself to be placed on display. I wanted to show her off to company like we do an accomplished child. I wanted Rusty to shine but she had no interest in performing on my cue. My motive for Mary's visit was to demonstrate how interactive Mom was with me still. I failed to prove my point. As Mary was leaving the room, she commented on Mom's coloring, remarking that her complexion was a little grayish. I guess she was trying to indicate that gray is not a healthy color for a human, but I couldn't see it. I was blind. Getting in her car, Mary said gently to me, "She's not engaged in life here anymore, Marsha. There's little interaction between her and her environment." I didn't want to hear this but Mary will not lie. I got the message. Before Dad died, Mom told me that it was time to find a way to let him go; now Mary made the same point concerning Mom.

During our next discussion, Mary explained the importance for caregivers to pay attention to aspects of their own life. I felt guilty when I was not with Mom because I was convinced that she needed me to help her through every step of her difficult journey.

"Are you doing it for your mother or for yourself?" Mary asked. "Does sitting with your mother, night after night, make you feel better or make your Mom feel better?"

"Sitting with her is killing me," I replied. "Mom is in her own little world whether I'm there or not. But I cannot play this out any other way."

"What would you do for fun if you could do anything at all right now?"

"I went to Disney World a couple of months ago, and it was

good to get away." I admitted. "But I'm pretty sure fun is something I'll never have again. I have no energy, and I'm too tired to go or do anything right now." I sat in silence for a while as I considered the answer to her question further. "If there were no restrictions on me and I could do anything I wanted, I'd fly to England and hang out with my friend, Susie."

"I bet if you bought a ticket tomorrow, you'd find the energy to go."

I thought about it a day or two and then bought a ticket. While I awaited my departure date, some of my energy returned. In the mean time, I tried to adjust and adapt psychologically to Mom's dwindling presence here on earth but it remained essential to me to deal with Mom's physical health problems at a basic level. In doing so and within the typical confrontations connected with her care came more opportunities for learning lessons. For instance, when I arrived at the nursing home one night, Mom's face was flushed with fever. She needed help and quick. I rushed out into the corridor and down to the centralized nursing station, the heart of the building, to find the nurse on duty. I wanted Mom's temperature to be taken and some action performed on her behalf. A new nurse I had never seen before stood at the counter, writing instructions into a resident's file.

"My mom..," I addressed him breathlessly, "is Lottie Burris. She's in Room 223 and she's burning up with fever and..."

He cut me off with, "I'm in the middle of something right now and I will be with her as soon as I'm done."

Oh. Oh. I am not going to accept this new employee's brusque manner! I will not be brushed off... (is what went through my head).

"I don't think you realize the importance of this..." is what I was in the process of saying when he cut me off again.

"I will be with you as soon as I can." He was serious. "Now, please wait for me in your mother's room."

I huffed back down to Mom's room and stewed for the next ten minutes regretting that I had possibly made an enemy. Then the new nurse came in, extended his hand to me and said, "Hi, my name's Don and I am now your mother's nurse on the night shift. I'm sorry about earlier, but we were in the middle of an emergency. I can't go into details but one of our residents was taken to the hospital and I had to make sure all her papers were in order for the EMTs to take with them. It was serious. I think you and I got off on the wrong foot. Can we start over?"

I had eyes only for Rusty Burris. I was singularly focused on her and I had been incapable of recognizing that other residents may actually be sicker than she was, but Don's explanation helped me understand that at times other patients may need to get bumped to the head of the priority list. This exchange taught me the value of a 'do-over'.

This was not the only time I was impatient with the medical staff. By comparison Rusty had infinitely more patience. For once in her life. Her mind was totally clear of all trivialities - only the things that really mattered permeated her diseased mind. She found ways to appreciate and thank her caregivers as they tended to her. She patted their arms or she gazed at them lovingly as they worked. When Mom held my hand I felt like I had won the lottery. It was as if she were telling me that she was pleased with me. Her smile communicated to me that she was aware of my presence. And a faint twinkle in her eye told me that she was glad I was there. Nothing could have meant more to me than those things. Then the small connections, the casual acknowledgments, began to fade.

CHAPTER NINETEEN

Arden is born!

My world was shrouded in shades of gray while life danced in Technicolor everywhere else. As I plodded along in my job at the university and as a spectator in the nursing home, Andy and Andrea made a healthy commitment to the future. The birth of their second daughter was the newest reminder that life goes on. Arden was born one afternoon in mid-May but I had heard no news of her arrival since Andy's announcement earlier in the day that they were heading over to the hospital. When I finally got Andy's message that Arden had arrived, I danced a jig to the good news circulating in the Burris family.

Donna and I paid a visit to the hospital the following day and met this new niece. If Arden's big sister Ava was a dark-haired beauty like her father, Arden was the spitting image of Andrea down to her blonde hair and adorable tear drop chin. In time, Andy and Andrea brought Arden along with Ava to see Mom. What a wonderful gift that Mom was able to hold this newest grandchild in her arms. She would not have a chance to become better acquainted with Ava or Arden but their paths crossed briefly. Sadly, she did not have that same honor with her great grandson, Nico.

Only two days after Arden's birth Peggy's father passed away. I met Peggy when I was twenty-four and we played sports together in Newport News, Virginia. Donna, Josh and I lived there for eight years while operating the dental laboratory we established. Peggy has been a close and much loved member of the Burris family ever since. As Rusty said on many occasions, family is created by choice, and not only those who are related to us by blood. After getting the news, I sat in my study listening to the drizzling rain outside the window which added gloom to an already cheerless day. I contemplated mine and Barbara's conversation the day before when she relayed the message of John's death. She said that although Peggy felt deep sadness, she also felt a huge relief. I sympathized with that feeling. Donna, Gypsy and I drove up for the week-end to be with Peggy, her sister, and my sister. As I pondered Peggy's journey and any parallels we shared, I was struck once again by the randomness of illness and death. We had seen many loved ones become ill, decline, and pass away since our own journey began and yet, amazingly, Rusty kept ticking like a Timex. And yet, just because there is ticking, it doesn't mean the watch is keeping good time.

Mom was slipping away from us. Her progressive deterioration unfolded at an agonizingly slow pace and the thought crossed my mind that Arden's arrival could not have been more perfectly timed. Having Ava and Arden in our lives, and anticipating my nephew Tony's son in only two more months, held out the promise of brighter days ahead.

For now though, Donna and I focused primarily on Mom and her basic needs. When Donna used Reiki with Mom, it was like a warm, soothing bath and it continued to bring relief to the physical discomforts caused by Mom's inability to physically move and alter her positions on demand. The CNAs checked on Mom frequently and assisted her, but it's not at all the same as being able to shift and adjust yourself whenever the urge strikes. Did Mom suffer during this time? I do not think she was in any great pain. If she had been, we would have aggressively sought to remove it through any means open to us. It's possible that Mom's atrophied brain was unable to recognize, register, process and send messages of acute physical pain to her conscious awareness. Perhaps that's a small compensation of the disease. But through her facial expressions, she certainly appeared to be uncomfortable at times and we attempted to alleviate that as much as possible.

Occasionally, Mom was able to respond to something I said with a feeble shake of her head or a tentative nod. Once, Mom made fists with her hands then formed an X-shape with her arms over her chest in response to my goodbyes to her. I looked up the meaning of such a gesture. It is the American Sign Language symbol for 'love'. This small reaction gave me an irrational glimmer of optimism that she could still make a come-back. The trickle-down effect of hope is a reprieve from emotional pain, no matter how brief. Even open heart surgery can be endured with enough anesthesia. On one such hopeful visit, Mom and I connected. She was brighter and more alert than usual. She took my hand as if she didn't want to ever let it go. She mumbled some unintelligible words that were directed to *them* but I pretended they were meant for me anyway. After a few moments, she squirmed as if she was agitated or uncomfortable and then she slumped backwards into a sort of semi-paralysis. I briefly conjured an image of Mom passing on to a sweeter place than this one. The thought swept through my mind like a wisp of smoke, then disappeared. As soon as I realized that I wished for my mother to die, I immediately and selfishly reclaimed my desire for her to stay alive for no other reason than merely to hold my hand. I recalled Mary Bobis stressing to me the unlikelihood that I held that kind of power over life and death but I was pretty sure she was wrong on this matter. If I focused all my thoughts on Mom, I believed it was quite possible to postpone her destiny with death. To balance my self-serving intentions, I engaged in a little sleight-of-hand misdirection. I told Mom that if she wanted some rest from the cares of this world, and a release from the burdens of her failing body, and if she really wanted to go with *them*, then I would honor her decision and I assured her that everybody would be alright. Her *chickies* would be safe even if she was not here to watch over us herself.

 She smiled. I think she was calling my bluff. Although I half believed what I said, Mom knew better. She knew I was lying through my teeth. I asked her (tenderly, I hope) what she was waiting for and what I could do to help her. I genuinely wanted to know. I asked her the same question when Hospice was called in less than a year before. Although Mom's physician believed her days were few when he requested their services for her, Mom let us know then that she was in no big hurry to leave us. This night she simply said, "I don't know…" She said it quite clearly then squeezed my hand again.

 Mom could sometimes respond with a couple of words, appropriate words, after speaking what seemed to be gibberish mere moments earlier. Maybe electrical impulses shooting between her synapses made clear positive connections in her brain at times before reverting back to their faulty state. I relished each momentary reprieve. By my next visit, Mom's immobility and detachment had returned. She was physically here, but preoccupied by her invisible friends.

"Where *are* you, Mom?" I asked her. She moved her eyes in my direction without changing her expression.

"I love you, Mom," I said this to see if these were magic words. She made no indication that they were but she moved her lower jaw up and down, up and down. I thought maybe she wanted to tell me something just as magical – but she didn't. It was only reflex. Then she locked her gaze onto me, so I mirrored her in return and moved my mouth the same way she had done. She copied me. I copied her back. Then it was a little fuzzy who was copying whom. I looked silly but I'd been trained in the 400 Club. I took Mom's hand in my own. It was cold. She squeezed my fingers. I'd won a major coup. Since she spent much of her time with *them*, I was gratified to steal her attention back, even for an instant. Her eyes darted back and forth, from me to them and back again, as if she couldn't make up her mind who to be with. Finally, she chose to focus on *them*. I was envious that they won out. But I understood afterwards that when she gave me her attention, it was a big deal.

Mom wasted away before our eyes, and so I was astonished whenever she demonstrated a hint of awareness of this world and me in it. During another supper visit, she looked deeply into my eyes with apparent interest. I stared right back at her. Her eyes were bright and clear. I observed them with the curiosity and attention of a scientist and I memorized them. Everyone in our family has brown eyes except Mom. And me. Mine are the color of a newly mown grass. Mom's were hazel – a tinge of light brown in her green – and rich with rust-colored flecks dusted around the iris. It was as if the flecks were spattered by the Creator's brush in anticipation of the nickname she would earn in her early adulthood. They were denser near the pupil and more sparsely scattered toward the outer edge of the iris. The iris was framed with a thin band of blue – navy blue. Maybe the blue was vivid because the whites of her eyes were so white. A splendid contrast. And expressive still. Not expressive with intense emotion like sadness or happiness, though. I did see displeasure once when she rolled her eyes for the benefit of *them* when I got sentimental in her presence. She never hesitated to cut her eyes at me if I was being unkind or using vocabulary not to her liking. A few times, she looked at me with a hint of tenderness, ever so briefly, as she awoke from a nap. But I no longer saw joy reflected in her face. When Mom was healthy, she had a twinkle in her eyes, her facial expression open and engaging, and her smile reflected the joie de vivre with which she came into this world. If I had to describe her now, I'd say that she looked serious. No-nonsense serious. This final lap around the track before crossing the finish line and entering her place in eternity was important and of the greatest consequence. It was a solemn affair which warranted a dignified approach to the journey ahead, and it was not to be taken lightly.

As I noticed the absence of joy in Mom's eyes, I realized that my own eyes registered none of that emotion either. My thoughts were concentrated on Mom, any additional energy that remained after caring for her was invested in my career. But Mom came first and having the luxury to prioritize these two aspects of my day was made possible by my supervisor who allowed me to continue working a flexible schedule. I contemplated applying for the Family and Medical Leave benefit provided by the university as soon as I completed the summer academic term. I taught the five-week summer history course Monday through Thursday in the evenings. It meant that I arrived at Willow Lake later than usual but, as with my nieces, it was therapeutic to have these young people in my life. I enjoyed their vitality and I delighted in having conversations that did not include the words *bed sores* and it allowed me to wear a mask of normalcy during the horrible months we waited for Mom's end to come. I was in survival mode. Having Ava and Arden, my students, my family and my closest friends helped.

Mom's changes were incremental but I was intensely tuned into them. She sipped daintily at her protein drink, taking in no more than a bird, and she was collapsing in on herself like one of those plastic push-puppets which falls slack when the base is depressed. Rusty, too, was falling limply into a half-dozen pieces.

I crawled into the bed with Mom each night and held her fragile little body in my arms. With her head on my shoulder, I counted no more than three gray hairs. Phenomenally, her hair remained its original auburn color and the CNAs teased us about sneaking into her room in the middle of the night to dye it. As I touched my head to hers, I caught a whiff of her soured hair.

Mom was usually clean and smelled pleasantly sweet but she must have sweated her hair down during a nap. I didn't mind. It's how she smelled at that moment and I decided that it wasn't unpleasant. As I lay there I realized that I was following Jim's advice for confronting life's worst difficulties. The best I could do for Rusty through this time now was to *just ride it out* with her. After only a few minutes, she would shut her eyes, relax into me, then fall asleep. I know this because I watched her eyes move underneath her eyelids in REM sleep and I tapped into a tiny bit of altruism deep down and hoped she was dreaming of how wonderful heaven will be. I encouraged her to make things easy on herself, to follow Dad and Robert into Paradise. But I knew deep down she wouldn't go easy. It's not the Rusty way.

My silent encouragement cheered her onwards, but my fingers were secretly crossed behind my back. I didn't intend to be cruel and prolong her suffering, but in my fantasy thinking I imagined there was yet more for me to do for her, more to be said. Once she was gone, I would never feel Mom pat my hand or play with my hair again. I wanted her sweet energy here on earth. I wanted to be near her. As she slept she took such shallow breaths and was so quiet that I put my hand on her chest to see if she had followed my wishes after all.

For the next few days Mom slept through my visits and ate little food. I wondered if I needed to call in Barbara and Andy. I had called them to a bedside vigil before and they readily assembled at my request. Mom had actually improved then, and as she rallied she looked at us with a glimmer of recognition and resumed eating rather heartily. Was this a trick? Was Rusty trying, once again, to gather her children to her side?

Another suppertime. I had not seen Mom for three days but it felt longer. I greeted Mom by putting my cheek on her face and nuzzling her like a puppy trying to get its nose warm. And she kissed me. A dry, light buss, but unmistakable in its tenderness. She squeezed my hand three times, like Morse Code, and she didn't take her eyes off me. Dolly Parton sang "I will always love you," on the radio. I sang along. Mom was unimpressed but she wasn't critical either so I warbled on. Then she took on an expression that said that none of this mush had anything to do with her, that any drama being created out of this scenario was my own invention. She had always taken life's bumps in stride and left the drama to others. But in this case, Mom became the star of the show. I was a prop and the audience, too. But I was in no way ready for the curtain call. I wallowed in that sentimental state for a while recognizing that I had no more ability to control my emotions than I had over directing what was happening to my mother's body and mind. Mom looked at me for a long time. The longer she looked, the easier it was for me to see again the healthy-Rusty in this woman's eyes. She was not totally gone yet. Did she know I was with her, that I loved her? I watched every labored breath. She looked pale and delicate but she made an effort to let me know she was still with me.

"I'll go get you something to drink, Mom." I started to get up and she grasped my hand tighter. She didn't want me to leave her. She'd rather have physical contact with me than to have a drink of water.

I dropped in to see Mom after a Monday night class. My thoughts had dwelled on her since our visit the day before when she was more inanimate than usual. She didn't eat, not even the sweet baby food. And she didn't drink. She usually enjoyed the nutrient drink because of its chocolaty flavor, but she didn't have the strength to grasp a straw between her lips on that visit. She was a weary traveler and her instinctual responses were failing her. She didn't return hugs, her lips didn't react to a kiss, and her eyes followed no movements as they stared blankly into space. The key functional elements of communication in Mom's brain were sputtering into oblivion. The automatic stuff behind the scenes commanded by the autonomic nervous system, like breathing and swallowing would eventually cease operating. Andy and I had talked on the phone earlier in the day and he told me he visited Mom late Sunday afternoon after I had left.

"How did she look to you?" I asked him.

"Pitiful," he replied. I agreed with his assessment.

By the time I got to her room, it was already 8:30 p.m. I took a quick peek at her from the hallway. She lay on her side on the bed, staring passively at the floor. Until tonight, whenever Mom was awake, she was engaged at least at some basic level with her surroundings, casually glancing about the room, up to the ceiling, out toward the hallway, responding to sounds and movements in the *here-and-now* or somewhere over *there*. A lot of the time, she was interested in what she alone could see, but that wasn't the case tonight. I went in and sat down by her bed. She did not acknowledge my presence. I wondered what she saw, for it was certainly not me.

Her eyes were cast down at the floor, fixated on one spot. She didn't blink. Her face looked flushed. I walked over and spoke to her quietly. I touched her forehead with the back of my hand to see if she had a fever but it felt quite cool. I hugged her as usual. Nothing in return. She was immobile, like the proverbial wooden Indian at the antique store. She didn't shift her gaze to me and she made no facial movements indicating that she was aware that anyone was in the room with her. Only a few days earlier, she couldn't take her eyes off me while she fidgeted with the fabric of my shirt. She stroked my arm lovingly and held my hand with purpose, and if I attempted to pull it away in order to reach her food, she playfully squeezed it and wouldn't relinquish her grip. When I stretched out beside her in the bed that night, she seemed content enough to have me close-by while I flipped through a reference book that I was using in my class. But after a while, she sensed that I was not interacting with her and she began to pick at the pages. When she did that, down went the book. I needed nothing else in the world at that moment. I was happy and didn't mind in the least that she demanded my attention. It was proprietary. I was hers to direct. I liked it. On this night, I wasn't upset because she did not respond to me as before. I was upset because she was *incapable* of it.

She could not reciprocate with an embrace of her own because her arms were no longer at her command. I hugged her again, wanting her to know that someone was there for her, to love her, and care for her. She may have been beyond needing that assurance, and yet I hoped that deep in her subconscious, she could still perceive warmth and tenderness. I rearranged her position on the bed to make her comfortable. It looked like she had been in one position for a while. Her knees were drawn up and the stress on her joints must have been painful. I rolled her onto her back and tucked a pillow under her knees. I propped her elbows up on two of her soft stuffed animals to get the pressure off the shoulder joints. These are our typical evening practices so nothing new there, but the difference this time was that when Mom looked at me, at the person moving her, there was no recognition in her eyes. I would have welcomed even a grimace. That would at least mean that she associated me with the source of the disturbance. Me. It didn't need to be me – Marsha, daughter-of-Rusty. I would have settled for me – somebody-who-is-in-the-room-with-Rusty. Mom had seemed to understand, throughout this ordeal until now, that when her children and grandchildren were with her, she knew we were 'hers'. Not any longer. If she maintained a sense of that bond now, she exhibited no evidence of it.

We were in new territory. No matter how much I hugged Mom, nothing was going to be exchanged between us. I let her go and walked into the hallway to locate her dinner tray on the food cart. I recognized the futility in trying to feed her, but I needed to *do* something. I was upset. I was sad. I felt abandoned. After all we'd been through? After our ten-year long fight together through the various phases of this dreadful disease, was Mom simply going to turn her back on me now? I did not deserve this snub. Oh, how I hate goodbyes. Was Rusty going to leave us without even a fare-thee-well? As these thoughts flitted through my head, I was mindfully aware that Mom had no free will left to her under the circumstances. It was another sad example of my illogical, magical thinking. How could I honestly believe that she had any control over what her poor brain was doing to her?

On my bleak drive home afterwards, I stopped at the post office to check for mail. I sat in the parking lot dumbly with the motor idling and a song sung by Patty Loveless came on the radio as if specially ordered by Rusty herself and it helped ease my troubled mind. The last verse caught my attention:

Sittin' with Mama, alone in her bedroom
She opened her eyes, then squeezed my hand
She said "I have to go now, my time here is over"
And with her final words she tried to help me understand.
Mama whispered softly "time will ease your pain,
   life's about changing nothing ever stays the same"
And she said, "how can I help you to say goodbye? It's okay to hurt
   and it's okay to cry. Come let me hold you and I will try.
How can I help you to say goodbye"?

The departure date for my trip to London crept closer. I debated if I should stay home with Mom instead. I talked to Mom's nurse and she encouraged me to go, they considered this new phase more or less a holding pattern and there was a general consensus that she could maintain this state indefinitely.

On a Monday night in late July Donna and I met friends for dinner. My evening class was done and I looked forward to seeing Judy and Joyce with a little more energy than I had had in a while. Donna and I went by the nursing home to check on Mom before our rendezvous at the restaurant. Mom was lying in her bed, starring out into space. She did this more and more now, but there was a difference tonight although I couldn't put my finger on exactly what that difference was. Mom tasted her supper, took a sip of her nutrition drink and was exhausted from the activity. The faint toll of a warning bell sounded. I ignored it. We went to have our dinner.

Judy and Joyce and I had grown up together in Newell. Judy was the youth leader at church then even though she was not much older than we were. Joyce and I were closer in age and had shared many adventures in our young adult lives. Mom loved them both like daughters and had been friends with their mother who died as a result of complications associated with Alzheimer's a few years earlier. They knew what I was going through. We didn't spend our evening complaining, though - Judy would never allow that - but we told stories from our younger days and remembered what it was like to be care-free. I shared my plans to fly to England on Monday. It was fun. We promised to do it again.

After our meal, we said our good-byes. As Donna and I buckled up, I told her, "I'd feel better if we drove back over to the nursing home..."

"Let's go," she said.

We walked into Mom's room and once again, I sensed there was something very different about the place. *Something* was missing. It was as if the countless, colorful and intricate threads that wove the tapestry of Rusty were unraveling. Mom was threadbare. She lay on her left side starring at the wall, looking more uncomfortable than before. Her breathing was labored and she was feverish. Donna went to find the nurse to help us get Mom propped and fluffed and shored up with her pillows. Her temperature was taken, food and liquid intake amounts were consulted from her chart, an oxygen tank was brought in, and the tube delivering the oxygen tucked under Mom's nose. The oxygen mist would relieve a little of the effort it took for her to breathe.

"This is different," I told the nurse. I couldn't be more specific. "There's something different," I repeated myself.

"Yes," she agreed. "Miss Lottie's taken a turn".

I had not been able to place as fine a point on the situation as she had done. I didn't ask for more details because I knew what she meant. Donna proposed bringing Hospice back into the picture. The nurse agreed. I sat with Mom a while longer looking at her face and trying to divine through mental telepathy what she wanted, what she needed. It was futile. We went home. Donna called Hospice the following morning.

I took the next day off from work and met my friend Paula for coffee. As I told her what was going on, Donna called to let me know that Hospice had the information they needed and would meet me at the nursing home after lunch to sign the documents. They had been of considerable help to me before and I looked forward to their support.

The Hospice nurse assessed Mom's condition and assured me that everything that could be done for her was being done. The last time Hospice was called in, Mom rallied and I expected a repeat performance from her this time. I told the representative about my planned trip to England and she assured me that it was the very thing to do. I was to go and relax and come back rested. As before, Hospice would schedule sitters to come and stay with Mom each evening to be with her for suppertime and they would give me a regular report of their experiences. Her reassurance helped, but I did not pack. Usually, I drag my suitcase out of the closet well in advance of my travels to toss essentials into it as I think of them. I did not follow protocol in preparation for this trip. My heart just wasn't in it.

CHAPTER TWENTY

*I have been braver than I ever thought possible
and yet I have not been as brave as I've wanted to be.*
                                                -Susan Rose Blauner

Donna and I visited Mom every evening during the following week. With Hospice support I detected a slight improvement in Rusty's status that no one else seemed to notice. When we made our Sunday visit, we expected to find Mom up, dressed, and in her Geri-chair. But she was still in bed. Mouth gaping. She stared into space and was in a much deteriorated condition. Donna tracked down medical personnel for an explanation. The nurse on duty told us that Mom couldn't swallow her food at breakfast. She just held the food in her mouth without chewing.

"Why didn't you call us?" I asked her.

"We knew you'd be here for lunch and we wanted to talk to you in person. We called Hospice and the nurse is here. She wants to see you."

The hospice nurse told us basically the same thing. "Your mother's brain can no longer give her throat muscles the message to swallow. It's common in the late stages of Alzheimer's, I'm afraid."

"What does that mean?" I knew what it meant but I wanted to hear the words.

"It means she can't eat anymore. We don't want to force feed her because of the possibility of her choking on the food. Of course feeding tubes can be used but I see that her Healthcare Power of Attorney states that…"

"No, we're not going to do that to her. Her wishes are clear. My brother and sister and I agree to abide by them."

"Then we'll make your mother as comfortable as possible and we'll do all we can for her during this final stage."

A long pause. Awkward on my part. Not on hers. It's the job

of a hospice nurse to be in this spot and I relied on her to know what to do. Although I had been pretend-preparing for Mom's death for a couple of years now, I was uncertain of my role and what was expected of me. It was the nurse's job to confront this situation as a matter of course but this would be the only time I would ever experience the death of the woman who gave birth to me and my sibs.

"So, this is it..." I tried to comprehend it all. Moments of my life flashed like a silent film through my mind. It fast-forwarded then stopped at this point.

She nodded. "This is it."

"How long does it take to starve to death?"

"Without food or liquids, your mother's organs will begin to shut down rather quickly, two or three days. Maybe even quicker for your Mom. The starvation and dehydration will not cause your mother to suffer."

"I know. We've already been through that with my dad."

"Oh? When was that?"

"Three years and one month ago today. One room over from here."

"I'm sorry. So you know that her final days will be peaceful..."

She was professional and kind but I was feeling sorry for myself.

"I know that she will not be able to complain," I told her.

After this conversation, Donna and I sat quietly with Mom. Throughout the entire nursing home ordeal Mom showed a childlike trust in us. And even now she looked so sweet, so gentle, and content with her situation. To be honest, she may not have had the resources or the ability to comprehend her *situation*. Nevertheless, fear was not reflected in her face. Mom was rendered into a purely transcendent state which made Alzheimer's only slightly tolerable. Surely not everyone who has experienced this disease close up can say the same and I am grateful for the small mercy.

We left Mom in the hands of her devoted CNAs for the evening and went home to call Barbara and Andy with the new developments. I cancelled my flight to London and went to work on Monday as if it was any other work day. I wanted to tie up loose ends of any work-related projects that couldn't wait for a while. I expected to be out indefinitely since I thought this would be the last day of my mother's life. I was wrong. She would have one more.

I called Mary. "Looks like this is the end, Mary." I felt calm. It was strange to engage in a normal routine while believing it was likely the last day of your mother's life but running around in a panic would take energy that I did not have. "I'm not going to England. I'll have to rethink the trip."

"I'm sorry," she told me. Mary, never given to mawkish sentimentality, was genuinely sad for me and for this turn of events. "Let me know what I can do to help."

"I will." I hung up the telephone and shut down my computer. I walked out of the office as my work mates looked on helplessly. I would see them again in five days at Mom's service.

I met Donna at home and we drove over to Willow Lake together. We didn't think to pack any provisions. The lesson Andrea taught us, to have a go-bag ready for long waits in a healthcare facility, was lost in the shuffle. We dropped Gypsy off at our neighbor's house for a sleep-over. That was the extent of our long-term preparations.

At the nursing home, we went into Mom's room where she was sleeping peacefully. I stroked her cheek. I sat down on a chair close by and Donna settled in on the foot of the bed. We didn't attempt to feed her. For the next three hours we barely budged and the only sound was that of the oxygen machine pumping the elixir of life into Mom's nostrils. Around 5:30 or 6 o'clock, Donna suggested we split a pack of crackers for supper and I decided it was time to place *the call* to Barbara and Peggy to come down and be with us because I finally grasped the reality that Rusty would not pull out of this fix. There was no escape from the certainty that Mom was leaving us whether we were on board or not so I made the announcement. They got on the road within moments and walked into Mom's room at 2:30 in the morning.

While we waited for Barbara and Peggy to arrive, Donna and I began the vigil. I asked myself what I would want if it was me lying in bed trying to detach from my earthly body. I pretended that if I was Mom, I would want my daughter to crawl into bed with me and cradle me through the night until the hour of my death. I also pretended that if this same daughter would light a candle for me and play beautiful music then it would create a sacred space for me to pass from the heaviness of the physical world into the love and light of the spiritual world. In short, it would make death beautiful. I lit the candle in the glass container sitting on Mom's bedside table and tuned the radio to a classical radio station. I crawled into bed with her, slipped my arm under her shoulders as I had done many times before and held her in my arms. To be truthful, more than anything else I simply wanted to be physically near Mom. Donna, too. She curled up like a kitten at the foot of Mom's bed and together we settled in for the night. The sands of time had run their course. Mom was slipping further and further away from us and soon she would be gone forever.

We were asleep when Barbara and Peggy arrived but we rallied a bit and brought them up to date with the information as we knew it. The nurses had moved in and out of Mom's room regularly all evening taking her vital statistics. Pulse, oxygen, respiration, all monitored and noted on her chart. These quantitative units were indicators that meant something to the medical staff and Mom's fate would follow a pre-determined paint-by-numbers scheme for them. Based on these numbers, we expected Mom to make an easy and peaceful departure before morning's light so we settled in. Barbara took possession of the chair where I sat earlier. She laid her head on the edge of Mom's bed and patted on Mom throughout the night. Donna maintained her position on the end of the bed and Peggy found two chairs that she set up facing each other and stretched out. I returned to my position in the bed with Mom. Candle burning. Music playing. I fell into a light sleep a couple of times. So did Donna, Barbara and Peggy. Mom continued to breathe quietly, almost silently, but her vitals improved with the dawning of the day. Mom was still in some control. She was the master of her death as she had been the master of her life. *Yay, Rusty!*

As the sun came up, we stirred. I was surprised by how incredibly hungry I was. How in the world could I be hungry at a time like this? Historically speaking, grief has never stopped a Burris from eating, but Barbara and I were not going to leave Mom's side on this occasion, even for food. I made some noise to wake up Donna and Peggy.

"Go get us some food," I implored them.

"No," they replied in unison. "We're fine."

They didn't want to leave the room because they were afraid Mom would, through a cruel quirk of fate, choose that opportunity to make her exit and they needed to be here. But about this fine point, I did not care. I required food. Donna and Peggy, the best friends ever, went in search of breakfast biscuits. While they were away, Barbara and I talked about old times. We remembered our favorite game, 'If you had all the money in the world, and everybody else did too – what would you buy?' Money couldn't buy what we wanted today.

We kept the candle going and the music playing. When Donna and Peggy returned, we inhaled our breakfast. Just before midday, Barbara and Peggy went to our house to have naps and showers. They were exhausted and Mom's nurse assured us that with Mom's improved numbers, we had a little leeway in our comings and goings. Donna and I stayed with Mom. No way were we going to leave the ol' gal alone even for a moment. If the time of death is predestined and if I was meant to be with Mom at that moment, I was damn well going to be there. I would outwit fate and weight the odds to my side this one time. Not trusting fate to play fair, I stuck to Mom like glue.

As Donna and I hovered over Mom, the Hospice nurse came in and made her own vital statistics assessment. I followed her out into the hall and asked her what to expect and how long this part of the process would take. I waited to hear the date and time of Rusty's exodus. She looked at me suspiciously like I was late for a lunch date.

"I know you can't give me a precise time. I only ask because my sister is here from Virginia. She has started a new job only recently, and if it's going to be two weeks, she can go home then come back when it's more imminent."

"I truly can't say," the nurse puzzled over Mom's chart. "Her vitals tell me that her body is in the process of shutting down. By all indications, your mother's death should be soon. Today. But another indication that death is near is in the eyes. Usually, the patient's eyes will begin to cloud over, get dull. Your mother's eyes are as clear and bright as yours. I've never seen anybody's eyes so focused and crystal clear when they're supposed to be this close to the end."

I shook my head in amazement. *She's right*, I thought. Whether they looked at me or were cast upon her destination in a faraway dimension, Mom's eyes remained vibrantly clear. Even in death Rusty did not adhere to the norm. She was going to observe her transition from this world to the next with brilliant ocular clarity.

For the record, my sister did not ask for this information. I wanted to know for her sake but I also wanted to know for myself - I was afraid I had been premature in asking her to drop everything to come to Charlotte so I was fishing for concrete information from an expert. It has been my experience that Hospice personnel are more forthcoming with their assessments than the typical members of the medical staff who must be extremely guarded in what they tell the family. Hospice will lay the information on the line, and they are uncannily accurate in predicting outcomes. They are the ones who help us deal with death when it appears on our horizon. And thank God somebody does because I know I'm afraid of my own death. But Mom's words from my childhood popped into my head.

God does something to help us get ready when death approaches, she told me once when I expressed to her my fear of dying. *Something happens inside of us that makes us not so scared, not so frightened. Death is not horrible. It's just the other side of life.*

"Don't send your sister back home yet," the nurse conceded after a moment's thought. "She should stay here. You should stay with your mother today. It won't be two weeks. That much I know."

"I'd like to go home and get a nap."

"I think it's safe to do that."

About four in the afternoon, when Barbara and Peggy returned to the nursing home, Donna and I went home to nap and shower. We napped, but there was no time to shower. I turned my cell phone off while I slept, but woke up an hour later with a start. I jumped up to get in the shower and in the half dozen steps it took me to get to the bathroom, I turned the telephone back on and the voice message indicator was parked on the screen. I played it. *"Marsha, Andy's here,"* my sister's voice told me. *"Momma's breathing is shallow and rapid. The nurses think she's close. You might want to get back here as fast as you can."*

Donna drove us back to the nursing home as quickly as the law allowed. Andy, Barbara and Peggy were circled around Mom's bed. Now with Donna and me in the circle, we made five and yet Barbara, Peggy and Donna felt as if the room was full to over-flowing with the many souls gathering to welcome Mom home. I didn't feel it at all. I was focused on one thing - Mom's face. Nothing else in the world existed for me. A cold wet washcloth was placed on Mom's forehead. It looked funny, as if she were in a hospital ward in the Crimea with a head injury. I sat down in the chair that Barbara had occupied the night before. She sat with her back to the wall on the other side of the bed. Andy beside her and Peggy at Mom's feet. Donna was to my right and to my left was an adjustable bedside tray under which the oxygen machine pumped rhythmically. I asked Barbara to pass the candle over to me so I could have it close by. I placed it on the tray and hoped to use it as inspiration for me to try, once again, to wish Mom a peaceful, easy crossing over.

Since Thursday night Mom's light had begun fading. She resembled a deflated balloon and was not able to shift herself into more comfortable positions; she couldn't even scratch her nose. And yet now, she began to vigorously move her legs as if walking a difficult path. She was not running away from death, but walking toward it confidently, determinedly. The strenuous effort needed for this walk caused her to breathe like a marathon runner and the oxygen machine pumped overtime to keep up. Rusty was afraid of very little and on this occasion she saw death, not as an object of revulsion, but an old friend. She didn't hurry. She took her time. She expended every ounce of energy available to her in order to meet Saint Peter at the Pearly Gates at her designated time and embrace her life after life there. She was on her way.

I panicked. My nerve left me, and as the quotation states, *I had been braver than I ever thought possible and yet I was not as brave as I wanted to be.* The reality, the finality, the significance of the moment hit me full force and I silently begged my Guardian Angels for a do-over. Had I done everything possible for Mom? What if I had neglected something vital to her care? Did I overlook the one thing that would have saved her life? She was only seventy-three-years old. That's not old. That's nothing. Maybe, if I had only loved her enough, she wouldn't die...

I held Mom's right hand, Barbara held her left. I laid my head on the bed beside Mom and cried for the first time in days, and then I looked up at Barbara and Andy and decided to come clean. "I don't know if I did everything I could. I'm afraid I missed something...," I confessed.

I wasn't fishing for a pat on the back. I was truly afraid that I'd neglected something of such great importance that it literally meant the difference between life and death for our mother. They assured me that I had done all that was possible. I believed them. They don't say a thing unless they mean it. I calmed down. I did love her enough but she was going to die anyway. Incalculable numbers of us have been here at this point and felt the same. It was just our turn. Again.

Out of the corner of my eye, I saw the flame of the candle dancing brightly in our darkened, quiet room and I was quite pleased that I remembered to do this little ritual for Mom, to help elevate her spirit as she continued down the long arduous road to eternity. People came and went in the room, but quiet reverence permeated our little enclave. There was only the sound of the oxygen machine, droning, pumping, delivering, O_2 to Mom.

I looked more closely at the candle sitting on the table top, directly above the oxygen tank.

I looked at the oxygen tank.

I looked again at the flame.

I noticed the combustible warning sign on the oxygen machine.

Unlike my poor Momma, my synapses were healthy and unencumbered with plaques and tangles although the messages sent and received dawdled sluggishly. But the critical message eventually arrived in the proper area for evaluation. And a note of warning clicked at last. I bent over the candle and quickly blew out the flame. I hoped my action went unobserved. It didn't. My family didn't miss a beat.

"Oh, lord," Andy proclaimed. "If that had exploded, every one of us would have gone with Momma!"

"I'm sorry. I don't know what I was thinking," I told them. The break in the tension was welcomed but the symbolic benefits of burning a candle were less important than our continued survival.

Mom's breathing became more labored. At times she gasped for air but her eyes remained as clear as a mountain brook. I observed every nuance, every breath, and each infinitesimal facial expression. I held her hand and noticed her fingernails tinged blue. Donna rubbed on Mom's legs, keeping the covers pulled over them protectively, as they continued their motion of walking. Andy, Barbara and Peggy were tucked in around the bed. Mom expended great effort in taking each breath. Her legs, moving, moving, moving. Wouldn't you just know that the journey was a Sisyphean uphill one? How in the world did she have the energy to walk so far while the indicators pointed to her body shutting down?

We experienced no evidence of a 'death rattle' although she was cold to the touch where she had been feverish only an hour or two earlier. The body instinctively knows to conserve the last tiny flicker of life by economizing the meager portion of oxygen and redirecting it to the body's core and ultimately to the most important organ of the body, the brain. Rusty's eyes remained clear and focused on her destination. Edna St.Vincent Millay's words rang true - *more precious was the light in your eyes than all the roses in the world.*

Willie's daughters came to tell Rusty goodbye, but I had not an ounce of energy available to acknowledge them. I regret that. Mom's breathing became more shallow. My breathing was shallow too. The waiting and the hyper-vigilance was making me edgy. How far did she have to walk, for God's sake? Why was it that Dad slipped on over as easy as pie and Mom worked harder than she'd ever worked in her flower garden, if that can be believed. My sister supplied the answer: "To Momma's way of thinking, it's only as important as the effort you put into it."

Moving against the current. Swimming upstream. That was Rusty. In Dad's philosophy of *just-ride-it-out*, there was no reason to fight against the inevitable when you could go with the flow. Not Rusty. Rusty would make this journey on her own two legs, using every last ounce of steam left to her. Her breaths became fewer and farther between. She'd take a breath. Then nothing. Another one. Then nothing. Just one more. Then nothing. Nothing. Is this it? Nothing. One more. Nothing. If our breaths are numbered, how many did Rusty have left? Has she used up her allotment? There's no gauge to tell us how low her inventory was getting. She may already be dipping into the auxiliary tank. Nothing. Nothing. Nothing. Then one more. We held our breath waiting, watching. We watched her eyes. Clear. No breath. *There was no way we could live in a world that did not include Rusty.*

We looked at each other, frozen. No breath. Not from Mom

and not from us. I glanced at the clock. Eight twenty-six p.m. Mom had taken her last breath. We held ours. The long goodbye finally ended. After an eternity, we exhaled. And we just sat there. We *could* survive in a world without Rusty. How was it possible? Until this moment, I could not conceive of a world with no Rusty. And yet the world continued to rotate on its axis.

Andy stood at the foot of the bed and looked down at her. He shook his head and laughed a little. "I kind of expect her to do something. I wouldn't be surprised if she let out one of her big old sneezes like she used to do at the dinner table. *Chaw!* He mimicked her unique sneeze. We laughed.

Peggy went to fetch the nurse to make the time of death official. I asked to be the one to close Mom's eyes for the last time. Those eyes. Still clear. Still bright. Staring into eternity. All the burdens and pain of this world were washed away. Rusty was a young girl again.

As soon as the nurse made her pronouncement, I was ready to leave. I called the funeral home and they assured me they would be over within the hour. Contrary to my desire to stand watch over Dad on the morning of his death, I now felt no such obligation on Mom's behalf. My job was done. Mom was gone, no longer trapped in her failing body. She was free. She was once again just fine - better than fine. Her spirit did not hover and there was nothing for me to watch over. She was delivered safely into the capable hands of her Angels. At last, her mind, her soul, her very essence was liberated from the prison of her body that had malfunctioned for years as a result of Alzheimer's disease. Mom's death was a victory as she shed her body in preparation for the promise of renewal.

Barbara and Peggy stayed to see to the final details at the nursing home. As for me, I felt only relief and I couldn't get out of the nursing home fast enough. I had two objectives for the past few years: care for Mom and outlive her. I had fulfilled both. I felt free for the first time in a decade and I relaxed because neither Mom nor Dad needed assistance of an earthly nature any longer. I called my friend Paula to ask her to meet us at the house. When Barbara and Peggy arrived, we made a party and drank many glasses of wine to the memory of Rusty. We celebrated. I was happy for Mom. *She did it!* Her journey was an uncommonly long one. We stood by her side and cheered her on, but she walked the whole way by herself. We raised a glass to her success. Missing Rusty would take the rest of our lives. My loss (the loss we would all feel) would hit later, but not yet. We drank toasts to Mom's successful completion of her life. To be with her at the end when she took the last breath God gave her was an honor. She saw us into this world and we saw her out of it. Full circles are satisfying even while they are ripping our hearts out. Wrapped inside the blanket of numbed-disbelief is a welcomed reaction to extreme loss. It aids in performing the necessary duties in the days ahead.

On the day after Mom's death we sat down once again with our friends at the funeral home to work out the details of Mom's memorial service. We contacted Tony to ask him to come home for his grandmother's funeral. Since Josh was finishing exam week at college, we planned the service for Saturday when he could be home and to give Tony and our cousin Virginia in Minnesota time to get to town. We agreed on the wording of her obituary then we browsed the inventory of caskets on offer in the showroom. We wandered through the displays like automatons. We knew we were going to choose one made of wood - Rusty claimed often that a plain pine box would suit her. Several pine models fit the criterion but we also knew that pecan was her favorite wood of choice. She had filled her house with furniture made from it so we were open to that as well. One model in particular caught our eye - the one with a special secret hidden draw in the lid. Here we could store mementos appropriate to accompany Mom into her afterlife. We didn't place as many of Mom's belongings with her as, say, King Tutankhamun had done, but we packed in as much as space allowed. We included a pair of pinking shears for her sewing needs; garden clippers to neaten up any heavenly flower beds she came across; photos of her loved ones to show around and brag a little (we made sure names and dates were clearly marked on the back of each one); a pack of Camels and lighter; and Donna snuck in Mom's favorite snack, a Snickers Bar.

For her clothes, we chose a nice beige and navy linen pantsuit from her wardrobe. Mom preferred natural fibers and something comfortable, we knew. Nothing showy, although if an outfit from brocade had presented itself, I don't think she would have minded that. How we cling to rituals during our time of bereavement. It's comforting. I recommend it.

Thursday was a free day for us. We went to a movie and Andy shopped for a new dress shirt. Hey, we were together and that was what really mattered. Could the sales clerks and ticket-sellers tell that our mom had died and we had not even buried her yet? We were orphans. It must have been plain as day.

Although the visitation on Friday evening was a sad occasion, my sibs and I were pleased to greet friends and family members who shared their Rusty-stories with us. Many of her acts of kindness and generosity we had never heard before. Rusty was a character, she often went against the current, but Rusty was loved. It's a beautiful legacy that she and Dad left us.

For Mom's memorial service on Saturday, I asked for Proverbs 31:10-31 to be read. In this scripture the author describes the twin roles of mother and wife in her family. This particular scripture easily served as Rusty's template, her life plan. Mom excelled in these roles in her own life. It was her profession and she was good at it. I prefer the more poetic King James Version although I can understand why ministers hesitate to use the KJV in liturgical services. Seeketh, worketh, planteth, goeth and maketh, used in seventeenth-century language don't roll off the tongue now as it once did. But if the minister attempted only one verse it would have to be: *Her children arise up, and call her blessed; her husband also, and he praiseth her.*

I would give the eulogy for Mom although I wasn't sure my knees would hold me up long enough to say the things I wanted to say on her behalf. It was important to me to remember Rusty for who she was before the disease stole her from us, and honor the person who evolved because of the disease. I wanted us to celebrate and remember all of her. It was the last thing I could do for my mother. I looked out at the sea of loving faces and saw that I was in very good company. I felt the real and welcomed support of Mom and Dad on either side of me, and then I began:

Thank you for being here today. And thank you especially for the encouragement, acts of kindness and love you've shown the Burris family throughout this long and difficult journey.

I have some thoughts and reflections I'd like to share with you today - the first of which is something my brother and sister and I agree on and that is: We can't believe Rusty's gone. We actually never thought we'd see this day come. We believed that Mom would live forever because – she said she would. She always said to us: "I'm not going!" And she was serious. She wasn't afraid, it's just that she loved life so much, she never wanted to let go of it. My brothers and sister and I use to tease her about which possessions of hers we wanted to divide among ourselves, when her time came, and she'd tease back and say, "Don't even worry about that, because I'm not going". She finally conceded that if she did have to go, she certainly intended to live to be at least a hundred years old.

I believed her. Whenever Rusty said something, you believed her. Plus to me, Mom always seemed bigger than life, and certainly bigger than death. And I have to tell you, I'm glad I'm not the one greeting her at the Pearlie Gates. Imagine when she confronts her welcomer with the fact that his calculations are off by 27 years. I don't want to ponder that confrontation.

So yes, Mom always seemed bigger than life, and I think it's probably because she had so much spirit and an incredible zest for life. So, I'll honor her today by talking about her joy for life and what it meant to me.

We've all missed the old Rusty for a very long time now. The Rusty who emerged as a result of Alzheimer's was peaceful, calm, and content (a bit of irony that's not lost on any of us). So today I want to reclaim and remember the whole person, including the old Rusty who was spunky and relished life passionately, and who was not content and peaceful and thought perfection "was" attainable.

There's a song written and sung by Grace Slick of the rock group Jefferson Airplane called: Take Your Time. *She wrote it originally because her friends accused her of burning her candle at both ends, and they advised her to slow down. And if you knew Rusty at all, you know this could have been her theme song - it fits her. I'll read a couple of lines and you'll know what I mean:*

> I'm gonna make one hour fit into just a few minutes
> I'm gonna get two days for the price of one
> Everybody keeps telling me to take it easy
> But time doesn't sit down and wait while I'm try to get it done
> So, take your time, take your time, and I'll take my own time

That summarizes Mom's approach to life. She wanted, and she got, good value for the time she spent here with us. She certainly packed in a lot of living in her time. I believe she left this earth with only a few regrets. I know she always wanted to live in a house made out of stone, and that dream was never realized. And I know she regretted not being able to share her children with her parents, since they both died when she was young – a regret that I believe my brother Andy now shares with her. But I don't think she felt regrets for a life not *fully-lived. I think Mom lived her life* her *way, the Rusty-way. No one on earth had power over her and I think that's kind of cool.*

She always followed her heart and her path and she didn't mind a little controversy along the way. She listened to, and heeded only her own inner voice, that divine "source" within her. She never caved, or capitulated to outside forces. Some would call that being stubborn but I call it being true to her own heart. And I think that's kind of cool, too.

And while she was doing things her way she had an awful lot of fun - even though she didn't always have things easy. Like most everyone, she had her share of pain and sorrow, but you wouldn't necessarily have known it, because her spirit and her faith helped her triumph and rise above the sad events of life.

I feel like she met the challenges that life presented her with grace and love and acceptance. I know she loved and accepted each one of us, each one of her children and grandchildren, as the individuals that we are and fully supported us as we each followed our own paths in life. And, I'm here to tell you, it's a wonderful gift to have unconditional love and approval from your mom and dad.

I'd like to think that she triumphed over this horrible disease, Alzheimer's, in her own way, as well. There are many challenges associated with this disease. I'd venture to say that every person in this sanctuary has had or is having a very close-and-personal relationship with Alzheimer's in some capacity - so you know the challenges I'm talking about. But, I believe it's these challenges that help us grow. Challenges help build character; they help us draw on our faith; they require us to lean on each other which bring us closer together as a family and as a community; and challenges help build spirit

Even the challenges of this disease couldn't totally dampen Mom's spirit, as she continued (almost to the end) to find ways to reach out, to comfort those who were caring for her, and to smile at us as long as she could. She found a way to encourage and to show love and acceptance of life's tests throughout it all and I thank her for that. I thank her for setting that example.

I must tell you, she loved you all, very much. I know this because she told us. She would brag on you and your successes. She sang your praises often. I think you should know that. She thought of you, many of you, as her own kids. You were like sons and daughters to her. Mom had a way of including everyone she knew as part of her family. And there was room for everybody in her family. Family and friends were two words that were interchangeable to her. She made friends easily. And then she put them to work - usually pulling weeds.

> I looked out at the congregation and saw knowing nods and a sprinkle of gentle giggles.

Weeds, or gardening in general, can be used as a metaphor for Mom's life. If she had stated a philosophy of life, I think it might have been: Plant pretty things, tend them and love them, and clear out all the nasty weeds that impede growth. If you do this, you're assured that more blooms than brambles will grow in your life.

I'll close these remarks by saying that I hope we can take a little bit of Mom's strength of character, that spark she had, and keep it alive. One image that Donna shared with me, which is worth holding onto, took place during one of the Old Fashion Days that the church once hosted. When Mom's turn in the dunking booth rotated around, her grandsons paid good money, saved from their allowances, to have a chance to dunk her. And they tried. But they were unsuccessful, as I recall. No matter. A long line of people anxious to take their turns waited behind Tony and Josh. Then somebody – I'm not sure who but you can feel free to come clean now – finally hit the target and Mom took a dunk. When she came up for air, she was laughing so hard, in that big baritone, horse-laugh of hers, as if she'd never had that much fun in her life.

Another image that Andy, Barbara and I will always have of Mom, (I'll leave you with this… although it's not very glamorous) is of Rusty on these church grounds on work-day with red clay under her fingernails, sweat running down her face, hair tied up in a bandana, a filterless Camel cigarette clinched between her lips, one eye squinting in defense against the smoke, holding a cup of black coffee in her hands.

How odd. At last I reclaimed Rusty and it was as simple as looking around me and seeing that, everything within my sight, she had touched in some way. Whether she was mother, friend, wife, or sister - she did her very best at everything she attempted. She lived boldly. She loved fiercely.

Ken Burrows, a friend of Mom's, followed me at the podium. He and I both worked at the university and he mentioned to me a few weeks earlier that he was dedicating a chapter of his book, *Life as a Weed: Meditations on Plants Unbidden* to Rusty and agreed to say a few words describing their friendship and their shared love of gardening. Another dear friend, Mary Ann Green, sang a favorite song of gardeners for Mom called, *I Come to the Garden Alone* written by C. Austin Miles. It's a little on the sentimental side, I admit, but the image of a faithful soul meeting the Son of God in her garden "while the dew is still on the roses" was fitting for Rusty.

As the service came to an end, and Mom was rolled out of the sanctuary for the last time, the organist played Saint-Saëns Symphony No. 3 in C minor for organ. The song I had sung to Mom many times as she lay in her bed at the nursing home that began, *if I had words to make a day for you, I'd sing you a morning golden and new* was adapted from the melody in this piece. Today, however, instead of a sweet little theme song, it was played as it had always been meant, as an organ fanfare. After composing this work and later dedicating it to the memory of his friend, Franz Liszt, Saint-Saëns said "I gave everything to it I was able to give. What I have here accomplished, I will never achieve again." Rusty too, had given everything she had to give to this life of hers.

Our family filed out of church behind Mom's casket and walked behind the hearse as it carried her up a small hill to the cemetery. At the gravesite, the minister read the following letter written by my sister:

Andy and Barbara want to thank Marsha for the unwavering love and devotion that she has given to their parents, but most especially to their mother. For the little things - from answering the phone calls for more toilet paper (now!) to the big things - fighting bureaucracy at local and state levels. And winning. For answering the same question asked 20 times with the same patience. For always putting Rusty first and herself last.

Over the past several years, as Rusty's condition deteriorated, they watched Marsha's devotion and commitment, borne solely out of love, grow in proportion. Every hour of every day was, in some way, connected to her care for Rusty. Marsha never took "no" for an answer when it came to Rusty. It only made her more determined.

No mere words can express adequately the gratitude that Andy and Barbara have for Marsha. Nor can words express their love for her.

That gratitude and love extend to Donna, who, especially during the last few years, has provided the balance and support that has kept Marsha going. And whose own love for Rusty often put her squarely in the path of some unsuspecting administrator or clerk determined to sidetrack her with red tape.

When all is said and done and when the "thank-yous" are all said. Marsha will just blush and say that she did it because she loved Momma. And that she would do anything for Rusty. And that she only wished she could have done more. We think she has: She has made us, and Rusty, very proud.

No Burris memorial is complete without bagpipes playing the essential farewell, "Amazing Grace". We added one more, the gospel, "Goin' Home".

As we laid Mom to rest at last, gorgeous flowers, generously contributed by friends and family, would keep Mom's physical remains company on their first lonely night below ground. The colorful blooms were comforting to those of us who remained above. Mom always said, "Give me flowers while I'm alive. Don't wait until I'm gone." She didn't have her way on this and neither did she have her way concerning her 'no food in the church' rule.

The Women of the Church at Newell Presbyterian generously provide bereaved families with heaps of food on the day of their loved one's funeral service. For Mom's service I asked if they would provide sandwiches and other finger foods, buffet style, so everyone present could participate. They agreed. I had attended many memorial services at the Greek Church for my friend Paula's family and I loved how inclusive the meal afterwards is. It is meaningful to be able to enjoy the company of friends and family in a relaxed atmosphere so I adopted the tradition. Paula had asked what she could bring to contribute to the feast and without hesitation Donna and I requested Koulourakia (Greek cookies) which is a favorite made-from-scratch pastry from the Stathakis kitchen. After the gravesite service, tables were set up in the sanctuary in the space behind the pews. Paula's cookies, and the food prepared by the church ladies were displayed prominently on folding tables.

We ate and drank and swapped Rusty-stories. Phyllis, one of our dear friends at the church, casually mentioned as she set out several dishes, "It's funny that if Rusty was here we wouldn't be allowed to have food in the sanctuary. She'd say, *don't have all this food in the church, have it up at the fellowship hall in the old building where it's supposed to be.*

Food and love was showered on our family that day. Then we went home to begin life without Rusty.

EPILOGUE

Because of a pesky grain of sand, the oyster made a pearl.
- The Author

From the moment we're born, we get banged around while ups and downs weave their way through our lives. The *ups* we accept without question but the *downs* can stop us in our tracks. The point of going through tough times is to learn something from it. These are some of the lessons I learned.

I learned that when tragedy strikes, it's the way we respond to the experiences that contributes to our growth as human beings. If we have no control over the hand of cards we are dealt, we can at least choose *how* we play those cards. Occasionally we must confront the prospects of having no control over certain circumstances.

I learned that just showing up and being with Mom and Dad during their most critical time of need made a difference to them and to me. If I had taken on their care solely out of a sense of duty or obligation, I would have missed the miracles and unexpected gifts that were awarded me because of the experience. I was needed and what I did mattered. Caring for Mom and Dad was perhaps the most important thing I have ever done, it was certainly the hardest thing I was ever called to do. Caring for them was a selfless act of love on my part. I made sacrifices in my personal life and career, that's true, but I have no regrets. I would do it again. By their example I learned that we can choose to not give up, rather to take every breath given to us. We must trust that the universe can give us what we need.

Some deaths are agonizingly slow in claiming their victims. I did not learn why this must be. Despair killed my brother, a stroke killed my father, and a brain-wasting disease killed my mother. Each of these fatal conditions took its own sweet time to claim its victims. I used the time to seek and hold on to the few and fleeting things in life that are truly important: love, acceptance, a pat on the hand, and a twinkle in the eye of someone who loves you.

I learned there are some things too big to do alone - we can do almost anything we put our minds to, if we have some help. I'm a reluctant and unskillful help-seeker but aid and guidance found its way to me anyway. I could not have survived to tell the tale of these life-changing ordeals without the support of friends, Guardian Angels and other helpers. My experience was more meaningful because they stepped in when I needed them. Often, when darkness enveloped my soul and squeezed all joy from my life I was guided toward daylight again because Donna, like a beacon, illuminated the way with her steady and abiding love for me and for my family. Like a moth, I was drawn to the warmth of that love and it made all the difference.

Kindness and compassion followed in the wake of people moving in tandem with my life and spilled over onto my own path. These individuals showed me how to access an inner strength I was not aware I possessed. These gifts were answers to prayers I often thrust angrily into the void of the universe to test whether anyone was out there paying attention. I was humbled to find that even if I screamed in anger like a two-year-old brat at God, He sent help anyway.

I learned that Jim's consistent way of accepting people and circumstances, demonstrated by his 'ride it out' philosophy, is not mere passive capitulation as I once thought it to be. He was not able to explain to me what he meant by the statement but by living it and demonstrating its effectiveness in the face of great difficulty I came to learn that riding out any storm is in fact something profound. Some events in our lives are such that only patience will see us through them. There are situations where nothing else can be employed with any good outcome. Not everything can be fixed. Sometimes there's nothing at all to be done about a given problem, we must simply hang on. To survive our challenges is all we can hope for at times. This conclusion sounds fatalistic but Italians have a lovely expression for these times: *Il bel far niente*. It means *the beauty of doing nothing*. Stopping and assessing the predicament gives us some distance and helps us see more clearly what the next step is. Pretty smart.

I learned that although Rusty was a rebel and assumed she

could fix anything that didn't suit her, she never deceived herself. She recognized and accepted that life was not fair. Without ever calling the disease by name, Rusty faced her illness by choosing to live every day with dignity. It took more courage than climbing the highest mountain on earth. She fought diligently but when faced with this unbeatable foe, she surrendered graciously. Many hardships must be faced in the course of our lives and her aphoristic words of wisdom run through my head several times a day. *Wonderful things come from manure! We'll have no beautiful blooms without manure! And it's free!* Mom made this announcement when I was a kid. This, she assured us, was necessary because fertilizer by any other name, comes into our lives whether we like it or not, and offers opportunities for growth for all God's creations. So, I learned that when piles of manure drop uninvited into our lives it might be useful to blend a bit of Mom's stand-and-fight way with Dad's ride-it-out outlook to handle it.

I learned that looking for a silver lining in the rough bumps of life paid off. This approach made me stronger and helped me survive some horrible events without bitterness - I did not realize that would be the result. I now understand that we all do the best we can, and I'm no longer as inclined to judge an individual for his or her choices. I extend this understanding to myself and cut myself more slack now as I develop better coping skills and I protect my boundaries more diligently. I care a lot less about what other people think of me while caring a whole lot more about what I feel is right and wrong. I still have a long way to go but I dare to hope that when given an irritating grain of sand I can now, like the oyster, make a pearl from it.

I'd like to say a final word or two about Alzheimer's and suicide. Suicide is a choice of last resort. The pain of Robert's life and death is as acute today as the moment I learned a .22 bullet ploughed through his brain. He must have believed this action was the only way to stop his suffering. His last act on earth may have erased the memory of his troubles but they are now carved indelibly into our own. For some reason he was unable to tap into resources that would have made a life-saving difference to him. I question why he could not recognize or access help in his times of need, but answers elude me. Life is full of loose ends. We don't always get closure. Nothing will ever make the event of Robert's suicide okay. It's not meant to be okay. But he was loved. Maybe his cause of death should have been noted as the inability to feel that love.

Alzheimer's disease has no known cause and no known cure. Freedom from its devastating influences on a person's life comes only with death. We watched little bits of Rusty become lost to us each day over a span of the decade it took us to say our good-bye to each other. Since Mom's death was indeed a result of Alzheimer's (being otherwise healthy) it is some consolation that her death certificate lists Alzheimer's disease as the cause of death. Its inclusion in this particular population may aid researchers in understanding the anatomy of the disease and contribute to finding a cure for it. Every effort we can expend to eradicate Alzheimer's is essential.

Before the moment of our final farewell to Mom, I had erroneously thought that after she passed from this world that the worst would be over, and that I would feel only relief. And in many ways I am relieved, but to this day I feel the shadow of her death upon my heart. The pain of loss, the absence of my mother, father and brother, and the hole that remains in my life without them, cannot be filled. I must, therefore, take solace in their memory, remembering the good times with the bad and the lessons my parents taught me.

A Letter to the Caregiver of the Caregiver

This is what I dubbed myself, Caregiver of the Caregiver. If your loved one is the primary caregiver of an Alzheimer's patient then that is what you are as well. And I have some advice for you, to see you and your loved one down this rocky and treacherous road. I'm here to tell you they _will_ come back to you.

Be patient – this could be a long ride with lots of unexpected twists and turns. When your loved one comes home from work or a visit to the nursing home or the Medicaid office and they yell at you for looking at them, be patient with them. This is an extremely frustrating experience for them and a lot of their frustration and anger will be directed at you. Be a duck and let those things just roll off your back. It is not your fault or theirs; it is the fear, frustration and pain needing an outlet.

Be creative – to get a caregiver to take care of themselves you have to be creative in offering suggestions in a way that makes them feel like it is their idea or even the little white lie that you've been having it rough at work and need some time away (which you probably need too), would they please go with you.

Most important of all – be there. Be there when they need to cry, to yell, to tell the same stories over again, to fret, to worry, and yes even to laugh, it can happen. Go as often as you can to the nursing home, the doctors, the lawyers. You may feel like all you do is sit in the background but you are a second set of eyes and ears to remember what was said and done. You are giving your loved one precious time with their loved one, time for another pat on the cheek that they will cherish in the hearts forever. This experience is a roller coaster ride of emotions and fears and sometimes just being in the same room with your love one is all you can do for them and that is enough.

This Alzheimer's experience is a long, dark, unknown path. Walk it with your partner, be their anchor in the dark as well as their light at the end. Tell them you will be there on the other side waiting for them. They will get through it, they will come back to you. You will both be changed by the experience but you will be together again.

Rusty, you were my friend and I miss you.
Donna Chinnis

Acknowledgements

I was helped along a bleak and dark path by many individuals who, like stars against a velvet black sky, showed me the way through with their own beautiful light. Truly, a pinpoint of light illuminates most when it is darkest. For those of you who walked each step with me as events unfolded, you made it possible to survive a long and difficult ordeal. Many treasured friends joined me after the major events had played out and to them I offer a very special note of gratitude for listening to my story over and over. To those who generously gave their time to various iterations of the manuscript, I am more grateful than I can express for your support while I committed the story to paper.

To my sister Barbara and my brother Andy – we stuck it out together when our challenges seemed insurmountable. I'm proud of us. I bet Mom and Dad are too. Andrea, you were a god-send to our family. You open your home to the Burris clan without fail. You feed us and provide a home-base for these now-orphaned siblings. To my nieces, Ava and Arden, you are evidence that life goes on. What a delight and pure joy you both are! To my nephew Tony, you are an important link in the family story. Stay strong and brave. Peggy, you are always there for us with your willingness to help out with a cheerful smile.

To Paula, my friend who knows where all the bodies are buried, and to Susan and Rowanne, who provided me with a literary community of like-minded souls, I love you tremendously. Susie, your unique point of view helped remove some of my own blinders. And to Kirby, who never wavered in encouraging me to ride the wild horse, your help and support can't be measured. Mary Bobis, I am healthier and a better person because of you.

And finally, to Donna and Josh, my family of choice – someone once said, even when it's cloudy, the sun is still there, as you have always been for me. I am most fortunate that fate brought you into my life. You are my eternal sunshine.

Resources

ALZEIMER'S RELATED

Alzheimer's Association - www.alz.org
A voluntary health organization in Alzheimer's care, support and research.

Elegy for Iris by John Bayley [Picador: St Martin's Press] 1999

Keeping Mum by Marianne Talbot [Hay House UK] 2011

No More Words: A Journal of My Mother, Anne Morrow Lindbergh by Reeve Lindbergh [Simon & Shuster] 2002

Still Alice, A Novel by Lisa Genova [Gallery Books] 2009

The 36-Hour Day: A Family Guide to Caring for Persons with Alzheimer Disease by Nancy L. Mace and Peter V. Rabins [Johns Hopkins University Press] 2011

The Ivey - www.theivey.com
A not-for-profit adult day care in Charlotte, NC. Founded by Lynn Ivey, for individuals with Alzheimer's and other memory loss or related chronic illnesses.

END-of-LIFE RELATED

A Grief Observed by C.S. Lewis [HarperOne] 2009

Final Gifts: Understanding the Special Awareness, Needs, and Communications of the Dying by Maggie Callanan and Patricia Kelley [Simon & Schuster] 2012

STROKE RELATED

American Stroke Association
www.strokeassociation.org

SUICIDE RELATED

Suicide Prevention Hotline: 1-800-273-TALK (8255)
Suicide Prevention Resource Center   www.sprc.org

After Suicide: A Ray of Hope for Those Left Behind by E. Betsy Ross [DaCapo Press] 2002

How I Stayed Alive When My Brain Was Trying to Kill Me: One Person's Guide to Suicide Prevention by Susan Rose Blauner [William Morrow] 2003

Silent Grief: Living in the Wake of Suicide by Christopher Lukas and Henry M. Seiden [Jessica Kingsley Publishers] 2007

GOVERNEMENT RESOURCES
   Medicare: www.medicare.gov
   Medicaid: www.medicaid.gov
   National Council on Aging: www.ncoa.org
   North Carolina Div of Aging: www.ncdhhs.gov/aging

ATTORNEYS
   Connie J Vetter, Attorney at Law www.cjvlaw.com
   1208 The Plaza, Charlotte, NC 28205
   Specializing in community relations and equal rights for all individuals

   Christine J. Sylvester, P.A.
   2720 East WT Harris Blvd., Suite 100
   Charlotte, NC 28213
   Specializing in elder law and estate planning

www.ingramcontent.com/pod-product-compliance
Lightning Source LLC
Chambersburg PA
CBHW020732160426
43192CB00006B/197